Juridicum—Bochumer Schriften zur Friedenssicherung und zum Humanitären Völkerrecht | Bochum Studies on the International Law of Peace and Armed Conflict

Volume 72

In der Schriftenreihe des Bochumer Instituts für Friedensicherungsrecht und Humanitäres Völkerrecht werden regelmäßig Publikationen veröffentlicht, die sich mit aktuellen Fragen von Friedenssicherung und humanitärem Völkerrecht beschäftigen. Die Reihe erscheint seit 1988 unter dem Titel **Bochumer Schriften zur Friedenssicherung und zum Humanitären Völkerrecht**. Sie wurde 2017 nach einer Unterbrechung von zehn Jahren zunächst neu aufgelegt und wird seit 2025 bei Springer weitergeführt.

Die Bände behandeln vielfältige Themen der Friedens- und Konfliktforschung, etwa das Gewaltverbot und Selbstverteidigung, kollektive Sicherheit und das Recht der Vereinten Nationen, Friedenseinsätze, sowie die Menschenrechte, das Völkerstrafrecht, das Umweltrecht und – in all seinen Facetten – das humanitäre Völkerrecht und die humanitäre Hilfe.

This book series regularly publishes monographs and edited collections on current issues concerning the maintenance of international peace and security as well as international humanitarian law. The series has been published since 1988 under the title **Bochumer Schriften zur Friedenssicherung und zum Humanitären Völkerrecht**. It was reissued in 2017 after an interruption of ten years and has been continued by Springer since 2025.

The volumes cover a wide range of topics in peace and conflict studies, such as the use of force and self-defense, collective security and the law of the United Nations, peace missions, as well as human rights, international criminal law, environmental law and—in all its aspects—international humanitarian law as well as humanitarian action.

Benedikt Behlert

The Necessity of a Conversation between the Administration and the Individual

The Relevance of Administrative Procedure to International Human Rights

Springer

Benedikt Behlert
Ruhr-Universität Bochum
Düsseldorf, Germany

Inauguraldissertation zur Erlangung des akademischen Grades eines Doktors der Rechte durch die Juristische Fakultät der Ruhr-Universität Bochum

ISSN 3091-4477 ISSN 3091-4485 (electronic)
Juridicum—Bochumer Schriften zur Friedenssicherung und zum Humanitären Völkerrecht | Bochum Studies on the International Law of Peace and Armed Conflict
ISBN 978-3-658-50302-4 ISBN 978-3-658-50303-1 (eBook)
https://doi.org/10.1007/978-3-658-50303-1

This Springer imprint is published by the registered company Springer Fachmedien Wiesbaden GmbH, part of Springer Nature.
The registered company address is: Abraham-Lincoln-Str. 46, 65189 Wiesbaden, Germany

Acknowledgements

Completing this thesis has been both a challenging and profoundly rewarding journey—one that would not have been possible without the support, guidance, and encouragement of many remarkable individuals to whom I am deeply grateful.

First and foremost, I would like to express my heartfelt thanks to my supervisor, Professor Pierre Thielbörger, whose unwavering support extended far beyond regular feedback sessions and colloquia. His professional insight and consistent encouragement have been invaluable throughout this process.

I am also sincerely grateful to my second supervisor, Professor Wolfram Cremer, whose support exceeded all expectations, and to Professor Stefan Huster, the third member of my Rigorosum committee, for his time and engagement.

A special thanks goes to my former colleagues at the Institute for International Law of Peace and Armed Conflict (IFHV) at Ruhr-Universität Bochum. Their camaraderie and intellectual companionship made this academic journey not only stimulating but also joyful. In particular, I would like to thank Theresa Ackermann, Tobias Ackermann, Maximilian Bertamini, Rouven Diekjobst, Laura Hofmann, Robin Ramsahye, Sabine Mortimer, and Marion Zastepinski, among others, for their support and friendship. Moreover, I thank the staff and members of the Geneva Graduate Institute for making my research stay there an inspiring and enriching experience.

I gratefully acknowledge the financial support provided by the Ryoichi Sasakawa Young Leaders Fellowship Fund (Sylff) and the German Academic Scholarship Foundation (*Studienstiftung des deutschen Volkes*), without which this research would not have been possible.

To my family—Gabriele, Michael, and Henning—thank you for your patience, understanding, and steadfast support throughout this long journey. Your constant belief in me throughout my entirely life has always meant everything.

And finally, my deepest love and gratitude go to my wonderful and incredibly gifted wife Liza. You have been my inspiration since the day we met. Your strength, clarity, and unwavering belief in me have always helped me find my way back when I lost direction.

Treaties and Legislation

International Treaties

Charter of the United Nations (adopted 26 June 1945, entered into force 24 October 1945)

Convention Relating to the Status of Refugees (adopted 28 July 1951, entered into force 22 April 1954) 189 UNTS 137

International Covenant on Civil and Political Rights (adopted 16 December 1966, entered into force 23 March 1976) 999 UNTS 171 (ICCPR)

International Covenant on Economic, Social and Cultural Rights (adopted 16 December 1966, entered into force 3 January 1976) 993 UNTS 3 (ICESCR)

Vienna Convention on the Law of Treaties (adopted 23 May 1969, entered into force 27 January 1980) 1155 UNTS 331 (VCLT)

Convention on the Rights of the Child (adopted 20 November 1989, entered into force 2 September 1990) 1577 UNTS 3

Convention on Access to Information, Public Participation in Decision-Making and Access to Justice in Environmental Matters (adopted 25 June 1998, entered into force 30 October 2001) 2161 UNTS 447 (Århus Convention)

Convention of the Rights of Persons with Disabilities (adopted 13 December 2006, entered into force 3 May 2008) 2515 UNTS 3 (CRPD)

Regional Treaties

Convention for the Protection of Human Rights and Fundamental Freedoms (European Convention on Human Rights, as amended) (ECHR)

Inter-American Convention of Human Rights, Pact of San Jose, Costa Rica (B-32) (adopted 22 November 1969, entered into force 18 July 1978) OAS, Treaty Series, No. 36 (IACHR)

European Union Legislation

Parliament and Council Regulation (EU) 1367/2006 of 6 September 2006 on the application of the provisions of the Aarhus Convention on Access to Information, Public Participation in Decision-making and Access to Justice in Environmental Matters to Community institutions and bodies [2006] OJ L 264/13

Charter of Fundamental Rights of the European Union [2012] C 326/02

Laws of the Federal Republic of Germany

Basic Law for the Federal Republic of Germany in the revised version published in the Federal Law Gazette Part III, classification number 100-1, as amended by the Act of 19 December 2022 (Federal Law Gazette I p. 2478); translated by Professor Christian Tomuschat, Professor David P. Currie, Professor Donald P. Kommers and Raymond Kerr, in cooperation with the Language Service of the German Bundestag, accessible at https://www.gesetze-im-internet.de/englisch_gg/englisch_gg.html, accessed 26 August 2025

Act on the Federal Constitutional Court as published on 11 August 1993 (Federal Law Gazette I p. 1473), as amended by Article 4 of the Act of 20 November 2019 (Federal Law Gazette I p. 1724); translation provided by the Federal Constitutional Court and, on behalf of the Federal Ministry of Justice and Consumer Protection, by Iyamide Mahdi and Ute Reusch, accessible at https://www.gesetze-im-internet.de/englisch_bverfgg/#:~:text=Act%20on%20the%20Federal%20Constitutional%20Court%20(Bundesverfassungsgerichtsgesetz%20-%20BVerfGG), accessed 26 August 2025

Administrative Procedure Act in the version last promulgated on January 23rd 2003 (Federal Law Gazette I p. 102), amended by Article 4, para. 8 of the Act to Modernise the Law on Costs (Kostenrechtsmodernisierungsgesetz – KostRMoG) of May 5th 2004 (Federal Law Gazette I p. 718); translation accessible at https://www.bmi.bund.de/SharedDocs/downloads/EN/gesetztestexte/VwVfg_en.html, accessed 26 August 2025

Code of Administrative Court Procedure in the version of the promulgation of 19 March 1991 (Federal Law Gazette I page 686), as amended by Article 5, subsection 24 of the Act of 21 June 2019 (Federal Law Gazette I page 846); translation provided by Neil Mussett, accessible at https://www.gesetze-im-internet.de/englisch_vwgo/englisch_vwgo.html, accessed 26 August 2025

Jurisprudence and Other Documents

Federal Constitutional Court of Germany (FCC)

Decisions Published in the Official Collection (BVerfGE)

Order of 27 September 1951, BVerfGE 1, 4 – *Urteilsverfassungsbeschwerde*

Judgment of 3 June 1954, BVerfGE 3, 383 – *Chancengleichheit der Parteien*

Judgment of 20 July 1954, BVerfGE 4, 7 – *Investitionshilfe*

Judgment of 16 January 1957, BVerfGE 6, 32 – *Elfes*

Order of 17 January 1957, BVerfGE 6, 55 – *Ehegattensplitting*

Order of 18 June 1957, BVerfGE 7, 53 – *Zur Bedeutung von Art. 103 Abs. 1 GG in Verfahren mit Untersuchungsgrundsatz*

Judgment of 15 January 1958, BVerfGE 7, 198 – *Lüth*

Order of 13 February 1958, BVerfGE 7, 275 – *Revisionsgegenerklärung*

Order of 08 January 1959, BVerfGE 9, 89 – *Haftbefehlsverfahren*

Order of 20 December 1960, BVerfGE 12, 45 – *Kriegsdienstverweigerung*

Judgment of 28 February 1961, BVerfGE 12, 205 – *Erstes Rundfunkurteil*

Order of 25 July 1963, BVerfGE 17, 108 – *Hirnkammerlüftung*

Order of 10 June 1964, BVerfGE 18, 85 – *verfassungsgerichtlicher Prüfungsumfang, spezifisches Verfassungsrecht*

Judgment of 18 December 1968, BVerfGE 24, 367 – *Hamburger Deichordnungsgesetz*

Judgment of 18 July 1972, BVerfGE 33, 303 – *Numerus Clausus I*

Judgment of 29 May 1973, BVerfGE 35, 79 – *Hochschulurteil*

Judgment of 12 April 2005, BVerfGE 112, 304 – *GPS-Observation*

Order of 12 April 2005, BVerfGE 113, 29 – *Beschlagnahme von Datenträgern*

Judgment of 15 February 2006, BVerfGE 115, 118 – *Luftsicherheitsgesetz*

Order of 13 June 2007, BVerfGE 118, 168 – *Kontenabfrage*

Order of 16 June 2009, BVerfGE 124, 43 – *E-Mail-Beschlagnahme*

Order of 20 July 2010, BVerfGE 127, 87 – *Hamburger Hochschulgesetz*

Order of 23 March 2011, BVerfGE 128, 282 – *Medizinische Zwangsbehandlung*

Order of 21 June 2016, BVerfGE 142, 234 – *Cybercrime Convention*

Judgment of 19 December 2017, BVerfGE 147, 253 – *NC Humanmedizin*

Decisions Published Elsewhere

Chamber order of 28 May 1998, NJW 1998, 2663

Non-acceptance order of 24 February 2009, NVwZ 2009, 581

Non-acceptance order of 22 August 2016, NVwZ 2016, 1630

Non-acceptance decision of 24 October 2017, NVwZ 2018, 573

UN Human Rights Committee (HRC)

General Comments

General comment No. 3: Article 2 (Implementation at the national level) (1981) HRI/GEN/1/Rev.9 (Vol. I) p. 174

General comment No. 13: Article 14 (Administration of justice) (1984) HRI/GEN/1/Rev.9 (Vol. I) p. 184

General comment No. 14: Article 6 (Right to life) (1984) HRI/GEN/1/Rev.9 (Vol. I) p.188

General comment No. 15: The position of aliens under the Covenant (1986) HRI/GEN/1/Rev.9 (Vol. I) p. 189

General comment No. 18: Non-discrimination (1989) HRI/GEN/1/Rev.9 (Vol. I) p.195

General comment No. 21: Article 10 (Humane treatment of persons deprived of their liberty) (1992) HRI/GEN/1/Rev.9 (Vol. I) p. 202

General comment No. 23: Article 27 (Rights of minorities) (1994) HRI/GEN/1/Rev.9 (Vol. I) p. 207

General comment No. 25: Article 25 (Participation in public affairs and the right to vote) (1996) HRI/GEN/1/Rev.9 (Vol. I) p. 217

General comment No. 27: Article 12 (Freedom of movement) (1999) HRI/GEN/1/Rev.9 (Vol. I) p. 223

General comment No. 28: Article 3 (The equality of rights between men and women) (29 March 2000) HRI/GEN/1/Rev.9 (Vol. I) p. 228

General comment No. 31: The Nature of the General Legal Obligation Imposed on States Parties to the Covenant (2004) HRI/GEN/1/Rev.9 (Vol. I) p. 243

General Comment No. 32, Article 14: Right to equality before courts and tribunals and to a fair trial (23 August 2007) UN Doc CCPR/C/GC/32

General comment No. 34, Article 19: Freedoms of opinion and expression (12 September 2011) UN Doc CCPR/C/GC/34

General comment No. 35, Article 9 (Liberty and security of person) (16 December 2014) UN Doc. CCPR/C/GC/35

General comment No. 36 Article 6: right to life (3 September 2019) UN Doc. CCPR/C/GC/36

General comment No. 37 (2020) on the right of peaceful assembly (article 21) (17 September 2020) UN Doc. CCPR/C/GC/37

Views

C.F. et al *v. Canada* (Comm no 113/1981, HRC, 12 April 1985)

Broeks v. Netherlands (Comm no 172/1984, HRC, 9 April 1987)

L.G. Danning v. Netherlands (Comm no 180/1984, HRC, 9 April 1987)

Zwaan-de-Vries v. Netherlands (Comm no 182/1984, HRC, 9 April 1987)

Jouni E. Länsman et al. *v. Finland* (Comm no 671/1995, HRC, 22 November 1996)

Äärelä and Näkkäläjärvi v Finland (Comm no 779/1997, HRC, 7 November 2001)

Kazantzis v Cyprus (Comm no 972/01, HRC, 7 August 2003)

P.K. v. Canada (Comm no 1234/2003, HRC, 22 May 2007)

Grioua v. Algeria (Comm no 1327/2004, HRC, 10 July 2007)

Poma Poma v. Peru (Comm no 1457/2006, HRC, 24 April 2009)

Benali v. Libya (Comm no 1805/2008, HRC, 1 November 2012)

Sharma, Paudel et al. *v. Nepal* (Comm no 2364/2014, HRC, 6 April 2018)

Millis v. Algeria (Comm no 2398/2014, HRC, 6 April 2018)

S. F. v. Denmark (Comm no 2494/2014, HRC, 17 May 2019)

Concluding Observations

Concluding observations of the Human Rights Committee: Iraq (19 November 1997) UN Doc CCPR/C/79/Add.84

Concluding Observations of the Human Rights Committee: Czech Republic (9 August 2007) UN Doc CCPR/C/CZE/CO/2

Concluding observations on the fourth periodic report of Nicaragua (30 November 2022) UN Doc CCPR/C/NIC/CO/4

Concluding observations on the fifth periodic report of the Philippines (30 November 2022) UN Doc CCPR/C/PHL/CO/5

Concluding observations on the second periodic report of Ethiopia (7 December 2022) UN Doc CCPR/C/ETH/CO/2

Other

General Comments Adopted by the Human Rights Committee: Introduction (19 May 1989) HRI/GEN/ 1/Rev. 6 p. 123

Committee on Economic, Social and Cultural Rights (CESCR)

General Comments

General Comment No. 3: The nature of States parties' obligations (art. 2, para. 1, of the Covenant) (1990) HRI/GEN/1/Rev.9 (Vol. I) p. 7

General Comment No. 4: The right to adequate housing (art. 11 (1) of the Covenant) (1991) HRI/GEN/1/Rev.9 (Vol. I) p. 11

General Comment No. 5: Persons with disabilities (1994) HRI/GEN/1/Rev.9 (Vol. I) p. 17

General Comment No. 6: The economic, social and cultural rights of older persons (1995) HRI/GEN/1/Rev.9 (Vol. I) p. 27

General Comment No. 7: The right to adequate housing (art. 11 (1) of the Covenant): Forced evictions (1997) HRI/GEN/1/Rev.9 (Vol. I) HRI/GEN/1/Rev.9 (Vol. I) p. 38

General Comment No. 9: The domestic application of the Covenant (1998) HRI/GEN/1/Rev.9 (Vol. I) p. 47

General Comment 11 (1999): Plans of action for primary education (article 14 of the International Covenant on Economic, Social and Cultural Rights) (10 May 1999) UN Doc E/C.12/1999/4

General Comment 12 (Twentieth session, 1999): The right to adequate food (art. 11) (12 May 1999) UN Doc E/C.12/1999/5

General Comment No. 13 (Twenty-first session, 1999): The right to education (article 13 of the Covenant) (8 December 1999) UN Doc E/C.12/1999/10

General Comment No. 14 (2000): The right to the highest attainable standard of health (article 12 of the International Covenant on Economic, Social and Cultural Rights) (11 August 2000) UN Doc E/C.12/2000/4

General Comment No. 15 (2002): The right to water (arts. 11 and 12 of the International Covenant on Economic, Social and Cultural Rights) (20 January 2003) UN Doc E/C.12/2002/11

General comment No. 16 (2005): The equal right of men and women to the enjoyment of all economic, social and cultural rights (art. 3 of the International Covenant on Economic, Social and Cultural Rights) (11 August 2005) UN Doc E/C.12/2005/4

General Comment No. 17 (2005): The right of everyone to benefit from the protection of the moral and material interests resulting from any scientific, literary or artistic production of which he or she is the author (article 15, paragraph 1 (c), of the Covenant) (12 January 2006) UN Doc E/C.12/GC/17

General comment No. 18: Article 6 of the International Covenant on Economic, Social and Cultural Rights (6 February 2006) UN Doc E/C.12/GC/18

General Comment No. 19: The right to social security (art. 9) (4 February 2008) UN Doc E/C.12/GC/19

General Comment No. 20: Non-discrimination in economic, social and cultural rights (art. 2, para. 2, of the International Covenant on Economic, Social and Cultural Rights) (2 July 2009) UN Doc E/C.12/GC/20

General comment No. 21: Right of everyone to take part in cultural life (art. 15, para. 1 (a), of the International Covenant on Economic, Social and Cultural Rights) (21 December 2009) UN Doc E/C.12/GC/21

General comment No. 22 (2016) on the right to sexual and reproductive health (article 12 of the International Covenant on Economic, Social and Cultural Rights) (2 May 2016) UN Doc E/C.12/GC/22

General comment No. 24 (2017) on State obligations under the International Covenant on Economic, Social and Cultural Rights in the context of business activities (10 August 2017) UN Doc E/C.12/GC/24

General comment No. 26 (2021) on land and economic, social and cultural rights, Draft prepared by the Rapporteurs, Rodrigo Uprimny and Michael Windfuhr (3 May 2021) UN Doc E/C.12/69/R.2

General comment No. 26 (2022) on land and economic, social and cultural rights (24 January 2023) UN Doc E/C.12/GC/26

Views

I. D. G. v Spain (Comm no 2/2014, CESCR, 13 October 2015)

Trujillo v Ecuador (Comm no 10/2015, CESCR, 14 November 2018)

López Albán v. Spain (Comm no 37/2018, CESCR, 29 November 2019)

Report on follow-up to communications Nos. 2/2014 and 5/2015 against Spain (Comm nos 2/2014 and 5/2015, CESCR, 29 November 2019)

El Ayoubi and El Azouan v Spain (Comm no 54/2018, CESCR, 19 February 2021)

European Court of Human Rights (ECtHR)

Tyrer v The United Kingdom (App no 5856/72, ECtHR, 25 April 1978)

Airey v Ireland (App no 6289/73, ECtHR, 9 October 1979)

Loizidou v Turkey (Preliminary Objections) (App no 15318/89, ECtHR, 23 March 1995)

Goodwin v The United Kingdom (App no 28957/95, ECtHR, 11 July 2002)

Inter-American Court of Human Rights (IACtHR)

Velásquez-Rodríguez v Honduras (Series C No 4, IACtHR, 29 July 1988)

19 Tradesmen v Colombia (Series C No 109, IACtHR, 5 July 2004)

Gonzaléz et al. *("Cotton Field") v Mexico* (Series C No 205, IACtHR, 16 November 2009)

International Court of Justice (ICJ)

Territorial Dispute (Libyun Aruh Jamuhiriyu/Chad) [1994] ICJ Rep 6

Ahmadou Sadio Diallo (Republic of Guinea v. *Democratic Republic of the Congo)* [2010] ICJ Rep 639

Application of the International Convention on the Elimination of All Form of Racial Discrimination, (Georgia v. Russian Federation) (Preliminary Objections) [2011] ICJ Rep 70

Permanent Court of International Justice (PCIJ)

S.S. Lotus (French Republic v. Turkish Republic), PCIJ Rep Series A No 10

Court of Justice of the European Union (CJEU)

Kadi and Al Barakaat v Council and Commission (Joined cases C-402/05 P and C-415/05 P, CJEU, 3 September 2008)

Special Rapporteur on the Right to Adequate Food

Report on the right to adequate food as a human right submitted by Mr. Asbjørn Eide, Special Rapporteur (7 July 1987) UN Doc E/CN.4/Sub.2/1987/23

United Nations General Assembly

Universal Declaration of Human Rights (adopted 10 December 1948) UNGA Res 217 A(III) (UDHR)

Draft International Covenants on Human Rights: Report of the Third Committee (8 December 1960) A/4625

Responsibility of States for internationally wrongful acts (28 January 2002) UN Doc A/RES/56/83

United Nations Declaration on the Rights of Indigenous Peoples (2 October 2007) UN Doc A/RES/61/295

International Law Commission

Third Report of the Special Rapporteur, Sir Humphrey Waldock (Sixteenth Session of the ILC (1964)) A/CN.4/167 and Add.1-3, ILC Yb. 1964, Volume II, p. 5

Draft articles on states responsibility with commentaries thereto, Report of the International Law Commission Fifty-third session (23 April-1 June and 2 July-10 August 2001) (1 October 2001) UN Doc A/56/10(SUPP) p. 59

UNESCO

Mexico City Declaration on Cultural Policies, World Conference on Cultural Policies, Mexico City, 26 July-6 August 1982 (1982) CLT/MD/1 p. 41

Other UN Documents and Resources

Proclamation of Teheran, Final Act of the International Conference on Human Rights: Teheran, 22 April to 13 May 1968 (1 September 1968) UN Doc A/CONF 32/41 p. 3

Vienna Declaration and Programme of Action, Report of the World Conference on Human Rights, Report of the Secretary-General (13 October 1993) UN Doc A/CONF157/24 (Part I) p. 20

Status of Ratification Interactive Dashboard: Ratification of 18 International Human Rights Treaties, https://indicators.ohchr.org, accessed 26 August 2025

International Commission of Jurists

Maastricht Guidelines on Violations of Economic, Social and Cultural Rights (2 October 2000) UN Doc E/C.12/2000/13 p. 16

International Monetary Fund (IMF)

Governance of the International Monetary Fund: an evaluation / [prepared by an IEO team headed by Ruben Lamdany] (2008).

WTO Appellate Body

Korea – Definitive Safeguard Measure on Imports of Certain Dairy Products (WT/DS98/AB/R) [2000] 1 DSR 3

Contents

Abbreviations

ASR	Articles on State Responsibility
CESCR	Committee on Economic, Social and Cultural Rights
CJEU	Court of Justice of the European Union
CRPD	Convention of the Rights of Persons with Disabilities
ECHR	European Convention on Human Rights
ECtHR	European Court of Human Rights
FCC	Federal Constitutional Court of Germany
HRC	United Nations Human Rights Committee
ICCPR	International Covenant on Civil and Political Rights
ICESCR	International Covenant on Economic, Social and Cultural Rights
IHRL	International Human Rights Law
IMF	International Monetary Fund
UN	United Nations
UNDRIP	United Nations Declaration on the Rights of Indigenous Peoples
VCLT	Vienna Convention on the Law of Treaties

Introduction

1

In 1997, the Committee on Economic, Social and Cultural Rights (CESCR) issued General Comment 7 on the right to housing, and specifically on the issue of forced evictions. In it, the committee made a remarkable statement on the value of procedure to international human rights. "Appropriate procedural protection and due process", the committee stated, were "essential aspects of all human rights".[1]

When we think of procedural protection under IHRL, we immediately think of the right to a fair trial, which has always been a central element of civil and political rights. We think of provisions such as Article 14 of the International Covenant on Civil and Political Rights (ICCPR)[2] or Article 6 of the European Convention on Human Rights (ECHR)[3]. The right to a fair trial was included in the Universal Declaration of Human Rights (UDHR)[4] and has been a central and often discussed element of International Human Rights Law (IHRL) since.[5]

[1] CESCR, *General Comment No. 7: The right to adequate housing (art. 11 (1) of the Covenant): Forced evictions* (1997) HRI/GEN/1/Rev.9 (Vol. I) HRI/GEN/1/Rev.9 (Vol. I) p. 38, para. 15.

[2] International Covenant on Civil and Political Rights (adopted 16 December 1966, entered into force 23 March 1976) 999 UNTS 171.

[3] Convention for the Protection of Human Rights and Fundamental Freedoms (European Convention on Human Rights, as amended).

[4] *Universal Declaration of Human Rights* (adopted 10 December 1948) UNGA Res 217 A(III) (UDHR).

[5] For a recent and probably the most comprehensive discussion of the right, see Amal Clooney and Philippa Webb, *The Right to a Fair Trial in International Law* (Oxford University Press 2021).

B. Behlert, *The Necessity of a Conversation between the Administration and the Individual*, Juridicum—Bochumer Schriften zur Friedenssicherung und zum Humanitären Völkerrecht | Bochum Studies on the International Law of Peace and Armed Conflict 72, https://doi.org/10.1007/978-3-658-50303-1_1

It has even been described as "one of the fundamental pillars of international law to protect individuals from arbitrary treatment".[6] Moreover, there is the guarantee of an effective remedy under IHRL which also offers procedural protection in the sense of *ex post* review.[7]

However, the right to a fair trial and the right to an effective remedy alone do not sufficiently explain the statement of the CESCR that adequate procedural protection is a necessary element of all human rights. Firstly, the International Covenant on Economic, Social and Cultural Rights (ICESCR)[8], the observance of which the CESCR oversees, does not contain a provision guaranteeing the right to a fair trial. Secondly, the CESCR's statement is general. It does not only refer to procedural protection or due process before courts of law and *ex post* protection. It speaks of adequate procedural protection in abstract terms. There must be more to the "adequate procedural protection" of human rights than fair trial rights protecting individuals from unfair court procedures.

This thesis seeks to shed light on another aspect of adequate procedural protection that is almost not discussed at all: the procedural protection of individuals *vis à vis* the administration of a state. The lack of scholarly engagement with this aspect of adequate procedural protection is surprising. The encounters with administrative agents are arguably the most relevant encounters with the state in most people's (daily) lives. Firstly, the executive branch of government—of which the administration forms a part—has rightly been described as the "most direct manifestation of State power".[9] While a legislative prohibition (should) normatively affect(s) individuals once it is in force, they will often experience what these laws mean for the reality of their lives only once they are enforced. Secondly, encounters with the administration of a state are the most common encounters with the state for the great majority of people. Not everyone will find herself in front of a court of law or another judicial tribunal in the course of her life. Facing a judge is far from a common encounter for most human beings. Everyone, however, will face the administration of a state in one way or another.

---

[6] Louise Doswald-Beck, 'Fair Trial, Right to, International Protection' in Anne Peters (ed), *Max Planck Encyclopedia of International Law (MPEPIL)* (Oxford University Press 2013).

[7] See generally Dinah Shelton, *Remedies in International Human Rights Law* (Oxford University Press 2006).

[8] International Covenant on Economic, Social and Cultural Rights (adopted 16 December 1966, entered into force 3 January 1976) 993 UNTS 3 (ICESCR).

[9] James Crawford, *State Responsibility—The General Part* (Cambridge University Press 2013), 119.

It is in this sense that the administration of a state constitutes the "everyday life of rule" (*"Alltag von Herrschaft"*)[10]. How important it is that IHRL is effectively realised in the everyday reality of the individual is well encapsulated in the famous quote from Eleanor Roosevelt of 1958:

> *Where, after all, do universal human rights begin? In small places, close to home—so close and so small that they cannot be seen on any maps of the world. Yet they are the world of the individual person; the neighborhood he lives in; the school or college he attends; the factory, farm, or office where he works. Such are the places where every man, woman, and child seeks equal justice, equal opportunity, equal dignity without discrimination. Unless these rights have meaning there, they have little meaning anywhere.*[11]

Having a better normative grasp of the relationship with the administration and its importance for how individuals experience "the everyday life of rule" is of central importance to understanding how IHRL shapes the relationship of the individual as the bearer of human rights with the state as their addressee.

For the fundamental rights of the German constitution, the Basic Law[12], and in particular in the jurisprudence of the Federal Constitutional Court of Germany (FCC), it has long been recognised that these fundamental rights require certain procedural protection of the individual—also *vis à vis* the administration. In 1977, the FCC made the statement that gives this thesis its name when it held that "the necessity of a conversation between the administration and the citizen correspond[ed] to the constitutional understanding of the *position of the citizen in the state*".[13] In order to conduct a targeted and fruitful analysis of IHRL with regard to the stipulations it makes for administrative procedure, this thesis analyses the jurisprudence of the FCC and develops an analytical foil from it through

---

[10] Christian Waldhoff, '§ 11 Verwaltung und Verwaltungsrecht' in Wolfgang Kahl and Markus Ludwigs (eds), *Handbuch des Verwaltungsrechts*, vol I (C. F. Müller 2021) (n. 21), para. 7.

[11] The quote is cited from IR Online, 'In Small Places, Close to Home: The Beginnings of Universal Human Rights' <https://ironline.american.edu/blog/our-basic-human-rights/> accessed 26 August 2025.

[12] Basic Law for the Federal Republic of Germany, as amended by the by the Act of 19 December 2022 (Federal Law Gazette I p. 2478), translated by Professor Christian Tomuschat, Professor David P. Currie, Professor Donald P. Kommers and Raymond Kerr, in cooperation with the Language Service of the German Bundestag, available at https://www.gesetze-im-internet.de/englisch_gg/englisch_gg.html.

[13] BVerfGE 45, 297 (335): *"Die Notwendigkeit des Gesprächs zwischen Verwaltung und Bürger entspricht dem grundgesetzlichen Verständnis der Stellung des Bürgers im Staat."* Emphasis added.

which it then looks at the ICCPR and the ICESCR and the pronouncements of the respective treaty bodies.

A formal decision-making process shaped by the concerns for the effectiveness of IHRL implementation and respect for the autonomy of the individual is indeed the "sworn enemy of arbitrariness, the twin sister of freedom".[14] In this sense, this thesis seeks to provide a comprehensive overview of the relationship between IHRL and administrative procedure and to understand the role individuals must play in the decision-making processes that shape their everyday lives.

[14] Rudolf von Jhering, *Geist des römischen Rechts auf den verschiedenen Stufen seiner Entwicklung*, vol 3/4 (Breitkopf und Härtel 1858), 497: *"Die Form ist die geschworene Feindin der Willkür, die Zwillings-schwester der Freiheit."*

Part I
Preliminary Remarks

Definitions, Scope, and Methodology 2

Before we can begin with our analysis, we must clarify a few things. Firstly, we must develop a working definition for "administrative procedure" (2.1). Secondly, we must define the scope of this study, i.e., delimit the part(s) of IHRL we will look at (2.2). Thirdly, we will exclude unpromising paths to approach the connection between IHRL and administrative procedure (2.3). Fourthly, we will explain this thesis' methodological approach and outline the course of our study (2.4). And finally, we must make a brief note on translations (2.5).

2.1 A Working Definition of "Administrative Procedure"

This thesis seeks to answer the question of whether international human rights oblige states to have (certain) administrative procedures in place. As an important preliminary step, this requires defining what this thesis means when it speaks of "administrative procedure". To do so, we will firstly define the part of the state that this thesis is concerned with, i.e., the "administration" (2.1.1). Secondly, we will look at which acts of the administration matter to this thesis (2.1.2). Thirdly, we will define the respective formalised decision-making processes leading up to such acts as "administrative procedures" (2.1.3).

B. Behlert, *The Necessity of a Conversation between the Administration and the Individual*, Juridicum—Bochumer Schriften zur Friedenssicherung und zum Humanitären Völkerrecht | Bochum Studies on the International Law of Peace and Armed Conflict 72, https://doi.org/10.1007/978-3-658-50303-1_2

2.1.1 Defining "Administration"

Defining the term "administration" is a difficult, if not impossible, undertaking.[1] The term is used differently around the world in different jurisdictions. In the United States of America, the highest level of the federal government is often referred to as the "President's administration", e.g., "the Biden administration", while in other national contexts, the term refers to specific parts of a State that are not to be equated with the highest level of (federal) government. For example, in Germany, the literal translation *"Verwaltung"*, is not to be equated with the federal government, i.e., the German chancellor's cabinet. It describes entities of a lower level. Moreover, businesses have administrations, too. The academic degree of a "Master of Business Administration", for example, does not traditionally prepare someone for a career in state institutions. Given the uncertainty around the notion, clarification is needed as to what this thesis means when it speaks of "administration".

The first important clarification is that whenever we refer to "administration", it is in the sense of "public administration". For our purposes, "administration" refers to a branch of government and not to the administration of a business, a hospital, etc. This does, however, not exclude private entities from the notion. They can form part of a state's administration when they exercise public administrative functions. This is in line with general international law, which attributes the conduct of private entities to States when they exercise governmental power as authorized by law[2] or acts "on the instructions of, or under the direction or control of" a state[3]. From a human rights point of view, the inclusion of these "private" parts of the administration is important in light of a surge in the outsourcing of traditionally governmental functions by the modern State.[4] Examples of such "parastatal entities"[5] range from

[1] Forsthoff famously held that the administration can be "described but not defined", Ernst Forsthoff, *Lehrbuch des Verwaltungsrechts*, vol 1 (10th edn, C. H. Beck 1973), 1.

[2] *Responsibility of States for internationally wrongful acts* (28 January 2002) UN Doc A/RES/56/83 (Articles on State Responsibility—ASR), Article 5.

[3] Article 8 ASR.

[4] Crawford, 127. For the U.S., see Scott Shane and Ron Nixon, 'In Washington, Contractors Take On Biggest Role Ever' *The New York Times* (New York) <https://www.nytimes.com/2007/02/04/washington/04contract.html> accessed 26 August 2025.

[5] For a discussion of the elements of this term see ILC, *Draft articles on states responsibility with commentaries thereto, Report of the International Law Commission Fifty-third session (23 April-1 June and 2 July-10 August 2001)* (1 October 2001) UN Doc A/56/10(SUPP) p. 59, 92–94.

private military companies[6], over corporate entities controlling immigration[7] to private prison administrations[8]. Given that such private actors can have considerable power over individuals and the exercise of their rights, they must not be excluded from this thesis' purview as long as they fulfil public functions.

Which functions of the state, however, does this dissertation refer to when it refers to the "administration" of a state? Given its multifaceted nature, "administration" has traditionally been defined *via negationis*, i.e., delineated against other functions of the state. In the German context, this negative definition was most famously employed by German administrative law scholar Otto Mayer in 1895.[9] According to the negative definition, the administration of a State is defined by delimitation to the other parts of the State.[10] Following the separation of powers tripartite[11], the legislature and the judicial branch of government are excluded and what one is left with is the executive of a state. The executive, however, must be further broken down. Not all parts of it are part of the "administration" in the sense employed by the present thesis. The highest level of government, i.e., the gubernatorial function (*"Gubernative"*) shall be excluded from the executive, too. What one ends up with then is the "administration" of a state in the sense in which this study will use the word.

---

[6] See Chia Lehnhardt, 'Private Military Companies' in Anne Peters (ed), *Max Planck Encyclopedia of International Law (MPEPIL)* (Oxford University Press 2011).

[7] See Tilman Rodenhäuser, 'Another Brick in the Wall: Carrier Sanctions and the Privatization of Immigration Control' (2014) 26 International Journal of Refugee Law 223.

[8] See Alfred C. Jr. Aman, 'Privatization, Prisons, Democracy, and Human Rights: The Need to Extend the Province of Administrative Law' (2005) 12 Indiana Journal of Global Legal Studies 511.

[9] Otto Mayer, *Deutsches Verwaltungsrecht*, vol I, II (Unedited reprint of the 3rd edition published in 1924 edn, Duncker & Humblot 2004), 7.

[10] Hartmut Maurer and Christian Waldhoff, *Allgemeines Verwaltungsrecht* (20th edn, C.H. Beck 2020), para. 6; Steffen Detterbeck, *Allgemeines Verwaltungsrecht* (21st edn, C. H. Beck 2023), para. 9.

[11] The concept is employed here not as a normative postulate but descriptively as a functional distinction. In this sense, Article 1 (1) of the Fundamental Law of Vatican City State holds that "The Supreme Pontiff, Sovereign of Vatican City State, has the fullness of legislative, executive and judicial powers", obviously not to normatively delineate competences from one another but to distinguish modes of government.

Until today, this negative definition can be found in academic literature.[12] While commentators have—not without basis—highlighted the problems with this definition and the fact that it produces unsatisfactory results,[13] attempts at defining "administration" positively must be considered failed.[14] And the main problem that leads to the embarrassment of legal scholars when it comes to positively defining "administration", namely that it is too multifaceted to be amenable to a positive definition, is even more pertinent for a study such as ours, that is not limited to one jurisdiction. If it is already impossible to define a (sub-)branch of government for one state, it is even more impossible to do so for all states. Hence, we will have to do with the negative definition of the administrative function of a state as well. It is flexible, or "neutral", enough to apply to different legal orders and thus comply with the universal claim of IHRL.

2.1.2 Relevant Types of Action

Having defined what this study means by "administration", we must ask ourselves which types of action this thesis is interested in. The types of actions the administration of a state is typically engaged in range from economic activity governed by private law over policy- and law-making to what is typically referred to as law-application. Our next step will thus be to define which acts of the administration this study is concerned with.

Firstly, we must exclude purely fiscal activity from the purview of this study. This is a study in IHRL. As such, it is not interested in inquiring into general (democratic) standards of accountability for public administrations.[15] The study

---

[12] See, e.g., Benedict Kingsbury, Nico Krisch and Richard B. Stewart, 'The Emergence of Global Administrative Law' (2005) 68 Law and Contemporary Problems 15, 17 who refer to this negative definition in an international law context and cite a previous edition of Maurer's textbook.

[13] Maurer and Waldhoff, para. 6; Waldhoff, paras. 16ff.

[14] Waldhoff, paras. 16ff.

[15] In the 1990s, a human right to democratic governance was indeed discussed. For one of the most famous contributions to this discussion, see Thomas M. Franck, 'The Emerging Right to Democratic Governance' (1992) 86 American Journal of International Law 46. From today's point of view, however, the attempt to derive a right to democracy from IHRL must be considered failed. The discussion was a phenomenon that can best be explained by the optimism of 1990s, the time after the fall of the iron curtain when the *zeitgeist* was that Western liberal values would now take over the world. Today, IHRL scholarship has become more aware of cultural and political differences between states and hence more reserved towards making propositions like a derivative right to democratic governance. For an example, see Jean

is interested only in those actions of the administration that have a sufficiently direct effect on individual human rights. Hence, merely fiscal activities such as the purchase of office supplies or the rental of a building or parking space are excluded from the purview of this study. Secondly, acts of the administration which have no legal relevance for private individuals outside the administration must be excluded, too. Purely internal proceedings without external effects (*"Außenwirkung"*) do not matter to IHRL.

Thirdly, we must exclude policy- and law-making activities of the administration from the scope of this study. While these may have effects on individual rights and will often be important for the implementation of human rights at lower levels,[16] they can be excluded against the backdrop of the goal of this study. As it is the goal of this study to consider the most immediate confrontations of individuals with the States' administrations from a normative point of view, administrative policy- or rule-making—which is aptly described as following a "legislative model"[17]—does not fall within this scope. These acts do not lead to direct encounters between individuals and state power.[18]

What we are left with is what is commonly referred to as "law-application". But what exactly is meant by "law-application"? The distinction between "rule-creation" and "rule-application" is firmly upheld in the continental legal

---

d'Aspremont, 'The Rise and Fall of Democracy Governance in International Law: A Reply to Susan Marks' (2011) 22 European Journal of International Law 549. D'Aspremont argues that the years between 1989 and 2010 have constituted an "unprecedented epoch of international law during which most domestic governance [...] has been regulated by international law to an unprecedented extent, the latter going as far as to prescribe a given type of procedure for acceding to power at the domestic level" but that "recent practice is jeopardizing the consolidation of the above- mentioned practice in favour of a requirement of democratic origin of governments" and that "[a]fter almost two decades of care for the democratic origin of governments, it seems that we are witnessing a return to foreign policies centred on the manner in which governments exercise power". Reading these words against the backdrop of recent domestic as well as international developments, we must conclude that d'Aspremont's words are even more true today than they were in 2011 when the article was published.

16 In particular, the CESCR often recognizes that programs of action are important for the implementation of a right. Article 14 ICESCR even specifically regulates such an activity. See CESCR, *General Comment 11 (1999): Plans of action for primary education (article 14 of the International Covenant on Economic, Social and Cultural Rights)* (10 May 1999) UN Doc E/C.12/1999/4.

17 Javier Barnes, 'Three generations of administrative procedures' in Susan Rose-Ackerman and Peter L. Lindseth (eds), *Comparative Administrative Law* (2nd edn, Edward Elgar Publishing 2017), 310.

18 See *supra* Chap. 1 generally.

tradition.[19] According to this distinction, law application is construed—in contrast to law-making—as a mechanical process. The administration which applies the law is considered the "mouth of the law".[20] Its purpose is to "find what the law has previously established".[21]

Such a mechanical understanding of "law-application"—which negates its creative element—has rightfully been criticised as unconvincing and naïve.[22] The process of "applying" a norm to a specific case necessarily entails creative elements.[23] In a decision from 2016, the FCC expressed the creative element of law application well:

> *It is true that judicial law-making is not limited to the execution of given norms in the sense that the judge would act as a mere "bouche de la loi", i.e., as an "automatic subsumption machine". Rather, it is inherent in every judicial activity that it methodically interprets the content of legal norms and defines their scope of application in order to decide on its application in individual cases on the basis of the positive, abstract-general formulation of the law. In this respect, the application of law is also the creation of new, not yet existing law on the basis of and in accordance with applicable law, the specifications of which are to be ascertained by the practitioner of the law by means of legal knowledge.*[24]

---

[19] Barnes. See also Christoph Möllers, *The Three Branches: A Comparative Model of Separation of Powers* (Oxford University Press 2013), 82.

[20] Barnes, 310.

[21] Ibid, 310.

[22] Christoph Möllers, *Die drei Gewalten* (Velbrück Wissenschaft 2008), 93.

[23] See already Hans Kelsen, who called the process of interpretation and application "constitutive" as opposed to "declaratory", Hans Kelsen, *Reine Rechtslehre: Einleitung in die rechtswissenschaftliche Problematik (Studienausgabe der 1. Auflage 1934)* (Matthias Jestaedt ed, Mohr Siebeck 2008), 89–90. With more references, see also Wolfram Cremer, 'Rechtsanwendungsgleichheit im Mehrebenensystem' in Ute Sacksofsky (ed), *Veröffentlichung der Vereinigung der Deutschen Staatsrechtslehrer, Band 78, Gleichheit, Vielfalt, Technischer Wandel* (De Gruyter 2019), fn. 14.

[24] BVerfG NVwZ 2016, 1630 (1631): *"Zwar ist richterliche Rechtsfindung nicht auf den Vollzug vorgegebener Normen in dem Sinne beschränkt, dass der Richter dabei als bloße „bouche de la loi", dh als „Subsumtionsautomat" fungieren würde. Vielmehr ist es jeder richterlichen Tätigkeit immanent, dass sie den Inhalt gesetzlicher Normen methodisch interpretiert und deren Anwendungsbereich definiert, um auf der Grundlage des positiven, abstrakt-generell formulierten Gesetzes im Einzelfall über dessen Anwendung zu entscheiden. Auch Rechtsanwendung ist insofern die Erzeugung von neuem, noch nicht bestehendem Recht auf der Grundlage und nach Maßgabe von anzuwendendem Recht, dessen Vorgaben mittels Rechtserkenntnis vom Rechtsanwender zu eruieren sind."* Reference omitted.

The wording of the FCC hints at a categorisation of legal norms which can guide us towards a definition of "law application" and which acts of the administration are relevant for the present study: the categorisations of abstract versus concrete, and general versus individual law. According to this categorisation, abstract rules are rules which apply to an unlimited number of issues while concrete rules govern just one specific issue. General rules are rules that are directed at an unlimited number of persons while individual rules address a particular person. The two categorisations are combined to categorise legal action in the following way: abstract and general rules are rules that have an unlimited number of addressees and govern an unlimited number of situations. Laws fall under this categorisation. On the other end of the spectrum are concrete and individual forms of law which have only one addressee and govern only one specific situation. Judgments usually fall under this categorisation, as well as "administrative acts"[25].

Against the backdrop of this categorisation, we can describe the process of law application as the *transformation* of abstract and general laws or rules into concrete and individual rules in the form of administrative acts.[26] Defining law-application in this way recognises its creative aspect and it makes a good case for the relevance of prescribed procedures leading up to these decisions and thus ultimately of this study. If the application of a norm was an automatic process leading to entirely predetermined results, procedural norms such as those this study is interested in, would be superfluous. There would be no process to organize if the application of general and abstract norms was an automatism.[27] Moreover, a definition of law-application as the transformation of abstract and general rules into individual and concrete law explains why this type of administrative action is

[25] See Sect. 35 of the German Administrative Procedure Act (APA) which defines *"administrative act" as "any order, decision or other sovereign measure taken by an authority to regulate **an individual case** in the sphere of public law and intended to have a direct, external legal effect"* (emphasis added). Similarly, Article 2 (1) (g) of Parliament and Council Regulation (EU) 1367/2006 of 6 September 2006 on the application of the provisions of the Aarhus Convention on Access to Information, Public Participation in Decision-making and Access to Justice in Environmental Matters to Community institutions and bodies [2006] OJ L 264/1 defines "administrative act" as *"**any measure of individual scope** under environmental law, taken by a Community institution or body, and having legally binding and external effects"* (emphasis added). Importantly, these are definitions of non-universal scope of application. They are meant only to exemplify the concretisation and the individualisation this thesis focuses on.

[26] Möllers aptly describes this transformation as "concretisation", Möllers, *The Three Branches: A Comparative Model of Separation of Powers*, 106.

[27] Möllers, *Die drei Gewalten*, 93.

often likened to the judicial function.[28] Administrative acts represent "the end of a relation of concretisation" (*"Konkretisierungszusammenhang"*)[29] in the same sense as judgments.[30]

2.1.3 Administrative Procedure as the Required Process Leading up to an Administrative Act

> *When a public authority makes a decision, the substance of its decision is what it decided. In other words, the substance includes both the conclusion or outcome of the decision and the reasons used to support that outcome. The process by which the public body made the decision is the way in which it decided or, more precisely, the sum of the steps by which it decided.*[31]

For the purposes of this thesis, the substance is the decision reached in an individual case. And the process leading up to it is the administrative procedure, i.e., the "series of activities and acts, sequence of steps"[32] the administration must follow before reaching that decision. The word "must" is important here. This thesis approaches administrative procedures from a normative perspective. It is concerned with the (implicit) requirements of IHRL for the decision-making process of the administration of a state when it transforms abstract and general rules into concrete and individual ones: must the affected individual be involved in this process? And if so, which steps must be taken to realise her involvement? Hence, administrative procedure must not be equated with the actual (cognitive) decision-making process of the administrative official preparing a decision.

To conclude, we can define administrative procedure as a "series of activities and acts, sequence of steps" that an administrative officer of a state must follow whenever she "applies the law", i.e. whenever she transforms abstract and general law into concrete and individual law.

---

[28] Barnes, 304.

[29] Christoph Möllers, *Gewaltengliederung* (Mohr Siebeck 2005), 97.

[30] Möllers bases his insights (partly) on Kelsen who already wrote that large parts of the administration were "functionally no different at all" from courts, Kelsen, 90.

[31] Aileen Kavanagh, 'Reasoning about proportionality under the Human Rights Act 1998: outcomes, substance and process' (2014) 130 Law Quarterly Review 235, 247.

[32] Giacinto Della Cananea, *Due Process of Law beyond the State: Requirements of Administrative Procedure* (Oxford University Press 2016), 22.

2.2 The Scope of the Study: Analysing the ICCPR and the ICESCR

The field of IHRL is vast. There is a large number of human rights treaties of universal scope, many of which address specific issues or vulnerable groups. It is beyond the scope of this study to look at all parts of IHRL. In order to still be able to deduce results which will likely be of relevance to IHRL in general, this study looks at the ICCPR and the ICESCR.

The ICCPR and the ICESCR are central human rights treaties. They have been called "probably the most important and well-known instruments of their kind worldwide"[33], or even "the crown jewels of rights protection at the universal level"[34]. Together with the UDHR, these treaties represent the so-called "International Bill of Rights".[35] The UDHR was adopted by the United Nations General Assembly in 1948 and included "first and second generation" rights, i.e., it includes civil and political as well as economic, social and cultural rights. Its flaw was, of course, the fact that it was non-legally binding. So, after it had been adopted, the international community began the process of casting the human rights it stipulated into binding law.

This process, however, did not turn out to be easy. When the international community tried to translate those rights the UDHR had "outlined in utopian form"[36] into binding law, differences came to light that ultimately made it impossible for the international community to create one coherent legally binding document. Eventually, the drafters reached the compromise that shapes the landscape of IHRL until today: they created two different instruments, the ICCPR with civil and political rights, and the ICESCR with socio-economic rights.[37]

---

[33] Helen Keller and Daniel Moeckli, 'Introduction' in Daniel Moeckli, Helen Keller and Corina Heri (eds), *The Human Rights Covenants at 50: Their Past, Present, and Future* (Oxford Academic, Oxford University Press 2018), 4.

[34] Eibe Riedel, 'Reflections on the UN Human Rights Covenants at Fifty' (2016) 54 Archiv des Völkerrechts 132, 152.

[35] See on this notion and the historical development of the documents John P. Humphrey, 'The International Bill of Rights: Scope and Implementation Bicentennial Symposium: Constitutional Government—Strengths, Weaknesses, Future' (1975) 17 Wm & Mary L Rev 527.

[36] Walter Kälin and Jörg Künzli, *The Law of International Human Rights Protection* (2nd edn, Oxford University Press 2019), 36.

[37] For a summary of the discussions around which rights from the UDHR to be transferred to a binding instrument, see Maya Hertig Randall, 'The History of the Covenants: Looking Back Half a Century and Beyond' in Daniel Moeckli, Helen Keller and Corina Heri (eds),

The ICCPR has been called "probably the most important human rights treaty in the world".[38] It has quasi-universal coverage, with an astounding 173 state parties.[39] It is the most comprehensive codification of civil and political rights at the international level.[40] Its scope ranges from issues such as the protection of human life, Article 6, over the protection of privacy, Article 17, to the protection of a minimum of children's rights, Article 24, and minority rights, Article 27. While its scope *ratione materiae* is limited to civil and political rights, its general scope *ratione personae* is not limited. As per its Article 2 (1), the ICCPR applies to all individuals under the jurisdiction of a state.

The ICESCR is the most comprehensive instrument protecting economic, social and cultural rights at the universal level.[41] It has not less astounding 171 state parties, and thus enjoys similarly universal application as its civil and political counterpart.[42] It codifies diverse rights such as the right to work, Article 6, the right to an adequate standard of living, Article 11, or the right to take part in cultural life, Article 15.

Together, the covenants protect a large array of diverse rights which highlight different aspects of international human rights protection. While a categorical difference between the two generations of rights is no longer convincing,[43] the degree to which the rights enshrined in the covenants emphasise different types of obligations under IHRL varies considerably. The right to freedom of expression, e.g., is certainly more dependent on states' abstentions from interferences whereas the rights to adequate food or the highest attainable standard of health require much more positive action from states to be brought to fruition. Together, the two treaties and the pronouncements of the respective treaty bodies respectively cover a large array of state action. This allows us to reach conclusions which

The Human Rights Covenants at 50: Their Past, Present, and Future (Oxford University Press 2018), 14–17.

[38] Sarah Joseph and Melissa Castan, *The International Covenant on Civil and Political Rights: Cases, Materials, and Commentary* (3rd edn, Oxford University Press 2013), 3.

[39] See *Status of Ratification Interactive Dashboard: Ratification of 18 International Human Rights Treaties*, accessible at <http://indicators.ohchr.org/> accessed 26 August 2025.

[40] Kälin and Künzli, 37.

[41] Ibid, 37.

[42] See *Status of Ratification Interactive Dashboard: Ratification of 18 International Human Rights Treaties*, accessible at <http://indicators.ohchr.org/> accessed 26 August 2025.

[43] See only Randall, 19–20. For a discussion of the most prominent arguments for a categorical distinction and the respective counter arguments, see Riedel, 'Reflections on the UN Human Rights Covenants at Fifty', 136ff. For the argument that the difference between the two categories of rights is gradual rather than categorical, see *infra* 7.2.2.2.

are probably relevant to other fields of IHRL, too. At least, the results of this study can *prima facie* be considered relevant to other, more specialised parts of IHRL. With their quasi-universal geographical scope and their broad scope *ratione materiae*, the ICCPR and the ICESCR represent the best object of study for us to look into the relationship between IHRL and administrative procedure.

For the following analysis of the committees' approach to administrative procedure, this thesis relies mainly on the general comments of the Human Rights Committee (HRC) and the CESCR. In Philip Alston's words, a general comment is

> *a means by which a UN human rights expert committee distils its considered views on an issue which arises out of the provisions of the treaty whose implementation it supervises and presents those views in the context of a formal statement of its understanding to which it attaches major importance.*[44]

In the general comments, the committees aggregate, or "synthesize" their own jurisprudence on specific rights or specific issues.[45] Therefore, the general comments are particularly important sources for discerning the human rights doctrine developed by the committees.[46] Moreover, general comments help the committees to sharpen their understanding of their own work.[47] And the HRC has expressed its desire to support states in fulfilling their obligations with the General Comments.[48]

With these documents, the treaty bodies commit themselves to a certain understanding of the respective covenants and they will likely be guided in their application of the respective covenants by these interpretations.[49] In this sense,

[44] Philip Alston, 'The Historical Origins of the Concept of 'General Comments' in Human Rights Law' in Laurence Boisson de Chazournes and Vera Gowlland-Debbas (eds), *The International Legal System in Quest of Equity and Universality: Liber amicorum Georges Abi-Saab* (Brill | Nijhoff 2001), 764.

[45] Kälin and Künzli, 213.

[46] Ibid, 214. See also Jane Connors, 'United Nations' in Daniel Moeckli, Sangeeta Shah and Sandesh Sivakumaran (eds), *International Human Rights Law* (3rd edn, Oxford University Press 2018), 391–392.

[47] Eckart Klein and David Kretzmer, 'The UN Human Rights Committee: The General Comments—The Evolution of an Autonomous Monitoring Instrument' (2015) 58 German Yearbook of International Law 189, 199.

[48] HRC, *General Comments Adopted by the Human Rights Committee: Introduction* (19 May 1989) HRI/GEN/ 1/Rev. 6 p. 123.

[49] Christian Tomuschat, *Human Rights: Between Idealism and Realism* (3rd edn, Oxford University Press 2014), 235.

the general comments have "practical authority".[50] They can be considered "basic point[s] of reference" for the committees,[51] but not only for them. In contrast to views on individual communications and concluding observations on state reports, general comments are not restricted to individual cases or specific states. They are abstract, they are general, and it is precisely that which gives them a "significant potential to influence the understanding and development of human rights in a far-reaching and sustainable manner".[52] While general comments—like other documents of universal treaty bodies—are non-binding, they constitute "authoritative interpretations" of the covenants.[53] Given their role in clarifying treaty provisions, it was even suggested that they could be considered "secondary treaty law".[54]

Since they possess "normative significance [...] for the development of human rights law",[55] focusing on the general comments is a promising approach—especially for issues of general relevance such as ours. In fact, the statement that "[a]ppropriate procedural protection and due process are essential aspects of all human rights", the starting point of our analysis, comes from a general comment of the CESCR.[56] It is very likely that something that at least one of the committees considers so fundamental to the system of human rights protection is found in the general comments. As we will see, this is indeed the case. Beyond the analysis of the 63 general comments (37 produced by the HRC and 26 by

---

[50] Torkel Opsahl, 'The General Comments of the Human Rights Committee' in Jürgen Jekewitz and others (eds), *Des Menschen Recht zwischen Freiheit und Verantwortung: Festschrift für Karl Josef Partsch zum 75 Geburtstag* (Duncker & Humblot 1989), 284. See also Eibe Riedel, 'Einführung—Allgemeine Bemerkungen zu Bestimmungen des Internationalen Paktes über Wirtschaftliche, Soziale und Kulturelle Rechte der Vereinten Nationen' in Menschenrechte Deutsches Institut für (ed), *Die»General Comments« zu den VN-Menschenrechtsverträgen: Deutsche Übersetzung und Kurzeinführungen* (Nomos 2005), 164.

[51] Nigel S Rodley, 'The Role and Impact of Treaty Bodies' in Dinah Shelton (ed), *The Oxford Handbook of International Human Rights Law* (Oxford University Press 2013), 632.

[52] Klein and Kretzmer, 209.

[53] See ibid, 204–210.

[54] Christine Chinkin, 'Sources' in Daniel Moeckli, Sangeeta Shah and Sandesh Sivakumaran (eds), *International Human Rights Law* (3rd edn, Oxford University Press 2018), 69. Chinkin rightfully relativises this characterisation, however, by pointing to the fact that treaty bodies do not have law-making power.

[55] Kerstin Mechlem, 'Treaty Bodies and the Interpretation of Human Rights' (2009) 42 Vanderbilt Journal of Transnational Law 905, 929.

[56] CESCR, GC 7, para. 15.

the CESCR), this study includes other relevant documents produced by the committees, in particular views adopted in response to individual communications, but also concluding observations where they can contribute something to our understanding of the relevance of administrative procedure to IHRL.

2.3 Unpromising Paths Towards Obligations for Administrative Procedure Under IHRL

To define the scope of this study more precisely, we shall exclude some unpromising paths towards construing the importance of administrative procedure to IHRL. Firstly, we will give an overview of and exclude explicit procedural rights and obligations in the ICCPR and the ICESCR (2.3.1). Secondly, we shall exclude an (analogous) application to the administrative decision-making processes of Article 14 ICCPR guaranteeing the right to fair trial (2.3.2). Finally, we will exclude Article 25 ICCPR as a convincing basis for obligations of administrative procedure under IHRL (2.3.3).

2.3.1 Explicit Procedural Rights and Obligations in the Covenants

Procedures are rarely spelled out (in detail) in the two covenants. Explicit procedural rights and obligations are rare in IHRL generally—at least for those parts of the documents that govern the relationship between the state and the individual. The relative lack of concrete procedural obligations is no wonder given the necessarily vague terms of international human rights treaties.[57] Nevertheless, there are certain provisions in the texts of IHRL treaties that codify procedural rights and obligations.

In Part II of the ICCPR, which stipulates the general obligations of states parties, we find only two provisions which mention procedural obligations directly. According to Article 2 (3) (b) ICCPR, each state party must

[57] See on the necessarily vague wording in human rights law treaties Başak Çalı, 'Specialized Rules of Treaty Interpretation: Human Rights' in Duncan B. Hollis (ed), *The Oxford Guide to Treaties* (Oxford University Press 2012), 531ff. Moreover, for more elaboration on this, see *infra* 8.2.1.1.1.

> *ensure that any person claiming [...] a remedy shall have his right thereto determined by competent judicial, administrative or legislative authorities, or by any other competent authority provided for by the legal system of the State.*

This provision does concretize the right to an effective remedy, enshrined in Article 2 (3) (a) ICCPR by sketching out some organizational and procedural requirements for how to realize the right to an effective remedy. Notably—according to its wording –the provision applies only to cases in which an alleged human rights violation has already occurred.[58] It is thus questionable whether Article 2 (3) ICCPR provides a means to prevent unjustified interferences with human rights from happening or whether it is merely a means to fight those interferences that have already taken place.[59] The other provision that spells out procedural obligations explicitly is Article 4 (3) ICCPR. The provision obliges states that take emergency measures to inform the other states parties through the intermediary of the Secretary General of the United Nations (UN). This obligation, however, is clearly an inter-state obligation and thus of no relevance to the present study.

Part III which contains the specific rights protected by the covenant contains some more precise procedural provisions, most prominently in its Article 9 ICCPR that codifies the right to liberty. The provision contains by far the most detailed prescriptions on procedural obligations. It spells out quite specific procedural rights for someone deprived of her liberty. The first paragraph is yet very general when it prescribes that individuals may only be deprived of their liberty "on such grounds and in accordance with such procedures as are established by law". The following paragraphs then spell out some features which "such procedures" must contain, namely prompt information of the reasons for the arrest and the charges brought (para. 2), prompt hearing in front of a judge and the right to a trial within a reasonable time (para. 3), as well as the right to an immediate review of the deprivation of liberty (para. 4). Interestingly, however, these procedural obligations apply only once the right has already been interfered with, i.e. after the initial detention. They do not stipulate obligations for how the decision to detain somebody must be reached, e.g. to hear the affected individual. The individual only has a right to be heard in order to challenge the detention once the arrest has already taken place. Article 10 (2) (d) ICCPR then stipulates

---

[58] Joseph and Castan, 867; Kälin and Künzli, 182.

[59] We will return to this question *infra* 7.2.2.1, and exclude the provision as a doctrinal basis there.

what could be described as *lex specialis* to Article 9 (3) ICCPR for juvenile persons, namely that "accused juvenile persons shall be separated from adults and brought as speedily as possible for adjudication".

Another provision that explicitly mentions certain requirements for a procedure in which a given right is to be realized is Article 25 (b) ICCPR. The provisions is devoted to the right to vote and prescribes that elections "shall be held by secret ballot, guaranteeing the free expression of the will of the electors". Just like the procedural guarantees in Article 9, this provision prescribes procedures not as ends in themselves, but as means to an end. In this case, the provision is even rather specific about its objective, namely to guarantee "the free expression of the will of the electors".

Finally, the ICCPR contains provisions the very substance of which are procedures. Article 13 ICCPR prescribes that

> *[a]n alien lawfully in the territory of a State Party to the present Covenant may be expelled therefrom only in pursuance of a decision reached in accordance with law and shall, except where compelling reasons of national security otherwise require, be allowed to submit the reasons against his expulsion and to have his case reviewed by, and be represented for the purpose before, the competent authority or a person or persons especially designated by the competent authority.*

This provision is significant because it is *merely* procedural. It does not provide standards for when an expulsion is materially lawful. Importantly, however, its scope is limited to expulsion procedures of persons residing lawfully in the territory of a state.

The most prominent provision stipulating procedural guarantees explicitly is Article 14 ICCPR. The provision contains a number of fair trial rights which are all procedural in nature. Importantly, the provision is not supportive in the sense that it would serve the better protection of other rights. Article 14 ICCPR is—at least when regarded individually—an end in and of itself. The provision is sometimes construed to provide for procedural guarantees outside its explicit scope—most importantly in connection with the asylum procedure and non-refoulement. Hence, we will reflect on whether it could be a convincing doctrinal basis for the obligations of administrative procedure we consider in this study in the following section.

Turning to the ICESCR, we find that provisions stipulating explicit procedural protection and obligations in the ICESCR are even rarer. According to Article 2 (1) ICESCR, states must realize the rights recognized in the covenant progressively. One could understand this obligation of progressive realization as a "procedural obligation", in the sense that the realization of economic, social and cultural rights is envisaged by Article 2 (1) ICESCR as a process. However, it does not refer to a procedure in the sense of this thesis.

Article 14 ICESCR includes an obligatory decision-making process. It stipulates that

> *[e]ach State Party to the present Covenant which, at the time of becoming a Party, has not been able to secure in its metropolitan territory or other territories under its jurisdiction compulsory primary education, free of charge, undertakes, within two years, to work out and adopt a detailed plan of action for the progressive implementation, within a reasonable number of years, to be fixed in the plan, of the principle of compulsory education free of charge for all.*

This provision only obliges the states parties to go through a certain process and does not stipulate any necessary components of the procedure. And, importantly for our study, the decision-making process stipulated here is a process on the macro-level. Abstract and general normative considerations or even rules will stand at the end of the process, not a concrete decision in an individual case. Other than that, the ICESCR does not contain any procedural obligations like the ones in the ICCPR mentioned above.

There are no obviously promising paths for our endeavour in these procedural provisions in the covenants. The only provision we have just discussed which could potentially serve as a basis of obligations of administrative procedure is Article 14 ICCPR to which we will now turn.

2.3.2 Article 14 ICCPR—A More or Less Direct Way to Adequate Procedural Protection *vis à vis* the Administration?

Article 14 ICCPR is, perhaps, the most obvious norm in the two treaties to derive procedural rights of individuals *vis à vis* a state's administration from. But could it be a convincing doctrinal basis for obligations of administrative procedure? Parts of the literature construe Article 14 ICCPR—at least *inter alia*—as a supplementary right. James Hathaway, in his seminal textbook on the rights of refugees, for example, claims that Article 14 ICCPR offers a "sound basis for arguing the entitlement of refugees to a formal legal entitlement of their rights, at least by way of review or appeal if these rights are denied by more informal decision-making structures".[60] In this understanding, Article 14 ICCPR is (at least also) a supplementary right that supports other rights, in this case the rights of refugees.

Hathaway writes this in connection with the asylum procedure—a procedure that is usually executed by administrative bodies of a state, but acknowledges that the scope of the provision might pose a challenge to the application to procedures leading up to a first-instance administrative decision. And indeed, according to the wording of the provision, the right to equality before "courts and tribunals" applies to courts and tribunals. The wording thus excludes an application of the provision to administrative bodies. It would, however, not be the first time that a provision's scope was widened, e.g., by way of analogy. So, are there good reasons for applying Article 14 ICCPR to the administrative decision-making process?

In 1984, the HRC devoted its first general comment to Article 14 ICCPR and called it "Article 14 (Administration of justice)"[61]. Reading the body of the text, one soon realizes that the HRC does not construe Article 14 ICCPR as an all-encompassing provision providing for procedural protection applicable to all situations in which "justice" is at stake. Firstly, the term "administration" in the heading does not refer to the totality of all non-legislative and non-judiciary state organs. It is used here as a derivative of the verb "to administer", in a sense that is closer to "award", like someone administers medicine. Secondly, the general comment, already in its first paragraph clarifies that Article 14 ICCPR is "*aimed* at ensuring the proper administration of justice".[62] Thus, the title of the general comment reflects the object and purpose of Article 14 ICCPR and does not directly say anything about its scope. Beyond these observations, there is not much to gain from General Comment 13. It is still very general and does not give us much information with regard to a potential (analogous) application of the provision to administrative procedures.

In 2007, the HRC replaced General Comment 13 with General Comment 32. The new general comment is entitled "Right to equality before courts and tribunals and to a fair trial". Not only does the title of the new version signify the material scope of the provision, rather than its object and purpose. The general comment also describes the specific rights and contents of Article 14 ICCPR in

---

[60] James C. Hathaway, *The Rights of Refugees under International Law* (Cambridge University Press 2005), 647.

[61] HRC, *General comment No. 13: Article 14 (Administration of justice)* (1984) HRI/GEN/1/Rev.9 (Vol. I) p. 184.

[62] Ibid, para. 1 (emphasis added).

much greater detail, taking into account states' views and developments since the first general comment on the provision. General Comment 32 allows for a much better grasp of the HRC's understanding of Article 14 ICCPR. Given that paragraphs two to seven of the provision apply exclusively to criminal proceedings—and therefore do not offer a promising path for us, the following remarks focus on the first two sentences of Article 14 (1) ICCPR and what the general comment has to say on these.

The first sentence stipulates the guarantee of equality before courts and tribunals. This includes the right to equal access to courts and tribunals—if necessary facilitated via financial and legal assistance[63] –, the right to similar procedural treatment in similar cases[64], and the right to equality of arms, that includes *inter alia* that "each side be given the opportunity to contest all the arguments and evidence adduced by the other party"[65]. According to the HRC, the guarantee applies "whenever domestic law entrusts a judicial body with a judicial task".[66] This statement is sobering. It mentions only "judicial tasks" and thus excludes administrative functions. The guarantee of equality before courts and tribunals can thus not serve as a convincing doctrinal basis.

However, Article 14 (1) ICCPR also stipulates the right to a fair and public hearing, before a competent, independent and impartial tribunal established by law in case someone has her rights determined in a suit at law. Does this right warrant the derivation of standards for administrative decision-making from the provision? According to General Comment 32, "suit at law" encompasses not only "judicial proceedings aimed at determining rights and obligations pertaining to the areas of contract, property and torts in the area of private law" but also

> *equivalent notions in the area of administrative law such as the termination of employment of civil servants for other than disciplinary reasons, the determination of social security benefits or the pension rights of soldiers, or procedures regarding the use of public land or the taking of private property.*[67]

Moreover, the HRC leaves open the possibility of including "other procedures which, however, must be assessed on a case by case basis in the light of the

[63] HRC, *General Comment No. 32, Article 14: Right to equality before courts and tribunals and to a fair trial* (23 August 2007) UN Doc CCPR/C/GC/32, paras. 9–12.

[64] Ibid, para. 14.

[65] Ibid, para. 13.

[66] Ibid, para. 7.

[67] Ibid, para. 16.

nature of the right in question".[68] Although this statement at first glance seems promising for our purposes, the parallel that the HRC draws with private law claims which is also reflected in the examples the HRC refers to, is a first indication in the opposite direction. Private law relations are usually peer-to-peer relations in which the subjects are on equal footing. Situations in which individuals face administrative bodies, however, constitute typical public law relations in the sense that the individual is subjected to the power of the state official.

This becomes more apparent with the following two paragraphs. The HRC goes on to list cases that are not covered by the procedural protection which Article 14 (1) ICCPR offers. These include situations in which "persons concerned are confronted with measures taken against them in their capacity as persons subordinated to a high degree of administrative control, such as disciplinary measures not amounting to penal sanctions being taken against a civil servant, a member of the armed forces, or a prisoner".[69] Moreover, the HRC excludes the application to "extradition, expulsion and deportation procedures".[70] While those examples the HRC lists under measures taken against persons "subordinated to a high degree of administrative control" might in part be justified with the idea that state agents themselves need not be protected against the state, the example of prisoners make clear that the HRC's understanding of Article 14 ICCPR is not suitable for our purposes. Because of the "high degree of administrative control" that prisoners are subjected to, they are particularly vulnerable and thus—one could argue—in particular need of procedural protection. Moreover, the examples highlight the "private law comparability" requirement that the HRC established in the paragraph before.

Finally, in the following paragraph, the HRC defines "tribunal" as "a body [...] that is [...] independent of the executive and legislative branches of government or enjoys in specific cases judicial independence in deciding legal matters in proceedings that are judicial in nature".[71] This passage ultimately tells us that the HRC does not consider Article 14 (1) ICCPR to be applicable to administrative procedures. Surely, "tribunal" is not a requirement for Article 14 ICCPR to apply. Rather, it is a necessary legal consequence: Whenever someone finds themselves in a suit at law, they have a right to have it decided by a qualified tribunal. However, the fact that it needs to be "independent of the executive" makes it clear that the fair structuring of the first-instance administrative decision-making

[68] Ibid.

[69] Ibid, para. 17.

[70] Ibid.

[71] Ibid, para. 18.

process is not the end of Article 14 ICCPR. The provision is meant to secure the individual's position *vis à vis* those bodies of the state that exercise judicial functions.

2.3.3 Administrative Procedure as an Obligation Under Article 25 (a) ICCPR?

Another provision which does not invoke procedural guarantees directly but could—*prima facie*—nevertheless give rise to obligations of administrative procedure is Article 25 (a) ICCPR. The provision codifies the right to "take part in the conduct of public affairs". "Conduct of public affairs" has been interpreted very broadly by the HRC in its General Comment 25. While Article 25 (b) and (c) concern the specific aspects of access to voting and public service, the HRC held that

> *[t]he conduct of public affairs, referred to in paragraph (a), is a broad concept which relates to the exercise of political power, in particular the exercise of legislative, executive and administrative powers. It covers all aspects of public administration, and the formulation and implementation of policy at international, national, regional and local levels. The allocation of powers and the means by which individual citizens exercise the right to participate in the conduct of public affairs protected by article 25 should be established by the constitution and other laws.*[72]

This statement is remarkable. Firstly, whenever public power is exercised, citizens have "the right and the opportunity [...] [t]o take part" in the conduct that is the exercise of public power. Secondly, the HRC highlights those branches of government that are not the judiciary, explicitly including the administration of a state[73], making the statement explicitly transferable to the object of this study. The committee then continues that the conduct of public affairs covers "all aspects of public administration, and the formulation *and implementation* of policy at international, national, regional and local levels". This statement clarifies that the application of a certain policy to an individual and a specific case by the administration of a state—and thus the mode of exercise of public power in the constellation that this study is interested in—falls under the concept of conduct of

[72] HRC, *General comment No. 25: Article 25 (Participation in public affairs and the right to vote)* (1996) HRI/GEN/1/Rev.9 (Vol. I) p. 217, para. 5.

[73] The fact that the HRC does not highlight the judiciary here can arguably be attributed to the fact that the ICCPR contains a separate provision guaranteeing procedural rights *vis à vis* the judiciary, Article 14 ICCPR.

public affairs. The HRC dedicates the remaining paragraphs of General Comment 25 to the other guarantees enshrined in Article 25 ICCPR, especially the right to vote. Only the statement represented here is devoted to Article 25 (a) ICCPR. This could be an indication that the HRC considers Article 25 (a) ICCPR to be somewhat of a fallback provision.

Given that the right to participate in the conduct of public affairs is so far-reaching and includes those constellations this study is interested in, have we perhaps already found our doctrinal basis for procedural rights *vis à vis* a state's administration? There are two reasons why this is not the case. Firstly, a doctrinal construction relying on one specific right is arguably not the type of construction that the CESCR had in mind when it held that adequate procedural protection was an essential element of "all human rights". Given that Article 25 ICCPR applies only to those states that have ratified the ICCPR, it is not a convincing construction to substantiate the proposition that all human rights require procedural protection. Secondly, and more importantly, the right has a narrow scope *ratione personae*. It is applicable only to those persons who are citizens of the state in question.[74] Everyone not having the nationality of the state in question would not benefit from the procedural protection the provision offers. Asylum-seekers dealing with border control authorities, e.g., would not fall under the scope of the right. Migrant workers dealing with immigration authorities would not either. Thus, Article 25 (a) ICCPR cannot function as the doctrinal basis for an obligation to ensure adequate procedural protection of all human rights due to its narrow scope *ratione personae*.

2.3.4 Conclusion

As we have seen, there are no provisions in the two covenants from which we could convincingly derive obligations of administrative procedure. Even more so, there are no provisions explicitly codifying the kinds of obligations we are looking for. Hence, the basis for obligations of administrative procedure can only be found in the general doctrine of IHRL (in the sense of *"allgemeine Menschenrechtslehren"*). Such a construction is also in line with the CESCR's statement that procedural protection was an essential element of all human rights and with

[74] Paul M. Taylor, *A Commentary on the International Covenant on Civil and Political Rights: The UN Human Rights Committee's Monitoring of ICCPR Rights* (Cambridge University Press 2020), 693.

the aspiration of IHRL to provide a certain standard of protection to everyone, regardless of their nationality.

2.4 Methodological Approach and Course of the Study

So far, no comprehensive research has been done on the relationship between IHRL and the involvement of the affected individual in the decision-making process of a state's administration. The topic is rarely discussed and those remarks that exist are mostly limited to laconic sentences in hand- or textbooks.[75] In order to nevertheless think about the connection in a way that will lead to reasonable results, this thesis follows a two-step process. In this section, we will describe this two-step process, i.e., the development of an analytical foil from the jurisprudence of the FCC and the subsequent analysis of IHRL through the analytical foil (2.4.1) and explain why this is a promising and viable approach (2.4.2). Moreover, we will discuss how such an approach can contribute to more honest IHRL scholarship (2.4.3).

2.4.1 Analysing IHRL Through a Constitutional Law Analytical Foil

This thesis studies the relationship between IHRL and administrative procedure in a two-step process. In a first step (part II of this thesis), we will develop the analytical foil from the jurisprudence of the FCC. In Germany, the relationship between constitutional basic rights enshrined in Articles 1–19 of the Basic Law and administrative procedure has been the subject of an extensive debate since the 1970s. German scholars and German courts have developed elaborate explanations and justifications for the procedure-dependence of basic rights realization. And the FCC has been developing the idea of "fundamental rights protection

[75] For an example, see Andrew Byrnes and Catherine Renshaw, 'Within the State' in Daniel Moeckli, Sangeeta Shah and Sandesh Sivakumaran (eds), *International Human Rights Law* (3rd edn, Oxford University Press 2018), 495, who, after highlighting that the role of the executive in protection human rights is "also critical", devote but one sentence to the idea of procedural protection *vis à vis* the executive of a state.

through procedures and organization"[76] since the late 1960s. The jurisprudence of the court will provide us with insights into how individual rights and guarantees of administrative procedure are connected. From these insights, we will craft an analytical foil which will allow us to analyse the pronouncements of the committees in a more targeted way.

Chapter 3 will give a brief overview of the historical development of the idea of the procedural dimension of the fundamental rights under the German constitution. Chapter 4 will address the "detour via objective law"[77] necessary to derive positive procedural rights from the catalogue of originally negative fundamental rights of the Basic Law. Chapter 5 will show that the FCC relies on both, an instrumental and a dignitarian justification. Given that the procedural dimension of fundamental rights is not originally enshrined in the Basic Law but represents a "development under the constitution"[78], such justifications were necessary. Finally, Chapter 6 will address the issues of enforceability, implementation and the standard of review employed by the FCC. Importantly, part II of this thesis is not meant to make a substantive contribution to the academic discourse on German fundamental rights. It is only meant to allow us to sharpen our observations on the pronouncements of the HRC and the CESCR, and to develop new thoughts on the doctrine of IHRL and its relationship to administrative procedure.

In a second step (part III of the thesis), we will analyse the ICCPR and the ICESCR as well as the respective pronouncements of the HRC and the CESCR through the so-developed analytical foil. In doing so, part III will essentially mirror the structure of part II. Chapter 7 seeks to discuss and identify the (precise) doctrinal basis for an obligation of administrative procedure under IHRL. Chapter 8 asks how such an obligation could be justified, and Chap. 9 entertains reflections on implementation and enforceability of obligations of administrative procedure. At the end, we will have a comprehensive overview of the relationship between IHRL and administrative procedure, and in particular over the importance of involving affected individuals in the decision-making processes of states' administrations.

---

[76] This formula was first coined by Konrad Hesse, cf. Konrad Hesse, 'Bestand und Bedeutung der Grundrechte in der Bundesrepublik Deutschland' (1978) Europäische Grundrechtezeitschrift (EuGRZ) 427, 434.

[77] Hans D. Jarass, 'Grundrechte als Wertentscheidungen bzw. objektivrechtliche Prinzipien in der Rechtsprechung des Bundesverfassungsgerichts' (1985) 110 Archiv des Öffentlichen Rechts 363, 369.

[78] Ernst-Wolfgang Böckenförde, 'Grundrechte als Grundsatznormen: Zur gegenwärtigen Lage der Grundrechtsdogmatik' (1990) 29 Der Staat 1, 2.

2.4.2 Why the Approach is Possible and Promising

Why is such a two-step approach possible and promising? That is because of the (structural) similarities between (German) fundamental rights and international human rights (2.4.2.1) and because we are not drawing normative consequences from German constitutional law for IHRL (2.4.2.2).

2.4.2.1 "Something Inherently Constitutional" in IHRL

The historical origins of modern IHRL are contested.[79] Most accounts, however, link the development of human rights back to the development of catalogues of constitutional rights during the era of enlightenment, such as the Declaration of the Rights of Man and of the Citizen in France of 1789 and the American Bill of Rights of 1791.[80] In one way or another, it can certainly be said that international human rights are "an offspring of the human rights that were originally codified at national level".[81] Beyond this historical connection, constitutional rights and international human rights have a lot in common, functionally, content-wise and structurally. This section will explain these similarities in order to justify why developing an analytical foil from the FCC's jurisprudence on fundamental rights is a promising endeavour and why it is valuable for thinking about the relationship between administrative procedure and international human rights.

In his article "Human Rights as International Constitutional Rights", Stephan Gardbaum explores whether the Universal Declaration of Human Rights (UDHR), the ICCPR, and the ICESCR, are sufficiently similar to a constitutional bill of rights to justify their nickname "International Bill of Rights".[82] To this end, he identifies similarities and differences between the two categories of individual

[79] See instead of many Philip Alston, 'Book Review: Does the Past Matter? On the Origins of Human Rights, The Slave Trade and the Origins of International Human Rights Law' (2013) 126 Harvard Law Review 2043, and Christopher McCrudden, 'Human Rights Histories' (2015) 35 Oxford Journal of Legal Studies 179.

[80] Ed Bates, 'History' in Daniel Moeckli, Sangeeta Shah and Sandesh Sivakumaran (eds), *International Human Rights Law* (3rd edn, Oxford University Press 2018); Kälin and Künzli, 4ff. Tomuschat even calls IHRL an "offspring of the human rights that were originally codified at the national level", Tomuschat, *Human Rights: Between Idealism and Realism*, 12ff.

[81] Tomuschat, *Human Rights: Between Idealism and Realism*, 137.

[82] For a comparison between American constitutional rights and human rights see Louis Henkin, 'Rights: American and Human' (1979) 79 Columbia Law Review 405.

rights and comes to the conclusion that "[t]here is undoubtedly something inherently constitutional in the very nature and subject-matter of international human rights law"[83].

Firstly, constitutional rights and international human rights are functionally similar. They share the "same basic function of stating limits on what governments may do to people within their jurisdictions".[84] They are both means to limit the exercise of public power. Accordingly, they both apply between states and individuals. Both work under the same "public law paradigm".[85] Hence, both categories of rights have something to say about the relationship between states and individuals under their jurisdiction. For us, this similarity is important as it makes it reasonable to assume that both fields of law have something to say about the design of administrative procedures. After all this is how most individuals experience the exercise of public power by the state.

Secondly, they share content-wise similarities. Most catalogues of fundamental rights in constitutions protect—at least to a certain extent—the same rights which can be found in the ICCPR, the ICESCR, and the UDHR.[86] Thirdly, and most importantly, however, both groups of rights are structurally similar. Aside from a few absolute rights, i.e., the prohibition of torture—guaranteed only conditionally; they are "presumptive shields rather than absolute trumps".[87] This means that these rights can be curtailed if there is justification for the state to do so. For example, in the case of freedom of expression, the German Basic Law states that it finds its limits "in the provision of general laws, in provisions for the protection of young persons and in the right to personal honour", Article 5 (2) Basic Law. The norm provides for an opportunity to introduce laws which restrict the right to freedom of expression for the stated objectives. Article 19 (3) ICCPR similarly states that the right to freedom of expression "may [...] be subject to certain restrictions" in order to ensure respect of the rights of others and for reasons of national security, public order, public health or morals. Both, the fundamental rights of the Basic Law, and international human rights allow for compromises between the individual interests they are meant to protect and the interests of the public within which these interests are to be protected.

---

[83] Stephen Gardbaum, 'Human Rights as International Constitutional Rights' (2008) 19 European Journal of International Law 749, 752.

[84] Ibid, 750.

[85] Many rights, however, find their way into the (legal) relationships between private parties by way of indirect application (*"Drittwirkung"*) or regulation of private law.

[86] Gardbaum, 750–751.

[87] Ibid, 751.

Robert Alexy analysed and described this structure of constitutional rights brilliantly in his seminal book "A Theory of Constitutional Rights".[88] In the book, Alexy has shown how the principle of proportionality followed from constitutional rights' nature as principles, i.e., their nature as "optimisation requirements". They require "that something be realized to the greatest extent possible given the legal and factual requirements".[89] We will revisit his seminal theory in a later place in this study.[90] Here, it suffices to recall that his theory of constitutional rights, and with it his justification of the principle of proportionality, has been very influential across the world. It has been received by constitutional lawyers all over the world but has also become a prominent feature in the discourse on international human rights.[91] That a work originally written for German constitutional rights has gained such a prominence in the IHRL discourse, is further proof of the structural similarity between constitutional and international human rights.

Between different jurisdictions, their constitutions and different regimes of human rights protection, the specific content of rights as well as their scope and exceptions obviously vary considerably.[92] Again looking to the right to freedom of speech, we will find that the legal order of the United States of America makes much fewer restrictions on the right than European constitutions and European constitutional law practice.[93] Moreover, the scope and content of the human right to freedom of speech also varies between different international and regional human rights regimes.[94] However, the general structure of rights remains the

[88] Robert Alexy, *A Theory of Constitutional Rights* (Julian Rivers tr, Oxford University Press 2002).

[89] Ibid, 47–48.

[90] See *infra* 5.1.2.1.2.

[91] See, e.g., Yutaka Arai-Takahashi, 'Proportionality' in Dinah Shelton (ed), *The Oxford Handbook of International Human Rights Law* (Oxford University Press 2013).

[92] Dieter Grimm, 'Freedom of Speech in a Globalized World' in Ivan Hare and James Weinstein (eds), *Extreme Speech and Democracy* (Oxford University Press 2009).

[93] For an overview of different regulatory approaches for free speech online, see Oreste Pollicino, 'Judicial Protection of Fundamental Rights in the Transition from the World of Atoms to the Word of Bits: The Case of Freedom of Speech' (2019) 25 European Law Journal; Brittany Wolf, 'Free Speech versus Human Dignity: Comparative Perspectives on Internet Privacy' (2014) 23 Tulane Journal of International and Comparative Law 251.

[94] For an overview of how different human rights treaties address the edge case of extreme speech and attempts at explanations for the differences, see Ivan Hare, 'Extreme Speech under International and Regional Human Rights Standards' in Ivan Hare and James Weinstein (eds), *Extreme Speech and Democracy* (Oxford University Press 2009).

same. In fact, it is their shared structure that allows for their varied realisation, implementation, and application in different jurisdictions.

Prima facie, these similarities explain why the approach taken here, i.e., to turn to constitutional law doctrine to try to find clarity and inspiration for answering questions regarding human rights, is promising. It explains why we may expect it to be fruitful for a better understanding of the relevance of (administrative) procedure to IHRL. But are there differences that would prohibit such an endeavour? Of course, there are differences between constitutional law and IHRL. However, they are mainly institutional and concern the enforcement of rights.[95] These differences are important, they are arguably the reason for much of the frustration with international human rights, and they should play a role when appreciating the pronouncements of international human rights bodies and the jurisprudence of constitutional courts respectively. Moreover, they entail daunting questions about the potential enforcement of the suggestions made here which warrant further academic enquiries. However, these are questions that this work is only marginally concerned with. This study is a normative inquiry into the requirements of IHRL for the relationship between individuals and state administrations. Questions of enforcement arise on another level so that, at least for our purposes, the approach taken by this thesis is promising indeed. Nevertheless, remaining mindful of the differences between constitutional rights and human rights is important to prevent overreaching, biased and unconvincing results.

2.4.2.2 Inspiration, not a Necessary Normative Consequence

The methodological approach taken here, i.e., to draw inspiration from national law for IHRL, is by no means revolutionary. International human rights bodies regularly look to national constitutional rights and respective juridical practice.[96] That these courts which are mandated by parts of the international community do so, could provide another argument for considering constitutional rights doctrine.

---

[95] Gardbaum, 751. The other difference with Gardbaum notices is that bills of rights typically have constitutional status within national legal systems whereas human rights treaties do not necessarily enjoy such a high status. However, this might not be true for all systems of international human rights enforcement. Regional systems can be very sophisticated as the example of the European Court of Human Rights (ECtHR) shows, see Alec Stone Sweet, 'Sur la constitutionnalisation de la Convention européenne des droit de l'hommes: Cinquante ans après son installation, la Cour européenne des droit de l'homme conçue comme une Cour constituionnelle' (2009) 80 Revue trimestrielle des droits de l'homme 923.

[96] On the cooperation between the ECtHR and European constitutional courts, see Andreas Voßkuhle, 'Multilevel Cooperation of the European Constitutional Courts: Der Europäische Verfassungsgerichtsverbund' (2010) 6 European Constitutional Law Review 175.

Many states have "adjusted their constitutional methodologies", either by incorporating human rights treaties into their constitution or by their courts and judicial bodies' relying heavily on IHRL when interpreting constitutional rights.[97] When constitutional courts interpret constitutional rights in line with what they consider to be IHRL, they implicitly make statements about human rights treaties, too.[98] For such observations to carry any normative research and thus provide a justification for research such as ours, however, they would need to be backed up by a comprehensive and detailed analysis of a sufficiently large and diverse amount of constitutional courts' practice. Only such an analysis could potentially justify drawing normative consequences from what the examined national courts have said for IHRL. But it is obviously beyond what this thesis can deliver.

This thesis takes a different comparative approach. What we are seeking is analytical clarity and inspiration, not normative guidance. Such an approach is not in need of any justification beyond the similarities we have highlighted in the previous section. There are three ways in which comparative legal exercises can be approached.[99] It can firstly be used for merely ornamental purposes, when there is no obvious connection between the foreign law that is referred to and a reference is only made to increase an author's prestige.[100] Secondly, comparative law exercises can be undertaken for inspirational purposes, as a "source of fresh ideas".[101] Thirdly, comparative law can be used to make a direct normative argument. Such an argument can be empirical, e.g., when a certain approach has turned out badly in other jurisdictions and the argument is that it should thus be avoided. Or the foreign law becomes a normative argument itself. This is the case when a court or legislature wants to adopt a particular solution *simply because* others have done so, too.[102] Only the third variant needs particular justification

[97] See with examples Gerald L. Neuman, 'The Uses of International Law in Constitutional Interpretation' (2004) 98 The American Journal of International Law 82, 84–89.

[98] Such an approach for national courts is—at least from an international legal point of view—desirable given that states and their courts are bound by IHRL. Peter Häberle has thus argued for the comparative legal method as the "fifth interpretation method", Peter Häberle, 'Grundrechtsgeltung und Grundrechtsinterpretation im Verfassungsstaat — Zugleich zur Rechtsvergleichung als „fünfter" Auslegungsmethode' (1989) 44 JuristenZeitung 913, 916–918.

[99] Jan M. Smits, 'Comparative Law and Its Influence on National Legal Systems' in Mathias Reimann and Reinhard Zimmermann (eds), *The Oxford Handbook of Comparative Law* (Oxford University Press 2006), 525.

[100] Ibid, 527.

[101] Ibid, 525.

[102] Ibid, 526.

as only it draws direct normative consequences from observations about other jurisdictions.[103]

This thesis does, however, not make a normative argument for IHRL based on German constitutional law. It is in the second "inspirational" sense that this thesis takes a comparative approach. It does not seek to find definite answers to questions about international human rights in the practice of the FCC. Its outcome is not going to be that the FCC's jurisprudence should guide the HRC and CESCR in their interpretation of the ICCPR and the ICESCR respectively. The purpose of the approach taken here is to sharpen our view of the committees' pronouncements and to seek inspiration from a legal system in which the discussion of the procedure-dependence of individual rights has been going on for many years.

Moreover, our approach will allow us to learn something about international human rights also by contrasting German constitutional law with IHRL. By comparison, we will be able to highlight or even gain important insights about the nature of IHRL which will inform our normative construction advanced in the following chapter. Hence, not only "positive inspiration" will be possible, but also "negative inspiration" in the sense that we might also understand what might not work for IHRL.

2.4.3 An Attempt at Honest and Transparent Human Rights Scholarship

An important final point about the methodological approach of this study is that besides enabling a more targeted and clearer analysis, our approach is meant to lead to greater transparency and honesty. The interpretive process is always determined to some extent by the societal context within which it takes place,[104] and by the convictions of the interpreter[105]. Everyone who engages in the (academic) discussion on international law does so with certain normative preconceptions

103 Ibid, 527ff.

104 Andrea Bianchi, 'Textual interpretation and (international) law reading: the myth of (in)determinacy and the genealogy of meaning' in Michael Waibel, Pieter H. F. Bekker and Rudolf Dolzer (eds), *Making Transnational Law Work in the Global Economy: Essays in Honour of Detlev Vagts* (Cambridge University Press 2010).

105 For an overview of the (potential) contributions of philosophical hermeneutics to a better understanding of the process of interpretation, see Daniel Peat and Matthew Windsor, 'Playing the Game of Interpretation: On Meaning and Metaphor in International Law' in Andrea Bianchi, Daniel Peat and Matthew Windsor (eds), *Interpretation in International Law* (Oxford University Press 2015), 13–16.

about the (universal) norms and underlying values which they debate.[106] These preconceptions were formed during their legal education in law schools, the political system under which they grew up, the culture in the home country, etc. And these preconceptions will inevitably have an impact on how they look at international law.[107] In that sense, legal scholarship is "inescapably political"[108], it "can never be free of subjective, decisional elements"[109].

For IHRL, this is, perhaps, even more true. Firstly, IHRL is a particularly political subject matter. It raises questions about the legitimacy and the limits of power and goes to the very foundations of our political co-existence. It is thus unsurprising that the contents of these rules and their normative consequences are highly contested and that those who participate in arguments about it are—at least—also guided by their political views. Take, for example, the questions of forced migration, with which the human rights bodies around the world have been concerned in recent years. These go to the very question of who is worthy of protection by a state and, ultimately, who belongs under and benefits from a certain social contract.[110]

Secondly, IHRL is a particularly vague legal matter. Its provisions and their wording are characterized by a high level of generality. Given that they are meant to govern the vertical relation between states and individuals in a theoretically infinite number of situations, this vagueness is "a function of the non-mechanical context in which human rights claims arise".[111] However, this diminishes the usefulness of two of the three interpretation ingredients provided for by Article 31 of the Vienna Convention on the Law of Treaties (VCLT)[112], namely the "ordinary meaning of the wording" and the "context". In many cases, human rights lawyers

---

[106] Myres S. McDougal and Harold D. Lasswell, 'The Identification and Appraisal of Diverse Systems of Public Order' (1953) 53 American Journal of International Law 1, 2.

[107] Oscar Schachter, 'The Invisible College of International Lawyers' (1977) 72 Northwestern University Law Review 217, 216–217.

[108] Anne Peters, 'Realizing Utopia as a Scholarly Endeavour' (2013) 24 European Journal of International Law 533, 542.

[109] Knut Ipsen, 'Regelungsbereich, Geschichte und Funktion des Völkerrechts' in Volker Epping and Wolff Heintschell von Heinegg (eds), *Völkerrecht* (7th edn, C. H. Beck 2018), para. 41.

[110] See on the questions forced migrants pose for our social contracts and the question of *who we are* Itamar Mann, *Humanity at Sea: Maritime Migration and the Foundations of International Law* (Cambridge University Press 2016), 6–20.

[111] Çalı, 'Specialized Rules of Treaty Interpretation: Human Rights', 531.

[112] Vienna Convention on the Law of Treaties (adopted 23 May 1969, entered into force 27 January 1980) 1155 UNTS 331 (VCLT).

are left with the "object and purpose" of a human rights provision.[113] Teleological interpretation is, however, the least mechanical of the accepted interpretive methods. With good reason, the object and purpose of a treaty have even been called an "enigma".[114] Its indefinite nature makes this method of interpretation rather susceptible to being influenced by the preconceptions that anyway influence one's thinking about IHRL. The object and purpose of a human rights treaty and, therefore, its teleological interpretation will almost inevitably be influenced to some extent by the interpreter's background, even when the interpreter acts *bona fide* and might not notice this herself.

The consequence that must be drawn from this realisation is not that a universal discourse about international law cannot be fruitful. Otherwise, this thesis would be pointless to begin with. But it means that the discourse can be fruitful only if it is done in a transparent and honest manner. Figuratively, we can imagine the discourse as a large table at which the discussants come together and to which everyone engaging in the debate brings their backpack of ideas that have been packed over the course of their socialisation in a particular (political) culture, a particular school system, during their legal education at university, and their professional practice. When taking these ideas out of one's backpack and presenting them to the other discussants at the table, it is of utmost importance to be transparent about where they come from. One should not keep one's preconceptions in one's backpack but openly lay them out on the table, together with one's ideas. Only then can the other discussants adequately appreciate these ideas and react to them. As Cassesse put it in less figurative terms:

> *[T]he interpreter will necessarily have to rely upon his or her personal ideological or political leanings. What matters, however, is that he or she should make it explicit and clear that the choice between two conflicting values is grounded in a personal slant or bias, and not in any 'objective' legal precedence of one value over the other.*[115]

Importantly, this does not mean that one should abandon the strive for objectivity. But when openness and transparency are ensured, a more fruitful discourse about international (human rights) law is possible. It is as an attempt at this transparency and thereby at contributing to the most fruitful discourse possible, that the methodological approach of this thesis should also be seen.

---

[113] Çalı, 'Specialized Rules of Treaty Interpretation: Human Rights', 533.

[114] Isabelle Buffard and Karl Zemanek, 'The "Object and Purpose" of a Treaty: An Enigma?' (1998) 3 Austrian Review of International & European Law 311, 342.

[115] Antonio Cassesse, *Five Master of International Law: Conversations with R-J Dupuy, E Jiménez de Aréchaga, R Jennings, L Henkin and O Schachter* (Hart Publishing 2011), 259.

2.5 A Note on Translations

As a consequence of its methodological approach, this thesis contains a number of direct citations from the jurisprudence of the FCC and other German language sources. Initial translations of these passages were made with the help of the DeepL software[116]. The translations were then checked by the author, and corrected, adapted and refined where needed. To allow the reader to double-check the translations easily, the German originals of the longer passages translated are included in the respective footnotes.

[116] The software can be accessed at https://www.deepl.com/translator.

Part II

Developing an Analytical Foil from the FCC's Jurisprudence

A Brief Sketch of the Development in Jurisprudence and Academia

3

Relevant jurisprudence on the procedural dimension of fundamental rights and the relevance of those rights for the (administrative) decision-making processes appeared early on in the FCC's history. In fact, already in the 1950s, the court mentioned that it was important for individuals to be actively involved in procedures through which public power is exercised.[1] In the literature, the idea of the relevance of procedure to the realisation of fundamental rights gained traction somewhat later; the literature had long neglected or underestimated the importance of procedures for the protection of fundamental rights.[2] In the 1970s, however, the idea did gain significant traction, both in the jurisprudence of the FCC and in the literature.[3]

This chapter will briefly sketch out this historical development to provide the background for the following analysis. It will recall the beginnings in the jurisprudence of the FCC (3.1), discuss two influential scholarly contributions to the debate (3.2), and finally highlight significant decisions of the FCC which firmly established the procedural dimension of fundamental rights as part of general fundamental rights doctrine *("Allgemeine Grundrechtslehren")* (3.3).

[1] BVerfGE 7, 53 (58); BVerfGE 7, 275 (278–279). See also *infra* 5.2.2.

[2] Michael Dolderer, *Objektive Grundrechtsgehalte* (Duncker und Humblot 2000), 232.

[3] For a tracing back of the historical development, and in particular the interplay between the literature and the FCC, see Sebastian Hartwig, 'Grundrechtsschutz des Verfahrens: Der Mülheim-Kärlich-Beschluss' in Dieter Grimm (ed), *Vorbereiter—Nachbereiter?* (Mohr Siebeck 2019).

B. Behlert, *The Necessity of a Conversation between the Administration and the Individual*, Juridicum—Bochumer Schriften zur Friedenssicherung und zum Humanitären Völkerrecht | Bochum Studies on the International Law of Peace and Armed Conflict 72, https://doi.org/10.1007/978-3-658-50303-1_3

3.1 The Beginnings in the Jurisprudence of the FCC

Already in 1957[4] and 1958[5], the FCC held that it was important for individuals to have a voice in court procedures and that *inter alia* their dignity demanded this. A landmark decision on the relevance of procedure for fundamental rights was the first *"Rundfunkurteil"* of 1961. The case concerned a dispute between the Federal Government of Germany and the *Länder*. At its core was the question of which level of the German state had the competence to institute and regulate television broadcasting. In this context, however, the court also discussed whether Article 5 Basic Law set standards for the organization of public broadcasting in Germany. It held that, beyond the rights that Article 5 Basic Law conveyed on individuals, it was also an "institutional liberty" in the sense that it protected a free television broadcasting as an institution—*inter alia* because of its exceptional importance for public opinion-forming—and required Germany to make "special arrangements for the realisation and preservation of the free broadcasting guaranteed in Article 5".[6]

In the 1968 *"Hamburger Deichordnungsgesetz"* judgment concerning a law which regulated Hamburg's dykes, the FCC articulated the idea that effective legal protection was "an essential element" of fundamental rights themselves for the first time.[7] With the law, the city administration had directly expropriated some inhabitants of Hamburg. The expropriation had not been done through an administrative act *based on* the law, but was ordered by the law directly. In consequence, the affected inhabitants had not been able to challenge the decision before a court, as there is no regular procedure before German courts to challenge laws directly. Even though the FCC eventually concluded that the chosen method of an expropriation by law had been justified in the circumstances of the case, it held that such an approach may only be taken in exceptional circumstances because "effective legal protection" against the decision was decisively diminished when it was taken in the form of a law.[8] This idea of effective legal protection as an essential element of every fundamental right would later become one of the two justifications for the FCC's jurisprudence on the necessary procedural protection required by the fundamental rights of the Basic Law.

---

[4] BVerfGE 7, 53 (57–58).

[5] BVerfGE 7, 275 (278–279).

[6] BVerfGE 12, 205 (259–263).

[7] BVerfGE 24, 367 (401).

[8] Ibid, 402–403.

3.2 Two Significant Scholarly Contributions: Häberle and Hesse

In the 1970s, voices in the literature began discussing the relevance of the decision-making process to fundamental rights more and more prominently. Peter Häberle's lecture *"Grundrechte im Leistungsstaat"* of 1971 is often regarded as a crucial moment for the debate on the connection between fundamental rights and administrative procedure.[9] In the lecture, Häberle proposes ways to make the German *"Grundrechtsdogmatik"*[10]fit for the challenges posed by the modern welfare state.[11] He characterises the relation of the welfare state to fundamental rights as ambivalent. On the one hand, the welfare state sets out to realize fundamental rights. On the other hand, the welfare state creates new "danger zones" for fundamental rights.[12] Häberle's lecture has proven to be highly influential for the development of fundamental rights doctrine in Germany, and it provides some helpful background for understanding the development of the idea that procedures are important for fundamental rights' realisation in the jurisprudence of the FCC.

Häberle suggests an "open doctrine" which enables further development while preserving the validity of fundamental rights.[13] As fundamental rights are "freedom-securing answers to specific dangers", their interpretation and application must be adapted to new circumstances and conditions of their implementation.[14] The constitution must undergo "vivid realization [...] that takes

---

[9] Erhard Denninger, 'Government Assistance in the Exercise of Basic Rights (Procedure and Organization)' 12 German Law Journal 430; Hartwig, 271–272, 281.

[10] On the term *"Dogmatik"*, see Matthias Jestaedt, 'Die deutsche Staatsrechtslehre im europäisierten Rechtswissenschaftsdiskurs: Kennzeichen, Kernkompetenzen und Rezeptionshindernisse' (2012) 67 Juristenzeitung 1, 2–3. It is difficult to translate this rather peculiar term into English. The translation which comes closest would probably be "fundamental rights doctrine", although "doctrine" sometimes comes with a pejorative connotation in the English language which *"Dogmatik"* does not have. *"Dogmatik"* is somewhat similar to Koskenniemi's use of "doctrine" when he makes the distinction between theory and doctrine in Martti Koskenniemi, *From Apology to Utopia: The Structure of International Legal Argument* (Reissue with a new Epilogue edn, Cambridge University Press 2006), 2.

[11] Peter Häberle, 'Grundrechte im Leistungsstaat' (1972) 30 Veröffentlichungen der Vereinigung deutscher Staatsrechtslehrer (VVDStRL) 43.

[12] Ibid, 56.

[13] Ibid, 69.

[14] Ibid, 69–70.

into account social facts"[15]. Such a flexible approach is made possible by the "openness, wideness and indeterminacy" of the constitution.[16] In a brilliantly put passage, Häberle summarizes his approach to fundamental rights doctrine:

> *Doctrine has to develop rationality guarantees for jurisprudential decision-making in the service of fundamental rights guarantees; it does not live on recapitulations of classics or post-glossators and is not an end in itself. The departure from certain dogmas can make fundamental rights more effective. The questioning of the doctrine of fundamental rights leads to its "opening" within the framework of an open understanding of the constitution.*[17]

Notably, Häberle begins with the object and purpose of fundamental rights as "freedom-securing answers to specific dangers" and develops his *Grundrechtsdogmatik* from there. The purpose of fundamental rights needs to be realized effectively. This is possible only with a certain degree of flexibility and a constant questioning of the current state of doctrine.[18] To the international lawyer, this approach might seem similar to flexible, progressive approaches to international (human rights) law guided by the principle of effectiveness, in particular the "living instrument doctrine" of the ECtHR.[19]

---

[15] Here, Häberle recalls a lecture from seven years earlier: Ulrich Scheuner, 'Pressefreiheit' (1965) 22 Veröffentlichungen der Vereinigung deutscher Staatsrechtslehrer (VVDStRL) 1, 17.

[16] Häberle, 'Grundrechte im Leistungsstaat', 72.

[17] Ibid, 71: *"Dogmatik hat im Dienst der Grundrechtsverbürgungen Rationalitätsgarantien für die rechtswissenschaftliche Entscheidung zu entwickeln; sie lebt nicht von Reprisen der Klassik oder Postglossatoren und ist kein Selbstzweck. Der Abschied von bestimmten Dogmen kann die Grundrechte effektivieren. Die Hinterfragung der Grundrechtsdogmatik führt zu ihrer "Öffnung" im Rahmen eines offenen Verfassungsverständnisses."* See on this approach for the constitution as a whole Peter Häberle, 'Zeit und Verfassung: Prolegomena zu einen "zeit-gerechten" Verfassungsverständnis' (1974) 21 Zeitschrift für Politik 111, 114ff.

[18] Häberle, 'Grundrechte im Leistungsstaat', 74.

[19] For an explanation of the living instrument doctrine along the lines of relevant case law, see Alastair Mowbray, 'The Creativity of the European Court of Human Rights' (2005) 5 Human Rights Law Review 57, 60–71. In fact, a "principle of effectiveness" can be found in the FCC's jurisprudence relatively early on, in a decision from 1957, in which the FCC stated that preference was to be given to "the interpretation 'which most strongly develops the legal effect of the norm in question'", BVerfGE 6, 55 (72). Häberle has later described his *status activus processualis* and other constitutional developments as belonging to the category of fundamental rights effectivization, Häberle, 'Grundrechtsgeltung und Grundrechtsinterpretation im Verfassungsstaat — Zugleich zur Rechtsvergleichung als „fünfter" Auslegungsmethode', 914.

After developing his idea of an effective fundamental rights doctrine, Häberle moves on to suggest a revision of Jellinek's famous *status*[20], based on his diagnosis that the forms of government and administration of the modern welfare state pose new threats to fundamental rights. In his view, the relation between the state and the citizen is no longer characterized by subjection but increasingly by communication and cooperation.[21] Thus, the image of a citizen subjected to public power and thus in need of protection against that power in the form of negative freedoms does not sufficiently describe the relationship between the citizen and the state anymore. Moreover, he argues that a private entity or idle lawmakers can pose a much greater threat to the freedom of the individual than "classic interferences".[22] In light of this, he argues for expanding Jellinek's status teaching by a *status activus processualis*:

> *In addition to [Jellinek's] status, a new relation begins to emerge in the welfare state, which is to be characterized as status activus processualis. It means the procedural side of fundamental freedom, the "fundamental rights due process", procedural participation with the consequence of the reservation of benefits as a procedural reservation of law. It results from an understanding of the constitution, the law and the state that emphasizes the procedural side more strongly. [...] It is the epitome of all norms and forms that regulate the procedural participation (including requirements of publicity) of those affected by the benefit state in their fundamental rights.*[23]

The necessity of this supplementation of Jellinek's *status* derives from the fact that in the modern welfare state, the meaning of freedom under the fundamental rights catalogue of the Basic Law is no longer defined by "definite norms" with clear-cut preconditions and definite legal consequences. Instead, the meaning of

---

20 Jellinek famously categorized the different relations in which an individual can be with a state in four *status*: the passive *status subjectionis,* the negative *status libertatis*, the positive *status civitatis* and the *status activus.* For an overview, see Georg Jellinek, *System der subjektiven öffentlichen Rechte* (Reprint of 2nd edn, Scientia Verlag 1964), 86–88.

21 Häberle, 'Grundrechte im Leistungsstaat', 59.

22 Ibid, 70. In the same sense Hesse, 430.

23 Häberle, 'Grundrechte im Leistungsstaat', 81: *"Neben diesen status beginnt sich im Leistungsstaat eine neue Relation herauszubilden, die mit status activus processualis gekennzeichnet werden soll. Er meint die verfahrensrechtliche Seite grundrechtlicher Freiheit, den "grundrechtlichen due process", prozessuale Teilhabe mit der Konsequenz des Leistungsvorbehalts als verfahrensrechtlichem Gesetzesvorbehalt. Er resultiert aus einem die Verfahrensseite stärker betonendem Verfassungs-, Rechts- und Staatsverständis. [...] Er ist der Inbegriff aller Normen und Formen, die die Verfahrensbeteiligung (einschließlich Publizitätsvorschriften) der durch den Leistungsstaat in ihren Grundrechten Betroffenen regeln."*

freedom in accordance with these rights is discerned *"in processu"*, also because the relations determining the reality of fundamental rights are often not bipolar anymore but complex—at least triangular—ones.[24]

In light of these developments, Häberle argues, *ex post* legal protection is less and less adequate to protect fundamental rights. The more leeway the "actively shaping administration"[25] needs, the more judicial deference will be needed. The protection of fundamental rights must therefore be relocated to the realm before the decision-making. If *ex post* legal decision-making cannot effectively protect fundamental rights, compensatory legal protection *ex ante* is needed.[26] This form of protection can manifest itself in many different forms. Hence, the implementation of the new status must be discerned for every fundamental right and each decision individually and can range from transparency or publicity requirements to institutional or organisational design requirements.[27] As we will see, this compensatory function of *ex ante* legal protection in cases in which *ex post* legal protection is not sufficient has featured prominently in the jurisprudence of the FCC.[28]

Häberle's far-reaching suggestions were hotly debated in the subsequent discussion at the *Staatsrechtslehrertagung*.[29] The concept of the *status activus processualis* has been particularly impactful, and it is one of Häberle's lasting contributions to German constitutional law.[30] Notably, Häberle approaches the relationship between fundamental rights and procedure from the vantage point of subjective rights. He frames the consequences from his observations about the welfare state in a way that puts the individual and her agency at the centre of the argument. The relationship between the citizen and the state is "procedurally disciplined"[31] in a way that enables the individual to "represent herself"[32].

---

[24] Ibid, 87.

[25] Dolderer, 252.

[26] Häberle, 'Grundrechte im Leistungsstaat', 121ff. In another passage, Häberle expresses the consequence neatly: *"Dem Leistungsstaat ist vor allem von der verfahrensrechtlichen Seite beizukommen."*, ibid, 90.

[27] Ibid, 82–84.

[28] See *infra* 5.1.1.2.

[29] Alexander Hollerbach and et al., 'Grundrechte im Leistungsstaat: Aussprache und Schlussworte' 30 Veröffentlichungen der Vereinigung deutscher Staatsrechtslehrer (VVD-StRL) 142.

[30] Denninger, 'Government Assistance in the Exercise of Basic Rights (Procedure and Organization)', 431.

[31] Häberle, 'Grundrechte im Leistungsstaat', 122.

[32] Ibid, 130.

This focus on the individual and her procedural capacity represents a notable contrast to other approaches, in particular to that of Häberle's teacher Konrad Hesse. Hesse's article *"Bestand und Bedeutung der Grundrechte in der Bundesrepublik Deutschland"* is considered another "[k]ey element[s] of the discussion"[33]. As far as the discussion of the procedural dimension of fundamental rights is concerned, it commences from the same basic observations about the modern welfare state and the challenges it poses for fundamental rights.[34] Hesse's central argument, however, is more pragmatic. Organization and procedure, he argues, will oftentimes be the only means to achieve results which are in accordance with constitutional rights.[35] In the article, Hesse coined the now ubiquitous formula of "realisation and safeguarding of fundamental rights through organisation and procedures".[36]

Two differences to Häberle's approach are notable. Firstly, as was already mentioned, Hesse approaches procedural obligations under fundamental rights from a more objective vantage point. With that comes, secondly, his more pragmatic framing of the argument: the procedural involvement of individuals is conceived as a means to the end of addressing practical problems. While Häberle's argument has strong utilitarian elements, too, he seems first and foremost concerned with more fundamental questions about the relationship between the citizen and the state in the modern welfare state. The individual and her procedural capacities stand at the centre of his suggestions. In a way, the approaches of Häberle and Hesse foreshadow the two justifications the FCC employs for procedural obligations under the Basic Law.

Only seven years after Hesse had called the procedural dimension of constitutional rights "important, yet still less recognized"[37], Alexy claimed that "[n]o idea has attracted as much attention in recent discussion of constitutional rights as the thought that there is a connection between constitutional rights, organization and procedure".[38]

---

[33] Alexy, *A Theory of Constitutional Rights*, 314.

[34] Hesse, 430.

[35] Ibid, 435.

[36] Ibid, 434: *"Grundrechtsverwirklichung und -sicherung durch Organisation und Verfahren"*.

[37] Ibid, 434.

[38] Alexy, *A Theory of Constitutional Rights*, 314. Besides the here discussed works by Häberle and Hesse, Alexy cites a number of other scholarly contributions to present the then current state of the debate: Herbert Bethge, 'Grundrechtsverwirklichung und Grundrechtssicherung durch Organisation und Verfahren: Zu einigen Aspekten der aktuellen Grundrechtsdiskussion' (1982) Neue Juristische Wochenschrift (NJW) 1; Helmut Goerlich,

While the remainder of this chapter will focus on the jurisprudence of the FCC, this closer look at two examples of the academic debate at the time was instructive to understand the historical context and the societal and academic debate that provided the backdrop for the FCC's decisions. The development of the welfare state fundamentally reshaped the relationship between the German state and its citizens in ways that the classical liberal doctrine of fundamental rights as defensive rights was insufficient to address.

3.3 The Solidification of the Idea of Protection Through Procedure in the FCC's Jurisprudence and Its Transfer to the Administrative Procedure

The idea that effective legal protection was an "essential element" of fundamental rights featured prominently in a number of the FCC's judgments in the 1970s.[39] In these judgments, the FCC confirmed its assertion from the *Deichordnungsgesetz* judgment and solidified it until it ultimately became "settled case-law".[40] In 1975, the FCC abstracted the idea that effective legal protection was an essential element of a fundamental right from the property guarantee in Article 14 Basic Law.[41] However, at the time, the idea of "effective legal protection" was still only applied to *ex post* legal protection.

This changed in the late 1970s with two decisions on compulsory auctions.[42] The latter of these two of 1977 has aptly been described as "the first bridge from judicial to administrative procedure" given that the judiciary was not addressed in its judicial function but as an organising instance with a quasi-administrative

Grundrechte als Verfahrensgarantien (Nomos Verlagsgesellschaft 1981); Fritz Ossenbühl, 'Kernenergie im Spiegel des Verfassungsrechts' [1981] Die Öffentliche Verwaltung 1.

[39] See, e.g., BVerfGE 37, 67 (77); BVerfGE 37, 132 (148); BVerfGE 44, 105 (120); BVerfGE 45, 422 (430–433); BVerfGE 46, 325 (334); BVerfGE 49, 220 (225); BVerfGE 49, 252 (257); BVerfGE 52, 380 (389); BVerfGE 53, 30 (65); BVerfGE 63, 131 (143); BVerfGE 113, 29 (57); BVerfGE 124, 43 (70); BVerfGE 128, 282 (311), BVerfGE 142, 234 (260–261); BVerfGE 147, 253 (309). The FCC has not always used the exact same wording. It has, e.g., also referred to "enforceability" to describe essentially the same idea, BVerfGE 39, 276 (294): "*Zu den wesentlichen Bestandteilen eines verfassungsmäßigen Rechts gehört [...] seine Durchsetzbarkeit [...].*"

[40] See, e.g., BVerfGE 52, 380 (389).

[41] BVerfGE 39, 276 (294).

[42] BVerfGE 42, 64; BVerfGE 46, 325.

function.[43] Two years later, in a highly significant decision, the FCC abstracted its effective legal protection considerations from court proceedings altogether: In *Schweigender Prüfling*, it considered the decision of an exam commission to fail an examinee because of his decision to remain silent throughout the oral part of his law exam even though he had gained the required overall points in the previous written part of the exam. The FCC found that the examinee's rights had been violated because the commission had not warned him that his remaining silent would eventually lead to his failing the exam. To justify this decision, the court stated that the fundamental rights of the Basic Law "demand[ed] validity in the respective procedural law" and that this was by now "settled case law"[44]—an interesting contrast to Hesse's calling the procedural dimension of fundamental rights "still less recognised"[45] in 1978. In a rather nonchalant fashion, the court explained why this idea was not restricted to *ex post* legal protection through court proceedings:

> *Since these effects already follow directly from the respective fundamental right, they are not limited to the procedure of judicial review, but also influence the design of the administrative procedure insofar as the administrative decision affects a fundamental right.*[46]

The two judgments that are most associated with the idea of fundamental rights protection through organisation and procedure, however, are probably the *Hochschulurteil* of 1973[47] and the *Mülheim-Kärlich* order of 1979[48]. The *Hochschulurteil* of 1973 addressed the question of how governing bodies of universities must be organised. For our purposes, the judgment is particularly instructive with regard to the doctrinal construction of procedural obligations derived from fundamental rights. The 1979 *Mülheim-Kärlich* decision concerned the permit procedure for a nuclear power plant. It is arguably the one decision most often associated with the idea of the protection of fundamental rights through administrative procedure.[49] In their constitutional complaint, the applicants claimed that the judgment they appealed had not duly taken into account the influence of their fundamental right of physical integrity on the rules governing

---

[43] Dolderer, 243.
[44] BVerfGE 52, 380 (389).
[45] Hesse, 434.
[46] BVerfGE 52, 380 (390).
[47] BVerfGE 35, 79.
[48] BVerfGE 53, 30.
[49] Hartwig, 262.

the permit procedure for nuclear power plants. The court ultimately denied the application on the merits. The previous court, it held, had not based its decision on a wrong understanding of fundamental rights but on the prospects for success of the appeal.[50] Nevertheless, the judgment has become (one of) the central judgment(s) of the FCC when it comes to the protection of fundamental rights through procedure. Here too, the FCC invokes its "settled case law" that "the protection of constitutional rights was also to be realized through the design of procedures" again.[51] Latest with the *Mülheim-Kärlich* order, the idea of procedural protection of fundamental rights was firmly established in the jurisprudence of the FCC.

[50] BVerfGE 53, 30 (66).

[51] Ibid, 65: *"Bei der verfassungsrechtlichen Beurteilung dieser Frage ist von der gefestigten Rechtsprechung des Bundesverfassungsgerichts auszugehen, daß Grundrechtsschutz weitgehend auch durch die Gestaltung von Verfahren zu bewirken ist [...]."*

4 The FCC's Doctrinal Construction

The fundamental rights of the Basic Law were originally conceived in the Western liberal tradition as negative rights of defence against the state. Still today, the *status negativus* is the "basic function" of fundamental rights.[1] Procedural rights, however, are rights *to* something. They are directed not at the abstention of the state from unwarranted interferences but at positive state action. They require the state to *listen* to the potentially affected individual, to *give* her reasons for the decision, to *organise* agencies and environments relevant to the enjoyment of fundamental rights in certain ways and so on. Procedural rights require the state to *take action*. Hence, they cannot be derived from the negative dimension of fundamental rights. The "liberal basic understanding of fundamental rights that only holds an injunctive relief against public power available" is insufficient to explain those obligations.[2]

Accordingly, the FCC had to resort to a rather sophisticated doctrinal-legal construction. It had to derive procedural rights and obligations from the "objective system of values" which the catalogue of fundamental rights of the Basic Law constitutes. To explain this sophisticated construction, this chapter briefly recalls the development of the objective dimension of fundamental rights (4.1), before it analyses the FCC's *Hochschulurteil* of 1971 in which the court explicitly relied

[1] Josef Isensee, '§ 191—Das Grundrecht als Abwehrrecht und als Staatliche Schutzpflicht' in Josef Isensee and Paul Kirchhof (eds), *Handbuch des Staatsrechts*, vol IX (C. F. Müller 2011), para. 2.

[2] Hartwig, 274. With essentially the same argument also Dolderer, 246, and Alexy, *A Theory of Constitutional Rights*, 319–320.

B. Behlert, *The Necessity of a Conversation between the Administration and the Individual*, Juridicum—Bochumer Schriften zur Friedenssicherung und zum Humanitären Völkerrecht | Bochum Studies on the International Law of Peace and Armed Conflict 72, https://doi.org/10.1007/978-3-658-50303-1_4

on the "objective system of values" to derive procedural rights and obligations from a fundamental right (4.2).

4.1 The Fundamental Rights Catalogue as an Objective System of Values

To explain the sophisticated construction necessary to derive procedural obligations from the fundamental rights of the Basic Law, we must first recall the "development under the constitution"[3] that lead to the recognition of fundamental rights as an "objective system of values". The FCC introduced the concept into German fundamental rights doctrine with its famous *Lüth* judgment of 1958.[4] Before this judgment, the FCC had only referred to an objective dimension of a fundamental right in a 1957 decision addressing the protection of marriage under Article 6 (1) Basic Law. The court held that beyond the article's negative dimension (and the institutional guarantees it provides for), it constituted a *"Grundsatznorm"*, i.e., a fundamental norm with a "a binding value decision for the entire area of private and public law concerning marriage and the family".[5] From this "value-deciding legal principle" (*"wertentscheidende Grundsatznorm"*) the court then derived a legal limits to the legislature's discretion.[6] Given the way Article 6 (1) Basic Law is phrased, however, this was yet not too surprising. The provision is in fact one of only two fundamental rights provisions directly stipulating positive obligations "to protect", the other one being Article 1 (1) (2) Basic Law, the protection of human dignity.[7]

Less than a year later, the FCC rendered its seminal *Lüth* judgment that would turn out to be a fundamental rights big bang.[8] The FCC was confronted

[3] Böckenförde, 2.

[4] BVerfGE 7, 198.

[5] BVerfGE 6, 55 (72).

[6] Ibid, 76.

[7] See on the "special protection" the provision guarantees Gregor Kirchhof, 'Der besondere Schutz der Familie in Art. 6 Abs. 1 des Grundgesetzes: Abwehrrecht, Einrichtungsgarantie, Benachteiligungsverbot, staatliche Schutz- und Förderpflicht' (2004) 129 Archiv des öffentlichen Rechts, 554ff.

[8] See on the judgments significance Thomas Henne, '"Smend oder Hennis?": Bedeutung, Rezeption und Problematik der 'Lüth-Entscheidung' des Bundesverfassungsgerichts von 1958' in Robert Chr. van Ooyen and Martin H. W. Möllers (eds), *Handbuch Bundesverfassungsgericht im politischen System* (2nd edn, Springer VS 2015), 220ff.

with the following facts:[9] the publicist Erich Lüth, the applicant in the case, had called upon film distributors and audiences in Germany not to support the new movie of Veit Harlan, a director who had previously worked for the Nazi regime. He saw Harlan as "unfit to restore the reputation of the German film". The production company for Harlan's newest movie successfully lodged an application with a court in Hamburg and won an injunction which prohibited the applicant to publicly call for a boycott of Harland's movies. Given that Harlan had previously been acquitted of accusations against him in connection with his involvement with the Nazis, the Hamburg court concluded that the expressions of the applicant constituted an immoral appeal for a boycott. Erich Lüth lodged a constitutional complaint against this decision arguing that his criticism of Harlan was a legitimate exercise of his freedom of expression under Article 5 (1) Basic Law.

As the legal relationship at hand was of a private law nature, the FCC raised the question of whether and in how far constitutional rights applied horizontally between private individuals. The court did, however, not consider it necessary to provide a definite answer to the question. Instead, it developed the idea of the *"mittelbare Drittwirkung"*, the idea of indirect third-party effect. In doing so, the court referred to the catalogue of fundamental rights as an "objective system of values":

> *Without doubt, the fundamental rights are primarily intended to secure the sphere of freedom of the individual from encroachment by public authority; they are defensive rights of the citizen against the state. [...]*
>
> *It is equally true, however, that the Basic Law, which does not intend to be a value-neutral order [...], has also established an objective system of values in its section on fundamental rights, and that it is precisely in this that a principled strengthening of the validity of the fundamental rights is expressed [...]. This system of values, which finds its centre in the freely developing human personality and its dignity within the social community, must apply as a basic constitutional decision to all areas of law; legislation, administration and jurisprudence receive guidelines and impulses from it. Thus, of course, it also influences civil law; no provision of civil law may be in contradiction to it, each must be interpreted in its spirit.*[10]

[9] BVerfGE 7, 198 (199–203).

[10] BVerfGE 7, 198 (204–205): *"Ohne Zweifel sind die Grundrechte in erster Linie dazu bestimmt, die Freiheitssphäre des einzelnen vor Eingriffen der öffentlichen Gewalt zu sichern; sie sind Abwehrrechte des Bürgers gegen den Staat. [...] Ebenso richtig ist aber, daß das Grundgesetz, das keine wertneutrale Ordnung sein will [...], in seinem Grundrechtsabschnitt auch eine objektive Wertordnung aufgerichtet hat und daß gerade hierin eine prinzipielle Verstärkung der Geltungskraft der Grundrechte zum Ausdruck kommt [...]. Dieses Wertsystem, das seinen*

The fundamental rights of the Basic Law represent an "objective system of values" which applies to "all areas of law", and to all powers of government. State agents must make sure that whenever they apply the law, they pay due consideration to the fundamental rights at stake and how the objective system of values they constitute influences their application of ordinary law. Should they not do so, the FCC added, they would not only violate objective constitutional law, but also the subjective rights of the affected citizen.[11]

This development of the "objective system of values" was one of the most significant constitutional developments in the history of the Federal Republic of Germany. The "generalization of the fundamental right beyond the legal consequence of the negative right"[12] which the objective system of values represents was to become the FCC's "most important instrument for conjuring up new fundamental rights content"[13], a "hermeneutic primordial soup"[14]. Consequently, all doctrinal issues beyond the defensive dimension had as their starting point the objective dimension of fundamental rights.[15] In *Lüth*, the FCC referred to the "objective system of values" to establish the effect of fundamental rights on private law, the *"Drittwirkung"*. Afterwards, the court derived obligations to protect[16] and, as we will see, procedural obligations from it.

Alexy has illustratively described the objective dimension as a threefold abstraction: a fundamental right has to be abstracted from its holder, from the duty-bearer, and from the "modalities of the object of the right", i.e., their demand not to interfere with the right without justification.[17] After this threefold abstraction, the interpreter of the right is left with the "bare ought to be" *("bloßes*

Mittelpunkt in der innerhalb der sozialen Gemeinschaft sich frei entfaltenden menschlichen Persönlichkeit und ihrer Würde findet, muß als verfassungsrechtliche Grundentscheidung für alle Bereiche des Rechts gelten; Gesetzgebung, Verwaltung und Rechtsprechung empfangen von ihm Richtlinien und Impulse. So beeinflußt es selbstverständlich auch das bürgerliche Recht; keine bürgerlich-rechtliche Vorschrift darf in Widerspruch zu ihm stehen, jede muß in seinem Geiste ausgelegt werden." References omitted.

[11] BVerfGE 7, 198 (206).

[12] Jarass, 'Grundrechte als Wertentscheidungen bzw. objektivrechtliche Prinzipien in der Rechtsprechung des Bundesverfassungsgerichts', 368.

[13] Robert Alexy, 'Grundrechte als subjektive Rechte und als objektive Normen' 29 Der Staat 49, 49.

[14] Isensee, '§ 191—Das Grundrecht als Abwehrrecht und als Staatliche Schutzpflicht', para. 159.

[15] Böckenförde, 8.

[16] BVerfGE 56, 54 (73).

[17] Alexy, 'Grundrechte als subjektive Rechte und als objektive Normen', 57.

Gesolltsein") of the respective freedom.[18] However, the FCC does not stop at this abstraction. It comes back down to the individual level and derives individual rights from the objective dimension. Jarass aptly called this operation a "detour via objective law".[19] It is a "legal trick" the FCC must entertain to come up with positive rights and obligations under those norms which were originally designed exclusively as negative rights of defence. It is, thus, an important step towards an "open fundamental rights doctrine" such as the one envisaged by Häberle[20].

4.2 Deriving Procedural Obligations from the Objective Dimension of Fundamental Rights: The *Hochschulurteil*

It was "only a matter of time" for the FCC to begin expanding the effects of its jurisprudence in *Lüth* to the field of procedural law.[21] The first judgment in which the FCC deduced procedural obligations from a constitutional right was the first *Rundfunkurteil* of 1961 which we have already summarized in the previous chapter. It is important to note that, in that case, the FCC treated Article 5 Basic Law in the form of its "bare ought to be"[22], as mere objective law.[23] No immediate reconnection to Article 5 Basic Law as a subjective right was made. This treatment, however, was necessitated by the procedural constellation of the case which had not come to the court in the form of an individual constitutional complaint but in the form of a "disagreement concerning the rights and duties of the Federation and the *Länder*" under Article 93 (1) (3) Basic Law. Twelve years later, the FCC handed down a judgment which is particularly instructive to understand how it constructs procedural rights and obligations: the *"Hochschulurteil"*. In this section, we will analyse the doctrinal-legal construction, the FCC employs therein (4.2.1), reflect on it (4.2.2) and assess the value of the construction beyond Article 5 Basic Law (4.2.3).

---

[18] Ibid, 57.

[19] Jarass, 'Grundrechte als Wertentscheidungen bzw. objektivrechtliche Prinzipien in der Rechtsprechung des Bundesverfassungsgerichts', 369.

[20] See *supra* 3.2.

[21] Hartwig, 285.

[22] Alexy, 'Grundrechte als subjektive Rechte und als objektive Normen', 57.

[23] BVerfGE 12, 205 (262–263).

4.2.1 The Doctrinal-Legal Construction in the *Hochschulurteil*

In its 1973 *Hochschulurteil*, the court had the opportunity to tie on to the ideas of procedural protection it had developed in the first *Rundfunkurteil.* And this time, the case had reached it in the form of an individual complaint.[24] A group of professors of various career levels had lodged complaints against a law re-organizing representation in the governing bodies of universities. According to the new law, professors no longer had a majority in these bodies. In that, the applicants saw their right to academic freedom under Article 5 (3) Basic Law violated.

In the classic fashion of negative rights of defence, Article 5 (3) Basic Law declares that "[a]rts and sciences, research and teaching shall be free". So, in order to derive a positive right to a certain set up of governing bodies, the FCC had to have recourse to the objective dimension of that right. In its reasoning, the FCC made the way in which it derives procedural guarantees, i.e., the way in which it technically constructs a legal basis for such guarantees explicit. Hence, the passage shall be represented here almost in full:

> *Article 5 (3) (1) Basic Law declares science, research and teaching to be free. According to its wording and meaning, this establishes an objective, value-deciding fundamental norm regulating the relationship between science, research and teaching and the state [...]. At the same time, the constitutional provision grants an individual right of freedom to everyone who is active in these areas* [...].
>
> *1. The right to freedom contained in Article 5 (3) Basic Law protects scientific activity as a right of defense against state intervention and is available to anyone who is active in science or wishes to become active* [...]. [...]
>
> 2. *The fundamental rights provisions of the Constitution embody an objective value system "in which a principled reinforcement of the validity of fundamental rights is expressed" and which applies as a fundamental constitutional decision to all areas of law* [...]. *Even where the legislature - as in the area of granting state activity—has greater creative freedom, the special value decisions Basic Law restrict this freedom, e.g. by prohibiting "distinctions which would run counter to the intention of the constitutional legislature, expressed in the value decision, to grant its special protection to a particular area of life or relationship to life" [...]. Article 5 (3) Basic Law also contains such a value decision. It is based on the key function that free science has both for the self-realization of the individual and for the development of society as a whole. This value decision does not only mean the rejection of state interventions in the previously identified sphere of science; it rather includes the commitment of the state,*

[24] BVerfGE 35, 79.

which sees itself as a cultural state, to the idea of free science and its cooperation in its realization and obliges it to positively adjust its actions accordingly, i.e. to prevent an erosion of this guarantee of freedom by protecting and promoting it. This results in postulates in two directions:

a) The state shall enable and promote the cultivation of free science and its communication to the next generation by providing human, financial and organizational resources. This means that it has to provide functioning institutions for a free scientific enterprise. This requirement is of particular importance because without a suitable organization and without corresponding financial means, which are essentially only available to the state, independent research and scientific teaching can no longer be carried out in wide areas of science, especially in the natural sciences. Today, the state has a de facto monopoly in this field of science; the exercise of the fundamental freedoms under Article 5 (3) Basic Law is necessarily linked to participation in state services.

b) In the area of scientific operations established and maintained with public funds, i.e., in an area of service administration, the state must ensure by appropriate organizational measures that the fundamental right of free scientific activity remains untouched to the extent possible, taking into account the other legitimate tasks of the scientific institutions and the fundamental rights of the various participants. It follows from this that even in the area of participation in public science, at least the core area of scientific activity described above must in principle be reserved for the self-determination of the individual holder of a fundamental right [...]). In this respect, the individual right under Article 5 (3) Basic Law is not changed by joining the corporation of the university. Furthermore, the value decision of Article 5 (3) Basic Law strengthens the validity of the right to freedom in the direction of participation rights. This is justified by the consideration that, on the one hand, participation in public services is increasingly becoming a necessary prerequisite for the realization of academic freedom, and that, on the other hand, according to the conception of the Basic Law, the interest of the community in a functioning academic enterprise is best served if the academically active individual can develop creatively.

The individual bearer of the fundamental right under Article 5 (3) Basic Law has a right from the value decision to such state measures, also of an organizational nature, which are indispensable for the protection of his fundamentally secured freedom, because they enable him to engage in free scientific activity in the first place. If this were not the case, the value-deciding fundamental norm would be largely deprived of its protective effect. This power of the individual fundamental right holder to enforce the observance of the value-deciding fundamental norm against public authority is part of the content of the individual fundamental right, the effectiveness of which is thereby strengthened.[25]

---

[25] BVerfGE 35, 79 (112–116): "*Art. 5 Abs. 3 Satz 1 GG erklärt Wissenschaft, Forschung und Lehre für frei. Damit ist nach Wortlaut und Sinngehalt eine objektive, das Verhältnis von Wissenschaft, Forschung und Lehre zum Staat regelnde wertentscheidende Grundsatznorm aufgestellt [...]. Zugleich gewährt die Verfassungsbestimmung für jeden, der in diesen Bereichen tätig ist, ein individuelles Freiheitsrecht [...].*

This passage shows the construction of the FCC quite clearly. The court highlights Article 5 (3) Basic Law as an individual negative freedom. Then, the FCC moves on to the objective dimension of the catalogue of constitutional rights of the Basic

---

1. Das in Art. 5 Abs. 3 GG enthaltene Freiheitsrecht schützt als Abwehrrecht die wissenschaftliche Betätigung gegen staatliche Eingriffe und steht jedem zu, der wissenschaftlich tätig ist oder tätig werden will […]. […]

2. In den Grundrechtsvorschriften der Verfassung verkörpert sich eine objektive Wertordnung, „in der eine prinzipielle Verstärkung der Geltungskraft der Grundrechte zum Ausdruck kommt" und die als verfassungsrechtliche Grundentscheidung für alle Bereiche des Rechts gilt […]. Auch dort, wo der Gesetzgeber – wie im Bereich der gewährenden Staatstätigkeit – größere Gestaltungsfreiheit besitzt, schränken die besonderen Wertentscheidungen des Grundgesetzes diese Freiheit ein, indem sie z. B. „Unterscheidungen verbieten, die dem in der Wertentscheidung ausgedrückten Willen des Verfassunggebers zuwiderlaufen würden, einem bestimmten Lebensbereich oder Lebensverhältnis seinen besonderen Schutz angedeihen zu lassen" […]. Eine solche Wertentscheidung enthält auch Art. 5 Abs. 3 GG. Sie beruht auf der Schlüsselfunktion, die einer freien Wissenschaft sowohl für die Selbstverwirklichung des Einzelnen als auch für die gesamtgesellschaftliche Entwicklung zukommt. Diese Wertentscheidung bedeutet nicht nur die Absage an staatliche Eingriffe in den zuvor gekennzeichneten Eigenbereich der Wissenschaft; sie schließt vielmehr das Einstehen des Staates, der sich als Kulturstaat versteht, für die Idee einer freien Wissenschaft und seine Mitwirkung an ihrer Verwirklichung ein und verpflichtet ihn, sein Handeln positiv danach einzurichten, d. h. schützend und fördernd einer Aushöhlung dieser Freiheitsgarantie vorzubeugen. Hieraus ergeben sich Postulate in zweifacher Richtung:

a) Der Staat hat die Pflege der freien Wissenschaft und ihre Vermittlung an die nachfolgende Generation durch Bereitstellung von personellen, finanziellen und organisatorischen Mitteln zu ermöglichen und zu fördern. Das bedeutet, daß er funktionsfähige Institutionen für einen freien Wissenschaftsbetrieb zur Verfügung zu stellen hat. Diesem Gebot kommt deswegen besonders Bedeutung zu, weil ohne eine geeignete Organisation und ohne entsprechende finanzielle Mittel, über die im wesentlichen nur noch der Staat verfügt, heute in weiten Bereichen der Wissenschaften, insbesondere der Naturwissenschaften, keine unabhängige Forschung und wissenschaftliche Lehre mehr betrieben werden kann. Der Staat besitzt hinsichtlich dieses Wissenschaftsbetriebs heute weithin ein faktisches Monopol; eine Ausübung der Grundfreiheiten aus Art. 5 Abs. 3 GG ist hier notwendig mit einer Teilhabe an staatlichen Leistungen verbunden.

b) Im Bereich des mit öffentlichen Mitteln eingerichteten und unterhaltenen Wissenschaftsbetriebs, d. h. in einem Bereich der Leistungsverwaltung, hat der Staat durch geeignete organisatorische Maßnahmen dafür zu sorgen, daß das Grundrecht der freien wissenschaftlichen Betätigung soweit unangetastet bleibt, wie das unter Berücksichtigung der anderen legitimen Aufgaben der Wissenschaftseinrichtungen und der Grundrechte der verschiedenen Beteiligten möglich ist. Daraus ergibt sich einmal, daß auch im Bereich der Teilhabe am öffentlichen Wissenschaftsbetrieb jedenfalls der oben

Law. It cites *Lüth* and other judgments, and once again stresses the function of the objective dimension to amplify the content of the rights. For the freedom of academia specifically, the FCC postulates that the state actively contributes to the realization of a free academia. From the objective dimension of Article 5 (3) Basic Law, the FCC draws two conclusions: Firstly, the state must provide for financial means and for suitable organisation, as without these, a free academia cannot function. Secondly, the state must ensure through suitable organisational measures that the constitutional right remains untouched insofar as it is possible considering the other legitimate tasks of universities and the constitutional rights of third parties. The FCC then concludes that the individual holder of the right is entitled to such organisational measures as are necessary for the execution of the right.

This is an explicit and therefore illustrative example of the "detour via objective law"[26] that is necessary in order to derive positive rights from the originally negative rights of the German Basic Law. The courts starts from the subjective negative rights, takes the detour via the objective dimension to derive objective obligations from it, and returns to the subjective level with positive rights. The

umschriebene Kernbereich wissenschaftlicher Betätigung grundsätzlich der Selbstbestimmung des einzelnen Grundrechtsträgers vorbehalten bleiben muß [...]. Insoweit wird das Individualrecht aus Art. 5 Abs. 3 GG durch den Eintritt in die Korporation der Hochschule nicht verändert. Darüber hinaus verstärkt die Wertentscheidung des Art. 5 Abs. 3 GG die Geltungskraft des Freiheitsrechts in Richtung auf Teilhabeberechtigungen. Das rechtfertigt sich aus der Überlegung, daß einerseits die Beteiligung am öffentlichen Leistungsangebot zunehmend zur notwendigen Voraussetzung für die Verwirklichung der Wissenschaftsfreiheit wird und daß andererseits nach der Konzeption des Grundgesetzes auch dem Interesse des Gemeinwesens an einem funktionierenden Wissenschaftsbetrieb am ehesten gedient wird, wenn sich die wissenschaftlich tätige Einzelpersönlichkeit schöpferisch entfalten kann.

Dem einzelnen Träger des Grundrechts aus Art. 5 Abs. 3 GG erwächst aus der Wertentscheidung ein Recht auf solche staatlichen Maßnahmen auch organisatorischer Art, die zum Schutz seines grundrechtlich gesicherten Freiheitsraums unerläßlich sind, weil sie ihm freie wissenschaftliche Betätigung überhaupt erst ermöglichen. Wäre dies nicht der Fall, so würde die wertentscheidende Grundsatznorm ihrer Schutzwirkung weitgehend beraubt. Diese Befugnis des einzelnen Grundrechtsträgers, gegenüber der öffentlichen Gewalt die Beachtung der wertentscheidenden Grundsatznorm durchsetzen zu können, gehört zum Inhalt des Individualgrundrechts, dessen Wirkungskraft dadurch verstärkt wird." References omitted.

[26] Jarass, 'Grundrechte als Wertentscheidungen bzw. objektivrechtliche Prinzipien in der Rechtsprechung des Bundesverfassungsgerichts', 369.

FCC reiterated this construction in a judgment of 2010 addressing a Hamburg law regulating university governance.[27]

4.2.2 Two Reflections on the FCC's Construction

Two points about the *Hochschulurteil* are remarkable. Firstly, the law of Lower Saxony *took away* certain privileges of professors and lecturers. Thus, it was argued that the FCC could have easily construed the law as an interference with negative rights as well.[28] However, the Court did not make such a classification but decided to build its argument on the objective dimension and construe the new law as a violation of the positive dimension of the right to academic freedom.[29] What was affected in the view of the court was the right of the professors *to* a certain organisation of the governance of their universities, not their right *against* interference with their academic liberties. Hence, the court did not derive procedural rights from the negative dimension of Article 5 (3) Basic Law. Had it wanted to do so, the lengthy explanations about the objective dimension of fundamental rights would not have been necessary. This does not mean that the negative dimension did not play a role in the court's argument. Much to the contrary, the court develops its arguments in favour of organisational protection as conducive to academic *freedom ("funktionsfähige Institutionen für einen* ***freien*** *Wissenschaftsbetrieb")*.[30] This, however, refers to the justification and the function of the procedural guarantees rather than the construction of their legal-doctrinal basis.

This takes us to the second point: while the court explicitly mentions only the enhancing effect of the objective dimension for the right itself, the relationship works in the other direction as well. Article 5 (3) Basic Law prescribes certain procedural setups *in order to* strengthen academic freedom as an individual right. By framing organisational obligations of the state as enforceable individual rights, the court in turn also strengthens the objective value dimension of Article 5 (3) Basic Law. The procedural capability of individuals before the FCC,

[27] BVerfGE 127, 87 (114–115).

[28] Jarass, 'Grundrechte als Wertentscheidungen bzw. objektivrechtliche Prinzipien in der Rechtsprechung des Bundesverfassungsgerichts', 386.

[29] Such a construction would ultimately be unconvincing, however, as it would be "a matter of chance whether the acts leading to the existence of procedural positions in ordinary law have already been carried out". Hence, the "hypothetical right of enactment is more important than the right to non-removal", Alexy, *A Theory of Constitutional Rights*, 320.

[30] BVerfGE 35, 79 (115). Emphasis added.

in particular the constitutional complaint according to Article 93 (1) (4a) Basic Law, becomes instrumental to the realisation of the objective system of values. Because the FCC does not only derive objective obligations from originally subjective negative freedoms, but its "detour via objective law"[31] ultimately lands it at subjective rights again, the objective and the subjective dimensions are in a mutually reinforcing relationship.[32]

4.2.3 The Value of the Construction beyond Article 5 Basic Law

It was argued that the idea of protection through organisation could not be extrapolated to fundamental rights outside of Article 5 Basic Law. Instead, the idea "should be abandoned as a category that operates on the level of general fundamental rights doctrines and instead be understood solely as a special manifestation of Article 5 (1) (2) and Article 5 (3) Basic Law".[33] This argument is unconvincing for two reasons.

Firstly, "procedure and organisation" have traditionally been considered together in the context of the protection of fundamental rights. In fact, Hesse's famous formula of "realization and safeguarding of fundamental rights through organization and procedure"[34] has become somewhat of a heading under which the two phenomena are considered together as a phenomenon of general fundamental rights doctrine. This is justified as both procedure and organisation are "systems of rules and/or principle for the production of outcomes".[35] Both are meant to structure interactions between states and those individuals subjected to their power in a way that is in accordance with the constitution.

Secondly, and more importantly, the doctrinal construction the FCC explicitly relied on in its *Hochschulurteil* is indicative of the argument's applicability to all fundamental rights. The court derives rights to certain organisational set-ups from

---

[31] Jarass, 'Grundrechte als Wertentscheidungen bzw. objektivrechtliche Prinzipien in der Rechtsprechung des Bundesverfassungsgerichts', 369.

[32] We will return to this observation when discussing the justifications the FCC employs. See *infra* 5.3.

[33] Matthias Roßbach and Thomas Wischmeyer, 'Grundrechtsschutz durch Organisation: Das erste Fernsehurteil und das Hochschulurteil' in Dieter Grimm (ed), *Vorbereiter—Nachbereiter?* (Mohr Siebeck 2019), 258.

[34] Hesse, 434.

[35] Alexy, *A Theory of Constitutional Rights*, 316.

the "objective system of values" which the catalogue of fundamental rights constitutes. This construction has been worded in general terms since its very inception in *Lüth*. It is not a phenomenon restricted to specific rights. While different fundamental rights might be more or less dependent on certain organisational requirements,[36] the construction the FCC used shows us that such differences can only be of degree and not categorical. Moreover, as we will see in the following chapter, the justifications the FCC uses to derive procedural guarantees from fundamental rights are relevant to all fundamental rights equally. The fact that the FCC has not yet explicitly addressed organisational guarantees beyond Article 5 Basic Law does therefore not constitute a convincing argument that the remarks of the FCC in the *Hochschulurteil* have no relevance beyond said provision. Recalling the historical backdrop and the academic debates of the time, only the construction of a procedural dimension as part of a general doctrine of fundamental rights could address the challenges identified by Häberle, Hesse and others.

4.3 Conclusion

The FCC derives procedural rights and obligations from the objective dimension of fundamental rights. This complicated "detour via objective law" is necessary because the procedural rights are directed at positive state action and the originally negative nature of the fundamental rights of the Basic Law do not give rise to positive state action. The FCC has made this construction explicit in the *Hochschulurteil* when it held that the realisation of academic freedom required an organisational set-up of university governance that ensured to the bearers of the right sufficient influence. This construction is, however, extrapolatable to other forms of procedural protection.

[36] It is certainly true that ensuring academic freedom requires a relatively high degree of organisation. Hence, academic freedom under Article 5 (3) Basic Law has been called an "organisational basic right", see Eberhard Schmidt-Aßmann, 'Die Wissenschaftsfreiheit nach Art. 5 Abs. 3 GG als Organisationsgrundrecht' in Bernd Becker (ed), *Festschrift für Werner Thieme zum 70 Geburtstag* (Heymann 1993).

The FCC's Justifications

5

Given that administrative procedural rights and obligations under the fundamental rights of the Basic Law are positive in nature, and as such merely a "development under the constitution",[1] they are in need of justification. An analysis of the FCC's jurisprudence reveals essentially two justifications: on the one hand, the FCC construes administrative procedures as means to an end. They are a tool to facilitate "correct" decisions and the more effective implementation of fundamental rights. We will call this the "instrumental justification" (4.1). On the other hand, the court relies on the "position of the citizen in the state", on the human image of the Basic Law. According to this justification, the involvement of the affected individual in the decision-making processes of the state are ends within themselves. This justification is first and foremost defined by the idea of human dignity as enshrined in Article 1 (1) Basic Law. We will call this the "dignitarian justification" (4.2).[2] Importantly, the two justifications are not mutually exclusive but interconnected; they reinforce each other (4.3).

---

[1] Böckenförde, 2.

[2] The terminology follows that of Groves and Weeks, as well as Daly, see Matthew Groves and Greg Weeks, 'The Legitimacy of Expectations About Fairness: Can Process and Substance be Untangled?' in John Bell and others (eds), *Public Law Adjudication in Common Law Systems: Process and Substance* (Hart Publishing 2016), 172.

B. Behlert, *The Necessity of a Conversation between the Administration and the Individual*, Juridicum—Bochumer Schriften zur Friedenssicherung und zum Humanitären Völkerrecht | Bochum Studies on the International Law of Peace and Armed Conflict 72, https://doi.org/10.1007/978-3-658-50303-1_5

5.1 The Instrumental Justification

At the core of the instrumental justification lies an essentially pragmatic argument: accurate decision-making and the effective implementation of fundamental rights is possible only when the views of the affected individuals are adequately considered in the process. From this follows an instrumental understanding of procedural involvement. In the words of Hesse, administrative procedure is a "means to bring about an outcome in accordance with fundamental rights and thus to effectively secure these rights, even in the face of [...] modern problems"[3].

The FCC has developed this justification primarily under the notion of "effective legal protection". After discussing this general idea (5.1.1), we will focus on two features of general fundamental rights doctrine—the principles of proportionality and equality –, to make the instrumental value of procedural involvement for the implementation of fundamental rights more palpable (5.1.2).

5.1.1 Fundamental Rights and Effective Legal Protection

"According to the conception of the Basic Law, effective legal protection [...] is an essential element of the fundamental right itself."[4] This dictum, first uttered by the FCC in its *"Hamburger Deichordnungsgesetz"* decision of 1968, has long been a central feature of the FCC's jurisprudence on fundamental rights. Initially developed as a guarantee of *ex post* judicial protection (5.1.1.1), it was later extended to include *ex ante* legal protection, in particular the administrative procedure (5.1.1.2). After explaining these developments, we will discuss the interplay between *ex post* and *ex ante* legal protection highlighting the value of the individual's involvement in the administrative procedure (5.1.1.3).

5.1.1.1 Fundamental Rights and *Ex Post* Effective Legal Protection: A Pragmatic Argument

In the *Hamburger Deichordnungsgesetz* decision, the FCC held that expropriations *by* statute were permitted only in exceptional circumstances to ensure that citizens had the possibility of challenging the expropriation before a court. The court justified this ruling with a reference to effective legal protection, stating that "[a]ccording to the conception of the Basic Law, effective legal protection [...]

[3] Hesse, 435.

[4] BVerfGE 24, 367 (401): "*Nach der grundgesetzlichen Konzeption ist hiernach ein effektiver [...] Rechtsschutz ein wesentliches Element des Grundrechts selbst.*"

is an essential element of the fundamental right itself."[5] Since, this dictum has become a central element of the settled case-law of the FCC.[6]

Notably, the court also referred in its judgment to Article 19 (4) Basic Law which, it held, "expanded legal protection by the Constitution" and "conspicuously expressed" a change in meaning of the protection of property from a "*Sachgarantie*" to a "*Rechtsträgergarantie*".[7] In later judgments, however, the court derived the obligation to provide effective legal protection directly from fundamental rights themselves.[8]

The FCC justifies its jurisprudence in this regard by highlighting a positive, enhancing effect of procedural protection for the material contents of a fundamental right. Already in the *Deichordnungsgesetz* decision, the court qualified the legal protection necessitated by the fundamental right as one "securing the existence of property".[9] In 1978, the court stated that procedural law was "the means of helping the holder of the fundamental right to exercise his constitutional right in a specific case".[10] One year later, in a case concerning the right to asylum, it held that the state had a "constitutional obligation to work towards the *best possible protection* of the complainant's fundamental right under Article 16 (2) (2) Basic Law *when organizing proceedings*".[11] And in 1981, the FCC put it very poignantly:

---

[5] Ibid.

[6] See, e.g., BVerfGE 37, 67 (77); BVerfGE 37, 132 (148); BVerfGE 44, 105 (120); BVerfGE 45, 422 (430–433); BVerfGE 46, 325 (334); BVerfGE 49, 220 (225); BVerfGE 49, 252 (257); BVerfGE 52, 380 (389); BVerfGE 53, 30 (65); BVerfGE 63, 131 (143); BVerfGE 113, 29 (57); BVerfGE 124, 43 (70); BVerfGE 128, 282 (311), BVerfGE 142, 234 (260–261); BVerfGE 147, 253 (309). The FCC has not always used the exact same wording. It has, e.g., also referred to "enforceability" to describe essentially the same idea, BVerfGE 39, 276 (294): "*Zu den wesentlichen Bestandteilen eines verfassungsmäßigen Rechts gehört [...] seine Durchsetzbarkeit [...].*"

[7] BVerfGE 24, 367 (400–401).

[8] E.g., BVerfGE 46, 325 (334); BVerfGE 49, 252 (257). This renders the fact that the relationship between the need for legal protection as a direct consequence of a given fundamental right and the guarantee of legal recourse afforded by Article 19 (4) Basic Law has not been clarified conclusively harmless for our purposes. On this relationship, see Eberhard Schmidt-Aßmann, 'Art. 19 Abs. 4' in Günter Dürig, Roman Herzog and Rupert Scholz (eds), *Grundgesetz Kommentar* (107th EL edn, C. H. Beck 2025), para. 23; Helmuth Schulze-Fielitz, 'Art. 19 Abs. 4' in Horst Dreier (ed), *Grundgesetz Kommentar* (3rd edn, Mohr Siebeck 2013), para. 148.

[9] BVerfGE 24, 367 (401).

[10] BVerfGE 49, 252 (257).

[11] BVerfGE 52, 391 (408). Emphasis added.

> *Fundamental rights in general, if they are to fulfil their function in the social reality, require suitable forms of organization and procedural regulations as well as an application of procedural law in conformity with fundamental rights,* ***insofar as this is of importance for the effective protection of fundamental rights.***[12]

These passages reveal an instrumental understanding of procedural law. Procedural law is not an end in itself but a means to an end. Moreover, the FCC explicitly called procedural law a means to secure the enjoyment of individuals' rights and highlighted its "complementary function for the enforcement of substantive rights".[13] The procedural involvement of the affected individual is thus not an end in and of itself, it is a means towards the end of a more effective fundamental rights protection. According to this instrumental justification, procedural involvement has a "serving, an auxiliary function"[14]. In line with this, the FCC later on also spoke of the "strive for the procedural effectivization of fundamental liberties".[15]

5.1.1.2 The Inclusion of *Ex Ante* Procedural Protection

In the 1970s, the FCC abstracted the idea of "effective legal protection as an essential element of the right itself" from *ex post* judicial proceedings. With two judgments on auction procedures, it applied the reasoning to procedures leading up to an original decision for the first time.[16] It derived certain obligations to notify a person of an imminent threat to her property rights from the "effective legal protection" idea. In these decisions, courts were not addressed in their judicial but rather in a quasi-administrative function.[17] They did not review an act of public power but exercised public power originally. Hence, the judgments built the "first bridge from judicial procedures to administrative procedures".[18]

In the *Schweigender Prüfling* case, the FCC first made the application of the instrumental justification to administrative procedures explicit:

---

[12] BVerfGE 56, 216 (236): "*Indes bedürfen Grundrechte allgemein, sollen sie ihre Funktion in der sozialen Wirklichkeit erfüllen, geeigneter Organisationsformen und Verfahrensregelungen sowie einer grundrechtskonformen Anwendung des Verfahrensrechts, soweit dieses für einen effektiven Grundrechtsschutz von Bedeutung ist [...].*" Emphasis added in English translation. References omitted.

[13] BVerfGE 73, 280 (296).

[14] See Wolfram Cremer, *Freiheitsgrundrechte* (Mohr Siebeck 2003), 404.

[15] BVerfGE 69, 315 (356).

[16] BVerfGE 42, 64; BVerfGE 46, 325.

[17] Dolderer, 243.

[18] Ibid.

> *Since these effects [of fundamental rights on the necessity of procedural protection] already follow directly from the respective fundamental right, they are not limited to the procedure of judicial review, but also influence the design of the administrative procedure, insofar as the administrative decision affects a fundamental right.*[19]

As we have seen above, the FCC did not elaborate on this extrapolation. It did not elaborate on the specific value of procedural safeguards before a decision is reached. Rather, the court seems to have taken the transfer for granted, as if its jurisprudence on "effective legal protection" and the procedural dimension of fundamental rights had always included *ex ante* legal protection.

5.1.1.3 The Relationship Between *Ex Post* and *Ex Ante* Legal Protection: Complementation, Compensation, Facilitation

Just a little over a month later, in the seminal *Mülheim-Kärlich* order, however, the FCC made instructive remarks on why administrative procedure matters to the protection of fundamental rights. It stated that the involvement of the citizen already in the permit procedure for nuclear power plants "shift[ed] forward" legal protection.[20] Notably, the court portrayed this form of *ex ante* legal protection as additional or complementary. It stated that the citizen was "not only" entitled to have a decision reviewed by rescissory action or seek preliminary protection from administrative courts but may already raise her objections in the procedure leading up to the decision.[21] So, legal protection *ex ante* is justified as an addition to *ex post* legal review. It bolsters the position of the individual *vis à vis* the state by providing her with additional means to make her voice heard. Together, legal protection *ex ante* and legal protection *ex post* ensure the effective protection of the material contents of fundamental rights at different stages of state action.

The majority opinion of the judgment gave rise to a famous dissenting opinion by judges Simon and Heußner.[22] The very influential opinion was later even cited by the FCC in a majority opinion.[23] Most importantly for us, it contains more

---

[19] BVerfGE 52, 380 (390): *"Da diese Auswirkungen bereits unmittelbar aus dem jeweiligen Grundrecht folgen, beschränken sie sich nicht auf das Verfahren der gerichtlichen Überprüfung, sondern beeinflussen auch die Gestaltung des behördlichen Verfahrens, soweit die behördliche Entscheidung ein Grundrecht berührt."*

[20] BVerfGE 53, 30 (60).

[21] Ibid.

[22] Ibid, 69–96.

[23] The FCC cited it when arguing that procedural protection was necessary for fundamental rights to fulfil their function in society, cf. BVerfGE 56, 216 (236).

explicit elaborations on the justification of *ex ante* legal protection. In addition to the complementary function highlighted by the majority decision, it explains how procedural involvement *ex ante* can compensate for legal and factual uncertainties around a decision as well as the inadequacy of *ex post* review on the one hand, and how it can enable *ex post* legal review on the other.

Firstly, the dissenting judges address the connection between the (necessary) vagueness of material law and the regulation of decision-making procedures.[24] They diagnose a "regulation deficit" in the rules governing the planning and permission of nuclear power plants: as rules for a constantly and rapidly evolving technology, they had to be kept sufficiently flexible and vague to accommodate technological developments. It was the job of the administration and the judiciary to make up for this deficit. Considering this, the judges argued, the constitution could not be indifferent towards the design of the respective decision-making processes. They had to be designed with the regulation deficit in mind. And the suitability of these procedures to produce "correct" results was important for an effective protection of fundamental rights. The judges concluded this argument with the very poignant formula that "only procedural law [could] prevent the area between law and technology from becoming a legal no man's land"[25].

It must be mentioned here, that while the judges highlight the fact that regulations concerning new and developing technology were in play in the *Mülheim-Kärlich* decision, they are in fact describing a general characteristic of every legal rule and its application. Every general and abstract legal rule is vague, otherwise it would not be general and abstract. The vagueness might be particularly pronounced when it comes to developing technologies or other fields which require open-ended regulation. The difference, however, is gradual and not categorical. Hence, the passage in the dissenting opinion points to an important and general proportional relationship: the more flexible or vague the applicable legal regulations are, the more important is the procedure governing the application of these regulations to a given case. In other words, good, well-regulated procedures can become necessary in order to compensate for "regulation deficits" in the material law. They can provide a counter-weight against such vagueness.

Secondly, in an interconnected point, the judges addressed the connection between procedure and factual uncertainties. Given the many unknowns and risks involved in a permit procedure for nuclear power plants, the judges argued, the

[24] BVerfGE 53, 30 (75–76).

[25] Ibid, 76.

assessment of the administration could "hardly be kept free from [...] fundamental points of view and subjective interests".[26] Hence, "it seems all the more important to include the points of view, interests and fears of all those involved in the approval procedure in due time and [...] to ensure that all relevant aspects are properly taken into account".[27] This is a plausible point: the greater the uncertainties surrounding a decision, the more likely it is for the administration to come to a "wrong" decision, e.g., because it overlooks an essential interest. Hence, it becomes particularly important to discipline the administration, and make it pay great care to the views and arguments of everyone potentially affected *before* it makes its decision.

These arguments about the (necessary) vagueness of regulation in the modern state and the uncertainties in decision-making reflect concerns expressed in the literature of the time.[28] They exemplify the complex "conditions of the present" to which Hesse alluded when he argued that organisational and procedural rules were the only way to adequately address the dangers of the welfare state.[29] That the dissenting judges were influenced by this then contemporary scholarship is evident when they quote Häberle's lecture and explicitly refer to his *status activus processualis*.[30]

Finally, in another passage, the dissenting judges touch upon another facet of the compensatory function and add a facilitative function to the picture. A "fair application of procedural law", the judges argue,

> *enables the administrative courts to shift the focus of their review from the difficult assessment of technical and scientific disputes to a more behavioural and procedural review of the actual decision-makers and thus to a task for which the courts are better equipped and the diligent fulfilment of which at the same time ensures adequate legal protection for the citizen.*[31]

---

[26] Ibid, 77.

[27] Ibid.

[28] See *supra* 3.2.

[29] Hesse, 435.

[30] BVerfGE 53, 30 (80).

[31] Ibid, 81–82: "[Eine faire Anwendung des Verfahrensrechts] *ermöglicht es darüber hinaus der Verwaltungsgerichtsbarkeit, den Schwerpunkt ihrer Nachprüfung von der schwierigen Beurteilung technischer und naturwissenschaftlicher Streitfragen mehr auf eine Verhaltens- und Verfahrenskontrolle der eigentlichen Entscheidungsträger zu verlagern und damit auf eine Aufgabe, für die die Gerichte besser gerüstet sind und deren sorgfältige Erfüllung zugleich dem Bürger angemessenen Rechtsschutz gewährleistet.*"

Firstly, by stating that administration officials are "the actual decision-makers" and highlighting that courts are "better equipped" for other tasks, the FCC hints at a facet of the compensation argument which was already pondered in the literature of the 1970s and 1980s[32], and which we find clearly expressed in a 1991 decision dealing once again with the German legal state exam. Therein, the court holds that

> *[w]hether and to what extent guarantees for the administrative procedure are required by fundamental rights depends [...] on the extent to which the protection of fundamental rights is guaranteed by ex post review of the courts.*[33]

The process of assessing the quality of a student' achievements in an exam is "determined by numerous imponderables which are very difficult and in some cases impossible to grasp in an administrative court case", including "[s]ubjective impressions and the randomness of the examiners' professional preferences".[34] To keep these influences in check and ensure fair grading despite the relative inadequacy of *ex post facto* legal review, *ex ante* legal protection is necessary.[35] In other words, procedural safeguards *ex ante* not only compensate for factual uncertainties and legal vagueness but also for a lack of effective legal protection *ex post*.

Secondly, the quoted passage from the dissenting opinion in *Mülheim-Kärlich* suggests that *ex ante* procedural protection can facilitate legal protection *ex post*. Certain procedural guarantees applicable *ex ante* "enable" the courts to fulfil their review function. The FCC also referred to this function in subsequent jurisprudence to justify *ex ante* legal protection. In this regard, the court held that the state must record the notification of citizens of the processing of sensitive personal data,[36] or that the details of treatments of inmates against their will must

[32] Häberle, 'Grundrechte im Leistungsstaat', 88, 123 et seq., Jürgen Schwarze, *Der funktionale Zusammenhang von Verwaltungsverfahrensrecht und verwaltungsgerichtlichem Rechtsschutz* (Duncker & Humblot 1974), 44; later also Jürgen Held, *Der Grundrechtsbezug des Verwaltungsverfahrens* (Duncker & Humblot 1984), 42–49.

[33] BVerfGE 84, 34 (46): *"Ob und inwieweit Garantien für das Verwaltungsverfahren grundrechtlich gefordert sind, richtet sich zum einen nach Art und Intensität des Grundrechtseingriffs, zum anderen danach, inwieweit der Grundrechtsschutz durch die nachträgliche Kontrolle der Gerichte gewährleistet ist."*

[34] Ibid.

[35] Ibid, 46–47.

[36] BVerfGE 65, 1 (70).

be recorded[37]. In both instances, the court explicitly referred to the facilitation of judicial review as a justification. And it even called such documentation obligations a "pre-impact" (*"Vorwirkung"*) of the fundamental guarantee of effective judicial protection.[38] Against the backdrop of this "preparatory function", elements of administrative procedure—such as the giving reasons requirement—that have not featured as prominently in the FCC's jurisprudence as the *audi alteram partem* principle become more relevant.[39] For the courts, knowing the administration's reasons for an interference with a fundamental right is a prerequisite for reviewing the legality of that interference.[40]

To conclude, legal protection *ex post* and legal protection *ex ante* both contribute to the "best possible protection of fundamental rights"[41]. They are both a means for an effective implementation of fundamental rights. Importantly, they do not do so independently of each other; they do so *in tandem.* Legal protection *ex ante,* in particular through administrative procedure, does not only add to *ex post* legal protection by injecting the views of the affected individual at a different point in time, enabling the administrative agent to reach a correct decision in line with fundamental rights. It also facilitates *ex post* review and compensates for a lack of it, as well as for vagueness in the law and factual uncertainties surrounding a decision. In this sense, *ex post* and *ex ante* legal protection are "interrelated elements of a larger unified system serving legal protection"[42]. Together, they form a "differentiated overall legal protection system".[43]

---

[37] BVerfG 128, 282 (313–314).

[38] Ibid, 313.

[39] On the importance of the giving reasons requirement for effective ex post legal protection, see already BVerfGE 6, 32 (44) where the FCC held that a person whose rights are interfered with has a right to learn the reasons for the interference. In this very early judgment, however, the FCC justified this right primarily by reference to the "*Rechtsstaat*" principle.

[40] Held, 41–42.

[41] BVerfGE 52, 391 (408).

[42] Schwarze, 57. For a more recent reiteration of this argument, see also Jan Ziekow, '§ 14 Verwaltungsrecht und Verwaltungsprozessrecht' in Wolfgang Kahl and Markus Ludwigs (eds), *Handbuch des Verwaltungsrechts,* vol I (C. F. Müller 2021), paras. 79–81.

[43] Schwarze, 44.

5.1.2 Specific Ways in Which Administrative Procedure Furthers the Implementation of Fundamental Rights

To make the instrumental connection between the realisation of fundamental rights and the involvement of the affected individual in the administrative procedure more palpable, we will reflect on the instrumental value of involving the affected individual in the administrative decision-making process for two features of general fundamental rights doctrine. Firstly, we will look at how the involvement of the individual in administrative decision-making processes can contribute to a proportionate decision (5.1.2.1). Secondly, we will reflect on how the involvement of the affected individual can facilitate a fair and equal implementation of human rights (5.1.2.2).

5.1.2.1 Procedural Involvement and the Principle of Proportionality

Besides an important effect the principle of proportionality has on the implementation of procedural obligations,[44] the FCC referred to the principle also when justifying procedural obligations. After briefly sketching out the principle of proportionality and its necessary connection to the fundamental rights of the German Basic Law (5.1.2.1.1), we will reflect on the instrumental value of procedural involvement of the affected individual for the implementation of the proportionality principle (5.1.2.1.2).

5.1.2.1.1 Constitutional Rights, Principles and Proportionality

In a general sense, the principle of proportionality (*"Verhältnismäßigkeit"*) under German constitutional law with its three sub-principles of suitability, necessity and proportionality *strictu sensu* governs the relationship between the end the state pursues and the means it employs.[45] Not one decision of the FCC can be considered *the* inception of the principle under the Basic Law—the court has developed its jurisprudence on the principle *peu à peu*.[46] The court mentioned the

---

[44] See *infra* 6.3.2.

[45] Christian Hillgruber, '§ 201: Inhalt und Schranken der Grundrechte' in Josef Isensee and Paul Kirchhof (eds), *Handbuch des Staatsrechts*, vol IX (C.F. Müller 2011), para. 51–77.

[46] Peter Staubach, 'Das Verhältnismäßigkeitsprinzip' in Dieter Grimm (ed), *Vorbereiter—Nachbereiter?, Studien zum Verhältnis von Verfassungsrechtsprechung und Verfassungsrechtswissenschaft* (Mohr Siebeck 2019), 131.

principle of proportionality explicitly for the first time in 1954.[47] Since then, the FCC has been continuously developing a sophisticated doctrine of the principle.[48]

The constitutional status of the principle is often justified by reference to the *Rechtsstaatsprinzip* (roughly the German equivalent to the rule of law).[49] The source of the principle that is important to our endeavour, however, lies in the fundamental rights themselves:

> *This principle [proportionality], which has constitutional status, follows from the very nature of fundamental rights, which, as an expression of the citizen's general claim to freedom vis à vis the state, may be restricted by public authority only to the extent that is indispensable for the protection of public interests.*[50]

This connection between the "very nature of fundamental rights" and the principle of proportionality has been explained by Robert Alexy in his seminal study "A Theory of Constitutional Rights". Alexy's theory "illustrates the mechanisms of action of the principle of proportionality [...] in an unsurpassed manner".[51] At the heart of the theory of fundamental rights lies the distinction between principles and rules. On the one hand, rules are "definitive commands".[52] A valid rule is "always either fulfilled or not"[53]. Principles, on the other hand, are "norms which require that something be realized to the greatest extent possible given the legal and factual requirements". They are "optimization requirements, characterized by

---

[47] BVerfGE 3, 383 (399).

[48] For a detailed tracing-back of the historical development in the jurisprudence of the FCC, see Staubach, 132 ff.

[49] See, e.g., Eberhard Schmidt-Aßmann, '§ 26 Der Rechtsstaat' in Paul Kirchhof and Josef Isensee (eds), *Handbuch des Staatsrechts*, vol II (3rd edn, C. F. Müller 2004), para. 87; Michael Sachs, 'Art. 20 [Verfassungsgrundsätze; Widerstandsrecht]' in Michael Sachs (ed), *Grundgesetz Kommentar* (10th edn, C. H. Beck 2024), para. 146–148. For a comparative account of the historical development of the rule of law on the one and the *Rechtsstaat* principle on the other hand, see Bernado Sordi, 'Révolution, Rechtsstaat and the Rule of Law: historical reflections on the emergence and development of administrative law' in Susan Rose-Ackerman, Peter L. Lindseth and Blake Emerson (eds), *Comparative Administrative Law* (2nd edn, Edward Elgar 2017).

[50] BVerfGE 65, 1 (44): *"Dieser mit Verfassungsrang ausgestattete Grundsatz folgt bereits aus dem Wesen der Grundrechte selbst, die als Ausdruck des allgemeinen Freiheitsanspruchs des Bürgers gegenüber dem Staat von der öffentlichen Gewalt jeweils nur soweit beschränkt werden dürfen, als es zum Schutz öffentlicher Interessen unerläßlich ist."*

[51] Cremer, *Freiheitsgrundrechte*, 271.

[52] Robert Alexy, 'Constitutional Rights and Proportionality' (2014) 22 Revus [Online] 51, 52.

[53] Alexy, *A Theory of Constitutional Rights*, 48.

the fact that they can be satisfied to varying degrees".[54] Hence, principles can be fulfilled to varying extents.

The distinction between rules and principles becomes most apparent when norms collide. When two rules collide, the conflict can be solved only by recognizing an exception for one of the rules, or by declaring one of the rules invalid or inapplicable in a given situation.[55] This is why maxims such as *"lex specialis derogat legi generali"* or *"lex posterior derogat legi priori"* are needed to solve such conflicts.[56] Competitions of principles, on the other hand, "are played out in the dimension of weight".[57] One of the competing principles must be outweighed by the other. The solution to such a competition of principles is found in a "*conditional relation of precedence* between the principles in the light of the circumstances of the case".[58] This relation is conditional because different circumstances can lead to different relations between the competing principles. The extent to which the optimization of a principle is factually and legally possible varies depending on the factual and legal circumstances of a given case. How a collision of principles is resolved shows their *prima facie* character.[59]

The connection between principles as a class of norms and proportionality is "as close as it could possibly be".[60] In fact, "the nature of principles implies the principle of proportionality and vice versa",[61] and "[t]he definition of principles as optimization requirements leads straightaway to a necessary connection between principles and proportionality".[62] This becomes clear when looking at the three legs of the proportionality test: suitability, necessity and proportionality *strictu sensu*.[63] These sub-principles define what is factually and legally possible. They define the "conditional relation of precedence" between two principles under given circumstances. On the one hand, the elements of suitability and necessity relate to what is factually possible in a given situation.[64] Both, the

[54] Ibid, 47–48.

[55] Ibid, 49.

[56] Ibid, 49.

[57] Ibid, 50.

[58] Ibid, 52. Emphasis original.

[59] Ibid, 57.

[60] Ibid, 66.

[61] Ibid, 66.

[62] Alexy, 'Constitutional Rights and Proportionality', 52.

[63] See only BVerfGE 118, 168 (193) where the FCC calls this version of proportionality "settled case-law" (*"stRspr"*).

[64] Alexy, *A Theory of Constitutional Rights*, 67.

question of whether a means can potentially further the state's legitimate aim, and the question of whether a milder yet equally effective means exists to further the aim, relate to factual conditions.[65] Proportionality *strictu sensu*, on the other hand, is the "requirement of balancing".[66] It defines the extent to which optimization is legally possible.[67] In other words, it defines the relative weight of one principle against another: "[t]he greater the degree of non-satisfaction of, or detriment to, one principle, the greater must be the importance of satisfying the other".[68] This explains the FCC's remark that the principle of proportionality follows from the nature of fundamental rights.[69]

5.1.2.1.2 Proportionality and Procedure

Whenever a state official seeks to take a certain measure, she must "keep in mind the scale of intervention available" and choose the mildest measures available on that scale.[70] Involving the affected individual in the decision-making process allows the administrative official to fulfil her obligations under the principle of proportionality. In this regard, the FCC stated in the *Hamburger U-Bahn* order that an expropriation without a prior procedure involving the potentially affected individual excluded the principle of proportionality.[71] The court's rationale here was pragmatic, framing the conversation between the administrative and the individual as a means to the end of proportionate decision-making. The administration should have conducted negotiations with the affected individual to

[65] It shall be said, however, that—in contrast to the suitability test—the question of necessity is not exclusively factual. Determining whether one means is milder than another does involve normative judgment.

[66] Alexy, *A Theory of Constitutional Rights*, 67.

[67] Ibid.

[68] Alexy, 'Constitutional Rights and Proportionality', 54.

[69] It must be mentioned here that Alexy rejects a "model of pure principles" for constitutional rights norms and instead argues in favour of the "double aspect of constitutional rights norms", see Alexy, *A Theory of Constitutional Rights*, 69–86. In a later publication, he has, however, explained how this differentiated approach does not constitute a counter-argument to the necessary connection between constitutional rights norms and proportionality, see Alexy, 'Constitutional Rights and Proportionality', 62–63. In any case, for our purposes it suffices to explain the connection between constitutional rights and proportionality merely with the connection between principles and proportionality as this captures a large enough number of situations to explain the practical argument in favour of the need of involving the individual in decision-making processes.

[70] Detlef Merten, '§ 68 Verhältnismäßigkeitsgrundsatz' in Detlef Merten and Hans-Jürgen Papier (eds), *Handbuch der Grundrechte in Deutschland und Europa* (2009), para. 67.

[71] BVerfGE 45, 297 (335).

find out whether an expropriation was actually necessary. Perhaps, a negotiated agreement could have been reached as a less intrusive measure for the affected individual. Thus, involving the affected individual in the decision-making process is an instrument to explore possible milder means to reach the envisaged aim. In any case, the administrative official must know how gravely different measures affected the rights of an individual in order to choose the mildest one available. Involving the individual enables the state official to understand where on the scale of gravity a measure falls, whether other measures are available and whether those would be equally effective.

The same practical argument can easily be made for the sub-principles of suitability and proportionality *strictu sensu.* It will not always be possible for a state official to assess the suitability of a measure it wants to take without being aware of the precise circumstances of the case at hand. Involving the individual in the decision-making process can help her become aware of all relevant facts. The involvement of the individual in the decision-making process plays the same, if not an even bigger role for proportionality *strictu sensu.* Even though the test required under this third sub-principle of proportionality is a normative exercise, conducting it properly requires a solid factual basis. To properly balance the gravity of the interference with the expected benefit, the state official must know what to put into either pan of the scale. On the one hand, she must know precisely how a measure might affect the individual. For that, she might need certain information about the individual's situation which she can only receive from the individual herself. On the other hand, the official must possess all information necessary to assess which benefits to expect from the measure. This information, too, might only become available to her by involving the individual in her decision-making process.

In a nutshell, the procedural involvement of the individual is a prerequisite for the administration to exercise its duties under the principle of proportionality.[72] It helps the administrative agent to sound out what is factually and legally possible. Without a procedure, the administration might not be able to assess the proportionality of the measure it envisages; it might not be able to verify the constitutionality of what it is about to do.

5.1.2.2 Procedural Involvement and the Principle of Equality

The principle of equality provides another instructive example to illustrate the instrumental connection between administrative procedure and the implementation of fundamental rights. After briefly sketching out the general obligations

[72] In this sense also Hesse, 431.

of the administration with regard to the equal application of fundamental rights (5.1.2.2.1), we will highlight the instrumental value of involving affected individuals in decision-making processes for the implementation of the principle of equality (5.1.2.2.2).

5.1.2.2.1 The Principle of Equality Under the German Basic Law

The principle of equality under the Basic Law has been the subject of many seminal judgments and great academic debate. The result is a complex and highly sophisticated doctrine for the principle, in particular for its manifestation in Article 3 Basic Law.[73] This is not the place to unfold this intricate doctrine. Fortunately, this is not necessary in order to understand the instrumental value of procedures to the realisation of the principle of equality. It is enough to recall the essence of the principle: that the state must treat equal things equally and unequal things unequally.[74]

Traditionally, violations of the equality principle were assessed only against the prohibition on arbitrariness *("Willkürverbot")*.[75] "Reasonable factual grounds" were enough to justify a differentiation in treatment between equals. Only if such grounds were lacking, a differentiation constituted an illegal discrimination.[76] Today, the doctrine around prohibited discrimination under the Basic Law has evolved, and many, if not most, cases of differentiation are to be assessed by the "new formula" which is essentially a proportionality test.[77] Given the

[73] See for overviews Uwe Kischel, 'GG Art. 3 [Gleichheit vor dem Gesetz]' in Volker Epping and Christian Hillgruber (eds), *BeckOK Grundgesetz* (62th edn, C. H. Beck 2025); Ferdinand Wollenschläger, 'GG Art. 3' in Peter Huber and Andreas Voßkuhle (eds), *Grundgesetz Kommentar* (8th edn, C. H. Beck 2024); Sigrid Boysen, 'GG Art. 3 [Gleichheit vor dem Gesetz]' in Ingo von Münch and others (eds), *Grundgesetz Kommentar* (8th edn, C. H. Beck 2025); Alexander Thiele, 'GG Art. 3 Abs. 1 [Gleichheit]' in Frauke Brosius-Gersdorf (ed), *Dreier Grundgesetz-Kommentar* (4th edn, Mohr Siebeck 2023), Paul Kirchhof, 'GG Art. 3 Abs. 1 [Gleichheit vor dem Gesetz]' in Günter Dürig, Roman Herzog and Rupert Scholz (eds),*Grundgesetz-Kommentar* (107th EL edn, C. H. Beck 2025).

[74] Jost Pietzker, '§ 125 Der allgemeine Gleichheitssatz' in Detlef Merten and Hans-Jürgen Papier (eds), *Handbuch der Grundrechte in Deutschland und Europa* (C. F. Müller 2013), para. 16.

[75] Kischel, paras. 30–33.2; Pietzker, paras. 40–42.

[76] Instead of many, see Hans D. Jarass, 'Art. 3 [Gleichheit]' in Hans D. Jarass, Bodo Pieroth and Martin Kment (eds), *Grundgesetz für die Bundesrepublik Deutschland Kommentar* (18th edn, C. H. Beck 2024), paras. 18–19.

[77] See for a clear reconstruction Angelika Nußberger and Johanna Hey, 'Art. 3 [Gleichheit vor dem Gesetz]' in Michael Sachs (ed), *Grundgesetz Kommentar* (10th edn, C. H. Beck 2024), paras. 8–37; Pietzker, para. 44.

"original connection between the principle of proportionality and [...] rational decision-making"[78], this development has arguably enhanced the arbitrariness-reducing function of the principle of equality. Baer brought down the connection between equality, proportionality and rationality to a handy formula when she wrote that "[t]he more we consider a social distinction irrational, the more a right to equality prohibits making that distinction"[79].

Regarding fundamental rights, the principle of equality prohibits that some enjoy their fundamental rights to a greater extent than others without a rational justification. Such an obligation has three potential bases in doctrine. Firstly, Article 3 (1) Basic Law is an overarching guarantee of equal treatment that applies whenever the state treats equal things equally or unequal things unequally.[80] Secondly, the obligation has been derived from the *Rechtsstaatsprinzip.*[81] Thirdly, it was argued that every fundamental right has a non-discrimination dimension which obliges the state to realize constitutional rights without discrimination.[82] For our purposes, the question of where exactly the obligation to grant fundamental rights protection in a way that does not discriminate comes from, can be left aside. What matters is that such an obligation of the administration exists and that it applies to the administration in the form of "equality in the application of the law" *("Rechtsanwendungsgleichheit").*[83]

5.1.2.2.2 Equality and Procedural Participation

The FCC pointed to the relationship between the principle of equality and procedural regulations in its *numerus clausus* judgments which concerned the fair allocation of limited study places. In the first judgment of 1972, the FCC derived a material right to participation *("Teilhaberecht")* from Article 12 (1) Basic Law which was more important "the more the modern state turned to social security and furthering of culture".[84] In a second step, the FCC combined this right with Article 3 (1) Basic Law (and the *"Sozialstaatsprinzip"*) and held that every

[78] Staubach, 135.

[79] Susanne Baer, 'Equality' in Michel Rosenfeld and András Sajó (eds), *The Oxford Handbook of Comparative Constitutional Law* (Oxford University Press 2012), 986.

[80] Nußberger, para. 65.

[81] Karl-Peter Sommermann, 'Artikel 20' in Peter Huber and Andreas Voßkuhle (eds), *Grundgesetz Kommentar* (8th edn, C. H. Beck 2024), paras. 305–307.

[82] Hans D. Jarass, 'Bausteine einer umfassenden Grundrechtsdogmatik' (1995) 120 Archiv des öffentlichen Rechts 345, 348–349.

[83] For a discussion of the principle, see Cremer, 'Rechtsanwendungsgleichheit im Mehrebenensystem', 119–124.

[84] BVerfGE 33, 303 (330–331).

citizen in principle had the right to participate in the offered educational opportunities with the same chances.[85] The court then defined the problem about absolute admission restrictions, namely that there are not enough spaces to allocate a place at a university to everyone entitled.[86] The consequence is "the blatant inequality that one part of the applicants receives everything and the other part—at least for a more or less long period of time, possibly decisive for further decisions in life—receives nothing".[87] In other words, not every holder of the fundamental right to occupational freedom can enjoy this right equally.

Against this backdrop of individual entitlement to the equal enjoyment of rights and factual limitations, the FCC defined constitutional requirements for the legality of absolute admission restrictions. An absolute *numerus clausus* is only permissible if "it is arranged within the limits of what is absolutely necessary, making exhaustive use of the existing educational capacities created with public funds" and if the

> *selection and distribution take place according to appropriate criteria with a chance for every applicant who is ready for higher education and with the greatest possible consideration for the individual choice of the place of education.*[88]

While the requirements laid out here relate mostly to substantive admission criteria, the latter remark about *how* the administration must consider the choices of the applicants points to the decision-making process. The connection of a material participation right to procedural protection was made explicit, however, only much later in the third *numerus clausus* judgment:

> *In the area of fundamental rights claims to participation – especially in competitive situations – the realisation of the substantive content of fundamental rights requires a procedural design appropriate to the protection of fundamental rights, because it can have an influence on the outcome of the selection decision. Thus, not only the*

[85] Ibid, 331.

[86] Ibid, 332.

[87] Ibid, 332–333.

[88] Ibid, 338: "*Im einzelnen ist ein absoluter numerus clausus für Studienanfänger nach dem Stand der bisherigen Erfahrungen nur verfassungsmäßig, wenn er (1.) in den Grenzen des unbedingt Erforderlichen unter erschöpfender Nutzung der vorhandenen, mit öffentlichen Mitteln geschaffenen Ausbildungskapazitäten angeordnet wird […] und wenn (2.) Auswahl und Verteilung nach sachgerechten Kriterien mit einer Chance für jeden an sich hochschulreifen Bewerber und unter möglichster Berücksichtigung der individuellen Wahl des Ausbildungsortes erfolgen […].*"

> *substantive selection criteria, but also the admission procedure itself require an open design. This includes sufficient procedural transparency.*[89]

The statement is brief but the instrumental understanding of (administrative) procedures comes out clearly. Because procedures can influence the outcome, they must be "appropriate to the protection of fundamental rights". They must be designed with the purpose of better, fairer outcomes in mind.

Moreover, the FCC cites a number of previous decisions which have framed the relationship between fundamental rights and administrative procedure as instrumental, too.[90] Specifically, it cites a decision in which it dealt with the selection procedure for notaries. In that decision, the court held that "[t]hrough the design of the selection procedure, direct influence is exerted on the competitive situation and thus on the result of the selection decision."[91] The design of the selection procedure has an influence on the composition of the group of applicants.[92] In such a case, the court argues, the "complementary function of the procedure for the enforcement of substantive rights" requires the state to have in place procedural rules that secure the realisation of Article 12 Basic Law.[93]

And the instrumental rationale is clear in the third *numerus clausus* decision as well: if everyone has an equal right to participation in the education system

---

[89] BVerfGE 147, 253 (309): *"Im Bereich grundrechtlicher Teilhabeansprüche—gerade in Konkurrenzsituationen—erfordert die Verwirklichung des materiellen Grundrechtsgehalts eine dem Grundrechtsschutz angemessene Verfahrensgestaltung, denn sie kann Einfluss auf das Ergebnis der Auswahlentscheidung haben* [...]. *Einer chancenoffenen Gestaltung bedürfen somit nicht nur die materiellen Auswahlmaßstäbe, sondern auch das Zulassungsverfahren selbst. Dazu gehört eine hinreichende Verfahrenstransparenz* [...]." References omitted.

[90] For the statement that the "substantive content of fundamental rights requires a procedural design appropriate to the protection of fundamental rights", the FCC cites BVerfGE 39, 276, BVerfGE 52, 380, BVerfGE 53, 30, BVerfGE 73, 280.

For the explicit reference to transparency, the court cites its first *numerus clausus* judgment, BVerfGE 33, 303. This reference is, however, not understandable. In the cited passage of said judgment, the FCC merely states that a wide range of admission criteria "impairs the transparency of the admission system and the equality of opportunity for applicants, as it makes the prospect of admission partly dependent on which university the applicant is considered for". This is – at best – an indirect postulate of transparency for admission procedures. It does not warrant a transparency postulate as clear as the FCC's statement represented above.

[91] BVerfGE 73, 280 (296).

[92] Ibid.

[93] Ibid.

derived from occupational freedom, and if that right may only be limited according to appropriate criteria, the procedure must enable those who administer the allocation of limited resources to obtain the information necessary to make their decision in a non-arbitrary manner. In order to achieve an equal application of the law, the administration needs a solid factual basis for its decision-making. It needs to know what may or may not differentiate one case from others. It needs to know who fulfils the criteria it has established. Only then can it allocate the limited resources in a way that is not arbitrary. Very often, this will only be achievable by giving the affected individuals the opportunity to explain themselves, i.e., by granting them the right to be heard.

One final aspect about the quote from the third *numerus clausus* decision is notable. In dashes, the FCC states that procedural protection is required "especially in competitive situations". This remark, which the court does not further elaborate upon, refers to the multipolarity of situations in which multiple right holders with, in principle, the same constitutional entitlements compete for limited public resources. The state delineates areas of freedom from one another in these situations, in an effort to reconcile individual entitlements with factual and societal necessities. It acts as a kind of referee in these situations. In that sense, it operationalises the value decision the Basic Law makes in favour of the "community-relatedness" of the individual.[94] In Hesse's words, procedures and organisation

> *enable the delimitation, limitation and allocation of areas of freedom, which – particularly evident in the area of the property guarantee – is becoming increasingly necessary in the narrowing world of the present. [...] to a certain extent also the balancing of conflicting fundamental rights positions.*[95]

The connection between the proper implementation of the principle of equality and the involvement of the affected individual in the decision-making process

---

[94] We will discuss this feature of the human image of the Basic Law in the next section on the deontological justification, see *infra* 5.2.

[95] Hesse, 436: *"[Organisation und Verfahren] ermöglichen allgemein die Abgrenzung, Begrenzung und Zuordnung von Freiheitsbereichen, die—besonders deutlich im Bereich der Eigentumsgarantie—in der enger werdenden Welt der Gegenwart in zunehmendem Maße notwendig wird. [...], in gewissem Umfang auch den Ausgleich kollidierender Grundrechtspositionen."*

allows us to highlight specifically the compensatory function *ex ante* legal protection has in relation to legal protection *ex post*. Imagine a situation in which a limited resource is distributed by a state. After the distribution, it turns out that the distribution was illegal because the state overlooked that a person who did not receive the resource had actually fulfilled the criteria. Practically, this hindsight realisation poses a whole host of potential problems. What if the resource has been used up by now and is simply not available anymore? What if the others who have received the resource fulfilled the criteria as well, and did not receive it illegally? These questions show how difficult it will be to deal with the situation in hindsight. Courts and administrators would face great difficulties to "clean up the mess". A diligently executed decision-making procedure that involves all affected individuals can reduce the likelihood of such situations. In that sense, legal protection *ex ante* compensates for (practical) difficulties in connection with effective legal protection *ex post*.

5.1.3 Conclusion

One of the two justifications the FCC relies on when it derives procedural rights and obligations from the fundamental rights of the Basic Law is an instrumental argument: the involvement of the affected individual in the decision-making process is a means to the end of the better realisation of fundamental rights. Procedural protection *ex ante* complements *ex post* judicial review, facilitates it, and compensates for a lack of effective review possibilities. For example, the implementation of the principles of proportionality and equality may benefit greatly from a conversation with the affected individual. In some cases, the implementation may even be possible only after such a conversation has taken place.

5.2 The Dignitarian Justification

In addition to the instrumental justification, we find another justification for procedural obligations under fundamental rights in the FCC's jurisprudence. In its order in the *Hamburger U-Bahn* case, the FCC stated that "the necessity of a conversation between the administration and the citizen correspond[ed] to the constitutional understanding of the *position of the citizen in the state*".[96]

[96] BVerfGE 45, 297 (335). Emphasis added.

What, however, defines this understanding? In 1954, the FCC held that

> *[t]he Basic Law's conception of the human being is not that of an isolated sovereign individual; rather, the Basic Law has decided on the tension between the individual and the community in the sense of the community-relatedness and community-boundness of the person, without touching her intrinsic value. [...] the individual must accept those limits to her freedom of action which the legislature imposes in order to maintain and promote social coexistence within the bounds of what is generally reasonable in the given circumstances, provided that the autonomy of the person is preserved.*[97]

Wahl is right to highlight that this idea of community-relatedness is necessarily preceded by the "recognition of the fundamental freedom and the autonomy of the individual".[98] The individual is "the beginning of all political thinking", she must never be bereaved of her autonomy, she is "a subject throughout and in principle" and "a legal subject everywhere in law".[99] We find an early variation of this idea in the plain wording of the *Herrenchiemsee* draft: "the individual is not there for the sake of the state, but the state is there for the sake of the individual"[100]. This formula has never become binding law. Nevertheless, it has had great influence on the constitutional conception of the individual human being within the state.[101]

This idea, this "human image of legal subjectivity"[102], is visible throughout the catalogue of fundamental rights in the Basic Law. However, it is the guarantee of human dignity, Article 1 (1) Basic Law, in particular, that has cast it into law. The following section will therefore briefly recall the essence of human dignity

[97] BVerfGE 4, 7 (15–16): *"Das Menschenbild des Grundgesetzes ist nicht das eines isolierten souveränen Individuums; das Grundgesetz hat vielmehr die Spannung Individuum—Gemeinschaft im Sinne der Gemeinschaftsbezogenheit und Gemeinschaftsgebundenheit der Person entschieden, ohne dabei deren Eigenwert anzutasten. [...] der Einzelne muß sich diejenigen Schranken seiner Handlungsfreiheit gefallen lassen, die der Gesetzgeber zur Pflege und Förderung des sozialen Zusammenlebens in den Grenzen des bei dem gegebenen Sachverhalt allgemein Zumutbaren zieht, vorausgesetzt, daß dabei die Eigenständigkeit der Person gewahrt bleibt."*

[98] Rainer Wahl, *Herausforderungen und Antworten: Das Öffentliche Recht der letzten fünf Jahrzehnte* (De Gruyter Recht 2006), 21.

[99] Ibid, 21.

[100] Entwurf eines Grundgesetzes ("Chiemseer Entwurf"), Artikel 1, published in Peter Bucher, *Der Parlamentarische Rat 1948–1949, Band 2: Der Verfassungskonvent auf Herrenchiemsee* (Deutscher Bundestag and Bundesarchiv eds, Oldenbourg Wissenschaftsverlag 1981), 580.

[101] Wahl, 21–22.

[102] Ibid, 22: *"Menschenbild der Rechtssubjektivität"*.

under the Basic Law (5.2.1) before we can reflect on the role it plays in the dignitarian justification of procedural obligations (5.2.2).

5.2.1 Human Dignity Under the Basic Law

The two first sentences of Article 1 (1) Basic Law are perhaps the most famous words of the German constitution. Early on, the court called human dignity a "fundamental constitutional principle"[103] and the "supreme value in the Basic Law"[104]. Obviously, there has been vast engagement in the literature with Article 1 (1) Basic Law which probably fills thousands of pages of articles, monographs, and so on. For our purposes, however, it suffices to recall the gist of human dignity under the Basic Law—the object formula—(5.2.1.1), and the connection of human dignity with (other) fundamental rights, namely the idea of the "human dignity core" (5.2.1.2).

5.2.1.1 The "Object Formula"

Based on the work of Dürig[105], the FCC developed the so-called object formula. This development made a significant contribution to turning the abstract lofty principle of human dignity into a judicially manageable concept. According to this formula, all state activity which treats the individual as a mere object and deprives her of her subject-status is prohibited.[106]

A decision of 2006 that annulled the so-called "air safety act" *("Luftsicherheitsgesetz (LuftSiG)")*[107] illustrates the object formula and its legal consequences perhaps better than any other. The air safety act had been enacted in the aftermath of the terrorist attacks on the Twin Towers in September 2001, and its section 14 (3) essentially allowed the German military to shoot down planes

---

[103] BVerfGE 6, 32 (36): *"tragendes Konstitutionsprinzip"*.

[104] Ibid, 41. See also BVerfGE 12, 45 (53): *"höchster Rechtswert"*. For a compilation of the many different expressions, the FCC has used to express this, see Mathias Hong, *Der Menschenwürdegehalt der Grundrechte: Grundfragen, Entstehung und Rechtsprechung* (Mohr Siebeck 2019), 414.

[105] See, e.g., Günter Dürig, 'Der Grundrechtssatz von der Menschenwürde: Entwurf eines praktikablen Wertsystems der Grundrechte aus Art. 1 Abs. 1 in Verbindung mit Art. 19 Abs. 2 des Grundgesetzes' (1956) 81 Archiv des öffentlichen Rechts 117, in particular 127 ff.

[106] Cf. Friederike Wapler, 'GG Art. 1 Abs. 1 [Menschenwürde; Menschenrechte; Grundrechtsbindung]' in Frauke Brosius-Gersdorf (ed), *Dreier Grundgesetz-Kommentar Band I* (4th edn, Mohr Siebeck 2023), paras. 64 ff.

[107] BVerfGE 115, 118.

which had been captured by terrorists in order to commit attacks similar to those of 9/11. The situation envisaged by the norm is easily conceivable: A plane with 200 passengers and crew members is hijacked by terrorists and on its course towards a football stadium with 60,000 fans inside. The law, following a simplistic quantitative rationale, allowed for the shooting-down of the plane and thus for the killing of a little more than 200 innocent human beings in order to save 60,000 in the stadium.[108] The FCC took issue with this utilitarian approach. Helpless individuals already stripped of their agency by the terrorists would be relegated to mere objects of state action if the state shot them down *in order to* save other lives. It is precisely this "in order to" element of the rationale of the law that was problematic. The passengers and crew members would be relegated to means to an end. Such an approach, the FCC held, was irreconcilable with Article 1 (1) Basic Law, no matter the end—even if it is saving (many more) human lives.[109] The judgment provides a palpable example of how the Kantian object formula plays out in practice.

Häberle has turned the object formula around and developed it further into a subject formula: "the constitution state realises human dignity by making the citizens the subject of their acts".[110] If no individual must be relegated to a mere object of state action, she must always retain a certain level of agency, a certain room for manoeuvre *vis à vis* the state. This version of human dignity will be useful to understand the connection between this fundamental principle of the Basic Law and procedural involvement of the individual.[111]

---

[108] Ibid, 122–124.

[109] BVerfGE 115, 118 (151–160).

[110] Peter Häberle, '§ 22 Die Menschenwürde als Grundlage der staatlichen Gemeinschaft' in Josef Isensee and Ferdinand Kirchhof (eds), *Handbuch des Staatsrechts* (3rd edn, C.F. Müller 2004), para. 52. These remarks in this relatively late piece by Häberle reflect the idea that already influenced his lecture at the *Staatsrechtslehrertagung* in 1971, namely that, in the modern state, the citizen is not merely subjected to public power but that her relationship with the state is better understood as a communicative relationship in the shaping of which she actively participates.

[111] Hence, Denninger also relies on it to explain the connection between human dignity and necessary procedural involvement of the individual in administrative decision-making processes, see Denninger, 'Government Assistance in the Exercise of Basic Rights (Procedure and Organization)', 445.

5.2.1.2 The Human Dignity Core of the Fundamental Rights

Importantly, the fundamental rights under the Basic Law have a human dignity core.[112] They are "concretizations of the principle of human dignity".[113] In this sense, the fundamental freedoms in the Basic Law lay out specifically protected rooms for manoeuvre, specific concretisations of the idea that the individual under the Basic Law is a self-directing agent. This idea becomes particularly manifest when looking at those fundamental rights which are not explicitly recognised by the Basic Law but were crafted from the constitution's text by the FCC. There is, of course, the "right to informational self-determination", which the FCC derived from a combined reading of Articles 2 (1) and 1 (1) Basic Law.[114] However, we also find this idea in the way the FCC interprets explicitly guaranteed fundamental rights, e.g., in its interpretation of Article 14 Basic Law.[115]

If a fundamental right has a core of human dignity, every holder of such a right is a "subject" of that right in the sense that she is in a position to—in one way or another—contribute actively to the realization of that right. One must of course be careful not to overstretch such interpretations of the constitution, especially because as the court stated already in 1954, the individual is not isolated but integrated into society. Nevertheless, appreciating this agency aspect of fundamental rights will help us understand how the position of the citizen within the state factors into the FCC's justification of the necessary procedural protection of these rights.

5.2.2 Human Dignity and Procedural Participation

Human dignity has long been a central justification for the procedural dimension of fundamental rights.[116] When having in mind that human dignity requires the state to treat individuals under its jurisdiction as subjects, rather than objects, it is easily conceivable why "[i]t follows from Article 1 (1) Basic Law that the

---

[112] For a compilation of FCC decision that have made this statement in various forms, see Hong, 428 ff.

[113] BVerfGE 107, 275 (284).

[114] BVerfGE 65, 1 (41–42). For a discussion of the right, see Jörn-Axel Kämmerer, 'Art. 2 GG' in Ingo von Münch and others (eds), *Grundgesetz Kommentar* (8th edn, C. H. Beck 2025), paras. 75–80.

[115] Cf., e.g., BVerfGE 46, 325 (334).

[116] Cf. Denninger, 'Government Assistance in the Exercise of Basic Rights (Procedure and Organization)', 445.

citizen may not be disposed of without procedural safeguards."[117] When the state interferes with an individual's rights without somehow involving her in the decision, e.g., by giving her a chance to explain her view of the issue at hand, or by giving her the reasons for the decision, the state does not treat her as a subject anymore. Merely confronting a citizen with a decision would make her an object of state action. To do justice to the individual's active role in the shaping of the reality of her rights guaranteed by Article 1 (1) Basic Law, the state must involve her in the process of making a decision which will affect her rights.[118]

It is therefore no surprise that fair trial rights, in particular the right to be heard in court proceedings, have been "early fields of application"[119] of the obligation to respect and protect human dignity in the jurisdiction of the FCC. The first time the court invoked *an* object formula was in 1957 when it argued that a person who was not granted the procedural capacities to make her case in front of a court and be heard, would become "ultimately only the object of the procedure".[120] As in other decisions of the time, however, the FCC did not explicitly refer to human dignity to explain the formula.[121]

One year later, the FCC then connected the right to having a voice in a court procedure to the idea of human dignity.[122] It made clear that human dignity provided a distinct justification for hearing the affected individual in a court, applicable in addition to the instrumental justification for such a procedural involvement:

> *The strictness with which the Federal Constitutional Court repeatedly emphasizes the principle of the right to be heard in court is based not only on the fact that the hearing of the parties involved is generally unavoidable for an all-round clarification of the facts and that it must therefore be made possible for them, in the interest of a correct decision, to supplement or correct representations given by other parties; in addition to the interest in clarifying the facts, this is demanded by the dignity of the person of the litigants.*[123]

---

[117] Häberle, 'Grundrechte im Leistungsstaat', 122.

[118] With essentially the same postulate Erhard Denninger, '§ 193—Staatliche Hilfe zur Grundrechtsausübung durch Verfahren, Organisation und Finanzierung' in Josef Isensee and Paul Kirchhof (eds), *Handbuch des Staatsrechts*, vol IX (3 edn, C. F. Müller 2011), paras. 55, 67.

[119] Hong, 419.

[120] BVerfGE 7, 53 (58).

[121] Cf. Hong, 419–420.

[122] BVerfGE 7, 275 (278–279).

[123] Ibid: "*Die Strenge, mit der das Bundesverfassungsgericht den Grundsatz des rechtlichen Gehörs vor Gericht immer wieder betont, beruht nicht nur darauf, daß die Anhörung der Beteiligten für eine allseitige Aufklärung des Sachverhalts in der Regel unumgänglich ist*

In 1959, the court then brought the principle of human dignity, the object formula and the necessity of the involvement of the affected individual in judicial proceedings together in one instructive sentence:

> *Moreover, the dignity of the person demands that his right not be summarily disposed of by authority; the individual should not only be the object of the judicial decision, but he should have his say before a decision affecting his rights is made, in order to be able to influence the proceedings and their outcome.*[124]

In 1983, the court then generalized these statements when it held that no individual "may be made the mere object of a state procedure" as this would violate her dignity.[125] Notably, the court speaks of "a state procedure", not a "judicial procedure". This constitutes an important generalisation.[126] Together with the expression from the *Hamburger U-Bahn* decision, that the "necessity of a conversation between the administration and the citizen" followed "from the position of the citizen under the Basic Law", these decisions leave little doubt that the dignity-based argument in favour of having a say *vis à vis* state authorities in their decision-making processes can be extrapolated to the administrative procedure. The subject-status of the individual participating in such a procedure must be guaranteed in one way or another.[127] Involving citizens into the administrative decision-making processes that concern them can help alleviate their "anyway present experience of powerlessness"[128] in relation to the state. It can empower them to play their part under the German Basic Law that is so fundamentally shaped by the idea that they are dignified subjects endowed with agency, and not mere objects of public power.

---

und daß es daher im Interesse einer richtigen Entscheidung ihnen möglich gemacht werden muß, von anderer Seite gegebene Darstellungen zu ergänzen oder zu berichtigen; neben dem Interesse an der Aufklärung der Tatsachen fordert dies die Würde der Person der Rechtsgenossen".

124 BVerfGE 9, 89 (95): *"Darüber hinaus fordert die Würde der Person, daß über ihr Recht nicht kurzerhand von Obrigkeits wegen verfügt wird; der einzelne soll nicht nur Objekt der richterlichen Entscheidung sein, sondern er soll vor einer Entscheidung, die seine Rechte betrifft, zu Wort kommen, um Einfluß auf das Verfahren und sein Ergebnis nehmen zu können."*

125 BVerfGE 63, 332 (337).

126 In this way, see also Hong, 420.

127 Denninger, 'Government Assistance in the Exercise of Basic Rights (Procedure and Organization)', 445.

128 BVerfGE 53, 30 (70).

In this sense, an administrative procedure in which the affected individual plays an active role, operationalises the subject status of the individual in her relationship with the state's administration. It operationalises her human dignity.

5.2.3 Conclusion

According to the "dignitarian" justification for obligations of administrative procedure, the states must involve citizens in its administrative decision-making because of the "position of the citizen in the state"[129]. This position is shaped mostly by the idea of human dignity enshrined in Article 1 (1) Basic Law. According to this highest constitutional value[130], the individual must always be treated as a subject. She must never be relegated to being a mere object of state action. This subject quality necessitates the "conversation" between her and the administration of a state. It necessitates involvement in the public decision-making process, through a right to be heard, by being given reasons for the decision etc. In contrast to the instrumental justification, the dignitarian justification is not concerned with the result of the individual's involvement, but with the process itself. The individual's involvement does not serve a purpose other than doing justice to her being a dignified being *vis à vis* the state and thus operationalising her dignity.

5.3 Two Interconnected Strands of Justification

In this chapter, we have identified two justifications which the FCC relies upon to justify derivative procedural obligations under the fundamental rights of the Basic Law. On the one hand, it invokes what we have called the "instrumental justification". According to this justification, administrative procedures are instrumental to the effective realisation of fundamental rights. They are a means to the end of better, i.e., more relevant and more effective fundamental rights protection. In that sense, they have a "serving, an auxiliary function"[131] for the material contents of fundamental rights. Notably, at least quantitively, this practical justification is more prevalent in the FCC's jurisprudence.

---

129 BVerfGE 45, 297 (335).

130 BVerfGE 6, 32 (41).

131 Cremer, *Freiheitsgrundrechte*, 404.

On the other hand, the FCC invokes what we have called the "dignitarian justification" that relies on the "position of the citizen under the Basic Law" and thus mostly on human dignity. Because the guarantee of human dignity demands that the individual always be treated as a subject and never as a mere object of state action, she must not just be confronted with a decision but be involved in those processes that led up to it. According to this justification, the involvement of the affected individual through (administrative) procedures is an end in itself.

In the *Hamburger U-Bahn* judgment, the FCC has relied on both justifications simultaneously. The court first stated that the involvement of the individual in the decision-making process was a necessary instrument to achieving results in accordance with the principle of proportionality. It was in the same passage, that the court then held that an administrative procedure was required by the "understanding of the position of the citizen under the Basic Law".[132] Thus, the two justifications are not mutually exclusive. They can and do apply together.

Importantly, the instrumental justification and the dignitarian justification do not merely add to one another. They mutually reinforce each other. It would be a mistake to think of these two justifications as independent of each other. Allowing affected individuals to raise objections already in the administrative procedure, this "shifting forward" of legal protection, *enables* them to make use of their rights. Especially in those situations in which *ex post* legal protection is not sufficient or even impossible, an opportunity to raise objections beforehand becomes an essential requirement for the citizen to be the self-directing agent the constitution wants her to be. By participation in the shaping of the reality of her rights, she can work towards their better implementation.

Conversely, given that the fundamental rights under the Basic Law all derive from human dignity and all contribute to the human image of the German constitution, effective legal protection does not only serve a better implementation of each individual fundamental right. Supplementing the substantive content of fundamental rights with procedural possibilities for the individual to enforce them, helps the realisation of the individual's subjective quality. It makes them an actor in the realisation of their rights *vis à vis* the administration of a state. Rainer Wahl has described the relationship between the two justifications aptly when he called the (procedural) ability to enforce one's rights "the highest criterion of independence".[133]

---

[132] BVerfGE 45, 297 (335).

[133] Wahl, 23–24.

Enforceability, Margins of Discretion, and Implementation

6

The pronouncements of the FCC on the implementation of procedural obligations are fundamentally shaped by the context-dependence of the procedural protection of fundamental rights, the obligations' positive nature, a wide margin of discretion of the legislature, and judicial restraint. Detailed pronouncements on how the other branches of the German government must implement these are rare. This chapter recalls the problem resulting from the open-ended nature of positive obligations (6.1) and the procedural and material consequences for the FCC's jurisprudence (6.2). Some observations about the implementation of procedural obligations which will complement our analytical foil can be made despite the open-ended nature of positive obligations, however (6.3).

6.1 The Problem with Positive Obligations and their Enforceability

Positive rights and obligations create problems, especially for the judiciary of a state. Given their open-ended nature, they create the risk of judicial overreach. In this section, we will briefly recall this problem (6.1.1) and show how the FCC's decision in favour of the subjective enforceability of these obligations, in a way, exacerbates the problem (6.1.2).

B. Behlert, *The Necessity of a Conversation between the Administration and the Individual*, Juridicum—Bochumer Schriften zur Friedenssicherung und zum Humanitären Völkerrecht | Bochum Studies on the International Law of Peace and Armed Conflict 72, https://doi.org/10.1007/978-3-658-50303-1_6

6.1.1 The Open-Ended Nature of Positive Obligations

Positive obligations are relatively open-ended. They generally leave the obliged with great leeway for how to fulfil them. To exemplify this, Alexy discusses the example of an obligation to rescue a person from a dangerous situation. That the rescue of a person is imperative does not make any act which would save that person imperative too.[1] Rather, the addressee of the obligation can choose how to rescue a person as long as she rescues her in the end. Negative obligations on the other hand are more immediate and their content is—at least *prima facie*—clearly defined.[2] The court itself expressed the difference between negative and positive rights aptly in a decision from 1997:

> *The subjective rights of defence against state intervention, which are primarily derived from fundamental rights, on the one hand, and the duties to protect, which derive from the objective meaning of fundamental rights, on the other, differ fundamentally from one another in that the right of defence requires specific state conduct in terms of its objective and content, while the duty to protect is fundamentally indeterminate.*[3]

The development of open-ended positive rights and obligations derived from the originally negative fundamental rights of the German constitution has attracted considerable criticism. This criticism is mostly based on considerations of democracy,[4] and the separation of powers[5]. Some have even gone so far to call positive obligations the "inversion of the function of fundamental rights into their own opposite".[6] Others caution against their potential randomness, fearing that the objective legal dimension could be used to deduce all kinds of obligations from,

---

[1] Alexy, 'Grundrechte als subjektive Rechte und als objektive Normen', 62.

[2] Jarass, 'Grundrechte als Wertentscheidungen bzw. objektivrechtliche Prinzipien in der Rechtsprechung des Bundesverfassungsgerichts', 373.

[3] BVerfGE 96, 56 (64): *"Die primär aus den Grundrechten folgenden subjektiven Abwehrrechte gegen staatliche Eingriffe einerseits und die sich aus der objektiven Bedeutung der Grundrechte ergebenden Schutzpflichten andererseits unterscheiden sich aber insofern grundlegend voneinander, als das Abwehrrecht in Zielsetzung und Inhalt ein bestimmtes staatliches Verhalten fordert, während die Schutzpflicht grundsätzlich unbestimmt ist."*

[4] See, with regard to social rights, e.g., Josef Isensee, 'Verfassung ohne soziale Grundrechte: Ein Wesenszug des Grundgesetzes' (1980) 19 Der Staat 367, 379.

[5] For an account of these positions, see Cremer, *Freiheitsgrundrechte*, 298–300.

[6] BVerfGE 39, 1 (73), dissenting opinion judges *Rupp-v. Brünneck* and *Simon*. This strongly worded statement was made regarding an obligation to enact prohibitions in criminal law. The fact that criminal law represents one of the strongest interferences with fundamental liberties possible might explain the particularly harsh wording used by the dissenting judges.

making its application in the end somewhat arbitrary.[7] Moreover, Böckenförde has warned of a "levelling" of the differences between the legislature and the judiciary.[8] As originally only negative rights become "principles with an optimization tendency", the task of the judiciary is elevated from one of interpretation and application to one of "concretization".[9] According to Böckenförde, this development is inevitable if one accepts objective dimensions of fundamental rights and leads to a "constitutional jurisdictional state" (*"verfassungsgerichtlicher Jurisdiktionsstaat"*).[10]

6.1.2 The General Decision of the FCC in Favour of Enforceability as Subjective Rights and the Problems that Come with It

In particular with regard to procedural obligations, the dangers resulting from their open-endedness as positive obligations are exacerbated by the FCC's general recognition of corresponding enforceable individual rights.

Alexy attaches great significance to the question of what he calls the "subjectification" of procedural obligations. He convincingly points out that the fact that the procedural rights are derived from substantive constitutional rights constitutes a *prima facie* argument for their subjective nature.[11] Whoever raises the point that a constitutional right has only objective effect in a particular context, bears the onus of proof.[12] Criticising the literature for approaching the connection between the administration and the individual merely from an objective obligations perspective, Alexy moreover claims that the jurisprudence of the FCC contains interesting references going in the other direction of subjective rights.[13]

[7] Matthias Herdegen, 'Art. 1 Abs. 3' in Günter Dürig, Roman Herzog and Rupert Scholz (eds), *Grundgesetz Kommentar* (107th EL edn, C. H. Beck 2025), para. 27.

[8] Böckenförde, 24 ff.

[9] Ibid, 21–22, 25.

[10] Ibid, 25–26.

[11] Alexy, *A Theory of Constitutional Rights*, 318; Alexy, 'Grundrechte als subjektive Rechte und als objektive Normen', 61.

[12] Alexy, *A Theory of Constitutional Rights*, 333.

[13] Ibid, 317.

And indeed, already in *Lüth*—the starting point of all developments under the objective dimension of fundamental rights –, we find remarks supporting his argument. After highlighting that the objective system of values constitutes a "principled reinforcement of [fundamental rights'] binding force", the FCC held that a judge who neglects the influence of fundamental rights on private law "not only violates objective constitutional law by failing to recognize the content of the fundamental right norm (as an objective norm), but rather, as a public authority, he by his judgment violates the fundamental right".[14] Moreover, it held that such a violation could then be brought before the court in the form of a constitutional complaint.[15]

The court gave this interconnectedness of the objective and the subjective dimensions another, perhaps even stronger expression in a later judgment when it held that the objective dimension "could not be separated" from the subjective negative dimension and made an independent framework of objective norms[16].

The procedural set up of the cases dealing specifically with procedural guarantees which we have discussed above supports the argument of the subjectification of procedural rights as well. Almost all of these landmark cases came to the FCC in the form of constitutional complaints under Article 93 (1) (4a) Basic Law, i.e., applications of individuals arguing that their constitutional rights had been violated.[17] If the procedural guarantees derived from fundamental rights were to take the form of objective obligations, the court could not have accepted these constitutional complaints as admissible. And it would not—as in the *Schweigender Prüfling* case or the *Hochschulurteil*—have ruled in favour of the applicants on the grounds that they were not granted the procedural protection.

With this general acceptance in favour of enforceability, however, the court does not mitigate the dangers outlined above. In fact, recognising these rights as subjective rights and thereby making them individually enforceable, heightens the danger of judicial overreach. Importantly, this is not meant as criticism. The FCC's approach here is consequential and legally required by the subjective nature of fundamental rights. However, it is important to realise the heightened danger that enforceable positive obligations bring about.

---

[14] BVerfGE 7, 198 (205–207).

[15] Ibid, 207.

[16] BVerfGE 50, 290 (337).

[17] Examples are BVerfGE 35, 79, BVerfGE 45, 297, BVerfGE 52, 380, BVerfGE 56, 216.

6.2 Consequences: Procedural Restrictions and a Wide Margin of Discretion

The dangers created by enforceable positive obligations are balanced out by certain general procedural restrictions upon constitutional complaints (6.2.1) as well as a wide margin of discretion for the legislature (6.2.2).

6.2.1 Procedural Restrictions on Constitutional Complaints

For the procedural constellation of constitutional complaints pursuant to Article 93 (1) (4a) Basic Law, there are procedural restrictions in place which are meant to limit the court's powers. They mostly concern and shape the relationship between the FCC and the other parts of the judiciary as well as the legislature of the Federal Republic of Germany and they are (partly) regulated in the Act on the Federal Constitutional Court (AFCC)[18]. Some restrictions apply to constitutional complaints generally (6.2.1.1), whereas for positive obligations, the burden of substantiation is significantly heightened (6.2.1.2).

6.2.1.1 General Restrictions for Constitutional Complaints

Firstly, there is the requirement to exhaust all possible judicial remedies before filing a constitutional complaint. This requirement is codified in section 90 (2) AFCC which stipulates that "[i]f legal recourse to other courts exists, the constitutional complaint may only be lodged after all remedies have been exhausted". This requirement is supplemented by the so-called "principle of subsidiarity".[19] This principle requires every applicant to refer her case to otherwise competent bodies—courts and others—to avoid or eliminate a violation of her fundamental rights.[20] In the words of the FCC, it requires that the applicant

[18] Act on the Federal Constitutional Court as published on 11 August 1993 (Federal Law Gazette I p. 1473), as amended by Article 4 of the Act of 20 November 2019 (Federal Law Gazette I p. 1724); translation provided by the Federal Constitutional Court and, on behalf of the Federal Ministry of Justice and Consumer Protection, by Iyamide Mahdi and Ute Reusch.

[19] The principle of subsidiarity in German constitutional law must not be mistaken with the principle of subsidiarity under IHRL. The latter has a much wider scope and sits at a much higher level of abstraction. We will discuss the principle of subsidiarity in IHRL and what it means for our appreciation of positive procedural obligations under IHRL in the next part of this thesis, see *infra* 9.2.2.

[20] Hans Lechner and Rüdiger Zuck, 'BVerfGG § 90 [Antragsberechtigung]' in Hans Lechner and Rüdiger Zuck (eds), *Bundsverfassungsgerichtsgesetz—Kommentar* (8th edn, C. H. Beck

beyond the requirement of exhaustion of the legal process in the narrower sense, seize all procedural possibilities available according to the situation of the case in order to obtain the correction of the asserted violation of fundamental rights by the specialized courts.[21]

The principle is meant to ensure that the constitutional complaint does not become an alternative remedy but that it is admissible only "if it becomes necessary to prevent a violation of a fundamental right despite exhaustion of the regular procedural possibilities".[22] This is not the case "if there is or was another possibility to eliminate the violation of the fundamental right or to achieve the same result in practice without recourse to the FCC".[23]

Secondly, the constitutional complaint is "not an additional remedy for proceedings before the ordinary courts or administrative courts".[24] The FCC does not review the legality of a court decision, i.e., whether the decision is in accordance with the law on which it is based. It merely assesses whether a violation of "specific constitutional law" is given.[25] For a constitutional complaint against another court's judgment to be successful, the mistake of that court must "lie precisely in the non-observance of fundamental rights".[26] This fundamental principle of constitutional review by the FCC has found a catchy expression in the postulate that the FCC must not be a super revision authority (*"Superrevisionsinstanz"*).[27]

2019), para. 157. For a detailed discussion of the principle see André Niesler, 'BVerfGG § 90 Abs. 2' in Christian Walter and Benedikt Grünewald (eds), *BeckOK BVerfGG* (19th edn, C. H. Beck 2025), paras. 44–65.1.

[21] BVerfG NJW 1998, 2663 (2664): *"Dieser in § 90 II 1 BVerfGG zum Ausdruck kommende Grundsatz [der Subsidiarität] erfordert, daß ein Bf. über das Gebot der Erschöpfung des Rechtswegs im engeren Sinne hinaus alle nach Lage der Sache zur Verfügung stehenden prozessualen Möglichkeiten ergreift, um die Korrektur der geltend gemachten Grundrechtsverletzung durch die Fachgerichte zu erwirken."*

[22] Ibid.

[23] Ibid.

[24] BVerfGE 1, 4 (5).

[25] See Christian Walter, 'GG Art. 93 [Bundesverfassungsgericht, Zuständigkeit]' in Günter Dürig, Roman Herzog and Rupert Scholz (eds), *Grundgesetz Kommentar* (107th EL edn, C. H. Beck 2025), paras. 150–154. The FCC has been using the formula "specific constitutional law" to limit its jurisdiction and define its relationship with those courts which are part of the stages of appeal since 1952, BVerfGE 1, 418 (420).

[26] BVerfGE 18, 85 (93).

[27] The FCC has used this terminology already in *Lüth*, see BVerfGE 7, 198 (207). See on this term and its meaning Klaus Schlaich and Stefan Korioth, *Das Bundesverfassungsgericht: Stellung, Verfahren, Entscheidungen* (12th edn, C. H. Beck 2021), 283–285.

Thirdly, the FCC cannot prescribe specific state action upon a successful constitutional complaint. In case of a constitutional complaint against a judicial decision, the FCC can reverse a decision of another court pursuant to section 95 (2) AFCC. However, it cannot render a decision but must instead refer the case back to the competent court. In case of a constitutional complaint against a law, the court can void the law, but it cannot replace it, section 95 (3) AFCC.

These procedural safeguards contribute to ensuring that the FCC does not overstep its mandate and in fact functions as a "court of fourth instance". They are not specifically designed for the adjudication of claims based on positive rights. Instead, they apply to every challenge brought before the court by an individual based on her constitutional rights. However, given the specific dangers of an overstepping of the FCC arising in the context of positive rights, they are arguably particularly important in that context, and thus also with regard to procedural obligations.

6.2.1.2 A Heightened Burden of Substantiation for Violations of Positive Obligations

Specifically with regard to constitutional complaints claiming violations of positive obligations, the FCC has introduced another procedural restriction, namely an increased burden of substantiation for the applicant. In a decision on the storage of chemical weapons on German soil, the court argued that, in order to be admissible, a constitutional complaint based on a violation of a duty to protect must

> *conclusively demonstrate that the public authority has either not taken any protective measures at all or that the regulations and measures taken are obviously completely unsuitable or completely inadequate to achieve their protective objective.*[28]

Furthermore, if the applicant argues that there is only one specific measure that could fulfil the obligation to protect, she must further "conclusively demonstrate this and the nature of the measure to be taken".[29] These requirements represent significant obstacles for anyone seeking to lodge a constitutional complaint with

[28] BVerfGE 77, 170 (215): *"Um den Anforderungen an die Zulässigkeit einer Verfassungsbeschwerde zu entsprechen, die auf eine Verletzung der sich aus dem Grundrecht des Art. 2 Abs. 2 Satz 1 GG ergebenden Schutzpflicht gestützt wird, muß der Beschwerdeführer schlüssig dartun, daß die öffentliche Gewalt Schutzvorkehrungen entweder überhaupt nicht getroffen hat oder daß offensichtlich die getroffenen Regelungen und Maßnahmen gänzlich ungeeignet oder völlig unzulänglich sind, das Schutzziel zu erreichen."*

[29] Ibid.

the argument that the state did not fulfil a positive obligation. In line with this, it has rightfully been pointed out that violations of procedural obligations are a constitutional legal problem only if their fulfilment was specifically required by fundamental rights.[30]

6.2.2 A Wide Margin of Discretion Under Positive Obligations

Beyond these general and specific procedural safeguards, the legislature enjoys a relatively wide margin of discretion when it comes to the implementation of positive obligations under the fundamental rights of the Basic Law.[31] Based on this insight, the FCC has drawn consequences regarding its standard of review of alleged violations of positive obligations:

> *In fulfilling these duties to protect, the legislature and the executive authorities have a broad scope for assessment, evaluation and design, which also leaves room for taking into account competing public and private interests, for example. This broad scope of discretion can be reviewed by the courts only to a limited extent, depending on the specific nature of the subject matter at issue, the possibilities of forming a sufficiently reliable judgment and the significance of the legal interests at stake. The fundamental rights claim associated with such a duty to protect is, in view of this discretion, directed only at the fact that the public authority takes precautions for the protection of the fundamental right which are not wholly unsuitable or wholly inadequate. Only under very special circumstances can this freedom of action be restricted in such a way that the duty to protect can be satisfied by a specific measure alone.*[32]

---

[30] Elke Gurlit, '§ 109 Dienende Funktion des Verfahrens und Prozeduralisierung' in Wolfgang Kahl and Markus Ludwigs (eds), *Handbuch des Verwaltungsrechts*, vol IV (C. F. Müller 2022), para. 9.

[31] On the question of whether this margin is material in the sense that it results from the fundamental rights of the Basic Law or procedural in the sense that it is only judicial restraint see Cremer, *Freiheitsgrundrechte*, 294–298.

[32] BVerfGE 77, 170 (214–215): "*Dem Gesetzgeber wie der vollziehenden Gewalt kommt bei der Erfüllung dieser Schutzpflichten ein weiter Einschätzungs-, Wertungs- und Gestaltungsbereich zu, der auch Raum läßt, etwa konkurrierende öffentliche und private Interessen zu berücksichtigen. Diese weite Gestaltungsfreiheit kann von den Gerichten je nach Eigenart des in Rede stehenden Sachbereichs, den Möglichkeiten, sich ein hinreichend sicheres Urteil zu bilden und der Bedeutung der auf dem Spiele stehenden Rechtsgüter nur in begrenztem Umfang überprüft werden [...]. Der mit einer solchen Schutzpflicht verbundene grundrechtliche Anspruch ist im Blick auf diese Gestaltungsfreiheit nur darauf gerichtet, daß die öffentliche Gewalt Vorkehrungen zum Schutze des Grundrechts trifft, die nicht gänzlich ungeeignet oder völlig unzulänglich sind. Nur unter ganz besonderen Umständen kann*

The FCC tries to balance an effective protection of positive rights against the requirements of democracy and the separation of powers. In consequence, it defers the decision-making on how precisely to implement positive obligations to the legislature. It reserves the right to interfere with a decision only in case it finds it to be "wholly unsuitable or wholly inadequate". In another decision, the court held that the Basic Law provided only the "framework, not specific solutions", and that it could only find that a violation had taken place

> *if the public authorities have either failed to take any protective measures at all or if the regulations and measures taken are wholly unsuitable or completely inadequate to achieve the required objective of protection or fall considerably short of it.*[33]

6.2.3 Conclusion

Given the difficulties that come with the open-ended nature of positive obligations and given that the procedural obligations discussed in this thesis are positive in nature, the FCC's approach towards reviewing the implementation of procedural obligations derived from fundamental rights is shaped by large margins of discretion for the other branches of the German government, especially the legislature, and by corresponding judicial restraint. These observations on the general approach of the court are already an important takeaway for us. Despite this cautious approach, however, there are some more concrete points we can take away on the issues of implementation. We shall now turn to them.

---

sich diese Gestaltungsfreiheit in der Weise verengen, daß allein durch eine bestimmte Maßnahme der Schutzpflicht Genüge getan werden kann." References omitted. With the same bottom-line also BVerfGE 96, 56 (64).

[33] BVerfGE 92, 26 (46): *"Das Bundesverfassungsgericht kann [...] die Verletzung einer Schutzpflicht nur feststellen, wenn die öffentliche Gewalt Schutzvorkehrungen entweder überhaupt nicht getroffen hat oder die getroffenen Regelungen und Maßnahmen gänzlich ungeeignet oder völlig unzulänglich sind, das gebotene Schutzziel zu erreichen, oder erheblich dahinter zurückbleiben."* More examples in Hans D. Jarass, '§ 38 Funktionen und Dimensionen der Grundrechte' in Detlef Merten and Hans-Jürgen Papier (eds), *Handbuch der Grundrechte in Deutschland und Europa* (C. F. Müller 2006), para. 38. For a detailed discussion of the consequences the FCC draws from the openness of positive obligations in terms of enforceability and implementation and the standard of review, see Cremer, *Freiheitsgrundrechte*, 291 ff.

6.3 Observations on the Court's Jurisprudence on the Implementation of Procedural Obligations

Despite the FCC's generally cautious approach towards ruling on the implementation of positive obligations, some observations regarding implementation shall be made here. Firstly—and this is connected to the way the FCC justifies procedural obligations—we will point out how the effective protection of fundamental rights is the yardstick for assessing the constitutionality of implementation measures (6.3.1). Secondly, we will discuss one particular consequence of this realisation: that the principle of proportionality influences the way in which procedural obligations must be implemented (6.3.2).

6.3.1 Effective Fundamental Rights Protection as the Yardstick for the Implementation of Procedural Obligations

The implementation of procedural obligations derived from fundamental rights is—as we have already learned from Häberle's lecture of 1971[34]—highly context-dependent. What is required in one situation might not be in another constellation and *vice versa*. Importantly, however, as we have already seen in our analysis of the justifications relied upon by the FCC, the effectiveness of the implementation and protection of fundamental rights is the yardstick by which to assess procedural rules and their application. Already in 1963, the FCC stated that the protection of fundamental rights could require a concrete procedural design to ensure such protection. It held that

> *the procedural design is subject to the requirements of the protection of fundamental rights. It thus moves out of the realm of the merely expedient. In this sense, the constitution can enforce a certain procedural arrangement, whereby aspects of expedient procedure that are in themselves important may have to take a back seat to the need to protect fundamental rights, and procedural inconveniences may have to be accepted.*[35]

[34] Häberle, 'Grundrechte im Leistungsstaat', 82–84. See *supra* 3.2.

[35] BVerfGE 17, 108 (117–118): *"Insofern steht die Verfahrensgestaltung unter dem Gebot des Grundrechtsschutzes. Sie rückt damit aus dem Bereich des nur Zweckmäßigen hinaus. In diesem Sinn kann die Verfassung eine bestimmte Verfahrensgestaltung erzwingen, wobei u. U. an sich beachtliche Gesichtspunkte zweckmäßigen Verfahrensablaufes hinter das Gebot des Grundrechtsschutzes zurücktreten und auch verfahrensrechtliche Unbequemlichkeiten in Kauf genommen werden müssen."*

Notably, this statement was made five years prior to the *Hamburger Deichordnungsgesetz* decision in which the idea of effective legal protection that developed into the court's instrumental justification was first mentioned. The pronouncement is by no means surprising. The court derives the necessity of procedural protection from the fundamental rights and justifies it—at least also—by reference to their potential to enhance the better implementation of the rights. To connect the implementation of the procedural protection to "the requirements of the protection of fundamental rights" is the only logical consequence. The FCC encapsulated this consequence of the justification for the implementation in a decision of 1978:

> *[Procedural law] not only serves the purpose of ensuring an orderly course of proceedings, but in the area relevant to fundamental rights, it is also the means of helping the holder of the fundamental right to obtain his or her constitutional right in a specific case. Accordingly, procedural law must be interpreted and applied with regard to fundamental rights. If there are several possible interpretations, the one that enables the court to enforce and realise the fundamental rights of the parties to the proceedings must be chosen.*[36]

The highly instructive *Palästinenser* decision of 1973 provides an opportunity to see how these abstract points can play out in reality. Two Arab students had received an expulsion order related to official measures against Arabs and Palestinian organizations triggered by the terrorist attack on the Israeli Olympic team in Munich in September 1972. The competent authority had ordered the immediate execution of that order. To fend it off, the students lodged an application for provisional measures. The administrative courts rejected their application for provisional measures, and eventually the case arrived at the FCC.

The court discussed whether the applicants had a right to personally participate in the oral hearings of their cases. While the FCC held that Article 19 (4) Basic Law did not grant an unconditional right to be present in asylum hearings, the court stated that the protection of fundamental rights could require such a procedural right.[37] The court then went on to explain why in the specific case, the presence of the applicants was in fact required by the protection of fundamental rights. It argued that it was especially difficult to make oneself heard from

---

[36] BVerfGE 49, 252 (257): "*[Das Verfahrensrecht] dient nicht nur dem Ziel, einen geordneten Verfahrensgang zu sichern, sondern ist im grundrechtlich relevanten Bereich auch das Mittel, im konkreten Fall dem Grundrechtsträger zu seinem verfassungsmäßigen Recht zu verhelfen. Demgemäß muß das Verfahrensrecht im Blick auf die Grundrechte ausgelegt und angewendet werden. Bei mehreren Auslegungsmöglichkeiten ist diejenige zu wählen, die dem Gericht ermöglicht, die Grundrechte der Verfahrensbeteiligten durchzusetzen und zu verwirklichen.*"

[37] BVerfGE 35, 382 (406).

abroad due to the distance, language barriers and the general absence of lawyers familiar with the applicable German law. Moreover, expelled foreigners cannot exercise their right to question witnesses and cannot themselves be questioned by the court. Especially in cases that depend a lot on the credibility of affected individuals, the court held, personal hearings can be essential. In the following paragraph, the court even held that a foreigner will have greater problems seeking justice in Germany when she is in Syria or Jordan than she would if she were in a European country.[38]

The passage aptly shows how the protection of fundamental rights in a given situation can require certain procedural rights. It also shows how much the (specific) requirements in terms of procedural protection depend on the circumstances of a given case. The question the court raised was what it would mean for the applicants' rights and their effective protection if the applicants were not present in the court room. If the effective protection of their fundamental rights suffered too much, their presence could be mandatory. This illustrates how and when "aspects of expedient procedure that are in themselves important may have to take a back seat to the need to protect fundamental rights"[39].

6.3.2 The Influence of the Principle of Proportionality on the Implementation of Procedural Obligations

The principle of proportionality influences the implementation of the necessary procedural protection in two ways. One of them is obvious: whenever procedures constitute obstacles to the enjoyment of fundamental rights, they must comply with the principle of proportionality (6.3.2.1). The other way in which proportionality influences the implementation is less straightforward: the required intensity of procedural protection is proportionate to the intensity and the degree of irreversibility of a decision (6.3.2.2).

6.3.2.1 The Prohibition of Disproportionate Procedures

Whenever a procedure creates obstacles for the enjoyment of fundamental rights, the procedure itself constitutes an interference and, as such, is subject to the proportionality test. We find this—rather obvious—idea, e.g., in a decision from 1977 which dealt with impeachment proceedings against a notary. In that case, the FCC held that "[e]specially when ordering and maintaining provisional protective

[38] Ibid, 406–407.

[39] BVerfGE 17, 108 (118).

measures, […] it [was] necessary to avoid placing a disproportionate burden on the person concerned by the nature and duration of the proceedings".[40] This connection, however, is nothing but a procedural version of the general requirement that interferences with fundamental rights must be proportionate.

6.3.2.2 Necessary Compensation for Intensity and Irreversibility

Another connection between the principle of proportionality and procedural obligations is more interesting: there is a proportionate connection between the intensity and the irreversibility of an envisaged interference and the importance of procedural protection. The FCC highlighted this connection in the already mentioned *Palästinenser* decision. The FCC made some interesting remarks in connection with the application procedure for provisional measures under section 80 (5) of the Code of Administrative Court Procedure (CACP)[41] which we shall briefly recall before discussing what the FCC said about it.

Normally, applications against decisions of the administration have suspensive effect on the enforceability of the measures, section 80 (1) CACP. This "fundamental principle of public law court procedure"[42] is meant to allow for judicial review of an administrative measure before facts are established. This, however, is not without exception. The authority that has issued a decision can order the immediate execution of the decision if there is a "special interest" in doing so, section 80 (2) (4) CACP. In such cases, the affected individual can apply for provisional measures and demand the suspensive effect of her application be restored by an administrative court according to section 80 (5) CACP.

In its reasoning in the *Palästinenser* decision, the FCC made interesting remarks about the required density of the procedural protection, after highlighting the importance of a case-by-case approach:

> *The purpose of the guarantee of legal protection and the constitutional principle of proportionality, however, at least provide this much: the more severe the burden imposed*

[40] BVerfGE 45, 422 (431). Reference omitted.

[41] Code of Administrative Court Procedure in the version of the promulgation of 19 March 1991 (Federal Law Gazette I page 686), as amended by Article 5, subsection 24 of the Act of 21 June 2019 (Federal Law Gazette I page 846); translation provided by Neil Mussett.

[42] BVerfGE 35, 263 (272).

> *on the citizen and the more the measures taken by the administration have an irreversible effect, the stronger is the citizen's right to legal protection and the less must it be allowed to take a back seat.*[43]

After this remark, the court went on to analyse the reasoning the administrative court had provided for its decision not to restore the suspensive effect of the application against the expulsion order. It concluded firstly that the administrative court had not sufficiently laid out that an overwhelming public interest in the immediate enforcement of the expulsion order existed.[44] Secondly, the FCC concluded that the administrative court had not adequately weighed the "serious and irreparable disadvantages for the complainants resulting from the immediate execution of the expulsion orders"[45]. In view of the gravity of an expulsion order and the potential irreversibility of the decision, the court's assessment of the order of immediate execution had to be much more thorough.

This proportionate connection between the intensity and the degree of irreversibility of a decision on the one hand, and the density of procedural protection on the other is of great importance for the implementation of procedural obligations. The greater the intensity of a measure, the greater the need for its procedural accompaniment, for "procedural compensation".[46] The more difficult a decision is to reverse, the more careful the concerned authority must be when making the decision. The FCC confirmed this approach for preliminary measures proceedings in later judgments.[47]

Why can this conclusion from the *Palästinenser* decision be extrapolated to administrative procedures? Firstly, as we have seen when we discussed the justifications, the FCC does not differentiate too much between *ex ante* and *ex post* legal protection when discussing the procedural dimension of fundamental rights. Both forms of legal protection follow the same instrumental function of enhancing the realisation of fundamental rights. Hence, the (proportionate) safeguard function of procedural guarantees makes just as much sense for the administrative procedure as it does for judicial proceedings.

---

[43] BVerfGE 35, 382 (402): "*Aus dem Zweck der Rechtsschutzgarantie und dem Verfassungsgrundsatz der Verhältnismäßigkeit ergibt sich aber wenigstens soviel: Der Rechtsschutzanspruch des Bürgers ist um so stärker und darf um so weniger zurückstehen, je schwerwiegender die ihm auferlegte Belastung ist und je mehr die Maßnahmen der Verwaltung Unabänderliches bewirken.*"

[44] Ibid, 402–404.

[45] Ibid, 404.

[46] Jarass, '§ 38 Funktionen und Dimensionen der Grundrechte', para. 55.

[47] BVerfGE 69, 315 (363); BVerfG NVwZ 2009, 581, para. 18.

Secondly, the preliminary measures procedure under section 80 (5) CACP is not a classical *ex post* judicial review procedure. As the FCC has made clear in the decision, the purpose of section 80 (5) of the CACP is to prevent an irreversible state of affairs.[48] In this sense, it bears certain parallels to the administrative procedure, especially in situations in which it compensates for a lack of adequate *ex post* review. The function of the procedure according to section 80 (5) CACP can be situated somewhere in between *ex ante* and the *ex post* legal protection we have carved out above. It provides *ex post* legal protection in the sense that it is a form of review of administrative action but it is *ex ante* in the sense that it is preliminary and takes place before a final judicial decision.

6.4 Conclusion

Positive obligations are open-ended. Hence, they harbour certain dangers for the competence structure of a state which are exacerbated by their enforceability. These dangers are addressed by general procedural restrictions which can be particularly important in the context of positive rights and a wide margin of discretion when it comes to the implementation of positive obligations. The idea of judicial restraint corresponds with these margins of discretion.

Despite this generally cautious approach two points of general relevance were worth noting at this point. Firstly, and unsurprisingly, the yardstick for reviewing the implementation of their procedural obligations of the other branches is the effectiveness of the protection of fundamental rights. The question the FCC poses is: what does this implementation mean for the enjoyment of fundamental rights?

Secondly, the principle of proportionality is connected to the implementation of procedural obligations in two ways. On the one hand, whenever procedures present obstacles to the enjoyment of fundamental rights, they must be designed so that they do not disproportionately interfere with the fundamental rights in question. On the other hand, there is a proportionate connection between the gravity and the irreversibility of an envisaged interference and the required procedural protection. The graver or the more irreversible an interference is, the more procedural protection, the more "procedural compensation"[49] is required.

[48] Hubertus Gersdorf, '§ 80 VwGO' in Herbert Posser and Heinrich Amadeus Wolff (eds), *BeckOK VwGO* (67th edn, C. H. Beck 2023), para. 1.

[49] Jarass, '§ 38 Funktionen und Dimensionen der Grundrechte', para. 55.

Part III
Obligations of Administrative Procedure Under IHRL

A Doctrinal Basis for Obligations of Administrative Procedure Under IHRL

7

This section is devoted to understanding what the precise doctrinal basis for obligations of administrative procedure under IHRL is. How must such a basis be crafted from the texts of the two covenants? To this end, we will analyse how the committees derive obligations of administrative procedure from the text of the treaties. Firstly, we will analyse how they construct the doctrinal basis for such obligations (7.1). Secondly, we will critically appraise the results of this analysis, assess whether the committees' approach is convincing and seek to add some finer detail to it, in particular by closing some gaps the committees' approach leaves (7.2). The goal of this section is to identify the correct "legal anchor"[1] onto which to attach textually the obligations of administrative procedure.

7.1 The Committees' General Construction

Our analyses of the pronouncements of the HCR (7.1.1) and the CESCR (7.1.2) in this section will demonstrate that, in laying out procedural obligations relating to specific rights recognised in the ICCPR and the ICESCR respectively, the committees follow a deductive approach. Both committees construe obligations of administrative procedure as part of the general doctrine of IHRL (in the sense of "*allgemeine Menschenrechtslehren*"). Consequently, both committees rely on a doctrinal construction the starting point of which are the general obligation provisions, Article 2 ICCPR and Article 2 ICESCR respectively. More precisely, both

[1] Pierre Thielbörger, 'Re-Conceptualizing the Human Right to Water: A Pledge for a Hybrid Approach' (2015) 15 Human Rights Law Review 225, 247.

B. Behlert, *The Necessity of a Conversation between the Administration and the Individual*, Juridicum—Bochumer Schriften zur Friedenssicherung und zum Humanitären Völkerrecht | Bochum Studies on the International Law of Peace and Armed Conflict 72, https://doi.org/10.1007/978-3-658-50303-1_7

committees approach these obligations as part of the general positive obligation. The committees then link the general procedural obligation to the specific rights in question to allow for a rights- and context-sensitive implementation. Beyond these insights, however, we find some gaps and inconsistencies in the committee's pronouncements.

7.1.1 The HRC's Pronouncements

The HRC relies on Article 2 (1) ICCPR—the obligations provision of the ICCPR—as the main "legal anchor" for procedural obligations (7.1.1.1). It construes the obligations as positive while highlighting their relevance to all dimensions of the covenant rights (7.1.1.2).

7.1.1.1 Article 2 ICCPR as the Main Legal Anchor for Procedural Obligations

The early general comments of the HRC were laconic, general, and rather reserved. In its General Comment 3, e.g., on the implementation of the covenant at the national level, the committee stated that Article 2 ICCPR "generally [left] it to the States parties concerned to choose their method of implementation in their territories within the framework set out in the article".[2] In the years since, however, the HRC's general comments have become more and more elaborate and explicit. We find the most insightful statement on how the HRC derives procedural obligations from the text of the ICCPR in its second most recent General Comment 36 on the right to life. Under the heading "Duty to protect life", the HRC addresses organizational and procedural obligations:

> *The duty to protect by law the right to life also requires States parties to* ***organize all State organs and governance structures through which public authority is exercised in a manner consistent with the need to respect and ensure the right to life****, including establishing by law* ***adequate institutions and procedures*** *for preventing deprivation of life, investigating and prosecuting potential cases of unlawful deprivation of life, meting out punishment and providing full reparation.*[3]

---

[2] HRC, *General comment No. 3: Article 2 (Implementation at the national level)* (1981) HRI/GEN/1/Rev.9 (Vol. I) p. 174, para. 1.

[3] HRC, *General comment No. 36 Article 6: right to life* (3 September 2019) UN Doc. CCPR/C/GC/36, para. 19. Emphases added.

The HRC references the "Cotton Field" judgment by the Inter-American Court of Human Rights (IACtHR) to support this argument.[4] The passage from said judgment—which the HRC quotes almost *verbatim*—reads:

> *With regard to the obligation to guarantee, the Court has established that it may be fulfilled in different ways, based on the specific right that the State must guarantee and on the specific needs for protection. This obligation refers to the duty of the States to organize the entire government apparatus and, in general, all the structures through which public authority is exercised, so that they are able to ensure by law the free and full exercise of human rights.*[5]

This passage which itself cites the seminal *Velásquez-Rodríguez* judgment[6] allows us to gain important insights. Firstly, the passage did not only concern the right to life protected by Article 4 ACHR. In fact, with this passage, the IACtHR recalls its jurisprudence on the obligations provision of the IACHR, Article 1 (1) ACHR.[7] This provision is very similar to Article 2 (1) ICCPR in that it also relates to all rights recognised in the ACHR.[8] Consequently, the organisational and procedural obligations from the above quote are general. They relate to all rights in the ACHR and, according to the IACtHR, "may be fulfilled in different ways, based on the specific right that the State must guarantee and on

---

[4] The author of this study agrees with Sarah Joseph that such "comparative jurisprudence" is laudable and has great potential to advance the protection of human rights arounds the globe, Sarah Joseph, 'Extending the Right to Life Under the International Covenant on Civil and Political Rights: General Comment 36' (2019) 19 Human Rights Law Review 347, 367–368. However, one argue that the fact that the HRC cannot cite its own jurisprudence is telling with regard to how settled the issue is. Nevertheless, the HRC uses strong language to express its interpretation of the states' obligations regarding the right to life ("requires"). Thus, this passage makes clear that the HRC does not consider this statement to be a suggestion *de lege ferrenda*. Instead, it deems the obligation to be binding and immediately applicable.

[5] IACtHR, *Gonzaléz et al. ("Cotton Field") v Mexico (Series C No 205, IACtHR, 16 November 2009)*, para. 236.

[6] See IACtHR, *Velásquez-Rodríguez v Honduras* (Series C No 4, IACtHR, 29 July 1988), para. 166. For more information on the seminal case and its enduring significance, see María Pía Carazo, 'Velásquez Rodríguez v Honduras Case' in Anne Peters (ed), *Max Planck Encyclopedia of Public International Law (MPEPIL)* (Oxford University Press 2008).

[7] IACtHR, *Gonzaléz et al. ("Cotton Field") v Mexico*, paras. 234–236.

[8] The provision reads: *"The States Parties to this Convention undertake to respect the rights and freedoms recognized herein and to ensure to all persons subject to their jurisdiction the free and full exercise of those rights and freedoms, without any discrimination for reasons of race, color, sex, language, religion, political or other opinion, national or social origin, economic status, birth, or any other social condition."*

the specific needs for protection"[9]. In the cited passage, the IACtHR thus follows a deductive approach. It derives specific obligations from the general obligation in a way that is sensitive to the rights in question and the circumstances of a given case.

Later in the judgment, the IACtHR does just that when it derives specific obligations from this general duty, after clarifying once more that the precise content of an obligation is "to be determined based on the specific needs of protection of the subject of law, either because of his or her personal situation or because of the specific circumstances in which he or she finds himself".[10]

By referencing the "Cotton Field" judgment, the HRC adopts this deductive approach. This suggests that the organisational and procedural obligation it mentions in General Comment 36 are—in the view of the committee—not limited to the right to life. Instead, the HRC, too, treats it as a general obligation relating to all human rights. In the cited passage of General Comment 36, the HRC merely "applies" this general obligation to the right to life. Two paragraphs later, the HRC confirms this interpretation when it refers directly to the overarching obligation in Article 2 ICCPR:

> *The duty to take positive measures to protect the right to life* ***derives from the general duty to ensure the rights recognized in the Covenant****, which is articulated in article 2 (1) when read in conjunction with article 6, as well as from the specific duty to protect the right to life by law, which is articulated in the second sentence of article 6.*[11]

This wording of "Article 2 (1) read in conjunction with Article 6" encapsulates in textual-legal terms how the IACtHR derived organisational obligations in its *Velasquez-Rodriguez* and *"Cotton Field"* judgments. Given that Article 2 (1) ICCPR stipulates obligations in relation to all rights enshrined in the ICCPR, the doctrinal construction reflects the CESCR's statement that adequate procedural protection is an essential element of *all* human rights. Finally, it is important to note that, in the last passage quoted here, the HRC, in line with human rights doctrine, connects the general obligation under Article 2 ICCPR to the specific rights in question.

---

[9] IACtHR, *Gonzaléz et al. ("Cotton Field") v Mexico*, para. 236.

[10] Ibid, paras. 243–248.

[11] HRC, GC 36, para. 21. Emphasis added.

7.1.1.2 Positive Obligations with Relevance for all Dimensions of the Rights

The fact that the committee holds that states must "organize the entire government apparatus and, in general, all the structures through which public authority is exercised" in a way that ensures the realisation of the right to life[12] under the heading of "the duty to protect" indicates that the committee considers this obligation to be positive in nature. In fact, the committee itself refers to it as an element of the "duty to take *positive measures* to protect the right to life".[13] This is unsurprising given that—as we have already discussed in the context of German fundamental rights above—the procedural obligations considered here require more than mere abstention from a state. They require the state to *listen*, to *give* reasons etc.[14] Another passage in General Comment 36 exemplifies this approach, too. In the context of palliative care and assisted suicide, the committee holds that states parties "must *ensure* the existence of robust legal and institutional safeguards to verify that medical professionals are complying with the free, informed, explicit and unambiguous decision of their patients, with a view to protecting patients from pressure and abuse".[15]

Pronouncements in earlier general comments confirm this understanding of procedural obligations as positive obligations. In its General Comment No. 3, in which the HRC discusses the ICCPR's implementation at the national level, the HRC highlighted that the covenant did not only require states parties to abstain from certain acts but also "call[ed] for specific activities […] to enable individuals to enjoy the rights".[16]

Moreover, in General Comment 34 on the right to freedom of opinion and expression, Article 19 ICCPR, the committee holds that

> *[t]o give effect to the right of access to information, States parties should* ***proactively*** *put in the public domain Government information of public interest. States parties should* ***make every effort*** *to ensure easy, prompt, effective and practical access to such information. States parties should also* ***enact the necessary procedures****, whereby*

---

[12] Ibid, para. 19.

[13] Ibid, para. 21. Emphasis added.

[14] See for the discussion in the context of German fundamental rights *supra* Chap. 4 generally.

[15] HRC, GC 36, para. 9. Emphasis added.

[16] HRC, GC 3, para. 1.

> *one may gain access to information, such as by means of freedom of information legislation.*[17]

Importantly, the highlighted words used in this passage all relate to state action rather than abstention. They all indicate that the states must *do* something rather than merely abstain from interfering with a liberty. In its most recent General Comment 37 on the right of peaceful assembly, Article 21 ICCPR, the HRC recalls that "[t]he obligation to respect and ensure peaceful assemblies imposes negative and positive duties on States before, during and after assemblies"[18]. After briefly discussing the negative obligations relating to the right, the committee moves on to positive obligations and states that, as part of the positive obligations relating to the right of peaceful assembly, states must "promote an enabling environment for the exercise of the right of peaceful assembly without discrimination, **and put in place a legal and institutional framework within which the right can be exercised**".[19] Four paragraphs later, the HRC elaborates on what this legal and institutional framework must look like when it holds that "[a] functioning and transparent legal and decision-making system lies at the core of the duty to respect and ensure peaceful assemblies".[20] These passages leave no doubt that the HRC construes procedural and organisational obligations such as the ones at the heart of the present thesis as positive obligations.

At the same time, the committee recognizes that these obligations are relevant to both dimensions, the negative and the positive ones. The decision-making system required by Article 21 ICCPR lies "at the core of the duty to respect *and* ensure"[21] and states must organize their institutions "in a manner consistent with the need to respect *and* ensure the right to life".[22] The doctrinal basis for procedural obligations lies in the positive dimension of the rights while their function, their *raison d'être* relates to all the rights dimensions.[23]

---

[17] HRC, *General comment No. 34, Article 19: Freedoms of opinion and expression* (12 September 2011) UN Doc CCPR/C/GC/34, para. 19. Emphases added.

[18] HRC, *General comment No. 37 (2020) on the right of peaceful assembly (article 21)* (17 September 2020) UN Doc. CCPR/C/GC/37, para. 23.

[19] Ibid, para. 24. Emphasis added.

[20] Ibid, para. 28. Emphasis added.

[21] Ibid, para. 28. Emphasis added.

[22] HRC, GC 36, para. 19. Emphasis added.

[23] This will become clearer in our analysis of the justifications the committees rely on when arguing in favour of procedural obligations. See *infra* Chap. 8 generally.

7.1.2 The CESCR's Pronouncements

Turning to the CESCR's pronouncements, there is good reason to assume that it, too, follows a similar deductive approach and relies on a similar doctrinal basis. After all, it was its General Comment 7 which stated that adequate procedural protection was an essential element of *all* human rights. This sub-section will verify this assumption (7.1.2.1), while highlighting inconsistencies beyond this general approach (7.1.2.2).

7.1.2.1 The CESCR's Deductive Approach

Just like the ICCPR, the ICESCR sets out the obligations of the state party in relation to the rights it protects in its Article 2. Accordingly, the CESCR follows the same deductive approach towards procedural obligations as the HRC. The quote from General Comment 7—that adequate procedural protection is an essential element of all human rights—is already indicative of that. Moreover, in said general comment, the committee holds that "the obligations of States parties to the Covenant in relation to forced evictions are based on article 11.1, read in conjunction with other relevant provisions", and that "[i]n particular, article 2.1 obliges States to use "all appropriate means" to promote the right to adequate housing"[24]. In the following paragraphs, the committee elaborates on these appropriate means to implement the protection against forced evictions. Generally, it states that "legislation against forced eviction is an essential basis upon which to build a system of effective protection" and that "[s]uch legislation should include measures which [...] (c) are designed to control strictly the circumstances under which evictions may be carried out".[25]

Some paragraphs later we find a catalogue of concrete procedural measures state parties are obliged to take in relation to forced evictions:

> *Appropriate procedural protection and due process are essential aspects of all human rights but are especially pertinent in relation to a matter such as forced evictions which directly invokes a large number of the rights recognized in both the International Covenants on Human Rights. The Committee considers that the procedural protections which should be applied in relation to forced evictions include: (a) an opportunity for genuine consultation with those affected; (b) adequate and reasonable notice for all affected persons prior to the scheduled date of eviction; (c) information on the proposed evictions, and, where applicable, on the alternative purpose for which the land or housing is to be used, to be made available in reasonable time to all those affected; (d) especially where groups of people are involved, government officials or*

[24] CESCR, GC 7, para. 8.

[25] Ibid, para. 9.

> *their representatives to be present during an eviction; (e) all persons carrying out the eviction to be properly identified; (f) evictions not to take place in particularly bad weather or at night unless the affected persons consent otherwise; (g) provision of legal remedies; and (h) provision, where possible, of legal aid to persons who are in need of it to seek redress from the courts.*[26]

This passage reveals the "deductive" approach. The CESCR first states that adequate procedural protection is an essential element of *all* human rights—effectively characterising it as part of general human rights doctrine (*"allgemeine Menschenrechtslehren"*)– and then derives from that a catalogue of procedural obligations specifically for the context of the right to housing and forced evictions. A general procedural obligation in relation to all human rights is applied to specific rights and specific situations and thereby concretised.

The CESCR's general comments on the right to water and the right to social security contain similar lists of procedural safeguards.[27] Notably, before these lists, the committee does not reiterate its statement that such procedural safeguards are essential to all human rights—it does not make the deductive approach explicit again. However, the committee stipulates similar, in large parts even equal, procedural safeguards in these lists. There is no reason to assume that the committee follows a different approach here.

The CESCR's most recent General Comment 26 on "Land and Economic, Social and Cultural Rights" confirms this inference. In it, the CESCR devotes an entire sub-section to "[p]articipation, consultation, and transparency".[28] It begins the sub-section by stating that "[p]articipation, consultation, and transparency are key principles for the implementation of covenant obligations, including in relation to land".[29] Interestingly, the draft version of the general comment of May 2021 had used a wording limited to "obligations relating to land".[30] The more general, more inclusive language the committee uses in the finalised document shows that it still follows the "deductive approach" it followed already in General

---

[26] Ibid, para. 15.

[27] CESCR, *General Comment No. 15 (2002): The right to water (arts. 11 and 12 of the International Covenant on Economic, Social and Cultural Rights)* (20 January 2003) UN Doc E/C.12/2002/11, para. 56; CESCR, *General Comment No. 19: The right to social security (art. 9)* (4 February 2008) UN Doc E/C.12/GC/19, para. 78.

[28] CESCR, *General comment No. 26 (2022) on land and economic, social and cultural rights* (24 January 2023) UN Doc E/C.12/GC/26, paras. 20 and 21.

[29] Ibid, para. 20.

[30] CESCR, *General comment No. 26 (2021) on land and economic, social and cultural rights, Draft prepared by the Rapporteurs, Rodrigo Uprimny and Michael Windfuhr* (3 May 2021) UN Doc E/C.12/69/R.2, para. 18.

Comment 7 as, after the general statement, the committee goes on to spell out what these general "key principles" mean in relation to land.

These pronouncements reveal a deductive approach towards procedural obligations, which is essentially the same as the HRC's approach. The CESCR, too, considers procedural obligations to be part of the general human rights doctrine, of the general obligations owed to individuals in relation to the guaranteed rights. Given that the ICESCR follows the same technique as the ICCPR in that it sets out the general obligation of states in its Article 2 ICESCR and then recognises specific rights in relation to which the states must fulfil these obligations, we can conclude that the CESCR, too, situates the doctrinal basis for procedural obligations in the general obligations provision, i.e., Article 2 ICESCR, in connection with the specific right in question.

7.1.2.2 Inconsistencies in the Details

Beyond this deductive approach, the specifics of the doctrinal basis for procedural obligations as viewed by the CESCR are unclear. The CESCR's statements on where precisely it locates the source for these procedural obligations are even somewhat contradictory at times. In different general comments, the committee discusses procedural obligations under different headings and locates those obligations in different contexts. We find expressions of procedural obligations as part of the positive obligations to protect and to fulfil and the negative obligation to respect, as well as in a variety of different other contexts.

Earlier general comments of the CESCR were relatively short and not clearly structured.[31] This makes it somewhat difficult to understand where precisely the CESCR locates the issues it discusses therein. Starting with its General Comment 9 on the implementation of the covenant of 1998[32], however, the committee has been making use of headings and sub-headings to structure its general comments more clearly. This makes it easier for us to understand where precisely in the

[31] It shall be noted here that General Comment 5 on persons with disabilities and General Comment 6 on economic, social and cultural rights of older persons already made use of structuring and headings. However, this was arguably since the documents addressed cross-cutting issues and not individual rights under the ICESCR. Accordingly, they are structured thematically rather than along the lines of doctrinal categories. See CESCR, *General Comment No. 5: Persons with disabilities* (1994) HRI/GEN/1/Rev.9 (Vol. I) p. 17; CESCR, *General Comment No. 6: The economic, social and cultural rights of older persons* (1995) HRI/GEN/1/Rev.9 (Vol. I) p. 27.

[32] CESCR, *General Comment No. 9: The domestic application of the Covenant* (1998) HRI/GEN/1/Rev.9 (Vol. I) p. 47.

"overarching framework of human rights protection"[33], the CESCR locates the doctrinal anchor for procedural obligations. At the same time, however, this practice reveals significant inconsistencies in the committee's approach. In fact, we find discussions of procedural obligations more or less all over the place.

In General Comment 14 on the right to health, Article 12 ICESCR, for example, the CESCR states that the "participation of the population in all health-related decision-making" is an "important aspect" of the right to health under the heading of "[n]ormative content of article 12".[34] It mentions a "right to seek, receive and impart information and ideas concerning health issues" under the sub-heading of "accessibility".[35] Under "[s]tates parties obligations", the committee then states that the obligation to fulfil "requires states to adopt appropriate legislative, administrative, budgetary, judicial, promotional and other measures towards the full realisation of the right to health".[36] Further down, it then specifies this by saying that the actions required by the obligation to fulfil the right to health include "supporting people in making informed choices about their health".[37] Finally, under the heading of "[i]mplementation at the national level", and under the sub-heading of "framework legislation", the CESCR holds that "the right of individuals and groups to participate in decision-making processes, which may affect their development, must be an integral component of any policy, programme or strategy developed to discharge governmental obligations under article 12".[38]

In General Comment 15 on the right to water, Articles 11 and 12 ICESCR, the CESCR discusses procedural protection *ex ante* in the sense of a "right of individuals and groups to participate in decision-making processes that may affect their exercise of the right to water" under the heading of "implementation at the national level" and under the sub-heading of "[l]egislation, strategies and

---

[33] HRC, *General comment No. 31: The Nature of the General Legal Obligation Imposed on States Parties to the Covenant* (2004) HRI/GEN/1/Rev.9 (Vol. I) p. 243, para. 5.

[34] CESCR, *General Comment No. 14 (2000): The right to the highest attainable standard of health (article 12 of the International Covenant on Economic, Social and Cultural Rights)* (11 August 2000) UN Doc E/C.12/2000/4, para. 11.

[35] CESCR, ibid, para. 12.

[36] CESCR, ibid, para. 33.

[37] CESCR, ibid, para. 37.

[38] CESCR, ibid, para. 54.

policies".[39] Moreover, under the sub-heading of "remedies and accountability"[40], the committee produces a list with procedural requirements similar to the one we found in General Comment 7. Three years later, in General Comment 16 on the equal rights of men and women, the committee speaks of the "right of individuals [...] to participate in decision-making processes that may affect their development" once more in the context of "implementation at the national level", under the very similar sub-heading of "policies and strategies".[41]

In General Comment 17 on the right to benefit from the protection of the moral and material interests resulting from scientific, literary or artistic production, Article 15 (1) (c) ICESCR, the committee discusses procedural obligations under the heading of "states parties obligations" and the sub-heading of "[s]pecific legal obligations". It mentions the principle of free, prior and informed consent as part of a specific protect obligation towards indigenous peoples.[42] Two paragraphs later, under the same sub-heading but in the context of the obligation to fulfil, the CESCR holds that states must "ensure the right of authors of scientific, literary and artistic productions to take part in [...] any significant decision-making processes that have an impact on their rights and legitimate interests, and to consult these individuals or groups or their elected representatives prior to the adoption of any significant decisions affecting their rights under article 15, paragraph 1 (c)."[43]

In General Comment 19 on the right to social security the committee discusses procedural obligations in various places. Like in the General Comments 15 and 16, it lays out procedural obligations under the heading of "implementation" and under the sub-heading of "remedies and accountability".[44] In this place, we

---

[39] CESCR, GC 15, para. 48: *"The right of individuals and groups to participate in decision-making processes that may affect their exercise of the right to water must be an integral part of any policy, programme or strategy concerning water. Individuals and groups should be given full and equal access to information concerning water, water services and the environment, held by public authorities or third parties."*

[40] Ibid, para. 56.

[41] CESCR, *General comment No. 16 (2005): The equal right of men and women to the enjoyment of all economic, social and cultural rights (art. 3 of the International Covenant on Economic, Social and Cultural Rights)* (11 August 2005) UN Doc E/C.12/2005/4, para. 37.

[42] CESCR, *General Comment No. 17 (2005): The right of everyone to benefit from the protection of the moral and material interests resulting from any scientific, literary or artistic production of which he or she is the author (article 15, paragraph 1 (c), of the Covenant)* (12 January 2006) UN Doc E/C.12/GC/17, para. 32. For a discussion of this principle, see *infra* 8.1.3.

[43] CESCR, GC 17, para. 34.

[44] CESCR, GC 19, para. 78.

find a list of procedural safeguards which must be ensured "[b]efore any action is carried out [...] that interferes with the right of an individual to social security".[45] Moreover, under "II. Normative content of the right to social security"—A. Elements of the right to social security—4. Accessibility—(d) Participation and information", the committee states that "[b]eneficiaries of social security schemes must be able to participate in the administration of the social security system".[46] In the following General Comment 20 on equality and non-discrimination, the CESCR mentions the "right to participate in decision-making processes" of individuals as part of the introductory paragraph to "national implementation".[47]

In General Comment 21 on the right to participate in cultural life, the CESCR again discusses procedural obligations in multiple places. Firstly, it calls the participation of affected individuals in decision-making processes a "necessary condition for the full realization of the right" under the heading of "[e]lements of the right to take part in cultural life" and "acceptability".[48] Secondly, it reiterates the importance of adherence to the principle of free, prior and informed consent in cases concerning indigenous peoples under the heading of "[n]ormative content of article 15, paragraph 1 (a)" and the sub-heading of "[p]ersons and communities requiring special protection".[49] Thirdly, the committee includes the rights "of all persons to have access to, and to participate in, varied information exchanges" and "[t]o take part freely in an active and informed way, an without discrimination, in any important decision-making process that may have an impact on his or her [...] rights under article 15, paragraph 1 (a)" under the negative obligation to respect the right to take part in cultural life.[50] Fourthly, the CESCR states that a persons must be able to "participate effectively in decision-making processes" as part of the obligation to fulfil.[51]

As we have already seen, in its most recent General Comment 26, the CESCR devotes an entire sub-section to "[p]articipation, consultation, and transparency"

---

[45] Ibid, para. 78.

[46] Ibid, para. 26.

[47] CESCR, *General Comment No. 20: Non-discrimination in economic, social and cultural rights (art. 2, para. 2, of the International Covenant on Economic, Social and Cultural Rights)* (2 July 2009) UN Doc E/C.12/GC/20, para. 36.

[48] CESCR, *General comment No. 21: Right of everyone to take part in cultural life (art. 15, para. 1 (a), of the International Covenant on Economic, Social and Cultural Rights)* (21 December 2009) UN Doc E/C.12/GC/21, para. 16.

[49] Ibid, para. 37.

[50] Ibid, para. 49.

[51] Ibid, para. 54.

under the heading of "[o]bligation of States Parties under the Covenant".[52] In the same general comment, the CESCR also addresses such obligations in connection with the obligation to fulfil human rights.[53] Hence, the newest general comment does not do away with but instead exacerbates the inconsistencies and uncertainties in the CESCR's approach towards procedural obligations, and in particular with regard to where the committee locates these obligations doctrinally.

7.1.3 Conclusion

The committees both follow a "deductive approach". They both understand procedural obligations as part of the general obligations of states in relation to all rights enshrined in the respective treaties. Both committees combine this general obligation with the specific rights in question to form the doctrinal basis for procedural obligations, thereby highlighting the rights- and context-sensitivity of this approach. Beyond this general approach, however, where precisely the committees attach the obligation is far from clear. While the HRC at least rather clearly construes procedural obligations as positive obligations and consequently locates them in the "ensure" dimension of the ICCPR, the CESCR's statements regarding procedural protection are somewhat "all over the place". It is not clear at all in which doctrinal category the CESCR roots the obligations. The CESCR has even discussed the procedural dimension of the right to participate in cultural life under the heading of the "obligation to respect" the right. However, the laconic pronouncements of the HRC leave considerable gaps, too. We will attempt to close these gaps in the following section and thus strengthen our understanding of how precisely IHRL gives rise to procedural obligations *vis à vis* the administration of a state.

7.2 A Convincing Doctrinal Construction?

In this section, we will reflect on the findings of the previous section. Is the doctrinal construction for procedural obligations employed by the committees convincing? How can the inconsistencies in their pronouncements be explained? How can the gaps be filled? Firstly, we will explain why the committees' understanding of procedural obligations as part of general human rights doctrine is

[52] CESCR, GC 26, paras. 20–21.

[53] Ibid, paras. 33–34.

convincing (7.2.1). Secondly, we will take a closer look at Article 2 ICCPR and Article 2 ICESCR and explain why these provisions should indeed be considered the correct "legal anchors" for obligations of administrative procedure (7.2.2). Thirdly, we will look beyond the general approach and discuss which elements of general human rights doctrine precisely give rise to procedural obligations (7.2.3). In particular, we will discuss which of the three general human rights obligations—respect, protect, fulfil—yield obligations of administrative procedure. The committees' pronouncements are relatively vague in this regard. Hence, our task here will be a more creative and less that of a critically appreciative task. Finally, we will reflect on the value of connecting the general obligations provisions to the specific rights in question (7.2.4).

7.2.1 Procedural Protection as Part of General Human Rights Doctrine

The committees construe procedural obligations as a feature of general human rights doctrine. They do not speak of a right to administrative procedure, a right to procedural protection or the like. Even in its most recent General Comment 26, in which the CESCR discusses "[p]articipation, consultation and transparency" in a separate sub-section, it calls these obligations "key principles for the implementation of Covenant obligations"[54]. In the academic discourse, however, we find voices that seek to frame obligations of administrative procedure as a "new human right". Such an approach contrasts with the committees' practice. Given that this section's goal is to critically appraise the committees' approach, however, we will give the approach a closer look.

In his article "A Right to Administrative Justice—'New' or Just Repackaging the Old?", Corder discusses the development of a standalone right to good administration in several post-colonial African constitutions.[55] He describes the shapes that the right has taken in the constitutions of Namibia, South Africa, Malawi, Nigeria, Kenya and Zimbabwe and juxtaposes the rights found in the mentioned African constitutions with Article 41 of the EU Charter of Fundamental Rights (CFR)[56]. The scope of Corder's analysis is not universal; he does not argue that

[54] CESCR, GC 26, para. 20.

[55] Hugh Corder, 'A Right to Administrative Justice—'New' or Just Repackaging the Old?' in Andreas von Arnauld, Kerstin von der Decken and Martin Susi (eds), *The Cambridge Handbook of New Human Rights—Recognition, Novelty, Rhetoric* (Cambridge University Press 2020).

[56] Charter of Fundamental Rights of the European Union [2012] C 326/02.

such a right has arisen in international (customary) human rights law. Nevertheless, against the background of his approach and the advantages Corder ties to the expression of right to administrative justice as a human right[57], the question arises of whether the committees' approach to construe procedural obligations as part of the general doctrine rather than speaking of a standalone right is the right approach.

The approach of deriving or creating a "new human right" is relatively *en vogue* in IHRL scholarship and practice.[58] The question of whether it was "time to recognise" a certain right has been a popular question in the last decades. And in some instances, such an approach was convincing and important. Such is the case, e.g., with the so-called right to water. Thielbörger has shown that a human right to water is "a plausible legal means to approach the basic human need for water"[59] and convincingly argued in favour of such a right.[60]

Besides the fact that it can be materially warranted, there is "something inherently appealing" to speaking of a "new human right".[61] Von Arnauld and Theilen have described five functions of such a call for new human rights in an article investigating the "added communicative value" of calling for new human rights. Claims for new human rights have an "appellative function" in that they "serve[s] to draw attention to certain situations which are deemed to be sufficiently unjust so as to qualify [...] as a human rights issue".[62] They have a "contesting function" in that they are meant to challenge the existing order and address existing injustices.[63] They can generate an opportunity for collaboration, a buzzword under

[57] Corder argues that the expression of a right to administrative justice as a human right "adds significantly to its weight and the prospects of compliance", Corder, 505.

[58] See Andreas von Arnauld, Kerstin von der Decken and Martin Susi (eds), *The Cambridge Handbook of New Human Rights—Recognition, Novelty, Rhetoric* (Cambridge University Press 2020).

[59] Pierre Thielbörger, *The Right(s) to Water: The Multi-Level Governance of a Unique Human Right* (Springer 2014), at 197. Notably, Thielbörger avoids an activist approach by limiting his claim already in the title of his book. By using a plural-s in parentheses that hints at the fact that "[i]t is [...] better to understand the right to water as a complex of different rights" he already clarifies his differentiated and prudent approach, ibid, 3.

[60] Thielbörger, 'Re-Conceptualizing the Human Right to Water: A Pledge for a Hybrid Approach'.

[61] Andreas von Arnauld and Jens T. Theilen, 'Rhetoric of Rights: A Topical Perspective on the Functions of Claiming a 'Human Right to ..." in Andreas von Arnauld, Kerstin von der Decken and Martin Susi (eds), *The Cambridge Handbook of New Human Rights* (Cambridge University Press 2020), 34.

[62] Ibid, 39–40.

[63] Ibid, 40–43.

which discussants can gather, share their thoughts and further their cause and thus have a "connecting function".[64] Moreover, they have a "triggering function" in that they represent an "the attempt to trigger particular institutions so that they may provide authoritative proclamations or interpretations, promote the right at issue with their resources and personnel or provide for remedies and reparations which might otherwise have been unavailable".[65] Finally, they have what von Arnauld and Theilen call a "jurisgenerative function": "by coaxing discourse surrounding the issue in a certain direction, the 'human right to …' becomes a kind of *discursive hub* which not only reinforces certain values and thus constrains discourse, but may also serve as a reference point for future (re)interpretations of international law".[66]

All of these functions can be beneficial for the human rights enterprise. And, insofar as scholars follow a *bona fide* human rights-based research agenda, they can even be legitimately intended by legal scholars. They can be valuable for an international human rights discourse that seeks to push the boundaries rather than be content with the state of the art. In other instances, however, such an approach seems inadequate. Speaking of "new human rights" has been called indicative of a "thirst for new epistemic territories as new human rights mean more areas of scholarly discussion".[67] It can also seem like the result of a reluctance to properly engage with (general) human rights doctrine. Simply putting a new name on something can sometimes be easier than engaging with it and framing it within known categories.

When new human rights are called for without the need for it, this can indeed harm the scholarly discourse and the human rights project as a whole. Already in 1984, Alston warned against an uncontrolled "conjuring up" of new human rights and the negative and de-legitimising effect it can have on IHRL.[68] One should therefore be mindful of this danger when engaging with phenomena that have not received comprehensive scholarly treatment and not call these phenomena "new human rights" hastily.

As we found in the previous section, the committees have so far withstood summarising the issues we are interested in under a notion of a "right to good

[64] Ibid, 43–45.

[65] Ibid, 45–47.

[66] Ibid, 47–48.

[67] Jean d'Aspremont, 'Expansionism and the Sources of International Human Rights Law' (2016) 46 Israel Yearbook on Human Rights 223, 228.

[68] Philip Alston, 'Conjuring Up New Human Rights: A Proposal for Quality Control' (1984) 78 American Journal of International Law 607.

administration", a "right to administrative procedure" or the like. And they did so rightfully. In our analysis of German constitutional law, we have seen that *ex ante* procedural protection can have an important function in enhancing the effectiveness of the realisation of individual rights in general. This general "serving, […] auxiliary function"[69] would not be adequately represented doctrinally if we framed procedural protection as a new standalone human right. Conceiving, instead, a procedural dimension of all human rights and obligations of administrative procedure in relation to all human rights, as an element of general human rights doctrine—as part of *"allgemeine Menschenrechtslehren"*—is more adequate. Such a conception reflects the importance of procedural involvement and procedural protection to *all* human rights.

7.2.2 The Obligation Provisions of the ICCPR and the ICESCR

A defining feature of human rights treaties is that the obligations they give rise to are set out in a "single, all-encompassing provision that assigns States duties to respect and ensure treaty rights".[70] It is therefore no surprise that most, if not all, of general human rights doctrine was developed based on these provisions. In the case of the ICCPR and the ICESCR, those provisions are the respective Articles 2. As we have seen, these provisions play a central role in the doctrinal bases for procedural obligations found in the pronouncements of the committees. Some questions, however, remain. In this section, we will take a closer look at the obligations provisions of the ICCPR (7.2.2.1) and the ICESCR (7.2.2.2) and pinpoint the legal anchor for procedural obligations more precisely.

7.2.2.1 The Precise Legal Anchor in Article 2 ICCPR

The obligations for states parties to the ICCPR are set out in the covenant's Article 2:

> *1. Each State Party to the present Covenant undertakes to respect and to ensure to all individuals within its territory and subject to its jurisdiction the rights recognized in the present Covenant, without distinction of any kind, such as race, colour, sex, language, religion, political or other opinion, national or social origin, property, birth or other status.*

[69] See Cremer, *Freiheitsgrundrechte*, 404.

[70] Çalı, 'Specialized Rules of Treaty Interpretation: Human Rights', 530.

2. Where not already provided for by existing legislative or other measures, each State Party to the present Covenant undertakes to take the necessary steps, in accordance with its constitutional processes and with the provisions of the present Covenant, to adopt such laws or other measures as may be necessary to give effect to the rights recognized in the present Covenant.

Each State Party to the present Covenant undertakes:

(a) To ensure that any person whose rights or freedoms as herein recognized are violated shall have an effective remedy, notwithstanding that the violation has been committed by persons acting in an official capacity;

(b) To ensure that any person claiming such a remedy shall have his right thereto determined by competent judicial, administrative or legislative authorities, or by any other competent authority provided for by the legal system of the State, and to develop the possibilities of judicial remedy;

(c) To ensure that the competent authorities shall enforce such remedies when granted.

Article 2 (1) ICCPR contains the general obligation for states to "respect and ensure" the ICCPR rights, as well as an obligation of non-discrimination. Article 2 (2) ICCPR then addresses practical implementation of the rights; states must take the necessary measures to give effect to the rights. Finally, Article 2 (3) ICCPR complements the provision by adding an obligation to have in place effective remedies to address violations of the rights recognized in the ICCPR. These provisions provide the "overarching framework within which the rights specified in the Covenant are to be promoted and protected"[71]. Which of these provisions precisely provides the anchor for procedural obligations?

As we have seen, the HRC has referred to Article 2 (1) ICCPR in its General Comment 36 as part of the doctrinal basis *inter alia* for the procedural obligations discussed here.[72] According to the committee, the doctrinal basis was "article 2 (1) [...] read in conjunction with article 6"[73]. As we will see, however, it would be more convincing to add Article 2 (2) ICCPR to the doctrinal basis as well. The two provisions should generally be read together whenever the obligations of states parties under the ICCPR are concerned. Accordingly, the precise textual basis for obligations of administrative procedure should be "Article 2 (1), (2) read in conjunction with the respective article". Before turning to this argument, we will exclude the third paragraph as the legal anchor.

[71] HRC, GC 31, para. 5.

[72] See *supra* 7.1.1.

[73] HRC, GC 36, para. 21.

While Article 2 (3) ICCPR contains a right to have one's right "determined by competent judicial, administrative or legislative authorities" and thereby makes a reference to an organisational requirement for public decision-making, it is clear that the provision is only concerned with remedying human rights violations that have already taken place. It provides for a right to legal protection *ex post* and not *ex ante*. The wording—"any person whose rights or freedoms as herein recognized *are violated*"—is clear in this regard. In its General Comment 31 on the general legal obligation of the states parties, the HRC confirms this view. It speaks of "mechanisms for addressing claims of rights violations under domestic law" and states that "[a]dministrative mechanisms are particularly required to give effect to the general obligation to investigate allegations of violations".[74] We find an even clearer expression of this stance in an early case of the committee:

> *The Covenant provides that a remedy shall be granted whenever a violation of one of the rights guaranteed by it has occurred; consequently, it does not generally prescribe preventive protection, but confines itself to requiring effective redress ex post facto.*[75]

While we have already seen that the second part of the statement in its absoluteness does not represent the view of the committee, the passage is a clear expression of the committee's understanding of Article 2 (3) ICCPR. There is no indication that the committee has changed its view on that provision meanwhile. Moreover, the literature concurs with the committees' view that the obligation under Article 2 (3) ICCPR is an obligation to provide *ex post* legal protection,[76] in particular by referring to the wording of the provision[77].

Having excluded Article 2 (3) ICCPR, we are left with Article 2 (1) and (2) ICCPR as potential legal anchors. In fact, the two must be taken together to provide for the correct doctrinal basis. This is because the two paragraphs of Article 2 ICCPR complement one another. Article 2 (1) ICCPR codifies the general obligation of states parties under international law and Article 2 (2) ICCPR prescribes—albeit vaguely—requirements for the "practical implementation" of these obligations.[78] As Joseph and Castan put it in their commentary to the ICCPR, "Article 2 (1) is fundamental; it is the 'obligation' provision that directs

---

[74] HRC, GC 31, para. 15.

[75] HRC, *C.F. et al v. Canada* (Comm no 113/1981, HRC, 12 April 1985), para. 6.2. Emphasis original.

[76] Joseph and Castan, 10, 882.

[77] Taylor, 81.

[78] Ibid, 59.

states immediately to implement the substantive ICCPR guarantees at the municipal level"[79] and "[p]aragraphs 2 and 3 of article 2 supplement paragraph 1 by requiring specific measures of national protection of ICCPR rights"[80]. Çalı expressed the connection between the two paragraphs well when she held that "Article 2 (1)-(2) of the ICCPR" provided an example for "a single, all-encompassing provision that assigns States duties" under IHRL.[81] Given this interplay between the two paragraphs, it is most convincing to construe both paragraphs, Article 2 (1) and (2) ICCPR, together as the correct "legal anchor" for obligations of administrative procedure. It allows us to not only frame administrative procedure as some component of an obligation to "respect and ensure human rights". Instead, we can more precisely characterise it as "such law[s] or other measure[s] as may be necessary to give effect" to the ICCPR rights. Moreover, this explicit reference to the principle of effectiveness provides an interesting connection to an important building block of a justification for obligations of administrative procedure under IHRL.[82]

7.2.2.2 Article 2 (1) ICESCR as the Legal Anchor in the ICESCR

Article 2 ICESCR fulfils the same function as the parallel provision from the ICCPR. It codifies the obligations of states in relation to the substantive rights enshrined in the ICESCR. It is the provision that sets out the general legal obligation states must fulfil in relation to the economic, social and cultural rights set out in the ICESCR. In comparison to Article 2 ICCPR, however, the provision uses much softer language. *Prima facie*, the provision therefore looks fundamentally different:

> *1. Each State Party to the present Covenant undertakes to take steps, individually and through international assistance and co-operation, especially economic and technical, to the maximum of its available resources, with a view to achieving progressively the full realization of the rights recognized in the present Covenant by all appropriate means, including particularly the adoption of legislative measures.*
>
> *2. The States Parties to the present Covenant undertake to guarantee that the rights enunciated in the present Covenant will be exercised without discrimination of any kind as to race, colour, sex, language, religion, political or other opinion, national or social origin, property, birth or other status.*

---

[79] Joseph and Castan, 9.

[80] Ibid, 10.

[81] Çalı, 'Specialized Rules of Treaty Interpretation: Human Rights', 530.

[82] See *infra* 8.2.1.1.

3. Developing countries, with due regard to human rights and their national economy, may determine to what extent they would guarantee the economic rights recognized in the present Covenant to non-nationals.

In contrast to Article 2 ICCPR, there are no paragraphs dedicated to the implementation of the general obligation or remedies. Instead, Article 2 (2) ICESCR codifies the non-discrimination obligation (which was part of the first paragraph of the parallel provision of the ICCPR), and Article 2 (3) ICESCR contains a concession to developing countries with regard to non-nationals. These two paragraphs of the provision can obviously not serve as the legal anchor we are looking for. Hence, Article 2 (1) ICESCR alone is the correct doctrinal hinge to tie the obligation to.

As mentioned, the provision evidently uses softer language than the ICCPR. It demands that the state "take steps [...] to the maximum of its available resources, with a view to achieving progressively the full realization of the rights recognized in the present Covenant". While the obligations under the ICCPR are clearly immediate for the states parties, the ICESCR obligations seem to be less immediate. According to the wording of the provision, the obligations must only be realised "progressively". Moreover, they are dependent on what the state can achieve.[83]

This perceived difference in the wording of Article 2 (1) ICESCR do not, however, make it a less adequate "legal anchor" for obligations of administrative procedure. In reality, the difference between the obligations under Article 2 (1), (2) ICCPR and Article 2 (1) ICESCR is gradual and not categorical.

Surely, the difference in language between the two provisions has given rise to debate about the differences between civil and political rights on the one hand, and economic, social and cultural rights on the other.[84] We even find writers emphasising differences in the quality of the obligation in relatively recent literature.[85] *Inter alia,* it has been argued that there was a general difference in the immediacy of the obligations[86] and a general difference in the nature of the obligations that the two covenants give rise to, namely that the obligations under

[83] For an in-depth discussion of what the concept of progressive realisation can mean in practice with extensive reference to the *travaux préparatoires*, see Philip Alston and Gerard Quinn, 'The Nature and Scope of States Parties' Obligations under the International Covenant on Economic, Social and Cultural Rights' (1987) 9 Human Rights Quarterly 156, 172–177.

[84] For a summary of those arguments, see ibid, 159–160.

[85] See, for example, Tomuschat, *Human Rights: Between Idealism and Realism*, 141.

[86] Ibid.

the ICCPR were negative and under the ICESCR positive in nature.[87] Today, however, it is widely accepted that, despite the textual differences, a fundamentally different approach towards ICESCR obligations has not arisen in practice. It is accepted today that both provisions stipulate multi-dimensional obligations.[88] And the positive obligations that arise from both treaties are limited to what is feasible for the state.[89] Alston and Quinn put it aptly when they held that the difference between the general obligations under the two covenants was gradual rather than categorical:

> *[T]he main difference between the rights recognized in the two Covenants consists of the fact that economic and social rights require relative greater state action for their realization than do civil and political rights. This difference separates the two sets of rights more in terms of degree than in kind [...].*[90]

Moreover, while many of the rights enshrined in the ICESCR are indeed subject to considerable leeway of states because of their positive nature[91] it is by now recognised that every right in the ICESCR contains elements which are immediately and unconditionally implemented.[92] Hence, Article 2 ICESCR is generally just as well-suited to serve as a doctrinal basis for procedural obligations as Article 2 ICCPR. It fulfils the same general function in that it, too, sets out the general legal obligations relating to the rights enshrined in the covenant.

---

[87] See Alston and Quinn, 159–160.

[88] Kälin and Künzli, 87; Frédéric Mégret, 'Nature of Obligations' in Daniel Moeckli, Sangeeta Shah and Sandesh Sivakumaran (eds), *International Human Rights Law* (3rd edn, Oxford University Press 2018), 97; see for a record of the development from understanding human rights as negative rights towards acknowledging their multi-dimensional nature also Sandra Fredman, *Human Rights Transformed: Positive Rights and Positive Duties* (Oxford University Press 2008), 1ff.

[89] Kälin and Künzli, 105.

[90] Alston and Quinn, 183–184.

[91] See on the necessary leeway that comes with the implementation of positive rights *supra* 6.2. as well as *infra* 9.2.1.

[92] Eibe Riedel, Gilles Giacca and Christophe Golay, 'The Development of Economic, Social, and Cultural Rights in International Law' in Eibe Riedel, Gilles Giacca and Christophe Golay (eds), *Economic, Social, and Cultural Rights in International Law* (Oxford University Press 2014), 13.

7.2.3 The Obligation of Administrative Procedure as an Obligation to Fulfil Human Rights

In our analysis of the German discourse, we have seen that the FCC derives the positive procedural obligations from the objective dimension of the Basic Law's fundamental rights.[93] Given that the fundamental rights were conceived as negative rights of defence, this rather sophisticated construction had been necessary for the FCC to situate positive obligations, including procedural ones, in the doctrine of fundamental rights. In contrast, international human rights have always been multi-dimensional. The multi-dimensional nature of civil and political rights is already enshrined in the wording of Article 2 (1) ICCPR when it provides that states must "respect and ensure" the rights recognised in the ICCPR. On the other hand, the CESCR has long made clear that social, economic and cultural rights entail a negative "respect" dimension as well.[94] Hence, the problem that forced the FCC to take the rather complicated "detour via objective law"[95] does not exist under IHRL.

After recalling the multidimensional nature of IHRL and the tripartite typology that is relied on to describe it (7.2.3.1), this sub-section will argue that the obligation "to fulfil" should be viewed as the general IHRL obligation that gives rise to obligations of administrative procedure (7.2.3.2).

7.2.3.1 The Multi-Dimensional Nature of IHRL

The modern doctrine of IHRL goes beyond the dichotomy of negative and positive obligations. Today, the obligations under IHRL are usually categorized by what has been called a "trias of State obligations"[96]: "respect, protect, fulfil". This typology is similar to that developed by Henry Shue in 1980.[97] Shue suggested a "very simple tripartite typology for duties" to shed light on distinctions

---

[93] See *supra* Chap. 4 generally.

[94] See, e.g., CESCR, *General Comment 12 (Twentieth session, 1999): The right to adequate food (art. 11)* (12 May 1999) UN Doc E/C.12/1999/5, para. 15.

[95] Jarass, 'Grundrechte als Wertentscheidungen bzw. objektivrechtliche Prinzipien in der Rechtsprechung des Bundesverfassungsgerichts', 369.

[96] Manfred Nowak, *UN Covenant on Civil and Political Rights: CCPR Commentary* (2nd revised edn, N.P. Engel, Publisher 2005), XXI.

[97] Despite the different wording for two of the obligations, his typology refers to essentially the same actions required of states, Henry Shue, *Basic Rights—Subsistence, Affluence and U.S. Foreign Policy: 40th Anniversary Edition* (40th anniversary edn, Princeton University Press 2020), 51ff.

"obscured by the dichotomy between negative and positive rights".[98] He exemplified his typology with the aid of the right to physical security and defined the state's duties in relation to that right as:

> *I. Duties not to eliminate a person's security—duties to avoid depriving.*
>
> *II. Duties to protect people against deprivation of security by other people—duties to protect from deprivation.*
>
> *III. Duties to provide for the security of those unable to provide for their own—duties to aid the deprived.*[99]

In 1987, Asbjørn Eide, then Special Rapporteur on the right to adequate food as a human right, included a similar tripartite typology in his report.[100] The report introduced the "respect, protect, fulfil" trichotomy which has since been adopted by human rights bodies[101] and become a "central resource in human rights commentary"[102].

States violate their negative obligation "to respect" whenever they interfere with a human right without justification. If one accepts that human rights have their origin in the emergence of national bills of rights during the enlightenment in the late eighteenth century,[103] one is probably right to call this "perhaps the most classical" human rights obligation.[104] It is at least largely similar to the negative defence dimension of German fundamental rights.

In addition to this negative obligation which states fulfil merely by abstaining from unjustified interference, they have the positive obligations "to protect" and "to fulfil". Under the obligation "to protect", states must "proactively ensure that persons within [their] jurisdiction do not suffer from human rights violations at the hands of third parties or even broad phenomena such as preventable environmental catastrophes".[105] In the words of the CESCR, the dimension "requires

---

[98] Ibid, 52.

[99] Ibid, 52.

[100] UN Special Rapporteur on the Right to Adequate Food, *Report on the right to adequate food as a human right submitted by Mr. Asbjørn Eide, Special Rapporteur* (7 July 1987) UN Doc E/CN.4/Sub.2/1987/23, paras. 66–69.

[101] Mégret, 97.

[102] Katharine G. Young, 'Rights and Obligations' in Daniel Moeckli and others (eds), *International Human Rights Law* (4th edn, Oxford University Press 2022), 138.

[103] For an example of this account, see Bates.

[104] Mégret, 97.

[105] Ibid, 97.

States to adopt measures to prevent any person or entity from interfering with the Covenant rights".[106] The dimension has a compensatory function. While human rights are not applicable horizontally between private entities and while they "cannot be viewed as a substitute for domestic criminal or civil law"[107], they require states to create "an environment in which rights are enjoyed".[108] The obligation comprises measures such as exercising "due diligence to prevent, punish, investigate or redress the harm caused by [...] private persons or entities".[109] With this dimension, international human rights also gains indirect third-party effect (*"mittelbare Drittwirkung"*).

Finally, under the obligation "to fulfil", states must "take positive steps that have as a consequence the greater enjoyment of rights".[110] It requires states "to create the legal, institutional, and procedural conditions that rights holders need in order to realize and enjoy their rights in full".[111] The obligation to fulfil has been broken down by the CESCR into three obligations which will be examined more closely in the following sub-section: "facilitate", "promote" and "provide".[112]

The obligation to fulfil is perhaps the dimension that requires most action on the side of the state.[113] Nevertheless, the traditional view that obligations under this dimension are relevant to socio-economic rights only has rightfully long been overcome. It is certainly true that the dimension is of particular importance to the mostly positive socio-economic rights. A state cannot implement the right to social security, for example, merely by remaining idle. Neither is it enough for the state to ensure that other individuals do not hinder the holder of the right to submit an application for social security. Instead, the state must *provide for* social security. It must provide for the necessary financial means and create a social security system, i.e., state structures through which the state can grant an individual her right.

However, the fulfil dimension is relevant to civil and political rights, too. There are several civil and political rights which logically presuppose active, "creative" behaviour on the side of the state. The right to a fair trial, Article 14 ICCPR,

106 CESCR, GC 26, para. 26.

107 HRC, GC 31, para. 8.

108 Mégret, 97.

109 HRC, GC 31, para. 8.

110 Mégret, 98.

111 Kälin and Künzli, 104.

112 Manisuli Ssenyonjo, *Economic, Social and Cultural Rights in International Law* (2nd edn, Hart Publishing 2016), 35.

113 Riedel, Giacca and Golay, 19.

provides an illustrative example. The state must have in place a functioning judicial system to fulfil its obligations under the right. It was therefore rightly called "mainly a 'positive' *fulfilment* right".[114] And if it does not have such a judicial system, it must create one. Another obvious example is the right to participate in public affairs, Article 25 ICCPR, in particular the aspect of the right to vote, Article 25 (b) ICCPR. The obligation on the side of the state is almost exclusively an obligation to facilitate votes in elections. States must do more than merely abstain from barring people to vote. Instead, the state must, e.g., set up polling stations. We could list more examples of positive obligations states must comply with under the ICCPR. However, these two examples shall suffice here to illustrate that civil and political rights are multi-dimensional in nature, too.

7.2.3.2 Administrative Procedure as Part of the Obligation to "Fulfil" Human Rights

Now that we have given an overview of the three dimensions of IHRL obligations, we can explain why the fulfil dimension is the correct legal anchor. In order to do so, we will first explain why the negative respect dimension is unsuitable (7.2.3.2.1). Secondly, we will address the protect dimension and argue that—properly conceived—it cannot be the precise legal anchor, either (7.2.3.2.2). Finally, we will turn to the fulfil dimension and explain why it is indeed the correct doctrinal basis for obligations of administrative procedure (7.2.3.2.3).

7.2.3.2.1 The Unsuitability of the Respect Dimension

In our analysis of the FCC's jurisprudence, we have seen that the FCC derives procedural obligations of the German administration from the objective dimension of the fundamental rights. This was necessary because the traditional negative dimension of German fundamental rights could not give rise to the need for positive state action.[115] The same is true for IHRL. The negative "respect" dimension merely requires states to abstain from interfering with a right without justification. It cannot, on its own, demand positive action from states. Hence, when the CESCR (or any other actor for that matter) seemingly derives procedural obligations from the respect dimension directly,[116] this is probably due to a technical mistake. It mixes up the function of procedural obligations with their precise basis in human rights doctrine.

---

[114] Ida Elisabeth Koch, 'Dichotomies, Trichotomies or Waves of Duties' (2005) 5 Human Rights Law Review 81, 95.

[115] See *supra* Chap. 4 generally.

[116] See, for example, CESCR, GC 21, para. 49.

As we have already seen in the context of the FCC's jurisprudence,[117] procedures can be an important (and oftentimes necessary) means to help or even achieve the realisation of negative obligations. The state agent hears the affected individual (and others) to find out whether a justification exists, to assess the gravity a measure would have in her particular case and so on. These steps can, of course, be crucially important to an effective implementation of the negative obligation under IHRL in complex political and societal realities. However, they are not a *conditio sine qua non* for the negative obligation's fulfilment. A state could theoretically decide not to interfere with the individual's rights at all. Instead of being careful not to overstep and justifying interferences with a terrorist's rights to liberty, it could just refrain from interferences entirely and thereby fulfil its obligations.

Surely, such a theoretical argument entirely disregards the complex societal reality within which human rights must be realised. Even though human rights have an individualist bias,[118] its subjects exist not in isolation but in relation to others. The relationship between individuals and the state is (virtually) never a pristinely bipolar relationship. Most of the time, the state's role is that of a referee, of a mediator delineating freedoms and entitlements of different individuals from one another seeking to fulfil negative and positive human rights obligations at the same time. Nevertheless, the theoretical argument that a state would fulfil its negative respect obligations merely by abstaining from interfering in someone's rights, shows that the precise doctrinal anchor for procedural obligations cannot be found in the negative respect dimension. The respect dimension in itself cannot give rise to procedural obligations.

7.2.3.2.2 The Unsuitability of the Protect Dimension

Some commentators define the obligation to protect so that it comprises administrative procedures. According to Mégret, e.g., states are obliged to create an "environment in which human rights are enjoyed".[119] Such an obligation would probably require states to have in place certain administrative procedures. Given their auxiliary function, their effect of providing *ex ante* legal protection, one might at least ask whether such an environment in which rights are enjoyed can exist without administrative procedures. Moreover, the HRC made the important

---

[117] See *supra* 5.1.

[118] Cf. Benedikt Behlert, 'The Protection of Human Rights in Times of Public Health Emergencies' in Pierre Thielbörger and Sascha Rolf Lüder (eds), *Die COVID-19-Pandemie als Herausforderung an das Völkerrecht, das Verfassungsrecht und das Verwaltungsrecht* (Berliner Wissenschafts-Verlag 2022).

[119] Mégret, 97.

and far-reaching pronouncement in General Comment 36 under the heading of "duty to protect life".[120] Similarly, Young has argued that the protect dimension focuses on "the state's role in [...] 'building infrastructures' and in organizing 'the governmental apparatus and, in general, all the structures through which public power is exercised, so that they are capable of juridically ensuring the free and full enjoyment of human rights'".[121]

Other accounts place procedural obligations under the fulfil dimension. Kälin and Künzli, for example, view the duty to "establish the legal, institutional, and procedural basis for full realization of the right concerned" as a necessary aspect of the obligation to fulfil human rights.[122] They also state that "[o]n the institutional level, the establishment of administrative bodies and tribunals providing legal protection [...] is particularly important".[123] Mégret subsumes an obligation "to organize the structure of the state apparatus in a way that ensures the full exercise of human rights" under the fulfil dimension.[124] When comparing Mégret's definition of the fulfil dimension to his definition of the protect dimension, the question arises whether an "environment in which rights are enjoyed" can exist without "the structure of the state apparatus [...] that ensures the full exercise of human rights".

Mégret is not the only author who defines the two obligation dimensions in a way that creates confusion when it comes to procedural obligations in one and the same article. Young, who has taken over his chapter on the nature of human rights obligations in a prominent human rights textbook, defines the fulfil dimension as the duty "to take appropriate legislative, administrative, budgetary, judicial and other measures towards full realization".[125] She goes on to state that the fulfil obligation "targets the follow-up (or last resort) actions of the state when obligations to respect or protect rights are not sufficient for their enjoyment".[126] Once again, we must ask: (how) can the organisation of "all the structures through

[120] HRC, GC 36, para. 19.

[121] Young, 136.

[122] Kälin and Künzli, 88.

[123] Ibid, 105.

[124] Mégret, 98. Note the similarity of Mégret's definition to the statement the HRC made in its General Comment 36. The similarity is presumably due to the fact that Mégret and the HRC both use the jurisprudence of the IACtHR as a reference for such an obligation.

[125] Young, 137. Young's definition follows the definition of the International Commission of Jurists: *Maastricht Guidelines on Violations of Economic, Social and Cultural Rights* (2 October 2000) UN Doc E/C.12/2000/13 p. 16, para 6.

[126] Ibid, 138.

which public power is exercised" in a way that "ensures the free and full enjoyment of human rights" be fulfilled in a way that is not insufficient to ensure the enjoyment of human rights?

The lines between the two positive human rights dimensions are obviously blurred, in particular when it comes to procedural or organisational obligations. The problem can be solved by refocusing on the *raison d'être* of the protect dimension. Its function is to compensate for the lack of direct horizontal applicability of international human rights. This is what the obligation was conceived for. Henry Shue already defined the second obligation of his tripartite typology as "[d]uties to protect people against deprivation of security *by other people*".[127] Eide, too, conceived the function of the obligation as preventing infringement on human rights by other individuals.[128] According to this function, the definitions by Mégret and Young appear to be too wide. The obligation is about "creating an environment in which rights are enjoyed" only insofar as this means effectively protecting against threats to human rights emanating from other private individuals. Such a narrow understanding of the protect dimension does not lead to definitional overlap and does therefore not create confusion.

And based on this narrow understanding, we can exclude the dimension as the precise legal anchor with the same hypothetical consideration with which we excluded the negative respect dimension. States can comply with their obligation to protect human rights without, e.g., hearing the affected individual. To exemplify this, let us recall the constellation in the FCC's *Mülheim-Kärlich* case. An operator of nuclear power plants applied for a permit to build and operate a new plant. In order to effectively take into account the right to physical integrity and the right to life of those living in the vicinity of the plant in its decision-making process, the authorities had to *inter alia* hear these individuals. However, looking at the obligation to protect the rights of those living in the vicinity in isolation, this obligation could have been fulfilled without hearing these individuals. The authorities could have just not permitted the construction of the plant. While this might have violated the operator's rights, the right to life and the right to physical integrity of those living close by would have been protected effectively.

Surely, this is another entirely theoretical and one-sided assessment. It does not take into account how the rights of the operator of the plant and the individuals are connected and how they must be balanced out within the complex social realities. However, it shows us that the protect dimension should not be regarded as the precise legal anchor for procedural obligations under IHRL, either, even in

[127] Shue, 52. Emphasis added.

[128] Special Rapporteur on the Right to Adequate Food, Eide Report, para. 68.

cases where the administration's task is that of balancing different private interests against each other. While the effective implementation of the obligation to protect human rights within complex social realities can necessitate or presuppose a conversation between the administration and the individual, we cannot derive obligations of administrative procedure directly or solely from it.

As we have seen, the HRC subsumed procedural obligations under the "obligation to protect" the right to life in its General Comment 36.[129] This can be explained, however, by the HRC's failure to consequently adopt the tripartite typology. In fact, it subsumes all positive obligations relating to the right to life under an obligation to protect, including such obligations that would clearly fall under the "fulfil" dimension when following Eide's tripartite typology, e.g., the right to live in dignity. According to the committee, the measures necessary to ensure the right to live in dignity can include the provision of "essential goods and services such as food, water, shelter health care, electricity and sanitation, and other measures to promote and facilitate adequate general conditions, such as the bolstering of effective emergency health services, emergency response operations (including firefighters, ambulance services and police forces) and social housing programmes".[130] When using the tripartite terminology, however, one should not subsume procedural obligations under the obligation to protect.

7.2.3.2.3 The Obligation to Fulfil as the Precise Legal Anchor

We are left with the obligation to fulfil human rights as the precise legal anchor for obligations of administrative procedure. In its most recent General Comment 26 on land issues, the CESCR has defined the obligation to fulfil as requiring states to "adopt legislative, administrative, budgetary, and other measures and establish effective remedies aimed at the full enjoyment of Covenant rights".[131] In the paragraphs following the definition of the obligation to fulfil the CESCR directly addresses *how* states must administer land-related issues. It subsumes the proper administration of land issues under the obligation to fulfil. The committee states that this administration must be free from discrimination, accessible, prompt and effective and that marginalised groups must be supported in using those land-related administrative services.[132] With these paragraphs, it is clear that the CESCR situates obligations relating to the design of the administrative

[129] HRC, GC 36, para. 19.

[130] Ibid, para. 26.

[131] CESCR, GC 26, para. 32.

[132] Ibid, paras. 33–34.

decision-making process within the obligation to fulfil human rights. By discussing "[p]articipation, consultation, and transparency" in a stand-alone section before turning to the "specific obligations" to respect, protect and fulfil, the CESCR seeks to highlight the functional relevance of administrative procedure to all three dimensions. It does not conceive of obligations of administrative procedure as additional, stand-alone human rights obligations. The same interpretation should be applied when the committee mentions procedural obligations under headings like "implementation" or "remedy".

Zooming in a bit closer on the obligation to fulfil, the reason for the CESCR's situating obligations of administrative procedure there becomes clearer. The obligation to fulfil human rights consists of three sub-obligations: the obligations to facilitate, provide and promote.[133] In its General Comment 14 on the right to health, e.g., the committee defines these three elements of the obligation to fulfil as obligations "to take positive measures that enable and assist individuals [...] to enjoy the right to health" (facilitate), "to fulfil [...] a specific right contained in the [ICESCR] when individuals [...] are unable, for reasons beyond their control, to realize that right themselves by the means at their disposal" (provide), and "to undertake actions that create, maintain and restore the health of the population" (promote).[134]

Given what we have learned about the *raison d'être* of (administrative) procedures from the FCC's jurisprudence, the "facilitate" dimension of the obligation to fulfil is the appropriate legal anchor. We have seen that the FCC considers the involvement of the individual in the decision-making process of the administration as a means to empower the individual. Through involvement in the administrative decision-making process, individuals are given the opportunity to make their case. In other words, *ex ante* legal protection, i.e., the involvement of the affected individual in the decision-making process, is a means to "enable and assist" individuals to enjoy their rights and thereby make the realisation of their rights more effective.[135] Hence, obligations of administrative procedure should be viewed as part of the states' obligation to fulfil, and in particular, as a part of their obligation to facilitate the enjoyment of human rights.[136]

---

133 See for example CESCR, GC 14, para. 37.

134 Ibid, para. 37.

135 See *supra* Chap. 5 generally.

136 This assessment will arguably become even more convincing when we look at how the committees justify procedural involvement of affected individuals, see *infra* 8.1.

7.2.4 The Necessity of Including the Specific Rights Provisions

As we have seen, the HRC defines the legal basis for an obligation of administrative procedure relating to the right to life as "article 2 (1) [...] read in conjunction with article 6".[137] This connection is not only necessary doctrinally. It also ensures that individuals can invoke their procedural right and thus makes the procedural protection more effective.

International human rights treaties set out general obligations in one general provision and then include specific provisions that codify the rights in relation to which states must fulfil these general obligations. Due to this regulation technique, the content of a right and the corresponding obligation can only be discerned by looking at the general obligations provision and the specific provision guaranteeing the right in question together. The general obligations provision is empty, even meaningless on its own. Human rights obligations receive their content only when read together with specific human rights provisions. The measures necessary to respect, protect, and fulfil the right to life will largely be different from those required by the right to education.

The interdependence is already acknowledged in the text of the obligations provisions themselves. Article 2 ICCPR establishes the obligations of states by reference to the rights set out in the covenant: states must "respect and ensure [...] *the rights*", they must take "the necessary steps [...] to give effect to *the rights*". The same is true for Article 2 (1) ICESCR: states parties must take steps towards the "full realization of *the rights* recognized in the [ICESCR]". The CESCR has expressed this in the first sentence of its General Comment 3, when it stated that Article 2 ICESCR had a "dynamic relationship" with the other provisions of the covenant.[138] Because of this relationship between the general part of human rights law and the specific provisions, those who interpret and apply will always move from those provisions codifying the states' obligations to the individual rights provisions and back in a way that resembles a hermeneutic circle[139].

---

[137] See *supra* 7.1.1.

[138] CESCR, *General Comment No. 3: The nature of States parties' obligations (art. 2, para. 1, of the Covenant)* (1990) HRI/GEN/1/Rev.9 (Vol. I) p. 7, para. 1.

[139] For an explanation of this concept, see Theodore George, 'Hermeneutics' in Edward N. Zalta (ed), *The Stanford Encyclopedia of Philosophy* (Winter 2021 edn, Metaphysics Research Lab, Stanford University 2021) <https://plato.stanford.edu/archives/win2021/entries/hermeneutics/> accessed 26 August 2025.

We must account for this "unavoidable intersection"[140] between the obligations provisions and the specific rights provisions when reflecting on the doctrinal basis for obligations of administrative procedure under IHRL, too. This must be done by including specific rights provisions together with the general obligations provision in the doctrinal basis. The precise content of the obligation to conduct an administrative procedure to safeguard someone's right to privacy may look entirely different than the content of the obligation to conduct an administrative procedure to safeguard the same person's right to health. The specific provisions guaranteeing the human right in question must therefore be part of the doctrinal basis for obligations of administrative procedure. The doctrinal basis for obligations of administrative procedure, the precise legal anchor would not be complete without it. Practically, this means that the doctrinal basis for procedural obligations relating to the right to housing, e.g., is not just Article 2 (1) ICESCR or Article 7 ICESCR but Article 2 (1) *in connection with* Article 7 ICESCR.

Moreover, this connection enables individuals to effectively benefit from the "adequate procedural protection" as an essential element of every human *right*. The HRC has made clear that Article 2 ICCPR alone cannot give rise to a claim under Article 2 of the Optional Protocol to the ICCPR.[141] It is not possible for a state to violate its obligations *in abstracto*. They can only be violated in relation to a right. The same goes for Article 2 (1) ICESCR as this provision, too, obliges the states parties to take measures to progressively realize the rights of the covenant, too. The inclusion of specific rights provisions in the doctrinal basis of obligations of administrative procedure ensures the enforceability of these obligations. This enables individuals to bring claims based on the argument that—for example—they were not heard before a decision that interfered with their human rights, and this—in turn—is crucially important for obligations of administrative procedure to fulfil their purpose. We will learn that obligations of administrative procedure—similarly to the obligations under German fundamental rights—serve to enhance the effective implementation of human rights obligations and that they arguably also serve to enable individuals to actively participate in the realisation of their rights. Fulfilling these purposes were *a priori* denied the possibility to invoke their procedural rights before an (inter)national court or other (quasi-) judicial body.

---

[140] Ben Saul, David Kinley and Jaqueline Mowbray, *The International Covenant on Economic, Social and Cultural Rights: Commentary, Cases and Materials* (Oxford University Press 2014), 137.

[141] HRC, *P.K. v. Canada* (Comm no 1234/2003, HRC, 22 May 2007), para. 7.6.

7.3 Conclusion

This section has analysed the committees' pronouncements with regard to obligations of administrative procedure. We have seen that the committees construe these obligations as positive obligations which are part of the general doctrine on international human rights. Consequently, the committees considered Article 2 ICCPR and Article 2 ICESCR in conjunction with the provision protecting the specific right in question to be the textual basis for the obligations. Beyond this general deductive approach, there were significant gaps in the committees' constructions.

After a critical reflection on the committees' approach, we have further refined the doctrinal basis. Obligations of administrative procedure should be construed as part of the general obligation to fulfil, in particular of the "sub-obligation" to facilitate human rights. When this aspect of Article 2 (1), (2) ICCPR and Article 2 (1) ICESCR is connected to the specific right in question, we have a precise and robust doctrinal basis. Moreover, it reflects the *raison(s) d'être* for administrative procedures under IHRL to which we will turn in the next chapter.

Justifying Procedural Obligations Under IHRL

8

Deriving obligations from IHRL treaties not explicitly recognised in their texts is always in need of justification. In this section we will analyse the committees' pronouncements with a view to identifying which justifications they rely on when discussing obligations of administrative procedure (8.1). We will find that the committees rely almost exclusively on instrumental justifications. In a second step, we will reflect on these justifications, explain, and contextualise them and argue that, additionally, a dignitarian justification is conceivable under IHRL, too (8.2).

8.1 The Committees' Justifications

This section analyses the pronouncements of the committees with a view to understanding which justifications the committees rely on when stipulating procedural obligations *vis à vis* the individual. We will first look at the—rather scarce—remarks found in the pronouncements of the HRC (8.1.1), and then turn to the remarks of the CESCR which grant more insights (8.1.2). Finally, we will briefly explain why the deontological justifications found in the committees' pronouncements on indigenous rights will be disregarded for the purposes of the present thesis (8.1.3).

B. Behlert, *The Necessity of a Conversation between the Administration and the Individual*, Juridicum—Bochumer Schriften zur Friedenssicherung und zum Humanitären Völkerrecht | Bochum Studies on the International Law of Peace and Armed Conflict 72, https://doi.org/10.1007/978-3-658-50303-1_8

8.1.1 The HRC's Justification

The HRC's pronouncements are relatively thin on the justification of obligations of administrative procedure. Yet, in some places, we can find instructive remarks which show that the HRC construes procedural capacities of the individual as means to empower the individual. However, according to the committee, this is not an end in itself. Rather, the individual must be empowered to challenge exercises of public power that violate her rights in order to contribute to an effective exercise of her rights.

In General Comment 15 on "[t]he position of aliens under the Covenant" from 1986 the HRC stated:

> *Article 13 directly regulates only the procedure and not the substantive grounds for expulsion. However, by allowing only those carried out "in pursuance of a decision reached in accordance with law", its purpose is clearly to prevent arbitrary expulsions.*[1]

While the scope of Article 13 ICCPR is rather specific—it governs only the expulsions of foreigners lawfully in the territory of a state, the connection to the notion of arbitrariness the HRC draws is interesting. Considering the centrality of the notion of arbitrariness to IHRL,[2] and the fact that human rights are meant to prevent the arbitrary exercise of public power, the statement highlights the idea that procedures can support the realisation of the material contents of human rights in an interesting way.

In General Comment 21 on the humane treatment of persons deprived of their liberty, the committee highlights the enabling function of "legal means" when it holds that

> *[i]t would [...] be appropriate to specify whether arrested or detained persons have access to such information and have effective legal means enabling them to ensure that those rules are respected, to complain if the rules are ignored and to obtain adequate compensation in the event of a violation.*[3]

---

[1] HRC, *General comment No. 15: The position of aliens under the Covenant* (1986) HRI/GEN/1/Rev.9 (Vol. I) p. 189, para. 10.

[2] For an early discussion of the notion in the Universal Declaration of Human Rights (UDHR) see Parvez Hassan, 'The Word "Arbitrary" As Used In The Universal Declaration Of Human Rights: "Illegal" Or "Unjust"?' (1969) 10 Harvard International Law Journal 225. See also *infra* 8.2.1.1.2.2.

[3] HRC, *General comment No. 21: Article 10 (Humane treatment of persons deprived of their liberty)* (1992) HRI/GEN/1/Rev.9 (Vol. I) p. 202, para. 7.

The effective legal means mentioned—which can only refer to procedural or procedure-initialising capacities—shall enable the individual to ensure that rules, and ultimately her human rights, are respected. Despite the recognition of the enabling function of procedural rights, the justification relied on here is predominantly instrumental. The procedural capacities of the individual are not ends in themselves. They are means "to ensure" that human rights are respected and "to obtain adequate compensation" in the event of a violation. Nevertheless, it is notable that the HRC highlights the individual's active role in the realisation of her rights.

General Comment 35 on the right to liberty and security elaborates on this idea of enabling the individual to contribute to the effective realisation of her rights. Besides codifying the substantive right to liberty, Article 9 ICCPR stipulates explicit procedural obligations that supplement the right to liberty. Against the backdrop of these guarantees, the HRC held that administrative detentions were permissible only in exceptional circumstances and that the state party bore the burden of proof for such circumstances whenever it wanted to deprive a person of her liberty based not on criminal grounds.[4] This obligation applies "broadly to the reasons for any deprivation of liberty"[5], and it flows from Article 9 (2) ICCPR which establishes an obligation to give the reasons for any arrest or detention "at the time of arrest". The committee then went on to make detailed remarks about the purpose of this giving reasons requirement:

> *One major purpose of requiring that all arrested persons be informed of the reasons for their arrest is to enable them to seek release if they believe that the reasons given are invalid or unfounded. The reasons must include not only the general legal basis of the arrest, but also enough factual specifics to indicate the substance of the complaint, such as the wrongful act and the identity of an alleged victim.*[6]

Once again, enabling the individual is not an end in itself. The individual need not be given reasons because she is a dignified human being. Rather, she is recognised as a kind of control instance here. In this sense, the passage highlights the important facilitative function which the giving reasons requirement can have for the guarantee of an effective remedy and which we have already found in the FCC's jurisprudence.[7] Nevertheless, the individual is put in a position to play an

---

[4] HRC, *General comment No. 35, Article 9 (Liberty and security of person)* (16 December 2014) UN Doc. CCPR/C/GC/35, para. 15.

[5] Ibid, para. 24.

[6] Ibid, para. 25. Emphasis added.

[7] See *supra* 5.1.1.3.

active role in the realisation of her rights by mounting a legal challenge against her arrest.

The enabling function comes out in a passage in the committee's most recent General Comment 37 on the right of peaceful assembly, too. After recalling that "[t]he obligation to respect and ensure peaceful assemblies imposes negative and positive duties on States before, during and after assemblies"[8], the committee holds that states must "put in place a legal and institutional framework within which the right can be exercised effectively"[9]. Some paragraphs later, the committee then elaborates on what such a framework must look like:

> *A functioning and transparent legal and decision-making system lies at the core of the duty to respect and ensure peaceful assemblies. Domestic law must [...] clearly set out the duties and responsibilities of all public officials involved, be aligned with the relevant international standards and be publicly accessible. States must ensure public awareness about the law and relevant regulations, including any procedures to be followed by those wishing to exercise the right, who the responsible authorities are, the rules applicable to those officials, and the remedies available for alleged violations of rights.*[10]

In this passage, the committee does not point to the enabling function of procedures as explicitly as in the passages previously cited here. Notably, however, it demands that states ensure public awareness *inter alia* about the "procedures to be followed by those wishing to exercise the right". This awareness-raising obligation is not an end in and of itself. It does not flow from the position of the individual under IHRL or the like. Rather, the transparency of the decision-making system serves the implementation of the states' duty to respect and ensure human rights. It serves to facilitate the effective enjoyment of the right to peaceful assembly.

The connection between the effective implementation of human rights and procedure is addressed from a different angle regarding the right to freedom of information. In General Comment 34, the committee holds that states should adopt adequate procedures as a measure to "give effect to the right to freedom of information".[11] Here, the connection between the implementation of a human right and procedures is not "supportive" in the sense that it can enhance the implementation. Rather, the procedure is a requirement to exercise the right to

[8] HRC, GC 37, para. 23.

[9] Ibid, para. 24.

[10] Ibid, para. 28.

[11] Ibid, para. 19.

freedom of information. This is an important potential justification for procedures which we must keep in mind as well and which can play an important role in the exercise of "procedure-dependent" rights such as the right to participate in public affairs. It is, however, nothing but a variant of the instrumental justification for the particular purpose of those procedures which are logical prerequisites for the exercise of a right.

To conclude, while the HRC's pronouncements do not give away much about why the HRC derives procedural obligations from the text of the ICCPR, our main takeaway from those passages where it does say something about the *raison d'être* of procedural protection *(ex ante)* must be that the committee considers procedures to be means to the end of a better and more effective implementation of the rights enshrined in the ICCPR. Even the enabling moment of procedural participation which featured—at least also—as an end in itself in the jurisprudence of the FCC is presented as a *means to ensure* that ICCPR are respected and ensured.

8.1.2 The CESCR's Justification

The CESCR's justifications are even more clearly instrumental justifications. There is less emphasis on the active role individuals can or should play in the realisation of their rights. Instead, the CESCR focuses almost exclusively on the relevance enhancing (8.1.2.1) and the remedy facilitating functions (8.1.2.2) of administrative procedure. Given the lack of relative emphasis on an individual's autonomy under socio-economic rights, it is perhaps unsurprising that the CESCR does not so much highlight the enabling function that participation in public decision-making has for individuals, but rather the positive practical consequences it has for states' administrative bodies.

8.1.2.1 Enhancing Relevance and Legitimacy of Decision-Making Through Participation

In the pronouncements of the CESCR, the participation of potentially affected individuals plays a larger role than in the pronouncements of the HRC. In its early General Comment 4 on the right to housing, the CESCR held that in order to properly implement the right to housing, states must "take immediate measures aimed at conferring legal security of tenure [...], *in genuine consultation with affected persons and groups*".[12] In another passage in the same general comment, the CESCR refers to "genuine consultation" again, when it holds that states must adopt national housing strategies which "should reflect extensive genuine consultation with, and participation by, all of those affected, including the homeless, the inadequately housed and their representatives".[13] The CESCR mentions "relevance and effectiveness" as the two reasons for the consultation requirements.[14] While these statements relate to policy-making rather than law application, we should take note of the fact that they construe participation as a means to the end of the more relevant and better realisation of human rights.

When discussing the rights of persons with disabilities in General Comment 5, the CESCR highlights the importance of "policy-making and programme implementation [...] on the basis of close consultation with, and involvement of, representative groups of the persons concerned".[15] One paragraph before, the committee holds that states must adopt "appropriately tailored policies and programmes" necessary to address problems of persons with disabilities and highlights "the need to legislate where necessary and to eliminate any existing discriminatory legislation".[16] This context makes clear that the ends pursued by requiring participation are once again "relevance and effectiveness". The rationale here is instrumental: consultation with affected groups is necessary to identify and effectively address problems. Moreover—and in contrast to General Comment 4 –, the CESCR does not only refer to macro-level policymaking but to "programme implementation" as well. It therefore builds a bridge towards law-application. We find the same reasoning in the following general comment on the rights of older persons when the CESCR holds that "[o]lder persons should [...] participate actively in the formulation and implementation of policies that directly affect their well-being".[17]

The idea that participation can enhance the relevance and effectiveness of programmes, rules, and their implementation has since become a regular feature of the CESCR's general comments. For example, in General Comment 12 on the right to food, under the heading of "[i]mplementation at the national level", the committee states that the "formulation and implementation of national strategies

---

[12] CESCR, *General Comment No. 4: The right to adequate housing (art. 11 (1) of the Covenant)* (1991) HRI/GEN/1/Rev.9 (Vol. I) p. 11, para. 8 (a), emphasis added.

[13] Ibid, para. 12.

[14] Ibid, para. 12.

[15] CESCR, GC 5, paras. 14.

[16] Ibid, paras. 13.

[17] CESCR, GC 6, para. 39.

for the right to food requires full compliance with the principles of accountability, transparency, people's participation".[18] In General Comment 14 on the right to the highest attainable standard of health, the committee called "participation of the population in all health-related decision-making at the community, national and international levels" an "important aspect" of the right to health,[19] and stated that "the right of individuals and groups to participate in decision-making processes, which may affect their development, must be an integral component of any policy, programme or strategy developed to discharge governmental obligations under article 12"[20]. General Comment 15 contains a similar remark on the "right of individuals and groups to participate in decision-making processes that may affect their exercise of the right to water".[21] And we find similar remarks in subsequent general comments, too.[22]

The context of these statements reveals the reason behind the committee's stressing the necessity of participation in decision-making. The committee does not mention "relevance" and "effectiveness" as explicitly as in General Comment 4. However, the cited passages are about drawing up and implementing national strategies to further the realisation of human rights. The CESCR mentions how these strategies must address existing problems. For example, in General Comment 20, the CESCR states that "[i]n addition to refraining from discriminatory

---

[18] CESCR, GC 12, para. 23.

[19] CESCR, GC 14, para. 11.

[20] Ibid, paras. 54.

[21] CESCR, GC 15, para. 48.

[22] CESCR, *General comment No. 18: Article 6 of the International Covenant on Economic, Social and Cultural Rights* (6 February 2006) UN Doc E/C.12/GC/18, para. 42: *"The formulation and implementation of a national employment strategy should involve full respect for the principles of accountability, transparency, and participation by interested groups. The right of individuals and groups to participate in decision-making should be an integral part of all policies, programmes and strategies intended to implement the obligations of States parties under article 6. The promotion of employment also requires effective involvement of the community and, more specifically, of associations for the protection and promotion of the rights of workers and trade unions in the definition of priorities, decision-making, planning, implementation and evaluation of the strategy to promote employment."*; CESCR, GC 19, para. 69: *"The formulation and implementation of national social security strategies and plans of action should respect, inter alia, the principles of non-discrimination, gender equality and people's participation. The right of individuals and groups to participate in decision-making processes that may affect their exercise of the right to social security should be an integral part of any policy, programme or strategy concerning social security."*; CESCR, GC 20, para. 36: *"Individuals and groups of individuals, who may be distinguished by one or more of the prohibited grounds, should be ensured the right to participate in decision-making processes over the selection of such measures."*.

actions, States parties should take concrete, deliberate and targeted measures to ensure that discrimination in the exercise of Covenant rights is eliminated".[23] And in General Comment 12, the committee states that national strategies for the implementation of the right to food must meet the requirements of the population for which they are designed.[24] The justification for the procedural participation of the affected individuals is thus instrumental: states need information in order to target problems, in order to ensure that their strategies and their implementation meet the requirements of the ICESCR. States need to be aware of the problems so that they can address them effectively. And in order to receive the necessary information, they must involve affected individuals in their decision-making processes. It is in this sense that the committee understands the involvement of affected individuals and groups in the cited passages as a requirement for relevant and effective human rights implementation.

This justification was most clearly expressed in the CESCR's draft general comment on the issue of land and socio-economic rights, written by rapporteurs Uprimny and Windfuhr. The two rapporteurs responsible for the draft held that

> *[i]ndividuals and communities must be informed and meaningfully participate in decision-making processes that may affect their enjoyment of covenant rights in land-related contexts,* ***otherwise their legitimate rights as land users might be overseen.***[25]

The rapporteurs could not have expressed the practical justification behind the involvement of affected land owners in the decision-making process more clearly. We shall note, however, that the half-sentence emphasised here has not made it into the final general comment published.[26]

In the CESCR's General Comment 21 on the right to take part in cultural life, we find an interesting angle to the practical justification. The committee lays out "necessary conditions for the full realization of the right" as "availability,

---

[23] CESCR, GC 20, para. 36.

[24] CESCR, GC 12, paras. 21–22.

[25] CESCR, GC 26, Draft of 3 May 2021, para. 18. Emphasis added.

[26] In the final version, the passage reads: "*Participation, consultation, and transparency are key principles for the implementation of Covenant obligations, including in relation to land. Individuals and communities shall be properly informed about and allowed to meaningfully participate in decision-making processes that may affect their enjoyment of Covenant rights in land-related contexts, without retaliation.*", CESCR, GC 26, para. 20.

accessibility, acceptability, adaptability and appropriateness".[27] Under the notion of "acceptability" it makes an interesting remark:

> *Acceptability entails that the laws, policies, strategies, programmes and measures adopted by the State party for the enjoyment of cultural rights should be formulated and implemented in such a way as to be acceptable to the individuals and communities involved. In this regard, consultations should be held with the individuals and communities concerned in order to ensure that the measures to protect cultural diversity are acceptable to them [...].*[28]

Once again, the committee uses the conjunction "in order to" highlighting the instrumentality of procedural involvement of the individuals affected. This time, however, the end is different. The consultations mentioned in this passage are not meant to enhance the relevance of a decision, they are meant to secure the acceptability of an exercise of public power to those over whom power is exercised. The committee thus hints at the legitimacy-enhancing function of procedures which we will discuss in the conclusion to this thesis.[29]

8.1.2.2 Effective Legal Protection

As we have seen in our analysis of the FCC's jurisprudence, the court frames its instrumental justification for the procedural participation of the affected individual in terms of "effective legal protection".[30] We can find a similar approach in the CESCR's pronouncements. In its early General Comment 9 on the domestic implementation of the Covenant, the CESCR recognised the importance of remedies for the effective implementation of the rights recognised in the ICESCR.[31] Some years later, in an individual opinion, the committee specified its pronouncements in this regard as meaning that there "cannot be a right without a remedy to protect it".[32] This is reminiscent of the FCC dictum from the *Hamburger Deichordnungsgesetz* judgment in which the court held that effective legal protection was an "essential element of the fundamental right itself".[33]

Importantly, in cases related to the right to housing, the committee highlights the importance of both, legal protection *ex post* and legal protection *ex ante.*

[27] CESCR, GC 21, para. 16.

[28] Ibid.

[29] See *infra* 10.3.

[30] See *supra* 5.1.1.

[31] CESCR, GC 9, para. 2.

[32] CESCR, *I. D. G. v Spain (Comm no 2/2014, CESCR, 13 October 2015)*, para. 11.3.

[33] BVerfGE 24, 367 (401). See also *supra* 5.1.1.1.

Already in its General Comment 7, where the committee included a catalogue of procedural requirements to be followed before going through with a forced eviction, the idea of legal protection is evident. In particular the requirements to give "adequate and reasonable notice [...] prior to the scheduled date of eviction", to provide, in due time, "information on the proposed evictions and, where applicable, on the alternative purpose for which the land or housing is to be used", and to provide legal remedies and legal aid to those who need it[34] have a rather direct connection to legal protection.

This connection is concretised in the CESCR's views in *I.D.G. v. Spain.* The committee recalls that "adequate procedural protection is central to all human rights, and that for forced evictions, adequate and reasonable notice for all affected persons prior to the scheduled day of the eviction and legal aid for their defence" was necessary.[35] Such notice must be conducted "properly and effectively so that the persons affected have the opportunity to participate in the proceedings in the defence of their rights".[36] The enabling moment of procedure which we have seen in the HRC's pronouncements analysed in the previous section is present here, too. The notification enables the affected individual to defend her rights. This becomes even clearer when the committee goes on to say that notification by public posting could be an appropriate means of notification only when it ensured "sufficient exposure and long enough notice that the affected person has the opportunity to take full cognizance of the start of the proceedings and can be a party to them".[37] The passage also highlights the facilitative function of *ex ante* legal protection for legal protection *ex post.*

In the final paragraphs of the views, in which the CESCR formulates "general recommendations", it holds that states must "[a]dopt appropriate legislative measures to ensure that the mortgage enforcement procedure and the procedural rules contain appropriate requirements [...] and procedures to be followed *before going ahead with auction of a dwelling, or with eviction*".[38] In its views in the case of *López Albán* of 2019, the committee solidifies this framing of procedural protection as legal protection *ex ante.* In its considerations of the merits of the case, the CESCR recalled its jurisprudence on the "[p]rotection against forced eviction" and mentioned that "persons concerned [by a forced eviction] must have had prior access to an effective judicial remedy" and that "there must be a real

[34] CESCR, GC 7, para. 15.

[35] CESCR, *I.D.G. v. Spain*, para. 12.1.

[36] Ibid, para. 12.2.

[37] Ibid, para. 12.3.

[38] Ibid, para. 17. Emphasis added.

opportunity for genuine and effective prior consultation between the authorities and the persons concerned".[39] With these remarks, the committee highlights the *ex ante* character of the procedural safeguard. It shall give the individual a means to intervene in the state's plan and to halt a potentially irreversible development.

8.1.2.3 Conclusion

The CESCR, too, construes procedural involvement of the affected individual as a means to achieve a more effective implementation of human rights. In contrast to the HRC's pronouncements, the idea of enabling the individual to play an active role in the realisation of her rights by granting her certain procedural capacities is much less explicit in the CESCR's pronouncements. The vantage point from which the CESCR approaches participation seems to be more objective: procedural participation facilitates more effective, more relevant human rights implementation. Only in the context of the right to housing do we find the active role the individual must play in the realisation of her rights.

8.1.3 Indigenous Rights and Procedural Involvement as an End in Itself

Despite the committees' almost exclusive reliance on instrumental justifications, there is one context in which the committees frame involvement of affected individuals as an end in itself: minority and indigenous peoples' rights. The HRC and the CESCR both refer to the right to "free, prior, and informed consent", a particularly strong form of a right to participate in decision-making processes, and both committees frame this form of procedural participation as an end in itself.

In General Comment 23 on minority rights, Article 27 ICCPR, the HRC held that "[t]he enjoyment of [minority] rights may require positive legal measures of protection and measures to *ensure the effective participation of members of minority communities in decisions which affect them*".[40] In its views in the *Poma Poma v. Peru* case of 2006, the committee stated that

> *the admissibility of measures which substantially compromise or interfere with the culturally significant economic activities of a minority or indigenous community depends*

[39] CESCR, *López Albán v. Spain (Comm no 37/2018, CESCR, 29 November 2019)*, para. 8.3.

[40] HRC, *General comment No. 23: Article 27 (Rights of minorities)* (1994) HRI/GEN/1/Rev.9 (Vol. I) p. 207, para. 7.

> *on whether the members of the community in question have had the opportunity to participate in the decision-making process in relation to these measures and whether they will continue to benefit from their traditional economy. The Committee considers that participation in the decision-making process must be effective, which requires not mere consultation but the free, prior and informed consent of the members of the community.*[41]

By defining "effective participation" as requiring "free, prior and informed consent of the members of the community", the HRC elevates affected individuals from mere participants in the decision-making process to actual decision-makers. It even goes beyond the wording of the United Nations Declaration on the Rights of Indigenous Peoples (UNDRIP)[42] which only requires states to consult and cooperate with indigenous peoples "*in order to obtain* their free, prior and informed consent".[43] In numerous concluding observations, the committee has reaffirmed this obligation.[44] Importantly, the committee does not frame procedural participation as a means to an end. It need not be ensured "in order to" facilitate a better protection of their material rights. Rather, it is an end in itself here.

We find the same stance in the CESCR's pronouncements. In its General Comment 24 addressing social and economic and business activities, the committee mentions indigenous peoples in several places.[45] One passage is of particular interest:

---

[41] HRC, *Poma Poma v. Peru (Comm no 1457/2006, HRC, 24 April 2009)*, para. 7.6. Emphases added.

[42] *United Nations Declaration on the Rights of Indigenous Peoples* (2 October 2007) UN Doc A/RES/61/295.

[43] Articles 19 and 32 UNDRIP. Emphasis added. For a discussion of the content of the obligation, see Mauro Barelli, 'Free, Prior, and Informed Consent in the UNDRIP: Articles 10, 19, 29 (2), and 32 (2)' in Jessie Hohmann and Marc Weller (eds), *The UN Declaration on the Rights of Indigenous Peoples: A Commentary* (Oxford University Press 2018), 252–253.

[44] Tara Ward, 'The Right to Free, Prior, and Informed Consent: Indigenous Peoples' Participation Rights within International Law' (2011) 10 Northwestern University Journal of International Human Rights 54, 56. For recent examples, see HRC, *Concluding observations on the second periodic report of Ethiopia* (7 December 2022) UN Doc CCPR/C/ETH/CO/2, para. 48; HRC, *Concluding observations on the fifth periodic report of the Philippines* (30 November 2022) UN Doc CCPR/C/PHL/CO/5, para. 52; HRC, *Concluding observations on the fourth periodic report of Nicaragua* (30 November 2022) UN Doc CCPR/C/NIC/CO/4, para. 42.

[45] CESCR, *General comment No. 24 (2017) on State obligations under the International Covenant on Economic, Social and Cultural Rights in the context of business activities* (10 August 2017) UN Doc E/C.12/GC/24, paras. 12, 17, 24, 38, 46, 48, 52 and 56.

> *In exercising human rights due diligence, businesses should consult and cooperate in good faith with the indigenous peoples concerned through indigenous peoples' own representative institutions in order to obtain their free, prior and informed consent before the commencement of activities. Such consultations should allow for identification of the potentially negative impact of the activities and of the measures to mitigate and compensate for such impact.*[46]

This postulate of procedural participation also gets by without reference to improving the implementation of substantive rights or to other principles.

Why do the committees frame participation in this particular context as an end in itself, and thus in contrast to the instrumental interpretation exposed in their pronouncements in general? The reason for this arguably lies in the debate on the rights of indigenous peoples, in particular in the connection between the principles of free, prior and informed consent and the right to self-determination of (indigenous) peoples. The principle of free, prior, and informed consent is most explicitly articulated in UNDRIP. Article 19 UNDRIP states that "[s]tates shall consult and cooperate in good faith with the indigenous peoples concerned [...] in order to obtain their free, prior and informed consent before adopting and implementing legislative or administrative measures that may affect them". Other references to the principle of free, prior and informed consent can be found in Articles 10, 29 (2) and 32 (2) of the Declaration. The document frames the principle of free, prior, and informed consent as an element of the right to self-determination.[47] This framing of the convention has been described as a result of the work of indigenous rights advocates who have long framed participation rights as derivative of indigenous peoples' rights to self-determination.[48] Hence, the emphasis in the discourse and the UNDRIP has been on autonomy, self-government, and political participation of indigenous peoples.[49]

This connection between the participation rights enunciated in documents on indigenous peoples' rights and their right to self-determination might explain why the committees put such an emphasis on indigenous peoples' rights to participate in the making of decisions which concern them. Such an argument is similar to the dignity-based argument brought forward by the FCC. While those individuals

---

[46] Ibid, para. 17.
[47] Barelli, 248.
[48] Ward, 58.
[49] Marc Weller, 'Self-Determination of Indigenous Peoples: Article 3, 4, 5, 18, 23 and 46(1)' in Jessie Hohmann and Marc Weller (eds), *The UN Declaration on the Rights of Indigenous Peoples: A Commentary* (Oxford University Press 2018), 143 et seq.

under the jurisdiction of the German state must be involved in the decision-making process because they must not be mere objects of the state's exercise of public power, indigenous peoples must be consulted because they are autonomous *vis à vis* the majority of their polity[50]. When involvement in the decision-making of the German state was the operationalisation of the agency of the individuals subjected to the power of the German state, the principle of free, prior and informed consent of indigenous peoples is the operationalisation of the autonomy which indigenous peoples enjoy under their right to self-determination. In this sense, the principle of free, prior and informed consent is a "key manifestation [...] of Indigenous peoples' right to self-determination"[51].

There is evidence that the debate on indigenous rights influenced the committees in their thinking about participation in the context of indigenous rights. For example, in the CESCR's General Comment 15 focusing on cultural rights, the committee refers *inter alia* to the UNDRIP to substantiate that states parties "should respect the free, prior and informed consent of indigenous peoples in all matters covered by their specific rights".[52] At least for the CESCR it is thus clear that it ties on to the debate around indigenous peoples' rights.

For us, this specific context of the committees' pronouncements framing procedural participation as an end in and of itself means that we cannot extrapolate this ratio to other human rights. The deontological justification employed in the context of indigenous peoples' rights is of limited use in the context of other human rights. It cannot be relied on to justify general obligations of administrative procedure under IHRL. The deontological justification that the committees rely on in the context of indigenous rights will therefore be disregarded in the present analysis.

---

[50] Indigenous peoples are *per definitionem* a non-dominant part of society, Joshua Castellino and Cathal Doyle, 'Who Are 'Indigenous Peoples'?: An Examination of Concepts Concerning Group Membership in the UNDRIP' in Jessie Hohmann and Marc Weller (eds), *The UN Declaration on the Rights of Indigenous Peoples: A Commentary* (Oxford University Press 2018), 37.

[51] Nathan Yaffe, 'Indigenous Consent: A Self-Determination Perspective' (2018) 19 Melbourne Journal of International Law 703, 708.

[52] CESCR, GC 21, para. 37. This reference is certainly not without its issues. Potential frictions between the individualistic IHRL and the collective or collectivised nature of indigenous peoples rights raise several questions that cannot be addressed here. For a discussion, see Martin Scheinin and Mattias Åhrén, 'Relationship to Human Rights, and Related International Instruments' in Jessie Hohmann and Marc Weller (eds), *The UN Declaration on the Rights of Indigenous Peoples: A Commentary* (Oxford University Press 2018), 67–69, 76–79.

8.1.4 Conclusion

We have seen that both committees construe procedural involvement as a means to an end, not an end in itself. States must involve affected individuals in their decision-making processes *in order to* effectuate a better implementation of human rights. We have not found a dignitarian justification similar to the one employed by the FCC. According to the committees, adequate procedural protection is an essential element of human rights because it facilitates the effective implementation of human rights, not because IHRL construes the individual as a dignified being that must be taken seriously.

Importantly, however, the HRC attaches great weight to the enabling moment of providing individuals with procedural capacities and the active role they may play in the realisation of their rights. The CESCR, on the other hand, uses wording that suggests a more objective approach. It does not make the enabling element as explicit but relies more on general notions of "relevance and effectiveness". It is only in its views on forced evictions, that we find a framing that highlights the enabling moment of procedural involvement.

8.2 Reflecting on the Committees' Justifications

Against the backdrop of our finding that the committees rely almost exclusively on arguments highlighting the instrumentality of procedures to the effective realisation of human rights, this section seeks to do two things. Firstly, it will reflect on the instrumental justification relied on by the committees in order to understand what lies behind it (8.2.1). Secondly, we will argue that a dignitarian justification for obligations of administrative procedure is conceivable under IHRL, too (8.2.2). In a third step, we will explain how the two justifications are potentially interconnected (8.2.3).

8.2.1 Instrumental Justifications for Procedural Obligations Under IHRL

As we have already stated prior to our analysis of the FCC's jurisprudence, instrumental justifications are justifications which construe administrative procedure and the involvement of the affected therein as means to an end. In the pronouncements of the committees, we find the better, more effective implementation of human rights as the end. Given the relative paucity of the committees on why and how exactly administrative procedure can contribute to this end, we will reflect on these questions. To this end, we will discuss the principle of effectiveness in international law and its relevance to IHRL (8.2.1.1). In a second step, we will highlight the role of the right to an effective remedy in securing the effective implementation of human rights, and how involving the affected individual in administrative decision-making processes can contribute to it (8.2.1.2).

8.2.1.1 Effectiveness

Effectiveness is the criterion that the committees use to assess whether states comply with their human rights obligations in their implementation of these obligations.[53] We find the criterion of effectiveness already in the text of the covenants. Article 2 (2) ICCPR, e.g., obliges states to take "measures as may be necessary to *give effect* to the rights recognized in the [...] Covenant". In contrast, Article 2 ICESCR does not hint at "effectiveness" in the same way as Article 2 (2) ICCPR. However, the CESCR has made up for that. In General Comment 9 on the implementation of the ICESCR rights, it holds that states have an obligation "to use all the means at its disposal to *give effect* to the rights recognized in the Covenant".[54] And Article 22 ICESCR refers to the "effective progressive implementation of the [...] Covenant" as well.

Effectiveness is first and foremost discussed as a principle of treaty interpretation. In this section, we will firstly explain how the principle is understood in general international law and what its specific relevance is to IHRL (8.2.1.1.1). This will provide us with the backdrop to make the argument that the involvement of affected individuals in the administrative decision-making process will often be required to realise human rights effectively (8.2.1.1.2).

8.2.1.1.1 The Principle of "Effectiveness" in (Human Rights) Treaty Interpretation

The principle of effectiveness is a central interpretive principle in international law. The ICJ even called the principle "one of the fundamental principles of interpretation of treaties"[55]. It is correctly understood as deriving from object and purpose interpretation.[56] To understand the principle, one must distinguish

[53] Tomuschat, *Human Rights: Between Idealism and Realism*, 174.

[54] CESCR, GC 9, para. 2 (emphasis added).

[55] *Territorial Dispute (Libyun Aruh Jamuhiriyu/Chad)* [1994] ICJ Rep 6, para. 51.

[56] Malgosia Fitzmaurice, 'Interpretation of Human Rights Treaties' in Dinah Shelton (ed), *The Oxford Handbook of International Human Rights Law* (Oxford University Press 2013), 746.

its two dimensions.[57] The first dimension is commonly referred to with the Latin maxim of *ut res magis valeat quam pereat*, or, in short, the *ut res* maxim. It requires the interpreter of a provision of international law to prefer an interpretation that gives a term a meaning and a role over one that does not.[58] According to the *ut res* maxim, an interpretation "reducing whole clauses or paragraphs of a treaty to redundancy or inutility"[59] is inadequate.[60]

The second dimension of the principle of effectiveness is of a more general nature. It demands that the interpreter go with the interpretation that realizes the aims—or the object and purpose—of the treaty best.[61] This dimension is arguably more important to IHRL given the field's necessarily heavy reliance on object and purpose interpretation. The reason for this was brilliantly explained by Başak Çalı in an article dealing with the suitability of the general rules of treaty interpretation for interpreting IHRL treaties. Çalı begins her argument about the particular reliance of IHRL on teleological interpretation from the observation that human rights treaties are necessarily vague.[62] Their vagueness is a "function of the non-mechanical context in which human rights claims arise".[63] Human rights apply "to a much larger universe of situations than many other international treaties".[64] If they were not relatively vague, they would not be able to govern the theoretically endless of situations in which individuals encounter the state. This vagueness, however, will often make relying on the textual and systematic interpretation rather fruitless.[65] To use the famous metaphor of the International Law Commission, textual and systematic interpretation will often not give us

[57] Richard Gardiner, *Treaty interpretation* (2nd edn, Oxford University Press 2015), 66.

[58] ibid, 168.

[59] WTO Appellate Body, Korea—Definitive Safeguard Measure on Imports of Certain Dairy Products (WT/DS98/AB/R) [2000] 1 DSR 3, paras. 80–81. Emphasis in original. Footnotes omitted.

[60] For an illustrative application of this dimension, see *Application of the International Convention on the Elimination of All Form of Racial Discrimination, (Georgia v. Russian Federation)* (Preliminary Objections) [2011] 59 Rep 70, paras. 133–134.

[61] Gardiner, *Treaty interpretation*, 168.

[62] The connection between the vagueness of human rights provisions and a necessity to pay particular attention to the object and purpose of a treaty has already been pointed to by Daniel Rietiker, 'The Principle of "Effectiveness" in the Recent Jurisprudence of the European Court of Human Rights: Its Different Dimensions and Its Consistency with Public International Law—No Need for the Concept of Treaty *Sui Generis*' (2010) 79 Nordic Journal of International Law 245, 254.

[63] Çalı, 'Specialized Rules of Treaty Interpretation: Human Rights', 531.

[64] Ibid, 531.

[65] Ibid, 531.

much to throw into the crucible[66] in which we melt the ingredients provided by Article 31 (1) VCLT into the interpretation of a rule or a treaty. In order to still achieve an interpretation, one must throw in more object and purpose.[67] The particular value of Çalı's argument is that it does not rely on metaphysical or political arguments about the nature of human rights but that it is—as she herself points out—"functional and descriptive".[68]

So, the second dimension of the principle of effectiveness which emphasises the object and purpose of a treaty is especially relevant to IHRL treaties because interpreters will often rely heavily on the object and purposes of these treaties. To better grasp the second dimension of the effectiveness principle in the context of human rights, we will have a look at the jurisprudence of the ECtHR. In its famous case of *Airey v Ireland*, the ECtHR held that "[t]he Convention is intended to guarantee rights that are *not theoretical or illusory*, but rights that are *practical and effective*"[69], a pronouncement it later upheld in several cases, e.g., in the case of *Loizidou v Turkey* in which the court held that the provisions of the European Convention of Human Rights (ECHR) must be "interpreted and applied so as to make its safeguards practical and effective"[70]. According to Çalı, these passages highlight the first dimension of the effectiveness principle because "the distinction between formalistic protection versus effective protection offers an animating reason to choose between conflicting understandings of the wording of the text".[71] However, as we have seen, the first dimension—the *ut res* maxim—is not a rejection of a formalistic understanding of words. It is rather the demand that the interpreter not disregard words entirely but give them any meaning at all. "Practical and effective" is not the opposite of human rights provisions devoid of meaning. Rather, it describes a general aspiration of human rights that are supposed to make the lives of their holders noticeably better. So,

---

66 On the crucible approach of the ILC generally, see Richard Gardiner, 'The Vienna Convention Rules on Treaty Interpretation' in Duncan B. Hollis (ed), *The Oxford Guide to Treaties* (Oxford University Press 2012), 480–481, as well as Mark Eugen Villiger, 'The Rules on Interpretation: Misgivings, Misunderstandings, Miscarriage? The 'Crucible' Intended by the International Law Commission' in Enzo Cannizzaro (ed), *The Law of Treaties Beyond the Vienna Convention* (Oxford University Press 2011), 113–114.

67 Çalı, 'Specialized Rules of Treaty Interpretation: Human Rights', 533.

68 Ibid, 533.

69 ECtHR, *Airey v Ireland* (App no 6289/73, ECtHR, 9 October 1979), para. 24. Emphases added.

70 ECtHR, *Loizidou v Turkey* (Preliminary Objections) (App no 15318/89, ECtHR, 23 March 1995), para. 72.

71 Çalı, 'Specialized Rules of Treaty Interpretation: Human Rights', 539.

when the ECtHR speaks of "practical and effective" rights, it speaks of the ECHR as a whole, and its object and purpose. The words of the judgment are more of a general statement about the Convention than about how to interpret particular words in order to retain their meaning. They thus relate to the second dimension of the effectiveness principle and provide a useful expression of it. Fitzmaurice therefore rightly argued that "the reliance on the 'object and purpose rule' to interpret human rights treaties can be viewed as having as its primary aim the effective application of such treaties".[72]

The similarities to Häberle's "open fundamental rights doctrine" are evident.[73] Häberle was concerned with how fundamental rights doctrine should adapt to challenges of the times in order to ensure that fundamental rights effectively keep fulfilling their function under changing circumstances. This becomes even more apparent when looking at the "living instrument" doctrine developed by the ECtHR. The doctrine is a specific application, or consequence, of the principle of effectiveness in treaty interpretation.[74] According to this doctrine, the ECHR is "a living instrument which […] must be interpreted in the light of present day conditions".[75] The doctrine makes clear that the "determinative point in time for the interpretation is the present and not the past".[76] Behind the doctrine is a concern for the efficacy of human rights protection.[77] Given that there was a

[72] Fitzmaurice, 764.

[73] For a discussion of what Häberle meant by this, see *supra* 3.2.

[74] Çalı, 'Specialized Rules of Treaty Interpretation: Human Rights', 539, Rietiker, 260–267. In Goodwin v UK, the ECtHR directly combines the *Airey* version of the effectiveness principle and the living instrument doctrine: *"since the Convention is first and foremost a system for the protection of human rights, the Court must have regard to the changing conditions within the respondent State and within Contracting States generally and respond, for example, to any evolving convergence as to the standards to be achieved* […]. *It is of crucial importance that the Convention is interpreted and applied in a manner which renders its rights practical and effective, not theoretical and illusory. A failure by the Court to maintain a dynamic and evolutive approach would indeed risk rendering it a bar to reform or improvement"*, ECtHR, *Goodwin v The United Kingdom* (App no 28957/95, ECtHR, 11 July 2002), para. 74. References omitted.

[75] ECtHR, *Tyrer v The United Kingdom* (App no 5856/72, ECtHR, 25 April 1978), para. 31.

[76] Christian Djeffal, *Static and Evolutive Treaty Interpretation: A Functional Reconstruction* (Cambridge University Press 2016), 302.

[77] Pierre-Marie Dupuy, 'Evolutionary Interpretation of Treaties: Between Memory and Prophecy' in Enzo Cannizzaro (ed), *The Law of Treaties Beyond the Vienna Convention* (Oxford University Press 2011), 136.

lively exchange between European constitutional law scholars in the 1970s,[78] it is perhaps not surprising that the "living instrument doctrine" has many similarities with Häberle's "open fundamental rights doctrine".

A word of caution is necessary here, too: While the focus on teleological interpretation in human rights law will generally mean "interpret[ing] in favour of the individual"[79], interpreters must be careful that an effectiveness approach towards treaty interpretation does not lead to unwarranted "expansionism" of treaty obligations.[80] We have already observed that the vagueness and flexibility of IHRL and the thus conditioned particular reliance on the object and purpose of IHRL treaties when interpreting them makes the field of law particularly susceptible to being influenced by the political and moral perceptions of the interpreter.[81] However, there is no automatism that an effective (and hence flexible) interpretation of IHRL will lead to illegitimate human rights overreach.[82] What matters, once more, is a transparent and honest approach to interpretation.[83]

8.2.1.1.2 Effective Human Rights Implementation and the Role of Legal Protection *Ex Ante*

While the principle of effectiveness is often discussed in the context of treaty interpretation, it is just as applicable to the implementation of treaties. If one would stop at the interpretation of a text when seeking to make rights "practical and effective", this goal would never be reached. One can come up with the most sophisticated interpretations of provisions of IHRL. If states do not implement them, if they do not put an effective interpretation of a human rights provision into practice, they will never become "practical and effective". They will

[78] Djeffal explains how, in the 1970s, concerns for the effective protection of individual rights and respective suggestions for flexible approaches were *en vogue* across the Western world, Djeffal, 303.

[79] IACtHR, *19 Tradesmen v Colombia* (Series C No 109, IACtHR, 5 July 2004), para. 173.

[80] For an example of this frequently made argument see Gerald Fitzmaurice, 'Vae Victis or Woe to the Negotiators—Your Treaty or Our Interpretation of It' (1971) 65 American Journal of International Law 358, 373. Moreover, Special Rapporteur Waldock in his report for the International Law Commission (ILC) was also concerned that an effectiveness approach towards treaty interpretation could result in unwarranted expansionism, *Third Report of the Special Rapporteur, Sir Humphrey Waldock (Sixteenth Session of the ILC (1964))* A/CN.4/167 and Add.1–3, ILC Yb. 1964, Volume II, 5, 60–61.

[81] See *supra* 2.4.3.

[82] Çalı, 'Specialized Rules of Treaty Interpretation: Human Rights', 540.

[83] See *supra* 2.4.3.

instead remain "theoretical and illusory". Hence, the committees use "effectiveness" as the criterion for an acceptable implementation of IHRL.[84] And hence, the idea of effectiveness can serve as a theoretical underpinning of the committees' instrumental justification for the conversation between the administration and the individual identified above.

We have already seen how the involvement of the affected individual in administrative decision-making can further the effective implementation of individual rights when analysing the jurisprudence of the FCC.[85] We have seen that an administrative agent will often only be able to conduct a proper proportionality test after having had an exchange with the individual whose legal position she is about the change. Moreover, we have discussed how an effective implementation of the principle of equality can require a conversation between the affected individual and the administration of a state, too. In the following sub-sections, we will argue that these utilitarian rationales are just as applicable to IHRL. To this end, we will emphasise the pragmatic nature of the arguments (8.2.1.1.2.1) and discuss the utility of involving the affected individual in administrative decision-making processes for the protection against arbitrary state action (8.2.1.1.2.2), as well as its utility for the implementation of the principles of proportionality (8.2.1.1.2.3), and equality (8.2.1.1.2.4).

8.2.1.1.2.1 The Pragmatic Nature of the Arguments

Before discussing the instrumentality of involving the affected individual in administrative decision-making for certain general aspects of IHRL, it is important to highlight the pragmatic nature of the arguments found in the FCC's instrumental justification.[86] Their pragmatic nature constitutes at least an important *prima facie* argument for the transferability of the arguments to IHRL. The arguments are not value-based. They do not relate to specific political, cultural, or metaphysical conditions but constitute, in essence, pragmatic arguments.[87] They merely highlight the instrumentality—or "utility"—of legal protection *ex ante* for

---

[84] Cf. Tomuschat, *Human Rights: Between Idealism and Realism*, 174.

[85] See *supra* 5.1.

[86] For the FCC's instrumental justification see *supra* 5.1.

[87] For a definition of pragmatic argument, see Chaïm Perelman, 'Pragmatic Arguments' (1959) 34 Philosophy 18, 18: *"[A]n argument is pragmatic when it consists in estimating an action, or any event, or a rule or whatever it may be, in terms of favourable or unfavourable consequences"*.

(other) fundamental features of general fundamental rights doctrine.[88] Because of their pragmatic nature, such arguments are inherently "capable of winning broader public allegiance—where the relevant public is global"[89]. The only theoretical precondition for these arguments to be convincing is that one accepts the importance of an effective realisation of IHRL—which is a premise non-critical research in international human rights such as the present thesis is necessarily built on.

8.2.1.1.2.2 Effective Human Rights Protection Against Arbitrariness

According to the ICJ, the protection against arbitrary treatment "lies at the heart of the rights guaranteed by the international norms protecting human rights.[90] Bjorge has pointed out that the ICJ rightfully focuses on the prevention of arbitrary treatment of individuals by the state and thereby takes the principle of effectiveness in the context of IHRL seriously.[91] The notion of arbitrariness has been enshrined in IHRL from its very inception.[92] Preventing arbitrary state behaviour has always been central to the project of IHRL. Dyzenhaus has rightfully pointed out that arbitrary behaviour is "an affront to human dignity", and its prevention is one of the fundamental principles of human rights law because it impairs one's ability to plan one's life.[93]

Importantly, in IHRL, arbitrary state behaviour must not be equated with illegal state behaviour. Rather, it "include[s] elements of inappropriateness, injustice, lack of predictability and due process of law, as well as elements of reasonableness, necessity and proportionality".[94] In other words, it is perfectly possible

88 Golder uses the word "utility" to explain a pragmatic justification of human rights, Ben Golder, 'Theorizing Human Rights' in Anne Orford and Florian Hoffmann (eds), *The Oxford Handbook of the Theory of International Law* (Oxford University Press 2016), 685.

89 Joshua Cohen, 'Minimalism About Human Rights: The Most We Can Hope For?' (2004) 12 The Journal of Political Philosophy 190, 192.

90 ICJ, *Ahmadou Sadio Diallo (Republic of Guinea* v. *Democratic Republic of the Congo)* [2010] ICJ Rep 639, para. 65.

91 Eirik Bjorge, *The Evolutionary Interpretation of Treaties* (Oxford University Press 2014), 52.

92 Cf. Hassan.

93 David Dyzenhaus, 'Dignity in Administrative Law: Judicial Deference in a Culture of Justification' in Dieter Grimm, Alexandra Kemmerer and Christoph Möllers (eds), *Human Dignity in Context: Explorations of a Contested Concept* (Nomos 2018), 244. We will return to this point at the end of this chapter as it provides an interesting connection between the instrumental justification discussed here, and the dignitarian justification suggested in the following section.

94 HRC, GC 34, para. 12. Reference omitted.

that an exercise of public power complies with the law of a state party but is nevertheless arbitrary.

Procedural rules have always been understood to aim at the prevention, or at least, the reduction of arbitrariness, too.[95] To illustrate this point, we can look to the duty to give reasons. In addition to the facilitative function it has for *ex post* legal protection,[96] it also aims at disciplining administrative decision-makers.[97] Knowing that one will have to justify one's decision makes it a lot harder for someone to reach a completely arbitrary decision.[98] The same goes for involving the individual in the decision-making process. Once the administrative official has been confronted with the views of the individual, it will be more difficult for her to disregard them. Moreover, an individual can also critically reflect upon and challenge the views of the administrative agent insofar as the agent is giving them away in the conversation already. This can also put the administrative agent in a position to justify herself and have a similar disciplining effect as the giving reasons requirement.

In that sense, administrative procedure and the involvement of the affected individual in administrative decision-making, in particular the duty to give reasons is a "formal commitment to a model of decision-taking which is rational"[99] and thus to a model of decision-making that is antithetical to arbitrariness. Hence, the involvement of the individual can help address the arbitrary ab(use) of public power and thus make an important contribution to what lies "at the heart of IHRL".[100]

8.2.1.1.2.3 Proportionality

We have discussed the utility of administrative procedure, of the involvement of the affected individual in the administrative decision-making process for an effective implementation of the principle of proportionality above.[101] Originally a German doctrinal concept, proportionality has long conquered legal thinking in other fields and jurisdictions, including IHRL. In fact, it has been so successful

[95] Della Cananea aptly describes administrative procedures as a "shield against arbitrariness", Della Cananea, 19.

[96] On this point, see *infra* 8.2.1.2.2.3.

[97] Michael Fordham, 'Reasons: The Third Dimension' (1998) 3 Judicial Review 158, 158.

[98] This certainly presupposes that the administrative official has a conscience. But we will have to operate based on this assumption.

[99] A. P. Le Sueur, 'Legal Duties to Give Reasons' (1999) 52 Current Legal Problems 150, 155.

[100] ICJ, *Diallo*, para. 65.

[101] See *supra* 5.1.2.1.

that it has been called "Germany's biggest exporting legal doctrine, the BMW of constitutional theory"[102]. Certainly, there are differences between the FCC's proportionality test and the proportionality tests found in the pronouncements of (quasi-)judicial human rights bodies.[103] However, the differences are in the details and the idea that limitations on human rights must be proportionate to the aim sought, is just as familiar to IHRL as it is to German constitutional law.[104] Notwithstanding regional and jurisdictional variations, proportionality has become the standard method for human rights decision-making.[105] To explain the connection between proportionality and human rights, we can therefore refer to what we have already found out about the connection between constitutional rights and proportionality in our analysis of the FCC's jurisprudence.[106]

In the face of the centrality of proportionality to IHRL as well, we can ask: Without having a conversation with the affected individual, how shall the administrative official have sufficient information to sound out what is legally and factually possible? How will she be able to conduct a proper proportionality test? The implementation of human rights is a constant delineation of freedoms. It always involves setting priorities—public goods over individual rights, the rights of one individual over the rights of another and so on. These questions must always be answered by proportionality analysis. Practically, this will more often than not require a conversation with the affected individual.

Another aspect we should highlight in connection with the proportionality principle is how administrative procedure—and this taps into the territory of the following section already—facilitates *ex post* legal review by making the proportionality test interpersonally comprehensible. The principle of proportionality has a rationalising function. It is "a framework based on a structured method

---

[102] George Letsas, 'Rescuing Proportionality' in Rowan Cruft, S. Matthew Liao and Massimo Renzo (eds), *Philosophical Foundations of Human Rights* (Oxford University Press 2015), 323.

[103] For an overview, see Arai-Takahashi, 453 ff.

[104] Kälin and Künzli, 92–93; Tomuschat, *Human Rights: Between Idealism and Realism*, 105–106. For a clear expression of this, see HRC GC 31, para. 6: *"Where [...] restrictions are made, States must demonstrate their necessity and only take such measures as are proportionate to the pursuance of legitimate aims in order to ensure continuous and effective protection of Covenant rights."*

[105] Charles-Maxime Panaccio, 'In Defence of Two-Step Balancing and Proportionality in Rights Adjudication' (2011) XXIV Canadian Journal of Law and Jurisprudence 109.

[106] See *supra* 5.1.2.1.

of thought"[107] that "emphasises the need to rationally justify a limitation of a constitutionally protected right"[108]. It rationalises the normative, otherwise mostly intuitive process of balancing by dividing it into steps and thus forces the decision-maker to "think analytically" and consider aspects that might otherwise be forgotten.[109] Involving the affected individual in that decision-making process by having a conversation with her, in particular by sharing the reasons for the decisions, makes this thought process understandable to others. It enables the individual to comprehend the decision and the way it was reached, to evaluate it, and to either accept it or try to take legal action against it. In the latter case, it ultimately enables the judiciary to exercise its function of reviewing (the rationality of) the decision. This facilitation of communication about an otherwise intuitive, and therefore unrelatable process of balancing two legal positions is existential to redeeming the principle of proportionality's commitment to rationality.

8.2.1.1.2.4 Equality

In our analysis of the FCC's jurisprudence, we have seen that the principle of equality, in particular in the form of equal application of the law (*"Rechtsanwendungsgleichheit"*) can require administrative procedures and the involvement of the affected individual therein.[110] This argument, too, was practical in nature: the principle of equality demands equal issues to be treated equally and unequal issues to be treated unequally. And to know what is equal and what is not, the administrative agent will need information which she will often only get from the affected individual herself. This argument can be extrapolated to IHRL with relatively little effort as well.

Equality is a fundamental principle of IHRL in the sense that the basic promise of human rights law is that *every*one enjoys human rights. This was human rights law's "point of departure".[111] The very idea of *human* rights was that *all* human beings enjoy them equally. This is reflected in the language of IHRL instruments. Article 1 UDHR, e.g., states that "[a]ll human beings are born free and equal in dignity and rights". The language of the covenants reflects that in almost all of their substantive provisions when they, e.g., state that "everyone enjoys" a certain right.

---

[107] Aharon Barak, *Proportionality: Constitutional Rights and their Limitations* (Cambridge University Press 2012), 459.

[108] Ibid, 458.

[109] Ibid, 461.

[110] See *supra* 5.1.2.2.

[111] Tomuschat, *Human Rights: Between Idealism and Realism*, 74.

This fundamental idea is concretized in obligations of non-discrimination and rights to equal legal protection under the ICCPR and the ICESCR. Both covenants include a prohibition of discrimination in their implementation provisions, Article 2 (1) ICCPR and Article 2 (2) ICESCR. Moreover, there are individual guarantees in the covenants which secure specific equality rights.[112] Most importantly, perhaps, the ICCPR contains an explicit general guarantee of equality before the law in its Article 26. In the words of the HRC, Article 26 ICCPR "does not merely duplicate the guarantee already provided for in article 2 but provides in itself an autonomous right".[113] In fact, Article 26 ICCPR goes beyond Article 2 in that it is "not limited to those rights provided for in the Covenant".[114] It does not only require states to provide consistent treatment to individuals under their jurisdiction regarding the rights enshrined in the ICCPR or in IHRL for that matter but for every legal position an individual has *vis à vis* a state[115].

Equality thus has a "multidimensional relationship" with IHRL.[116] On the one hand, it is a foundational principle. It has shaped human rights from their very inception and has important connections with human dignity as another foundational principle of IHRL. On the other hand, it has found immediately binding expressions in specific provisions of IHRL. Importantly, the principle of equality before the law is meant to prevent arbitrariness.[117] This can also be seen from the fact that the HRC has developed the "reasonable and objective" criterion to distinguish justified from unjustified differentiation.[118]

---

[112] The ICCPR contains specific guarantees of equal treatment for men and women, Article 3 ICCPR, a non-discrimination obligation for derogations from human rights obligations, Article 4 (1) ICCPR, a prohibition of certain acts which constitute incitement to discrimination, Article 20 (2) ICCPR, a specific provision prohibiting discrimination against children, Article 24 (1) ICCPR, a specific prohibition to discriminate based on certain grounds for the right to take part in public affairs, Article 25 ICCPR. The ICESCR refers to equality or non-discrimination specifically with regard to men and women, Article 3 ICESCR, and workers' rights, Article 7 ICESCR.

[113] HRC, *General comment No. 18: Non-discrimination* (1989) HRI/GEN/1/Rev.9 (Vol. I) p. 195, para. 12.

[114] Ibid, para. 12.

[115] Ibid.

[116] Jarlath Clifford, 'Equality' in Dinah Shelton (ed), *The Oxford Handbook of International Human Rights Law* (Oxford University Press 2013), 420.

[117] Manfred Nowak and William Schabas, *U.N. International Covenant on Civil and Political Rights: Nowak's CCPR commentary* (3rd revised edn, N.P. Engel, Publisher 2019), 746; Taylor, 730.

[118] The HRC de6veloped this criterion in three cases against the Netherlands from 1987: HRC, *Broeks v. Netherlands* (Comm no 172/1984, HRC, 9 April 1987), para. 13; HRC,

The practical considerations we have identified in the FCC's jurisprudence thus apply to IHRL, too. Equal implementation of IHRL, and a non-discriminatory implementation of national law will often require administrative agents of states to involve the affected individual in order to be aware of whether they fulfil certain criteria and of the consequences of their actions.

8.2.1.2 Effective Legal Protection

"[S]ecuring accountability is a major defining purpose of any legal order".[119] IHRL guarantees to every victim of a human rights violation a right to an effective remedy. This right to an effective remedy under IHRL is a right to effective legal protection *ex post* (8.2.1.2.1). However, the remarks of the committees as well as the findings of our analysis of the FCC's jurisprudence allow us to reflect on the value of legal protection *ex ante* for effective remedies and for an effective implementation of IHRL in general (8.2.1.2.2).

8.2.1.2.1 Legal Protection *Ex Post*: The Right to an Effective Remedy Under IHRL

We find the guarantee of an effective remedy already in Article 8 UDHR which stipulates that "[e]veryone has the right to an effective remedy by the competent national tribunals for acts violating the fundamental rights granted to him by the constitution or by law". Article 2 (3) ICCPR states that states parties undertake "[t]o ensure that any persons whose rights or freedoms as herein recognized are violated shall have an effective remedy" (lit. a)) and "[t]o ensure that any person claiming such remedy shall have his right thereto determined by competent judicial, administrative or legislative authorities, or by any other competent authority provided for by the legal system of the State, and to develop the possibilities of judicial remedy" (lit. b)). While the ICESCR does not contain an explicit stipulation of the right to an effective remedy, the CESCR has made up for this lack in its pronouncements. Already in its General Comment 3 on "[t]he nature of States parties' obligations", the committee held that the provision of judicial

Zwaan-de-Vries v. Netherlands (Comm no 182/1984, HRC, 9 April 1987), para. 13; HRC, *L.G. Danning v. Netherlands* (Comm no 180/1984, HRC, 9 April 1987), para. 13. For a discussion of the criterion and its development and application in the HRC's case law, see Taylor, 732–738.

[119] Heike Krieger and Anne Peters, 'Due Diligence and Structural Change in the International Legal Order' in Heike Krieger, Anne Peters and Leonhard Kreuzer (eds), *Due Diligence in the International Legal Order* (Oxford University Press 2020), 351–352.

remedies was among the measures necessary to implement the ICESCR whenever a right was considered justiciable.[120] Whenever a state chooses not to have in place effective remedies for potential violations, the onus to show that they were not necessary is on the state party to the covenant.[121] Other international human treaty regimes also recognise the right an effective remedy either in their text or, at least, through the practice of the respective committees.[122] The right to an effective remedy is a ubiquitous element of IHRL.

8.2.1.2.1.1 The Right to an Effective Remedy as a Right to Legal Protection *Ex Post*

The concept of "effective remedy" under IHRL refers only to *ex post* legal protection. Already the word "remedy" gives this away. The Oxford English Dictionary defines "remedy" as "[a] means of legal redress".[123] "Redress" in turn is defined as "reparation or compensation for a wrong or consequent loss"[124] or even "appeal against a decision"[125]. In line with this, Article 2 (3) ICCPR, for example, includes only persons whose rights "are violated" within its scope of application. According to the wording of the provision, an (alleged) human rights violation must have already taken place. The HRC's pronouncements in General Comment 31 further clarify this. In particular, with regard to the administration of a state, the HRC states that "[a]dministrative mechanisms are particularly required to give effect to the general obligation to investigate *allegations of violations* promptly, thoroughly and effectively through independent and impartial bodies."[126] This statement presupposes an alleged violation which the independent and impartial bodies mentioned here can look into. In this context, the HRC does not mention legal protection *vis à vis* the administration *ex ante*. The literature on

[120] CESCR, GC 3, para. 5.

[121] CESCR, GC 9, para. 3.

[122] For an overview, see Shelton, *Remedies in International Human Rights Law*, 114–119.

[123] Oxford English Dictionary, *remedy, n* (Oxford University Press 2023), entry no. 3.

[124] Oxford English Dictionary, *redress, n* (Oxford University Press 2023), entry no. 1.a.

[125] Ibid, entry no. 3.

[126] HRC, GC 31, para. 15. Emphasis added. The HRC further clarified that the right to an effective remedy is a right to effective legal protection ex post in HRC, *C. F. et al. v. Canada*, para. 6.2: *"The Covenant provides that a remedy shall be granted whenever a violation of one of the rights guaranteed by it has occurred; consequently, it does not generally prescribe preventive protection, but confines itself to requiring effective redress ex post facto."* For another example, see HRC, *Kazantzis v Cyprus* (Comm no 972/01, HRC, 7 August 2003), para. 6.6: *"article 2, paragraph 3, provides protection to alleged victims if their claims are sufficiently well-founded to be arguable to be arguable under the Covenant"*.

Art. 2 (3) ICCPR[127] and on the right to an effective remedy under IHRL more broadly[128] treats the right to an effective remedy as a right to *ex post* legal protection too. Moreover, the pronouncements of the CESCR also support such an assertion.[129] We have consequently already excluded Article 2 (3) ICCPR as the potential doctrinal basis for obligations of administrative procedure.[130] For the same reasons, the right to an effective remedy cannot function as a direct justification for legal protection *ex ante*.

8.2.1.2.1.2 Two Dimensions of the Right to an Effective Remedy

Shelton has rightfully highlighted that the right to an effective remedy under IHRL has two dimensions, a procedural and a substantive one.[131] In its substantive sense, the right to an effective remedy can demand a variety of actions from a state. It can demand "restitution, rehabilitation and measures of satisfaction, such as public apologies, public memorials, guarantees of non-repetition and changes in relevant laws and practices, as well as bringing to justice the perpetrators of human rights violations".[132] Remedies generally aim at restoring the situation of the harmed individual to how it was prior to the unwarranted interference with her rights.[133] They are primarily aimed at restitution. In cases where restitution is not possible, states have to resort to other measures such as financial compensation or apologies. Thus, the substantive content of the right to an effective remedy in a given case depends greatly on the nature of the violation.[134]

The procedural dimension of the right to an effective remedy, on the other hand requires that there are effective legal avenues in place for the individual who deems herself the victim of a human rights violation.[135] This dimension demands "appropriate judicial and administrative mechanisms for addressing claims of

---

127 Joseph and Castan, 867. Taylor also acknowledges that "[t]he text of Article 2 (3) (a) (through the words 'are violated') suggests that the right to an effective remedy only after a violation has been committed", Taylor, 81.

128 Kälin and Künzli, 182.

129 See, e.g., CESCR, GC 7, para. 13: *"Legal remedies or procedures should be provided to those who are affected by eviction orders."*; CESCR; GC 9, para. 3: *"remedies for violations of economic, social and cultural rights"*.

130 See *supra* 7.2.2.1.

131 Shelton, *Remedies in International Human Rights Law*, 7–8.

132 HRC, GC 31, para. 16.

133 Shelton, *Remedies in International Human Rights Law*, 10.

134 Ibid, 9–10.

135 Ibid, 8–9.

rights violations under domestic law".[136] Despite the open wording used by the HRC in the cited passage, there is a preference for a judicial remedy. In fact, judicial remedies can even be the only sufficient remedy in cases of allegations of particularly serious human rights violations.[137] What is important in any case is that the body deciding upon the remedy is independent from political constraints.[138]

The procedural dimension is about the *process* in which violations of human rights and how to address them materially are determined, i.e., which substantive actions must be taken to redress a violation. When the FCC states that "effective legal protection […] is an essential element of the fundamental right itself",[139] it refers to the German constitutional law equivalent of the procedural dimension of the right to an effective remedy under IHRL. Also, Article 19 (4) (1) Basic Law speaks of "recourse to the courts".[140] We will thus comprehend the right to an effective remedy also in this procedural sense here, unless explicitly indicated otherwise. Moreover, we will limit our considerations to access to justice against actions of administrative agents of a state. The procedural side of the right to an effective remedy has gradually been widened to include, e.g., a duty to investigate infringements of human rights by private parties.[141] For our purposes, however, we will focus on access to justice against alleged violations of human rights by the state.

8.2.1.2.1.3 *Raisons d'être* of the Right to an Effective Remedy

The right to an effective remedy is considered necessary to make sure that human rights are implemented fully and effectively.[142] It is a "necessary tool in order to

[136] HRC, GC 31, para. 15.

[137] Taylor, 78–79.

[138] Ibid, 79.

[139] See *supra* 5.1.1.

[140] See Schulze-Fielitz, paras. 39–42. Notably, Schulze-Fielitz argues that, regarding judicial protection, Article 19 (4) Basic Law as well as the procedural dimension of the fundamental rights themselves establish the same requirements.

[141] On the expansion, see Valeska David, 'The Expanding Right to an Effective Remedy: Common Developments at the Human Rights Committee and the Inter-American Court' (2014) 3 British Journal of American Legal Studies 259.

[142] Dinah Shelton, 'Human Rights, Remedies' in Anne Peters (ed), *Max Planck Encyclopedia of Public International Law (MPEPIL)* (Oxford University Press 2006), para. 1.

give full effect to the legal provisions enshrined in conventions and treaties".[143] The HRC has acknowledged that the purpose of the right to an effective remedy is to enable individuals to vindicate their human rights.[144] In that sense, the right to an effective remedy also contributes to an effective realisation of IHRL.[145] It is another building block within IHRL ensuring that human rights are "practical and effective". Moreover, the right to an effective domestic remedy is a consequence of the principle of subsidiarity, according to which states are first and foremost responsible for the realisation of international human rights.[146]

The right to an effective remedy enhances the effectiveness of human rights implementation in a number of ways. Shelton identifies four rationales for a right to an effective remedy under IHRL.[147] Firstly, there is what Shelton characterises as the primary function of remedies: compensatory or remedial justice. This, of course, refers to the function to restore the victim's situation as well as possible.[148] Secondly, effective remedies contribute to "condemnation or retribution". And in that sense, remedies "affirm, reinforce, and reify the fundamental values" enshrined in IHRL.[149] Thirdly, Shelton identifies "deterrence" as a function of remedies. The idea is that a cost-benefit analysis will deter rational actors from violating human rights if the price for violations is high enough.[150] Theoretically, this prevents human rights violations and thus contributes to a situation in which human rights are enjoyed effectively. Finally, there is the idea of "restorative justice" which relates to the ends of peace, societal healing, and the reintegration of perpetrators into society,[151] all of which are important elements of an "environment in which rights are enjoyed"[152].

---

[143] Vincent Couronne and Raphaël Maurel, 'Effective Domestic Remedy' in Hélène Ruiz Fabri (ed), *Max Planck Encyclopedia for International Procedural Law* (Oxford University Press 2019), para. 2.

[144] HRC, GC 31, para. 15.

[145] The HRC held that the right to an effective remedy must be granted "in addition to effective protection of Covenant rights", HRC, GC 31, para. 15.

[146] Couronne and Maurel, 2. Couronne and Maurel call it a "condition" of the principle of subsidiarity.

[147] Shelton, *Remedies in International Human Rights Law*, 10 ff. See also Michael Reiertsen, *Effective Domestic Remedies and the European Court of Human Rights* (Cambridge University Press 2022), 38–44.

[148] Shelton, *Remedies in International Human Rights Law*, 10–11.

[149] Ibid, 12–13.

[150] Ibid, 13–14.

[151] Ibid, 14–16.

[152] Mégret, 97.

The contributions which these functions of the right to an effective remedy make to the effective enjoyment of human rights are evident. They all significantly contribute to a societal reality in which individuals can enjoy their rights. The precondition for this contribution, however, is that the remedy is effective. And legal protection *ex ante* in the form of involving the individual in decision-making processes of the administration can make a significant contribution towards this goal. As we have seen from our analysis of the FCC's jurisprudence, sometimes legal protection *ex ante* can even be a precondition for effective *ex post* review. Or it can compensate for the potential ineffectiveness of legal protection *ex post*. It is the purpose of the next section to show that the practical arguments found in the practice of the FCC are extrapolatable to IHRL.

8.2.1.2.2 Legal Protection *Ex Ante* and its Relationship to Legal Protection *Ex Post*

In our analysis of the FCC's jurisprudence, we have identified three ways in which legal protection *ex ante* relates to legal protection *ex post*. It adds to the protection which *ex post* review offers, it can compensate for factual and legal complexities as well as for a lack of effective legal protection *ex post*, and it can facilitate *ex post* review. These functions make just as much sense in the context of IHRL. Thus, they can contribute to explaining the instrumental justification found in the committees' jurisprudence.

8.2.1.2.2.1 Additional Protection *Ex Ante*

The first function we have found in the jurisprudence of the FCC was that legal protection *ex ante* adds to legal protection *ex post*. For example, in the *Mülheim-Kärlich* judgment the court held that involving affected individuals already in the administrative decision-making process offers them opportunities to inject their views already in the procedure leading up to an initial decision.[153] This function is just as relevant under IHRL as it is under German constitutional law. Under IHRL, states are under an obligation to prevent human rights violations before they occur. While the right to an effective remedy is important for the effective enjoyment of human rights and also has a preventive deterrence function, it is necessary because the primary obligation is not always fulfilled. Not every human rights violation is prevented in the first place. In other words, the right to an effective remedy for human rights violations would be superfluous in an ideal world in which human rights violations do not occur to begin with. Hence, "state procedures that individuals are subject to need to be shaped in a way that

[153] See *supra* 5.1.1.3.

violations are avoided."[154] This includes administrative procedures as all parts of the government of a state are bound by human rights[155]. Involving the individual in the administrative decision-making process allows her to share her views and puts the administration in a position to pay appropriate consideration to her rights. In essence, the function of additional protection gives rise to a simple, quantitative argument: the more opportunities the affected individual has to present her views and to defend her case, the better the potential protection of her interests.[156]

8.2.1.2.2.2 The Compensatory Function of Legal Protection *Ex Ante*

The second function of involving the affected individual in the administrative decision-making process is compensatory. Procedural protection *ex ante* can compensate for factual and legal complexities and uncertainties revolving around a decision, as well as for the inaptness of legal protection *ex post* to address a situation. In our analysis of German constitutional law, we could find an example for the compensatory function regarding legal and factual difficulties in the dissenting opinion of judges Simon and Heußner to the *Mülheim-Kärlich* judgment. Because the permit procedure for a nuclear power plant was so fraught with practical and legal complexities, the judges argued, a careful procedure in which the views of the affected individuals are adequately considered was imperative. And we found an example of procedural safeguards in an administrative procedure compensating for a lack of appropriate hindsight protection in the FCC's jurisprudence on judicial review of exam decisions.[157]

The example of nuclear power plant permit procedures is directly extrapolatable to IHRL. In 1984, the HRC issued a general comment on the right to life in which it discussed the specific dangers resulting from the existence of nuclear weapons.[158] It has reiterated the concerns voiced therein in its recent General Comment 36 on the right to life.[159] While these documents deal with

---

[154] Anja Seibert-Fohr, 'Domestic Implementation of the International Covenant on Civil and Political Rights pursuant to its article 2 para. 2' (2001) 5 Max Planck Yearbook of United Nations Law 399, 459.

[155] HRC, GC 31, para. 4. In this regard, Kälin and Künzli rightfully point out that international law is no different from international law in general, Kälin and Künzli, 69.

[156] For a short overview of this argument in common law jurisprudence, see Paul Daly, *Understanding Administrative Law in the Common Law World* (Oxford University Press 2021), 82–84.

[157] For a discussion of these functions, see *supra* 5.1.1.3.

[158] HRC, *General comment No. 14: Article 6 (Right to life)* (1984) HRI/GEN/1/Rev.9 (Vol. I) p. 188.

[159] HRC, GC 36, para. 66.

the danger emanating from nuclear weapons and not nuclear power plants, the elaborations on the obligation to protect the right to life are extrapolatable to peaceful applications of nuclear technology. The Chernobyl disaster of 1986 and the Fukushima disaster of 2011 are examples of the dangers to the right to life that result from peaceful applications of nuclear technology. Hence, the complex questions regarding the balancing of the right to life and the potential public good of energy safety as well as operators' rights to run the power plant arise under IHRL just as pertinently as they did and do under German constitutional law. This is especially true when considering that IHRL never applies in a vacuum but always within a national legal system which adds a further layer of complexity.

While the jurisprudence of the FCC on limited review of exam decisions can be extrapolated to IHRL, too,[160] the asylum procedure provides a particularly good example for how the administrative decision leading up to the initial decision, and in particular the administrative procedure leading up to an eventual expulsion decision can compensate for the inadequacy of effective *ex post* legal protection. Asylum procedures are "ultimately [...] about expulsion".[161] If the decision to deny someone asylum, and eventually to expel someone, is made mistakenly, it will often be impossible to repair this *ex post facto.* Once an asylum seeker with a valid claim to international protection has unlawfully been expelled from the host state and is back in her country of origin, she faces grave dangers for her human rights.[162] Latest in this situation would the rights of the asylum-seeker be nothing more than "theoretical or illusory". And *ex post* protection in the state that has violated the asylum seeker's rights by expelling her would not be suitable to address this. After all, the state in which she is now would need

[160] The HRC has explicitly recognised education as a field of application of the non-discrimination guarantee of Article 26 ICCPR, see HRC, *General comment No. 28: Article 3 (The equality of rights between men and women)* (29 March 2000) HRI/GEN/1/Rev.9 (Vol. I) p. 228, para. 31. Moreover, claims against allegedly unfair exam decisions are also conceivable based on the right to education, Article 13 ICESCR, as well as the right to work, Article 8 ICESCR, both in connection with the ICESCR's prohibition on discrimination, Article 2 (2) ICESCR. As far as exam decisions affect chances of entry into systems of higher education, Article 13 (2) (c) ICESCR is of particular importance as it states that "[h]igher education shall be made equally accessible to all, on the basis of capacity".

[161] David James Cantor, 'Reframing Relationships: Revisiting the Procedural Standards for Refugee Status Determination in Light of Recent Human Rights Treaty Body Jurisprudence' (2015) 34 Refugee Survey Quarterly 79, 89.

[162] Benedikt Behlert, 'The Obligation to Conduct Individual Refugee Status Determination Procedures under the ICCPR—Constructing a Convincing Legal Basis' (2019) 2 Humanitäres Völkerrecht (Journal of International Law of Peace and Armed Conflict) 201, 209–210.

to cooperate to reinstate her position. And her inability to avail herself of the protection of her state of origin is a central element in the refugee definition, Article 1 (A) (2) of the Convention Relating to the Status of Refugees[163]. This potential inaptness of *ex post* legal protection must be compensated for by particularly thorough procedures *ex ante* and by paying close attention to the view of the affected individual in order to ensure that her human rights remain "practical and effective". This example illustrates well what Konrad Hesse meant when he made the point that "[t]he danger of devaluation of the substantive fundamental rights positions due to delayed protection can only be countered by procedural arrangements that take this situation into account."[164] And it highlights why Judge Böhmer, in his separate opinion from 1978 stated that "[i]n essence, due process [was] the only possibility to enforce or effectively guarantee fundamental rights"[165]

8.2.1.2.2.3 The Facilitative Function of Legal Protection *Ex Ante*

The facilitative function of legal protection *ex ante* has played a role in the committees' pronouncements, too. We have seen it in the case law of the CESCR on the right to housing, as well as in the HRC's remarks on the *raison d'être* of detainees being given the reasons for their arrest. The argument is the same as in the jurisprudence of the FCC: legal protection *ex ante* can facilitate remedies against alleged violations of human rights. While the compensatory and the enhancing function of legal protection *ex ante*, together with legal protection *ex post,* directly make the implementation of the material right itself (more) effective, the facilitative function describes how procedural involvement *ex ante* makes this implementation indirectly more effective by enabling an effective remedy.

Of particular relevance to the facilitative function is the giving reasons requirement. It facilitates accountability of public administrative bodies through the judiciary.[166] On the one hand, it enables individuals to challenge decisions which they consider unjustified.[167] By letting the affected individual know why and how a certain decision was reached, the individual is put in a position to challenge the decision effectively. Giving individuals the reasons for an administrative decision

---

163 Convention Relating to the Status of Refugees (adopted 28 July 1951, entered into force 22 April 1954) 189 UNTS 137.

164 Hesse, 436.

165 BVerfGE 49, 220 (235).

166 Della Cananea, 63–64.

167 Mark Elliott, 'Has the Common Law Duty to Give Reasons Come of Age Yet?' [2011] Public Law 56, 62.

is "an invitation to question" that decision.[168] Should the individual not agree with the decision, she can challenge it. Her right to an effective remedy becomes "practical and effective" when she is put in a position to argue against the decision in a targeted fashion. Her challenge will then not resemble a gamble but can be based on a rational estimation of its chances for success. In other words, "[i]n the absence of reasons to protest against, the right of appeal would be nugatory".[169] This enabling rationale for giving reasons requirements was also relied upon by the ICJ in the Diallo judgment.[170]

On the other hand, the giving reasons requirement enables courts and other bodies to effectively conduct their review function. For courts, the duty to give reasons provides "the lens through which compliance with [...] the law is evaluated".[171] Administrative procedure therefore does not only facilitate judicial review by enabling the individual to challenge a decision. It also facilitates judicial review by enabling courts to exercise their review function. Given the unequivocally accepted value of effective remedies for IHRL, it is no surprise that the facilitative function of legal protection *ex ante* has been highlighted in the literature[172].

8.2.1.3 Conclusion

The committees rely on instrumental justifications to explain why procedural guarantees are necessary, why they constitute "essential elements of all human rights". To them, the participation of the affected individual in the decision-making process is a means to an end. However, they do not elaborate upon that instrumental justification. In this section, we have attempted this in the committees' stead. We found that the principle of effectiveness can provide us with the theoretical underpinnings for the instrumental justification. To make human rights

---

168 Le Sueur, 156.

169 Daly, 98. Notably, Daly explains that a general right to be given reasons for an administrative decision does not exist in most common law systems due to reasons of efficiency and effectiveness in administrative decision-making, but that—whenever a statue explicitly provides for judicial recourse against a decision, the giving reasons requirement is accepted as a necessary facilitation of that recourse.

170 ICJ, *Diallo*, para. 84.

171 Dyzenhaus, 264. Ahmed and Perry have made the interesting argument that, in addition to enabling the reviewing bodies to comprehend the administration's reasons for the decision, it enables these bodies to understand when to defer to the administration, see Farrah Ahmed and Adam Perry, 'Expertise, Deference, and Giving Reasons' [2011] Oxford Student Legal Research Paper Series.

172 Jarrod Hepburn, 'The Duty to Give Reasons for Administrative Decisions in International Law' (2012) 61 International and Comparative Law Quarterly 641, 655–661.

"practical and effective", involving the affected individual in the decision-making process will often be necessary. Moreover, we have seen that the pragmatic arguments about the function of legal protection *ex ante* in relation to the legal protection *ex post* identified in the jurisprudence of the FCC apply to IHRL, too. Involving the individual in the administrative decision-making process adds to the protection *ex post* review provides, it can compensate for factual and legal complexities as well as for the potential inaptness of *ex post* review, and it can facilitate *ex post* legal protection, and in that sense contribute to a "larger unified system serving legal protection"[173] of international human rights domestically. Against the backdrop of this instrumental justification, we can say that obligations of administrative procedure under IHRL suggest an answer to what Alston has identified as a central challenge to IHRL, namely "how to enhance the likelihood that domestic legal systems will give effect to the international obligations undertaken by states".[174] This passage has shown why involving the affected individual in the administrative decision-making process will enhance this likelihood significantly.

8.2.2 A Dignitarian Justification Under IHRL?

Apart from the context of indigenous peoples' rights, the committees construe the procedural involvement of affected individuals as a means to the end of more relevant and effective human rights implementation. They do not rely on a dignitarian justification based on the human image of IHRL. This section seeks to show that such a dignitarian justification is, however, conceivable. Not unlike the German Basic Law, IHRL also conceives the individual as a "self-directing agent"[175] (8.2.2.1). Based on this human image of IHRL, we will argue that administrative procedures are operationalisations of this human image *vis à vis* the administrations of states (8.2.2.2).

8.2.2.1 The Individual as a "Self-Directing Agent" Under IHRL

Before the advent of IHRL, individuals were not subjects under international law. Their legal position was merely a derivative of their home states' sovereignty

[173] Schwarze, 57.

[174] Alston, 'The Historical Origins of the Concept of 'General Comments' in Human Rights Law', 766.

[175] Charles R. Beitz, 'Human Dignity in the Theory of Human Rights: Nothing but a Phrase?' (2013) 41 Philosophy & Public Affairs 259, 288.

rights, and for any claims based on alleged maltreatment by other states, they were entirely dependent on their home states' benevolence.[176] The arrival of IHRL changed this. Today individuals enjoy genuine rights under international law because they are human beings, not because they are citizens. With the origin of international fora, they are not even dependent on their home states' support in enforcing the rights anymore. In fact, the procedural capacity of human beings has been permanently evolving.[177] Consequently, today, human beings are considered "partial subjects" of international law.[178] Given the developments in IHRL since World War II, some have even claimed that "in the circumstances of today the individual human being takes centre stage within the international system".[179] While one might consider this statement to be an exaggeration, one cannot deny that individuals have gained more and more legal significance on the international level, and in general international law. Through the advent of IHRL and the developments within that field and others[180], the human being has been transformed from a mere object to a (partial) subject of international law.

Given that IHRL has contributed so much to the international legal personality of human beings and their potential agency, it is reasonable to assume that IHRL itself construes the human being as a self-directed agent. Many rights from the catalogues of the ICCPR and the ICESCR can be referred to prove this assumption (8.2.2.1.1). However, most importantly, it is the idea of human dignity, which has been called the "most pervasive and fundamental"[181] idea of IHRL, that shapes this understanding as it can be boiled down to the idea of agency and self-directedness, too (8.2.2.1.2).

---

[176] See Hollin Dickerson, 'Minimum Standards' in Anne Peters (ed), *Max Planck Encyclopedia of Public International Law (MPEPIL)* (Oxford University Press 2010) as well as Kay Hailbronner and Jana Gogolin, 'Aliens' in Anne Peters (ed), *Max Planck Encyclopedia of Public International Law (MPEPIL)* (Oxford University Press 2013).

[177] Katrin Fenrich, *The Evolving International Procedural Capacity of Individuals* (Springer 2019).

[178] Christian Walter, 'Subjects of International Law' in Anne Peters (ed), *Max Planck Encyclopedia of Public International Law (MPEPIL)* (Oxford University Press 2007), paras. 15–18.

[179] Tomuschat, *Human Rights: Between Idealism and Realism*, 2.

[180] For an analysis of how developments in fields other than IHRL have contributed to the current role of the human being in international law, see Anne Peters, *Beyond Human Rights: The Legal Status of the Individual in International Law* (Cambridge University Press 2016).

[181] Paolo G. Carozza, 'Human Dignity' in Dinah Shelton (ed), *The Oxford Handbook of International Human Rights Law* (Oxford University Press 2013), 345.

8.2.2.1.1 A Systematic View on the Rights in the Covenants

Given their historical origin, it is not surprising that civil and political rights are about empowerment. Hence, many rights can be found in the ICCPR which are meant to contribute to the ideal of the individual as a self-directed agent (8.2.2.1.1.1). However, we can identify more or less direct connections between the idea of human agency and socio-economic rights, too (8.2.2.1.1.2).

8.2.2.1.1.1 The Idea of Human Agency in the ICCPR

Given their origin in the Enlightenment and their initial *raison d'être* as preventing subjugation, civil and political rights as such are concerned with protecting individual autonomy. It is unsurprising that civil and political rights protect freedoms and rights of particular importance to exercising human agency. We shall nevertheless highlight some of those rights of particular importance for protecting human autonomy in the ICCPR at this point.

First and foremost, Article 16 ICCPR which provides that "[e]veryone shall have the right to recognition everywhere as a person before the law" is a central piece in our argument in favour of an autonomous conception of the individual. The "short but profound"[182] provision is "intended to ensure that every person would be a subject, and not an object, of the law"[183]. This becomes clear when considering the fields of application of the provision that the committee has addressed so far. An example is the HRC's jurisprudence on enforced disappearances where the committee held that depriving someone of "their capacity to exercise entitlements under law [...], and of access to any possible remedy [...] must be interpreted as a refusal to recognize such victims as persons before the law".[184] The committee has invoked a similar formula for incommunicado detentions.[185] Moreover, the HRC was concerned whether confinement in psychiatric hospitals "based on mere 'signs of mental illness'" were in accordance with Article 16 ICCPR.[186] These stark examples show how Article 16 ICCPR protects individual human autonomy by protecting their legal personality and their ability to exercise their rights.

---

[182] Taylor, 445.

[183] *Draft International Covenants on Human Rights: Report of the Third Committee* (8 December 1960) A/4625, para. 25.

[184] HRC, *Grioua v. Algeria* (Comm no 1327/2004, HRC, 10 July 2007), para. 7.8. For restatements see also HRC, *Millis v. Algeria* (Comm no 2398/2014, HRC, 6 April 2018), para. 7.10; HRC, *Sharma, Paudel et al. v. Nepal* (Comm no 2364/2014, HRC, 6 April 2018), para. 9.10.

[185] HRC, *Benali v. Libya* (Comm no 1805/2008, HRC, 1 November 2012), para. 6.9.

[186] HRC, *Concluding Observations of the Human Rights Committee: Czech Republic* (9 August 2007) UN Doc CCPR/C/CZE/CO/2, para. 14.

Beyond Article 16 ICCPR, it is immediately clear that the prohibition on torture and cruel, inhuman or degrading treatment and punishment, Article 7 ICCPR, as well as the prohibition on slavery, Article 8 (1), (2) ICCPR, which are non-derogable and do not allow for limitation, protect a person's autonomy against the starkest forms of its deprivation.

Moreover, those rights which are concerned with securing certain communicative freedoms recognise human agency, too—most importantly, the freedoms of opinion and expression, Article 19 ICCPR, the freedom of assembly, Article 21 ICCPR and the freedom of association, Article 22 ICCPR. These rights have a clear connection to human autonomy as well. In this regard, the HRC held that the "[f]reedom of opinion and freedom of expression are indispensable conditions for the full development of the person"[187] and that the freedom of assembly enables people "to exercise individual autonomy in solidarity with others".[188] Article 18 ICCPR, the freedom of thought, conscience and religion, must be considered in this context as well. Manfred Nowak and William Schabas aptly highlight the autonomy dimension of these rights when they state that

> *freedom of thought and religion is not infrequently termed, along with freedom of opinion, the core of the Covenant, since this nucleus demonstrates that that the international Bill of Rights is based on the philosophical assumption that the individual as a rational being is master of his or her own destiny.*[189]

These communicative freedoms are "cardinal to the proper functioning of democracy, free participation in public affairs and accountability of those wielding power".[190] In this context, Article 25 ICCPR which is concerned with the rights of citizens to *actively* participate in the conduct of public affairs[191] must be highlighted here as well. This provision even envisages institutionalised forms of the exercise of individual human autonomy, e.g., through elections.

And finally, we must highlight those rights that guarantee the individual legal means to enforce their rights. There are the fair trial rights enshrined in

---

[187] HRC, GC 34, para. 2.

[188] HRC, GC 37, para. 1.

[189] Nowak and Schabas, 498. See also Christian Tomuschat, 'Human Rights in a World-Wide Framework—Some Current Issues' (1985) 45 Zeitschrift für ausländisches öffentliches Recht und Völkerrecht 547, 565, as well as John P. Humphrey, 'Political and Related Rights' in Theodor Meron (ed), *Human Rights in International Law: Legal and Policy Issues* (Oxford University Press 1986).

[190] Taylor, 539.

[191] For a more detailed discussion of the provision, see *supra* 2.3.3.

Article 14 ICCPR, procedural rights of those deprived of their liberty, Article 9 (3), (4) ICCPR, as well as the right to an effective remedy under Article 2 (3) ICCPR. Against the backdrop of what we have already observed about the enabling moment of procedural participation and one's ability to enforce one's rights as the "highest criterion of independence"[192], it is immediately understandable how these rights recognise individual autonomy and how these rights help individuals vindicate their agency.

After this brief overview of ICCPR rights that recognise and support human agency, we may conclude that the covenant (unsurprisingly) has the image of an autonomous individual in mind. On the one hand, it presupposes the right-holders' autonomy, and on the other hand the realisation of the covenant rights significantly contributes to an individual's ability to exercise her autonomy.

8.2.2.1.1.2 Rights with an Agency Dimension in the ICESCR

An agency facet of economic, social and cultural rights cannot be discerned as easily. The idea that the right-holder is and should be autonomous is not as prevalent in the text of the ICESCR as it is in the ICCPR. Yet, there are provisions in the ICESCR which (implicitly) recognise human autonomy. Moreover, the idea of indivisibility of human rights establishes a strong, albeit less direct connection between the rights of the ICESCR and the human autonomy presupposed and envisaged by the ICCPR.

As for the rights in the ICESCR which refer to human autonomy, Article 6 (1) ICESCR specifically includes the "right of everyone to the opportunity to gain his living by work which he freely chooses or accepts". According to the CESCR, the inclusion of this right "underlines the fact that respect for the individual and his dignity through the freedom of the individual regarding the choice to work".[193] With this inclusion, the CESCR recognises a certain connection between work, self-determination, and self-fulfilment. Accordingly, a correlative duty to work is not referred to in the covenant despite some fears of "social parasitism" by some states parties.[194]

With the right to form trade unions, the ICESCR recognises a right which is at the same time socio-economic and civil and political in nature.[195] It is recognised in Article 8 ICESCR as well as Article 22 ICCPR. The purpose of the right is

[192] Wahl, 23.

[193] CESCR, GC 18, para. 4.

[194] Saul, Kinley and Mowbray, 282–283.

[195] Ibid, 487.

defined by Article 8 (1) (a) ICESCR as "the promotion and protection of [the individual's] economic and social interests".

Moreover, the idea that education is a prerequisite for human beings to fully develop their potential is a commonplace. That is not to say that it is trivial or banal. The CESCR has rightfully called the right to education enshrined in Article 13 ICESCR an "empowerment right" and recognised—in somewhat lofty terms—that "a well-educated, enlightened and active mind, able to wander freely and widely, is one of the joys and rewards of human existence".[196]

Finally, Article 15 ICESCR must be mentioned here. It firstly protects the active participation in cultural life. The connection between this right and the idea of an autonomous human being becomes clear when recalling that the UNESCO Mexico City Declaration on Cultural Policies rightfully recognised

> *that it is culture that gives man the ability to reflect upon himself. It is culture that makes us specifically human, rational beings, endowed with a critical judgement and a sense of moral commitment. It is through culture that we discern values and make choices. It is through culture that man expresses himself, becomes aware of himself, recognizes* his incompleteness, questions his own achievements, seeks untiringly for new meanings and creates works through which he transcends his limitations.[197]

In its General Comment 21, the CESCR included in the definition of the right to take part in cultural life the right of everyone "to act freely, to choose his or her own identity, to identify or not with one or several communities or to change that choice, to take part in the political life of society, to engage in one's own cultural practices and to express oneself in the language of one's choice" as well as the right "to seek and develop cultural knowledge and expressions and to share them with others, as well as to act creatively and take part in creative activity".[198]

Secondly, Article 15 ICESCR also protects the right of the individual "[t]o benefit from the protection of the moral and material interests resulting from any scientific, literary or artistic production of which he is the author" and thereby rewards the capacity of human beings to be autonomous in the sense that they can make free, creative choices.

Hence, while socio-economic rights are not as a whole derived from the idea of the human being as a self-directed agent, there are a number of ways in which

---

[196] CESCR, *General Comment No. 13 (Twenty-first session, 1999): The right to education (article 13 of the Covenant)* (8 December 1999) UN Doc E/C.12/1999/10, para. 1.

[197] UNESCO, *Mexico City Declaration on Cultural Policies, World Conference on Cultural Policies, Mexico City, 26 July-6 August 1982* (1982) CLT/MD/1 p. 41, preamble.

[198] CESCR, GC 21, para. 15.

they presuppose and endorse this idea. Finally, the idea of the indivisibility of human rights adds a more indirect connection between socio-economic rights and the idea of the autonomous individual. The idea was recognised by several important international IHRL documents[199] and refers to the realisation that civil and political rights cannot be realised meaningfully when (some) socio-economic rights, such as the right to food, are not realised.[200] In other words, "the full realization of civil and political rights without the enjoyment of economic, social and cultural rights is impossible".[201] The enjoyment of socio-economic rights is therefore also a necessary precondition for the autonomous human being envisaged by civil and political rights.

8.2.2.1.2 Human Dignity as Agency

While civil and political as well as socio-economic rights presuppose and endorse human agency, the central element, the centrepiece to IHRL's human image as that of a self-directed, autonomous individual lies in the principle of human dignity. The principle is so much present in this body of law that it has been called the "most pervasive and fundamental"[202] idea of IHRL, even though there is no binding general guarantee of human dignity under IHRL. To show why human dignity is the centrepiece of IHRL's human image and thus of a dignitarian justification for obligations of administrative procedure, we will first give a brief overview of where and in which forms the concept of human dignity appears in IHRL (8.2.2.1.2.1). Afterwards, we will argue that the idea of agency stands at the centre of human dignity (8.2.2.1.2.2).

8.2.2.1.2.1 Human Dignity and International Human Rights—An Overview

The concept of human dignity has found multiple expressions in IHRL. After the Second World War, the concept first appeared in the preamble to the Charter

---

[199] The ICCPR and the ICESCR recognise the idea in the preambles. For other examples, see *Proclamation of Teheran, Final Act of the International Conference on Human Rights: Teheran, 22 April to 13 May 1968* (1 September 1968) UN Doc A/CONF 32/41 p. 3, para 13; as well as *Vienna Declaration and Programme of Action, Report of the World Conference on Human Rights, Report of the Secretary-General* (13 October 1993) UN Doc A/CONF157/24 (Part I) p. 20, para. 5.

[200] For an instructive set of questions illustrating the idea Ssenyonjo, 18.

[201] Proclamation of Tehran, para 13.

[202] Carozza, 'Human Dignity', 345.

of the United Nations[203]. In 1948, it was then introduced in the preamble and Article 1 of the Universal Declaration of Human Rights which states that "[a]ll human beings are born free and equal in dignity and rights". The ICCPR and the ICESCR have then taken up "this lofty provision"[204] in their preambles which both "recognize" that the rights they set out derive from the "inherent dignity of the human person". Today, virtually all other human rights instruments contain references to human dignity, mostly, however, in their non-binding preambles.[205] Carozza even speaks of a "nearly exceptionless canonical inclusion of references to dignity".[206] The only major human rights treaty which does not include an explicit reference to human dignity is the ECHR.[207] However, the ECtHR made up for this blank spot by continuously referring to the concept in its judgments.[208]

Notably, there is no enforceable general guarantee of human dignity in IHRL. This is an important difference to the German constitution and thus to the dignitarian justification of the FCC. When treaties contain references to human dignity in their operative parts, they do so either in relation to specific rights,[209] or in relation to specific groups. The Convention on the Rights of Persons with Disabilities (CRPD)[210] of 2006, for example, contains a significant number of references to human dignity. In the very first sentence of its preamble, the document refers

---

203 Charter of the United Nations (adopted 26 June 1945, entered into force 24 October 1945).

204 Tomuschat, *Human Rights: Between Idealism and Realism*, 86.

205 See for an extensive overview of the mentions of the concept in international conventions see Aharon Barak, *Human Dignity: The Constitutional Value and the Constitutional Right* (Cambridge University Press 2015), 37–48.

206 Carozza, 'Human Dignity', 350.

207 However, the ECtHR has made up for this in its jurisprudence. For an analysis of the relevance of the concept in the European regional human rights system, see Sebastian Heselhaus and Ralph Hemsley, 'Human Dignity and the European Convention on Human Rights' in Paolo Becchi and Klaus Mathis (eds), *Handbook of Human Dignity in Europe* (Springer Nature 2019).

208 For an overview of the ECtHR's jurisprudence on human dignity and its fundamental role for the European system of human rights, see Catherine Dupré, 'Human Dignity in Europe: A Foundational Constitutional Principle' 19 European Public Law 319.

209 Article 10 ICCPR, for example, provides that "[a]ll persons deprived of their liberty shall be treated with […] respect for the inherent dignity of the human person". Another example is Article 13 ICESCR which mentions dignity in connection with the right to education, when it stipulates that "education shall be directed to the full development of the human personality and the sense of its dignity".

210 Convention of the Rights of Persons with Disabilities (adopted 13 December 2006, entered into force 3 May 2008) 2515 UNTS 3 (CRPD).

to the "inherent dignity [...] of all members of the human family". Moreover, it *inter alia* declares the promotion of dignity its purpose in Article 1, and obliges states to "foster respect for the rights and dignity of persons with disabilities" in Article 8. While Article 3 CRPD does contain a general guarantee of human dignity when it defines "[r]espect for inherent dignity, individual autonomy including the freedom to make one's own choices, and independence of persons" as one of the convention's principles, the CRPD is applicable only to persons with disabilities. A similar provision can be found in Article 23 of the Convention on the Rights of the Child[211] which states that "mentally or physically disabled children should enjoy a full and decent life, in conditions which ensure dignity, promote self-reliance and facilitate the child's active participation in the community".

Other than these references, we find general references to dignity mostly in non-binding preambles to IHRL treaties,[212] or soft law documents such as the UDHR or the Vienna Declaration and Programme of Action. These non-binding parts of IHRL, in particular the preambles of human rights treaties, sometimes refer to human dignity as the source of human rights.[213] Hence, and not surprisingly, the argument that human dignity is a, or even *the* foundation of IHRL is a rather common feature in IHRL literature.[214] The ubiquity of human dignity in IHRL has prompted commentators to observe that the *topos* is on the rise internationally.[215]

---

[211] Convention on the Rights of the Child (adopted 20 November 1989, entered into force 2 September 1990) 1577 UNTS 3 rhus.

[212] For an overview of the mentions of human dignity in human rights law instruments and the functions the concept fulfils in international human rights jurisprudence, see Carozza, 'Human Dignity', and Barak, *Human Dignity: The Constitutional Value and the Constitutional Right*, 34–48.

[213] The ICCPR, the ICESCR, e.g., which both state that the rights they stipulate "derive from the inherent dignity of the human person".

[214] Tomuschat, *Human Rights: Between Idealism and Realism*, 85 ff. Similarly, Kälin and Künzli argue that IHRL is "rooted in the acknowledgment that the entitlements in question are necessary to safeguard human dignity [...] and serve to protect fundamental characteristics of the human person and his or her dignity", Kälin and Künzli, 28–29.

[215] Jochen von Bernstorff, 'The Dispute About Human Dignity and Ethical Absolutism in the Field of Fundamental and Human Rights Protection: Defending a Deontic Understanding of Rights' in Dieter Grimm, Alexandra Kemmerer and Christoph Möllers (eds), *Human Dignity in Context: Explorations of a Contested Concept* (Nomos 2018), 271–273.

Despite the central role the idea of human dignity plays in IHRL documents, the concept remains undefined by these instruments.[216] The exact scope, content and legal value of human dignity remain contested.[217] Some commentators have therefore cautioned against overestimating the legal value of the concept.[218] Others even declared the concept "useless".[219] Against this backdrop of ubiquity and challenge, the next section will argue that the minimum content of the concept of human dignity can be understood as the idea of the "status of a self-directing agent"[220].

8.2.2.1.2.2 Autonomy as the Central Meaning of Human Dignity

The precise meaning and specific implications of human dignity in the context of (international) human rights have long been the subject of an extensive and ongoing debate in the academic literature.[221] This is not the place to recall this debate. Instead, this section will focus on the very gist of the concept of human dignity, on its "current canonical expression"[222], namely the idea that the human being is "a self-controlling, self-developing agent [...] in contrast to [...] a dependent, passive recipient of the agency of others"[223], and that individuals must be taken seriously as such. Exploring different expressions and facets of this basic idea will help us understand how it provides the centre-piece to IHRL's human image and the basis for a dignitarian justification of procedural obligations.

In an influential article of 2008, McCrudden shares a rather sceptical view on the principle of human dignity and its objective worth for IHRL. He presents

---

[216] Christina Binder, 'Human Dignity in International Human Rights Law' in Philipp B. Donath and others (eds), *Der Schutz des Individuums durch das Recht: Festschrift für Rainer Hofmann zum 70 Geburtstag* (Springer 2023), 230.

[217] Christopher McCrudden, 'Human Dignity and Judicial Interpretation of Human Rights' (2008) 19 European Journal of International Law 655.

[218] Ibid, 680.

[219] Ruth Macklin, 'Dignity is a Useless Concept: It Means no More than Respect for Persons or Their Autonomy' (2003) 327 British Medical Journal 1419; in a similar direction calling the concept "empty" Justin Bates, 'Human Dignity—An Empty Phrase in Search of Meaning?' (2005) 10 Judicial Review 165, 168; and calling the concept "vacuous" Mirko Bagaric and James Allan, 'The Vacuous Concept of Dignity' (2006) 5 Journal of Human Rights 257, 269. Although it shall be mentioned here that Bates, Bagaric and Allan have qualified their classification to be true only until the meaning of human dignity is discerned.

[220] Beitz, 288.

[221] For a recent contribution, see Binder.

[222] Jürgen Habermas, 'The Concept of Human Dignity and the Realistic Utopia of Human Rights' (2010) 41 Metaphilosophy 464, 465.

[223] Alan Gewirth, 'Rights and Virtues' (1985) 38 The Review of Metaphysics 739, 743.

dignity as a concept that—at least when it comes to its application in actual cases—is so malleable that it is "often found on both sides of the argument" and that it can support different conclusions.[224] Despite his sceptical stance towards the concept, McCrudden identifies three elements of a "minimum core" of human dignity: the "ontological claim", according to which every person possesses an intrinsic worth because she is a human being; the "relational claim", according to which this intrinsic worth requires that every individual must be recognised and respected by others in one way or another; and the "limited-state claim", i.e. the idea that the state exists "for the sake of the individual human being" and not *vice versa*.[225] These elements, McCrudden argues, constitute the discernible "central meaning of dignity".[226]

In particular the relational and the limited-state claim, evoke the Kantian idea that the human individual shall not be treated as a means to an end but always as an end in herself. This Kantian principle is often referred to in discussions of human dignity.[227] Oscar Schachter, e.g., takes it as the starting point for a discussion of "human dignity as a normative concept" in an editorial for the American Journal of International Law:

> *One general answer to our question [of what human dignity means] is suggested by the Kantian injunction to treat every human being as an end, not as a means. Respect for the intrinsic worth of every person should mean that individuals are not to be perceived or treated merely as instruments or objects of the will of others.*[228]

Schachter ties this Kantian idea to an individual's "capacity to make choices" and states that it reflects their "individual autonomy and responsibility".[229] Notably, he also recognises a "procedural implication" of human dignity, namely that "every individual [...] should be recognised as having the capacity to assert claims and to protect their essential dignity",[230] after having stated that human autonomy does not separate the individual from the society within which she exists, but

[224] McCrudden, 'Human Dignity and Judicial Interpretation of Human Rights', 698.

[225] Ibid, 679.

[226] Ibid, 724.

[227] Niels Petersen, 'Human Dignity, International Protection' in Anne Peters (ed), *Max Planck Encyclopedia of Public International Law (MPEPIL)* (Oxford University Press 2020), para. 6.

[228] Oscar Schachter, 'Editorial Comment: Human Dignity as a Normative Concept' (1983) 77 American Journal of International Law 848, 849.

[229] Ibid, 850–851.

[230] Ibid, 851.

that human dignity instead "involves a complex notion of the individual".[231] This reminds us of the early connections between human dignity, the object formula and the right to participate in procedures made by the FCC.[232]

Another, more recent example of a direct invocation of Kant comes from Jürgen Habermas. He, too, argues that human dignity's "current canonical expression" lies in the Kantian idea that human beings must never be treated as mere objects.[233] Schachter's and Habermas' accounts are both similar to the understanding of human dignity and the consequences (for procedural obligations) we have identified in the FCC's jurisprudence.[234] They, too, use an object formula to describe the normative implications of human dignity. And they are in line with what McCrudden identified as the minimum core of the meaning of human dignity which actors in the international community can agree on.

Other accounts which do not resemble the FCC's approach so clearly have human autonomy or human agency at the centre of the meaning of human dignity as well. Joel Feinberg, e.g., argues that rights are "to be claimed, demanded, affirmed, insisted upon".[235] He defines claiming as "the manner of assertion" the point of which is to "*make sure* people listen".[236] Feinberg then connects these points to an understanding of what it means to be human:

> *[I]t is claiming that gives rights their special moral significance. This feature of rights is connected in a way with the customary rhetoric about what it is to be a human being. Having rights enables us to "stand up like men", to look others in the eye, and to feel in some fundamental way the equal of anyone. [... A]nd what is called "human dignity" may simply be the recognizable capacity to assert claims. To respect a person then, or*

231 Ibid.

232 See *supra* 5.2.2. That Schachter justifies the procedural implications by reference to the community-boundness of the individual, also reveals parallels to the discussion in the German literature. In particular, we are reminded of Häberle's notion that a person's rights may only be realised "in processu" given the complex relations between her, the state and other individuals in the modern (welfare-)state. See *supra* 3.2.

233 Habermas, 465. Habermas rather directly invokes an object formula: "The respect for the dignity of every person forbids the state to dispose of any individual merely as a means to another end., even if that end be to save the lives of many other people." The wording of the formula evokes the FCC's judgment in the *Luftsicherheitsgesetz* case. For a summary of the case, see *supra* 5.2.1.1.

234 See *supra* 5.2.

235 Joel Feinberg, 'The Nature and Value of Rights' (1970) 4 The Journal of Value Inquiry 243, 252.

236 Ibid, 250–252.

> *to think of him as possessed of human dignity, simply is to think of him as a potential maker of claims.*[237]

Here, human dignity as human autonomy or agency already has an institutional-legal form. Having rights and the (procedural capacity) to assert them is what "human dignity" is about. What follows from this is that human beings cannot be thought of as mere beneficiaries of IHRL. If possessing human dignity means to be thought of as a potential maker of claims, human beings must be viewed and treated as such. By making claims, or deciding not to claim their rights, they play an indispensable active role in the realisation of these rights. To put it perhaps somewhat pathetically they are agents of their own fate.

Another agency-based interpretation of human dignity that highlights a different facet can be found in Rainer Forst's "intersubjective justification theory" of human rights. According to this theory, human rights are political expressions of human autonomy.[238] Consequently, human rights should provide the individual with those rights necessary to be "someone who 'counts', who is seen and recognized as someone with 'dignity', that is, with an effective right to justification".[239] Hence, the claim underlying all human rights is "to be respected as autonomous agents who have the right not to be subjected to certain actions or institutional norms that cannot be adequately justified to them."[240] Such a right to justification forms the "normative basis for a conception of human rights".[241]

From there, Forst develops a "relational" meaning of human dignity:

> *[T]he notion of "dignity" that lies at the heart of such a conception of human rights is not a metaphysical or ethical one, combined with a doctrine about the good life. Rather, dignity means that a person is* ***to be respected as someone who is worthy of being given adequate reasons for actions or norms that affect him or her in a relevant way****. And this kind of respect requires us to regard others as autonomous sources of normative claims within a justificatory practice. Each person is an "authority" in the space of reasons, so to speak.*[242]

---

[237] Ibid, 252.

[238] Rainer Forst, 'The Justification of Human Rights and the Basic Right to Justification: A Reflexive Approach' (2010) 120 Ethics 711, 712.

[239] Ibid, 717.

[240] Ibid, 712.

[241] Ibid, 734.

[242] Ibid. Emphasis added.

The similarity of Forst's language here to one of the most prominent features of administrative procedure—the giving reasons requirement—is striking. It makes the procedural implications of his angle to human dignity immediately apparent. To do justice to the dignity of the human person, the state must justify what it does to her. It must give her the reasons for the decision that affect her negatively. The link between a human person's autonomy, her right to be taken seriously, and the way in which the administration of a state must treat that individual becomes immediately palpable when reading Forst's words.

Finally, another interesting take on human dignity and human autonomy can be found in the works of Jeremy Waldron. Waldron defines human dignity as a "high-ranking status".[243] To him, the concept is about an "upwards equalization of rank".[244] Today, dignity is accorded to every human being, and not just to high-ranking members of society, i.e., to the nobility. An important part of the set of rights previously only enjoyed by the nobility was "a right to have [their] voice reckoned with and counted".[245] As a result of the upwards equalisation, such a right to be heard is now enjoyed by everyone. Today, it is part of what it means to be human. While Forst's account emphasised the giving reasons requirement, Waldron's way of approaching or defining human dignity makes the principle of *audi alteram partem* particularly palpable. Individuals and their views must be taken seriously, they must not only be heard, but they must also be "reckoned with and counted".[246]

The accounts of human dignity represented here differ from each other in their approaches, the methodology they rely on, and their emphases. However, they all agree on the basic point that human dignity means "the status of a self-directing agent"[247]. Because of her human dignity, a human person can "demand that her agency and her presence among us as a human being be taken seriously and accommodated in the lives of others, in others' attitudes and actions towards her, and in social life generally."[248]

---

[243] Jeremy Waldron, 'Dignity and Rank' in Jeremy Waldron and Meir Dan-Cohen (eds), *Dignity, Rank, & Rights* (Oxford University Press 2012), 22.

[244] Ibid, 33.

[245] Ibid, 35.

[246] Ibid.

[247] Beitz, 288.

[248] Jeremy Waldron, 'How Law Protects Dignity' (2012) 71 Cambridge Law Journal 200, 202.

8.2.2.2 Administrative Procedure as the Operationalisation of the Human Image of IHRL

What does this understanding of human dignity as human autonomy or agency imply for our question of whether a dignitarian justification for obligations of administrative procedure can be derived from IHRL? Given what we have learned about the dignitarian justification of the FCC and given the similarities of human dignity in IHRL and human dignity in the Basic Law, the consequence seems obvious. The normative implication for IHRL must essentially be the same: if IHRL requires that the individual be taken seriously as a "self-directed" agent, if her voice must count and be reckoned with, she must not be relegated to an object of state power but retain subject quality when confronted with it. Hence, the administration of a state must have some sort of a "conversation" with her whenever it plans to curtail her rights. Simply taking a decision without paying due regard to her view and confronting her with it without sharing the reasons with her would violate her dignity. In other words, because the individual is endowed with dignity, because she is an autonomous agent, she must be treated as such, and decisions cannot be taken over her head. This is what a dignitarian justification of obligations of administrative procedure under IHRL could look like.

So far, so good. However, this is only a justification for the necessity of a "conversation" of any kind. It does not provide a compelling reason for obligations of administrative *procedure* in the sense of a "series of prescribed steps that the administration must follow before making a decision"[249]. It does not tell us why the exchange between the administration and the individual must be formal and structured and organised by law. Are there no other ways to involve individuals in decision-making processes that affect them? Could a member of a state's administration not simply invite the affected individual for a cup of tea to inquire about her view on a matter? Could she not make a casual phone call to tell the affected individual the reasons for her decision? How can we justify formal, sometimes complicated procedures which may delay or even prevent the effective exercise of rights?

To understand why only a formalised, only an institutionalised conversation can satisfy the requirements of human dignity we must highlight the principle's equality dimension. This dimension is particularly evident in Waldron's conceptualisation of human dignity as an "upwards *equalization* of rank"[250]. *Every*one nowadays possesses the rights which used to belong only to the nobility. *Every*one

[249] Della Cananea, 22.

[250] Waldron, 'Dignity and Rank', 33.

must be reckoned with. And *every*one must enjoy this right to the *same* extent. Consequently, a state must make sure that its implementation of the human dignity's autonomy aspect does not lead to arbitrary unequal treatment. This can only be achieved by a formalised procedure in which everyone generally participates in the same way and to the same degree.

Building on Waldron's account of dignity and emphasising its equality aspect, Dyzenhaus even defines the right to dignity as "nothing more than the principle that individuals must be treated as equal before the law"[251] and as "the right of individuals to equal treatment in the way in which the law was administered"[252]. Given what we have established about the meaning of human dignity above, Dyzenhaus' account of "dignity as equality" puts too little emphasis on its autonomy aspect. Nevertheless, his emphasis of the equality dimension is helpful to understand why a casual conversation would not do justice to the requirements of human dignity.

For the same reason, there is a more straightforward systematic argument to be made for a "formal" conversation: a (potentially) unequal implementation of the requirements of human dignity would not sit well with the standalone principle of equality under IHRL. As we have seen above, the principle requires states to realise human rights without unwarranted discrimination.[253] Together with the equality dimension of human dignity, the principle of equality provides us with the answer of why the dignitarian justification developed here can give rise only to administrative procedural obligations. They justify the "conversation between the administration and the individual" only in a formalised form. Only such a form of involving the individual in state decision-making can take the individual seriously while guaranteeing that the formerly noble right of having one's view considered is indeed enjoyed by *every*one equally. Regulating the decision-making process in a legally binding way is thus an essential means to ensure that those subjected to their power do not depend on the goodwill of the state official they are confronted with. It is a means to limit arbitrariness and thus "affronts to human dignity"[254].

To conclude, administrative procedure is a way to operationalise the requirements of human dignity *vis à vis* the administration of a state. It is the appropriate answer to the demand of the individual "that her agency and her presence be taken

---

[251] Dyzenhaus, 241.

[252] Ibid, 242.

[253] For an overview of this principle in IHRL, see *supra* 8.2.1.1.2.4.

[254] Dyzenhaus calls "arbitrariness" an "affront to human dignity because it removes from those subject to the law the ability to plan their lives in advance, and the ability to plan one's life in this way is a necessary (though not a sufficient) condition for a life of dignity", Dyzenhaus, 244.

seriously" by the administration of a state, an appropriate means to implement the subject formula for everyone who now benefits from noble rights equally and thereby inject human dignity into the everyday experience of the individual with the state. It is a way for the state to ensure that the individual's voice is heard, reckoned with, and counted. The giving reasons requirements takes the individual seriously as the bearer of the right to justification. The principle of *audi alteram partem* provides the infrastructure which enables individuals to be "makers of claims". In short, administrative procedure is an operationalisation of the "high-ranking" and "equalised" status of a "self-directing agent", of the status of human dignity.

In his lecture "Law, Dignity, and Self-Control", Waldron aptly outlines the relevance of court hearings for the agency dimension of human dignity. The passage can easily be extrapolated to administrative procedure. It neatly encapsulates a dignitarian justification for procedural obligations under IHRL and shall therefore conclude our reflections on the possibility of developing a dignitarian justification for IHRL:

> *Another way in which law respects the dignity of those who are governed is in the provision that it makes for hearings in cases where an official determination [of the content and application of a norm] is necessary. [...] By hearings, I mean formal events, like trials, tightly structured in a procedural way in order to enable an impartial tribunal to determine rights and responsibilities fairly and effectively after hearing evidence and argument from both sides. Those who are immediately concerned have an opportunity to make submissions and present evidence, and confront, examine, and respond to evidence and submissions presented from the other side. Not only that, but both sides are listened to by a tribunal that is bound to respond to the arguments put forward in the reasons that it eventually gives for its decision.*
>
> *[...] Applying a norm [...] involves paying attention to a point of view. In this way it embodies a crucial dignitarian idea – respecting the dignity of those to whom the norms are applied as beings capable of explaining themselves. [...]*
>
> *In this way too, then, law conceives of the people who live under it as bearers of reason and intelligence. They are thinkers who can grasp and grapple with the rationale of the way they are governed and relate it in complex but intelligible ways to their own view of the relation between their actions and purposes and the actions and purposes of the state. This too is a tribute to human dignity.*[255]

8.2.2.3 Conclusion

Even though the committees do not rely on a dignitarian justification when they derive procedural requirements from the rights of the covenants, we have shown

[255] Waldron, 'Law, Dignity and Self-Control', 54–55.

that such a justification is conceivable. IHRL envisages the individual not as a passive beneficiary of rights, but as an agent with an active role to play in the realisation of these rights. This image can be found in many of the rights under the two covenants, but it is first and foremost encapsulated by the concept of human dignity. While the precise meaning of human dignity in IHRL is contested, the "minimum core" meaning can be defined as the idea of the human being as a "self-directed agent", a "maker of claims", someone whose voice needs to be heard and "reckoned with" and who is deserving of justification. Involving the individual in those decision-making processes that affect her, provides a way to operationalise this position of the individual as an actor *vis à vis* a state's administration. However, the conversation between the administration and the individual must be formalised. This way, human dignity can be operationalised in a way that does justice not only to its agency, but also to its equality dimension, and the principle of equality in IHRL. Lastly, the dignitarian justification provides an interesting connection to recent calls for comprehending humans more as subjects endowed with agency and less as passive beneficiaries of IHRL.[256]

8.2.3 Interactions Between the Instrumental and the Dignitarian Justification

As part of our analysis of the FCC's jurisprudence on obligations of administrative procedure derived from the fundamental rights of the Basic Law, we have reflected upon the relationship between the instrumental and the dignitarian justifications employed by the constitutional court. We have found that the justifications do not apply in parallel but that the functions of administrative procedure at which the two justifications hint mutually enforce each other.[257] These reflections apply in the context of IHRL, too.

---

[256] For an example see Mann, 16. Mann postulates that individuals must be conceived as participants with agency in the realisation of their rights and even in the shaping of international law. In contrast to our justification, however, Mann's argument is inductive. Mann conducts a "careful description and phenomenological characterization of the actions of those who have no state protection and the experience of being confronted by their claims". From this, he develops what he calls a theory of human rights as "rights of encounter" through "careful description and phenomenological characterization of the actions of those who have no state protection and the experience of being confronted by their claims". The dignitarian justification of administrative procedure developed here can be seen as a complementation to such theories of human rights, or as a normative consequence thereof.

[257] See *supra* 5.3.

Firstly, empowering the individual to be the self-directed agent contributes to the effective realisation of her rights. We have already encountered this connection—albeit not explicitly—in the HRC's justifications whenever the committee referred to the necessity of "empowering" individuals to challenge alleged violations of their human rights. In that sense, operationalising the position of individuals as active participants in the realisation of their rights at least bears the potential of making that realisation more effective.

Conversely, making the realisation of an individual's rights more effective contributes to the realisation of her dignity. Carozza made an argument based on the observation that human dignity served as the theoretical foundation that the drafters of the UDHR could agree on. If this is true, he asks, why do we not read the declaration as the authoritative, internationally accepted expression of the concept?[258] The totality of the rights enshrined in the UDHR would then make up human dignity. By realising the totality of the rights enshrined in the UDHR, states would realise human dignity. While such an argument is only *prima facie* convincing—it wrongfully presents those rights as sufficient conditions for the realisation of human dignity, while they actually are only necessary conditions –, the argument has merit insofar as it highlights the contribution of each human right to the dignity of a person. In this sense, it has been argued that the principle of access to justice should not be understood as a tool to empower courts to fulfil their function in a legal system but rather as a means to empower humans.[259]

Finally, we have seen that human rights and administrative procedures are both "shields against arbitrariness"[260]. And Dyzenhaus has convincingly argued that arbitrariness is "an affront to human dignity" because it impairs one's ability to plan one's life.[261] If the individual never really knows what to expect from a state, does not get the opportunity to make her case before those who decide it and is not provided reasons in situations for those decision that affect her, the ensuing uncertainty inhibits her freedom to direct herself. In that sense, the notion of arbitrariness aptly highlights the connection between the instrumental and the dignitarian justification.

---

258 Paolo G. Carozza, 'Human Dignity and Judicial Interpretation of Human Rights: A Reply' (2008) 19 European Journal of International Law 931, 937.

259 Se-Shauna Wheatle, 'Access to Justice: From Judicial Empowerment to Public Empowerment' in Mark Elliott and Kirsty Hughes (eds), *Common Law Constitutional Rights* (Hart Publishing 2020).

260 Della Cananea, 19.

261 Dyzenhaus, 244.

Implementation and Scope of Review 9

In this chapter, we will analyse the committees' pronouncements as to how obligations of administrative procedure must be implemented and how their implementation can be reviewed. We will firstly look at what the committees have held in this regard and how the abstract requirements stipulated in general comments can play out in practical cases (9.1). Secondly, we will assess the findings against the backdrop of the risks that come with positive obligations under IHRL (9.2). Finally, we will reflect on how robust procedural obligations under IHRL could potentially contribute to a better implementation of the principle of subsidiarity (9.3).

9.1 The Committees' Pronouncements on Implementation and Review of Procedural Rights

This section analyses what the committees have said with regard to implementation of procedural safeguards under IHRL and their approach to review. The pronouncements of the CESCR are of particular importance and help in this endeavour. Firstly, we will see that the implementation of obligations of administrative procedure is context-dependent (9.1.1). Secondly, we will look at how the obligations play out in practice and how effectiveness in the realisation of human rights must be the yardstick for their implementation (9.1.2). Thirdly, we will see how the principle of proportionality influences the implementation (9.1.3).

B. Behlert, *The Necessity of a Conversation between the Administration and the Individual*, Juridicum—Bochumer Schriften zur Friedenssicherung und zum Humanitären Völkerrecht | Bochum Studies on the International Law of Peace and Armed Conflict 72, https://doi.org/10.1007/978-3-658-50303-1_9

Finally, we will discuss whether the procedural obligations discussed here are individually enforceable (9.1.4).

9.1.1 The Context-Dependence of Procedural Protection

In contrast to a noticeable paucity of its sister committee as regards the implementation of procedural obligations, the CESCR has made some rather insightful remarks when it comes to the elements of administrative procedures required by IHRL. These remarks highlight what we have already stated in our analysis of the FCC's jurisprudence,[1] namely that the implementation of procedural obligations—like that of all positive obligations—is highly context-dependent.

In its General Comment 7, after stating that adequate procedural protection was an important element of all human rights, the CESCR lists elements that such protection should include with regard to forced evictions:

> *(a) an opportunity for genuine consultation with those affected; (b) adequate and reasonable notice for all affected persons prior to the scheduled date of eviction; (c) information on the proposed evictions, and, where applicable, on the alternative purpose for which the land or housing is to be used, to be made available in reasonable time to all those affected; (d) especially where groups of people are involved, government officials or their representatives to be present during an eviction; (e) all persons carrying out the eviction to be properly identified; (f) evictions not to take place in particularly bad weather or at night unless the affected persons consent otherwise; (g) provision of legal remedies; and (h) provision, where possible, of legal aid to persons who are in need of it to seek redress from the courts.*[2]

The first requirement on this list is the "genuine consultation" requirement which had already featured in the committee's earlier General Comment 4 on housing rights, albeit in a more general sense and in relation to policy-making.[3] In General Comment 7, the CESCR now applies this criterion to individual cases of forced evictions. Moreover, the CESCR lists the requirement of "adequate and reasonable notice for all affected persons prior to the scheduled date of eviction". Thirdly, the information on the eviction and the alternative use of the dwelling must be given "in reasonable time to all those affected".

We find similar lists in two other general comments on different rights. In General Comment 15 on the right to water, the committee states that

[1] See *supra* 6.3.

[2] CESCR, GC 7, para. 15.

[3] CESCR, GC 4, para. 12.

> *[b]efore any action that interferes with an individual's right to water is carried out by the State party, or by any other third party, the relevant authorities must ensure that such actions are performed in a manner warranted by law, compatible with the Covenant, and that comprises: (a) opportunity for genuine consultation with those affected; (b) timely and full disclosure of information on the proposed measures; (c) reasonable notice of proposed actions; (d) legal recourse and remedies for those affected; and (e) legal assistance for obtaining legal remedies (see also General Comments No. 4 (1991) and No. 7 (1997)).*[4]

Moreover, in a passage in General Comment 19 on the right to social security which resembles the passage in General Comment 15 almost word-for-word, the committee states that

> *[b]efore any action is carried out by the State party, or by any other third party, that interferes with the right of an individual to social security the relevant authorities must ensure that such actions are performed in a manner warranted by law, compatible with the Covenant, and include: (a) an opportunity for genuine consultation with those affected; (b) timely and full disclosure of information on the proposed measures; (c) reasonable notice of proposed actions; (d) legal recourse and remedies for those affected; and (e) legal assistance for obtaining legal remedies.*[5]

The following synopsis highlights the commonalities and differences between the catalogues:

GC 7 (forced evictions)	**GC 15 (right to water)**	**GC 19 (right to social security)**
a) opportunity for genuine consultation with those affected	a) opportunity for genuine consultation with those affected	a) opportunity for genuine consultation with those affected
b) adequate and reasonable notice for all affected persons prior to the scheduled date of eviction	c) reasonable notice of proposed actions	c) reasonable notice of proposed actions

(continued)

[4] CESCR, GC 15, para. 56.

[5] CESCR, GC 19, para. 78.

(continued)

GC 7 (forced evictions)	GC 15 (right to water)	GC 19 (right to social security)
c) information on the proposed evictions, and, where applicable, on the alternative purpose for which the land or housing is to be used, to be made available in reasonable time to all those affected	b) timely and full disclosure of information on the proposed measures	b) timely and full disclosure of information on the proposed measures
d) especially where groups of people are involved, government officials or their representatives to be present during an eviction	*- no equivalent -*	*- no equivalent -*
e) all persons carrying out the eviction to be properly identified	*- no equivalent -*	*- no equivalent -*
f) evictions not to take place in particularly bad weather or at night unless the affected persons consent otherwise	*- no equivalent -*	*- no equivalent -*
g) provision of legal remedies	d) legal recourse and remedies for those affected	d) legal recourse and remedies for those affected
h) provision, where possible, of legal aid to persons who are in need of it to seek redress from the courts	e) legal assistance for obtaining legal remedies	e) legal assistance for obtaining legal remedies

Elements of procedural protection under the right to housing, the right to water, and the right to social security.

As this table shows, five of the eight elements of procedural protection stipulated in General Comment 7 in the context of forced evictions re-appear in General Comment 15 on the right to water and General Comment 19 on the right to social security: the requirement to provide an opportunity for genuine consultation with those affected, reasonable notice of the proposed actions, and timely and full disclosure of information on the proposed measures, the provision of legal remedies, and provision of legal assistance for it. Importantly, the first three requirements directly relate to legal protection *ex ante*. And they include the classical elements of administrative procedure, namely the *audi alteram partem* principle, and the giving reasons requirement. The three requirements that the persons carry out the eviction be properly identified, that government or representatives be present during the eviction, and that evictions do not take place in bad weather do not reappear on the lists regarding the right to water and the right to social security.

What can we infer from this? Notably, the substantive rights in the context of which the committee mentions those procedural elements are substantively different from each other. They govern different subject matters and become relevant in very different situations. Hence, the procedural protection that is needed for individuals in those situations in which these rights are at stake, can vary. For example, an equivalent requirement that evictions do not take place in particularly bad weather or at night would not make sense in the context of the right to social security. This requirement is specifically tailored to forced evictions, i.e., to situations in which individuals and their livelihoods are particularly vulnerable to inhospitable weather conditions.

The other differences can be explained with the different dimensions of human rights that can be at stake in a decision. Forced evictions relate to the negative obligation of states not to interfere with individuals' rights in unjustified ways. A forced eviction is, perhaps, the classic example of an interference with the negative dimension of socio-economic rights. And normally, it will be a rather severe interference with the "respect" dimension of the right to housing. Moreover, as the CESCR rightfully highlights, forced evictions endanger not just one but many human rights at once.[6] Hence, it is no wonder that the committee establishes additional requirements of representation and transparency. The lists with elements of procedural protection regarding the rights to water and social security are not tailored to measures interfering with the negative dimensions of these rights. Instead, they relate to all dimensions these rights give rise to. Hence, the three elements from the list in General Comment 7 which were not included in later lists show us the context-dependence of adequate procedural protection.

At the same time, those five elements of adequate procedural protection which are included in all three lists, and in particular those three elements which relate to legal protection *ex ante* show us that basic features of the conversation between the administration and the individual are generally relevant to all forms of state

[6] CESCR, GC 7, para. 15.

action. Given the relevance of these procedural means for the effective implementation of subjective rights,[7] this is unsurprising. The committees' pronouncements allow us to take a closer look at how two of the three requirements, i.e., the adequate and reasonable notice requirement, as well as the genuine consultation requirement play out in practice in the following sections.

9.1.2 Effective Realisation of Human Rights as the Yardstick for the Implementation of Procedural Obligations

In this section, we will analyse how the requirement to give adequate and reasonable notice (9.1.2.1) and the genuine consultation requirement (9.1.2.2) can play out in practice. Perhaps, unsurprisingly, we will see that the requirements must be implemented in a way that does justice to the justification(s) we have identified and suggested in the previous chapter.

9.1.2.1 Adequate and Reasonable Notice

As we have seen, one of the procedural requirements that features in all three lists of the CESCR is that of "adequate and reasonable notice". This requirement is important as notifying individuals prior to a decision enables them to participate in the decision-making process and to give their view of the situation. In that sense, the requirement is a precondition for participation in administrative procedures. It stood at the centre of two individual cases considered by the CESCR—*I. D. G. v. Spain* and *Trujillo v. Ecuador*. We will now have a closer look at these cases.

9.1.2.1.1 I. D. G. v. Spain

In *I.D.G. v. Spain*[8], the committee had to look at a mortgage enforcement procedure. The author had purchased property in Madrid. By 2012, she had been behind on several mortgage payments. This led the lending institution to apply for a mortgage enforcement procedure against her. In September and October of 2012, the Madrid Courts Central Notification and Enforcement Service tried to notify the author of the decision to admit the mortgage enforcement application unsuccessfully four times. Finally, the notification was posted on the Court notice board at the end of October 2012. On 11 February 2013, the court ordered

[7] See *supra* 8.2.1.1.2 as well as 5.1.2.

[8] CESCR, *I.D.G. v. Spain*.

to arrange for an auction of the property of the author. On 1 and 21 March 2013, the Notification and Enforcement Service attempted to notify the author of the planned auction but was unsuccessful again. They left a message for the author so that she could pick up the notice which she eventually did by proxy on 4 April 2013. The author claimed that only then—more than half a year after the admission of the lending institution's application—had she become aware of the mortgage enforcement proceedings against her. She argued that because of the court's "lack of diligence" she had not been notified of the proceedings against her and that this failure of notification had made it impossible for her to mount a defence against the proceedings and violated her right to housing under the ICESCR.[9]

While some aspects of the case concerned proceedings in front of a court, the notification procedure was "administrative in nature"[10]. Moreover, the committee explicitly noted that its statements regarding the necessary involvement of the individual in the proceedings were applicable to procedures regardless of whether they were conducted by parts of a state's judiciary or executive.[11]

Before beginning its analysis of the facts of the case, the CESCR states that "the main legal problem posed by [the] communication [was] whether the author's right to housing [...] was violated by the State party as a consequence of a mortgage enforcement process in which, according to the author, she was not properly notified of the application, thus preventing her from defending her rights under the Covenant".[12]

When laying out the abstract legal requirements against which to test the facts of the case, the committee begins by recalling some general aspects of the right to housing before discussing the obligation to ensure access to an effective and immediate remedy in the context of notification procedures which the CESCR derived *inter alia* from Article 2 (1) ICESCR.[13] The committee then turns to the "adequate notice" requirement, and recalls that "appropriate procedural protection and due process are essential aspects of all human rights".[14] It then goes on to state that states' authorities

---

[9] Ibid, paras. 2.1–2.6.

[10] Leonie Huijbers, *Process-based Fundamental Rights Review* (Intersentia 2021), 74.

[11] CESCR, *I.D.G. v. Spain*, para. 12.2.

[12] Ibid, para. 10.6.

[13] Ibid, paras. 11.2–11.4.

[14] Ibid, para. 12.1.

> *should* take all reasonable measures and make every effort to ensure that the serving of notice of the most important acts and orders in an administrative or judicial procedure is conducted properly and effectively so that the persons affected have the opportunity to participate in the proceedings in defence of their rights.[15]

Finally, the committee states that the public posting of information may fulfil the adequate notice requirement, but that it may do so only as an absolute last resort[16] and that, given the importance of the notification requirement for enabling the individual to defend her rights, an insufficient notification would amount to a violation of the right to housing[17].

Against this legal background, the CESCR evaluates the facts of the case. It "acknowledges the repeated efforts" to notify the author of the communication in person but reaches the conclusion that the Spanish authorities could have done more. The committee states that they could, e.g., have left a note in her letter box or that they could have left the notification with the caretaker or a neighbour. Hence, the committee concludes, the state party had not established that publicly posting the notification was actually a means of last resort and that it was therefore not in accordance with the requirements for adequate notice it had laid out before.[18]

Notably, in 2019, the CESCR issued a report on follow-up communications to *I.D.G. v. Spain* in which it held that Spain had "satisfactorily implemented" the views when it had changed the provisions in its Civil Procedure Act that dealt with public posting of notices. The public posting of a notification was only possible now after more exhaustive attempts to notify the affected individuals personally, such as sending the notice to their workplace or investigating for their current address.[19] The case of I.D.G. v. Spain shows us that the committee takes the notice requirement very seriously given its importance for enabling the individual to defend her rights *vis à vis* state authorities. It thus connects the requirement of timely notification to the instrumental justification we have outlined above. In particular, we can see how requirements of administrative procedure can facilitate legal protection—this time *ex ante*—but allowing the affected to defend her rights in the process.

---

[15] Ibid, para. 12.2.

[16] Ibid, para. 12.3.

[17] Ibid, para. 12.4.

[18] Ibid, para. 13.3.

[19] CESCR, *Report on follow-up to communications Nos. 2/2014 and 5/2015 against Spain* (Comm nos 2/2014 and 5/2015, CESCR, 29 November 2019), p. 2–4.8

9.1.2.1.2 Trujillo v. Ecuador

Another interesting case is that of *Marcia Cecilia Trujillo Calera v. Ecuador*[20]. The case is one of the few individual cases decided by the CESCR that does not concern the right to housing. Instead, the case deals with the right to social security. The author had tried to retire from work under a "special reduced retirement scheme" after she had paid contributions to the retirement system for several years. When she finally applied for early retirement, the authorities told her that her payments had been invalid and that she had no right to receive early retirement in Ecuador. The author's claim and the views of the CESCR directly addressed the administrative procedure that led up to the decision to deny her entry to the pension scheme which makes the case particularly relevant for our purposes.[21]

The author claimed that "everyone should have access to information on eligibility for social benefits and to an administrative process that guarantees due process".[22] Moreover, she denounced the administrative procedure in question as "not efficient, prompt or effective".[23] The state party of Ecuador directly reacted to this claim by arguing that the right to due process was regulated in the ICCPR, not the ICESCR and that therefore the claim was inadmissible before the CESCR.[24] It then went on to bring an alternative argument, namely that "[p]roceedings between individuals and the administration are governed by the principle of good faith and based on presumption of knowledge of law", and that, because the law was clear on the question of her eligibility and because she could have figured her non-eligibility out herself, the author's communication was to be dismissed.[25] The author answered to these arguments that it was the responsibility of the Ecuadorian Social Security Institute "to determine, in a timely and efficient manner, whether its affiliates' contributions are made within the established time frame". In her case, the officials had failed to inform her of the problems with her payments and the proceedings had not been timely as they took 14 years.[26]

In the merits part of the view, the CESCR defines the "central question" of the case as

---

[20] CESCR, *Trujillo v Ecuador* (Comm no 10/2015, CESCR, 14 November 2018).

[21] Ibid, paras. 2.1–2.4.

[22] Ibid, para. 3.2.

[23] Ibid, para. 3.2.

[24] Ibid, para. 4.5. See *supra* 9.1.4.

[25] Ibid, para. 4.8.

[26] Ibid, para. 5.4–5.5.

> *whether the denial of the author's request for special retirement constitutes a violation of the right to social security under article* 9 of the Covenant ***because the Ecuadorian Social Security Institute not only did not inform her in a timely manner that her voluntary affiliation had terminated in August 1989 and that the subsequent contributions made by her until February 1995 were invalid*** but also continued to receive her contributions.[27]

The CESCR clarifies that a lack of timely information can in theory lead to a violation of the human right to social security under Article 9 ICESCR. When turning to the issue of "access to a retirement pension" as an aspect of the right to a retirement pension[28], the committee recalls organizational and procedural requirements that are highly interesting for our purposes. Firstly, the committee mentions that states enjoy a "certain margin of discretion" in ensuring access to a retirement pension.[29] Then, it moves on to generally concur with Ecuador's argument that there should be an assumption that everyone knows the law. However,

> *States must ensure the right of all affiliates to request, seek and receive information on their right to social security, including their retirement pension or future retirement pension, and take the necessary steps to ensure that the institutions, whether public or private, responsible for managing the social security system provide affiliates with timely and appropriate information on, among other things, the validity of their contributions and any changes to their affiliation status.*[30]

Later on in the views, the committee gets to a point that is essential for our study, a part entitled "Lack of adequate and timely information and disregard of legitimate expectations".[31] In this part, the committee addresses why it is so important for the affected individual to be given timely information on their case. The committee argues that individuals must be informed of their (legal) situation in a timely fashion not only because they have a right to be given an opportunity to present their own views and legal arguments but also to make certain life arrangements. In the constellation of the case, the author had lived the last 20 years of her life with the expectation that she would benefit from the early retirement regime offered by the Ecuadorian state. These remarks are particularly interesting as they provide a connection to the dignitarian justification. The

[27] Ibid, para. 10.6. Emphasis added.

[28] Ibid, para. 12.1–12.3.

[29] Ibid, para. 12.1.

[30] Ibid, para. 12.2.

[31] Ibid, para. 16.1–16.4.

"ability to plan one's life" has been called a "necessary condition for human dignity".[32] And the case of *Trujillo v. Ecuador* shows us a very interesting way in which the conversation between the administration of a state and an individual can be a condition for that ability to plan, and thus ultimately for human dignity.

9.1.2.2 Meaningful Participation and Genuine Consultation

The second procedural requirement from the CESCR catalogues on which we find some remarks in the committees' pronouncements is the genuine consultation requirement. We find an example of this in the HRC's pronouncements on minority rights, e.g., in the seminal case of *Länsman et al. v. Finland*. The case concerned a communication lodged by a member of a minority group against logging in an area the group had traditionally used for reindeer herding. The HRC reaffirmed the obligation to ensure effective participation which it had stipulated in its general comment on minority rights in 1994.[33] However, after reaffirming the principle, the HRC went on to declare that the minority group

> *was* consulted in the process of drawing up the logging plans and in the consultation, the [minority group] did not react negatively to the plans for logging. That this consultation process was unsatisfactory to the authors and was capable of greater interaction does not alter the Committee's assessment.[34]

Notably, the committee defers the assessment of whether the procedure was satisfactory largely to the state party. The fact that the authors were not satisfied with the consultation and there was room for more interaction was explicitly labelled irrelevant to the committee's assessment. This statement is a lot more reserved than the CESCR's calling for an opportunity for "genuine consultation".

More recently, the committee has dealt with the genuine consultation requirement differently. In its views to *Äärelä and Näkkäläjärvi v Finland* of 2001, the HRC discussed the question of whether an interference with reindeer husbandry was so substantial that the state party had "failed to properly protect the authors' right to enjoy their culture".[35] The committee found in favour of Finland, *inter alia* with the argument that "the authors, and other key stakeholder groups, were

---

[32] Dyzenhaus, 244.

[33] HRC, *Länsman et al. v. Finland* (Comm no 671/1995, HRC, 22 November 1996), para. 10.4.

[34] Ibid, para. 10.5. Emphasis original.

[35] HRC, *Äärelä and Näkkäläjärvi v Finland* (Comm no 779/1997, HRC, 7 November 2001), para. 7.5.

consulted in the evolution of the logging plans [...], and that the plans were partially altered in response to criticisms from those quarters".[36] Two interpretations are conceivable here, however. The passage can be read as an *argumentum a fortiori*: if it is enough for the state party to hear the affected individual's criticism, it is certainly enough to respond to that criticism by altering plans. Alternatively, it can be read as the committee requiring active engagement with criticism offered by the affected individual. The second reading would certainly be more in line with the instrumental justification, i.e., the principle of effectiveness, and the deontological justification suggested by this thesis, i.e., administrative procedure as the operationalisation of human dignity. Ultimately, however, the passage is inconclusive.

As we have seen above, the CESCR developed the idea of letting affected persons or groups participate in decision-making processes already in its early general comments. We find this idea of participation in relation to broader policy-making in the general comments on the right to housing[37], the rights of persons with disabilities[38], the rights of older persons[39], the right to food[40] and the right to the highest attainable standard of health[41]. From General Comment 7 onwards, the committee has applied the reasoning to individual decision-making and has been circumscribing the obligations as providing for an "opportunity for genuine consultation". However, is has not specified in greater detail what "genuine consultation" must look like.

Only in the newest general comment on issues of land and socio-economic rights do we find some more specific remarks. The CESCR states that "[i]ndividuals and communities shall be [...] allowed to meaningfully participate in decision-making processes that may affect their enjoyment of Covenant rights".[42] It states that "sufficient and transparent information [...] are key for human rights based participation in decision making", and that "decision-making processes should be transparent, organized in the relevant languages, without barriers and with reasonable accommodation for all involved".[43] While these statements are not particularly specific, either, they highlight what the

[36] Ibid, para. 7.6.

[37] CESCR, GC 4, para. 12.

[38] CESCR, GC 5, paras. 13–14.

[39] CESCR, GC 6, para. 39.

[40] CESCR, GC 12, para. 24.

[41] CESCR, GC 14, paras. 11, 17 and 54.

[42] CESCR, GC 26, para. 20.

[43] Ibid.

term already suggests: that the "genuine consultation" requirement cannot be implemented by merely formalistic consultation procedures. Instead, procedures directed at the involvement of the affected individual must be meaningful. The affected individual must have a voice; she must be heard and reckoned with. Only then is the consultation *genuine*. The state must put in place conditions for such meaningful participation. What precisely the consultation must look like in order to be meaningful will depend on many factors. It is, as we have already seen, context-dependent. The rationale(s) behind the requirement, however, must guide its implementation and—ultimately—its review.

9.1.2.3 Conclusion

In this section, we have looked at how the obligation to involve the affected individual in the decision-making process must play out in practice. Most importantly, we have seen that the CESCR has highlighted the effectiveness justification as a yardstick for the implementation of obligations of administrative procedure. Given that we have identified essentially the same instrumental justification in the pronouncements of the HRC and that a dignitarian justification can be applied to human rights in general[44], this idea that the implementation must be guided by these justifications must be extrapolated to civil and political rights as well, despite the HRC's relative paucity on the issue of implementation.

9.1.3 Proportionality and Procedural Obligations

In our analysis of the FCC's jurisprudence, we have identified two ways in which the principle of proportionality relates to the implementation of procedures, both of which we find in the committees' pronouncements as well. Firstly, the principle of proportionality prohibits procedures from presenting disproportionate obstacles to the effective enjoyment of human rights (9.1.3.1).[45] Secondly, the intensity of an envisaged interference with a right has a proportionate relationship with the required procedural protection (9.1.3.2).[46]

[44] See *supra* 8.2.2.

[45] See *supra* 6.3.2.1.

[46] See *supra* 6.3.2.2.

9.1.3.1 The Obstructive Potential of Procedures for the Enjoyment of Human Rights

When the realisation or the enjoyment of a right, depends on the completion of a procedure, the procedure presents an interference with that right. In that sense, procedures can have an obstructive potential for human rights. They can theoretically be abused by governments to limit their enjoyment. We have found this realisation in the jurisprudence of the FCC,[47] and it can be found in the committees' pronouncements, too.

The HRC in particular has highlighted the obstructive potential of procedures which necessitates one of the two material consequences of the principle of proportionality for procedural obligations: procedures may limit the enjoyment of human rights only to the extent necessary for and proportionate to the respective purpose of the procedure.

The HRC invoked the obstructive potential of procedures for the first time in its general comment on the freedom of movement in 1999. In the document, the committee makes two remarkable statements. Firstly, the committee holds that

> *[t]he principle of proportionality has to be respected not only in the law that frames the restrictions, but also by the administrative and judicial authorities in applying the law. States should ensure that any proceedings relating to the exercise or restriction of these rights are expeditious and that reasons for the application of restrictive measures are provided.*[48]

The HRC makes these remarks under the heading of "Restrictions (paragraph 3)" and with direct reference to the principle of proportionality. The connection between the principle of proportionality and procedures that must be fulfilled before a right can be exercised is evident: the more burdensome and longer a procedure is, the more it interferes with the enjoyment of a right. And the more a procedure interferes with a right, the weightier the justification must be.

In another interesting passage in the same general comment, the committee elaborates on the factors which can make a procedure particularly burdensome for the individual:

> *A major source of concern are the manifold legal and bureaucratic barriers unnecessarily affecting the full enjoyment of the rights of the individuals to move freely, to leave a country, including their own, and to take up residence. Regarding the right to*

[47] See *supra* 6.3.2.1.

[48] HRC, *General comment No. 27: Article 12 (Freedom of movement)* (1999) HRI/GEN/1/Rev.9 (Vol. I) p. 223, para. 15. Emphases added.

> *movement within a country, the Committee has criticized provisions requiring individuals to apply for permission to change their residence or to seek the approval of the local authorities of the place of destination, as well as delays in processing such written applications. States' practice presents an even richer array of obstacles making it more difficult to leave the country, in particular for their own nationals. These rules and practices include, inter alia, lack of access for applicants to the competent authorities and lack of information regarding requirements; the requirement to apply for special forms through which the proper application documents for the issuance of a passport can be obtained; the need for supportive statements from employers or family members; exact description of the travel route; issuance of passports only on payment of high fees substantially exceeding the cost of the service rendered by the administration; unreasonable delays in the issuance of travel documents; restrictions on family members travelling together; requirement of a repatriation deposit or a return ticket; requirement of an invitation from the State of destination or from people living there; harassment of applicants, for example by physical intimidation, arrest, loss of employment or expulsion of their children from school or university; refusal to issue a passport because the applicant is said to harm the good name of the country. In the light of these practices, States parties should make sure that all restrictions imposed by them are in full compliance with article 12, paragraph 3.*[49]

The passage is an unusually explicit expression of what the committee considers to be "bureaucratic barriers unnecessarily affecting the full enjoyment of the rights of the individuals [under Article 12 ICCPR]". Many of the examples on the list are procedural. The passage gives us a comparatively clear idea of what the committee considers to be problematic procedural obstacles. *E contrario*, we can infer from these statements that the HRC is of the opinion that Article 12 ICCPR requires states to ensure speedy decision-making processes and that access to such procedures and the competent authorities is not made difficult by obstacles such as complicated application requirements, high administrative costs, etc. While the level of detail of this passage in General Comment 12 is certainly remarkable, the issue of high administrative hurdles for freedom-of-movement-related matters already appeared in earlier concluding observations of the HRC.[50]

Another context in which the HRC clarifies its stances on administrative hurdles for the enjoyment of human rights is that of peaceful assemblies. In General Comment 37 on the right of peaceful assembly, the HRC discusses the compatibility of notification regimes with Article 21 ICCPR.[51] The passage begins with the assertion that "[h]aving to apply for permission from the authorities

---

49 Ibid, para. 17. Emphases added.

50 HRC, *Concluding observations of the Human Rights Committee: Iraq* (19 November 1997) UN Doc CCPR/C/79/Add.84, para. 14.

51 HRC, GC 37, para. 70–73.

undercuts the idea that peaceful assembly is a basic right".[52] In particular the danger of notification becoming *de facto* permission procedures is expressed by the committee when it makes clear that notification regimes must not in practice be authorization regimes.[53] This highlights the committee's awareness and its cautious approach towards procedural obstacles in the way of the realisation of human rights. Certainly, notification regimes represent a much less intrusive interference with the right of peaceful assembly than a regime which would make the exercise of the right dependent on an official permit would be.

However, the HRC has not only addressed the obstructive potential for the enjoyment of negative freedoms. It has also discussed the obstructive potential of procedures for positive rights. In its General Comment 34, in the context of the right of access to information, the committee held that, in order to give effect to the right of access to information,

> *States parties should make every effort to ensure easy, prompt, effective and practical access to such information. States parties should also enact the necessary procedures, whereby one may gain access to information, such as by means of freedom of information legislation. The procedures should provide for the timely processing of requests for information according to clear rules that are compatible with the Covenant. Fees for requests for information should not be such as to constitute an unreasonable impediment to access to information.*[54]

The procedures discussed in this passage enable individuals to vindicate their right to information by applying for access to the piece of information held by public bodies they are interested in. To discharge this facilitative function, however, the procedures must not impede the individual's right of access to information in an unreasonable way. Explicitly, the committee states that the temporal and financial obstacles must not be such that they would unnecessarily impede access to information. The rationale is essentially the same as in the examples discussed above: the longer it takes for the authorities to reach a decision on something an individual has a right to and the more costly it is for her to get such a decision, the more the decision-making process interferes with her rights. Obviously, the principle of proportionality is at work here, too.

Moreover, in General Comment 36, in the context of the "right to live a life in dignity", the HRC raised the issue of timeliness of decision-making again. The committee discusses obligations to provide easy access to conditions needed for a

[52] Ibid, para. 70.

[53] Ibid, para. 73.

[54] HRC, GC 34, para. 19.

life in dignity. It holds that measures to implement the right to live in dignity must be "designed to ensure access without delay".[55] These measures will necessarily include procedures that regulate the allocation of (limited) resources. As with the procedures in place to facilitate the right to freedom of information, we are dealing with procedures that constitute prerequisites to the enjoyment of positive rights. So, the same rationale applies here.

The obstructive potential of the procedures plays a role in the pronouncements of the CESCR, too, albeit less prominently and less explicitly. In its General Comment 22 on sexual and reproductive health, for example, the CESCR holds that states are prohibited from enacting laws and policies "that create barriers in access to sexual and reproductive health".[56] Moreover, in General Comment 19, under the heading of "accessibility", the committee mentions that social security benefits must be provided in a "timely manner".[57] Given that the right to social security depends on procedures for its realisation, this is the same constellation as in the HRC's General Comment 34, when the committee held that procedures were necessary to realise the right of access to information. Generally, the idea of "access" to a right plays a great role in the pronouncements of the CESCR.[58] Hence, the rationale that the effective enjoyment of a right must not be impeded by unrealistically high procedural requirements is easily extrapolatable to socio-economic rights.

To conclude this section, we shall characterise the phenomenon we have described here once again as an application of the doctrine governing the limitation of human rights. The consequences resulting from the obstructive potential of the procedure are nothing more than a straightforward application of the principle of proportionality. When the enjoyment of a human right is made dependent upon the completion of a procedure, that procedure limits the right. In other words, the procedure presents an interference with a human right that is *prima facie* guaranteed independently of the completion of a procedure. Hence, the procedure must comply with the general doctrine governing the limitation of human rights.

---

55 HRC, GC 36, para. 26.

56 CESCR, *General comment No. 22 (2016) on the right to sexual and reproductive health (article 12 of the International Covenant on Economic, Social and Cultural Rights)* (2 May 2016) UN Doc E/C.12/GC/22, para. 41.

57 CESCR, GC 19, para. 27.

58 Latest since GC 12, the CESCR has regularly put emphasis on the notion of "access" to socio-economic rights in its general comments.

9.1.3.2 A Proportionate Connection Between the Intensity of the Interference and the Scope of Procedural Protection?

In our analysis of the FCC's jurisprudence, we have seen how the principle of proportionality can influence the required level of procedural protection. In the *Palästinenser* decision, the FCC held that the greater the degree of irreversibility of an envisaged decision, the greater the need for procedural protection *ex ante*.[59] Given the relevance of proportionality to IHRL,[60] one would assume that the proportionate relationship between the intensity with which the envisaged act interferes with human rights and the requirements of procedural protection plays a role here as well.

Surprisingly, remarks in this regard by the committees are rare. In the general comments, we find the idea that procedural protection, especially *ex ante* procedural protection becomes more important, the more the envisaged decision will interfere with human rights in the CESCR's pronouncements only in one place. In its General Comment 7 the CESCR stated that

> *appropriate* procedural protection and due process are essential aspects of all human rights but are especially pertinent in relation to a matter such as forced evictions which directly invokes a large number of the rights recognized in both the International Covenants on Human Rights.[61]

Notably, the CESCR relies on a "quantitative" understanding of intensity here. The committee does not say that procedural protection is especially pertinent whenever an interference with one human right is particularly grave or irreversible but when an interference negatively affects multiple human rights at once. We can only speculate why that is. Is it because the CESCR thinks that the more human rights are implicated, the worse the situation for the affected individual? Is it because the more human rights are implicated, the more complex the situation becomes for the agent of the administration to assess? Any deeper reflection on this issue would lead to great—perhaps unsurmountable—doctrinal challenges

[59] See *supra* 6.3.2.2.

[60] See on this already *supra* 8.2.1.1.2.3.

[61] CESCR, GC 7, para. 15.

that cannot be tackled here.[62] Importantly, however, this passage points to a proportionate connection between the worsening of the situation of the individual and the procedural protection that such a change must be accompanied by. Moreover, the fact that the committee relies on this quantitative understanding here does not exclude the extrapolation of this thought to a criterion of the qualitative intensity of an envisaged interference.

Beyond this reference, we do not find an explicit reference to the idea that the procedural protection must be particularly strong whenever the envisaged interference is particularly intensive or irreversible. This is surprising as we find this idea of a proportionate connection between an envisaged interference and necessary precautions in the literature. In fact, it has been discussed in IHRL scholarship, e.g., with regard to the standard of due diligence.[63] Moreover, at least the relation that procedural protection must be particularly strong when the interference is irreversible, follows directly from the compensatory function of legal protection *ex ante* for a lack in adequate legal protection *ex post*.[64] In accordance with the compensatory function of *ex ante* procedural protection, it could easily be argued that if *ex post* procedural protection is not available to remedy a human rights violation—and that a decision is irreversible in this sense –, *ex ante* procedural protection must be particularly thorough to make up for it.

9.1.3.3 Conclusion

The principle of proportionality influences the implementation of obligations of administrative procedure in two ways. Firstly, whenever the enjoyment of human rights is made dependent upon the completion of a procedure, the procedure represents a limitation of that right. Thus, it must comply with the general requirements for limiting a human right, in particular, with the principle of proportionality. In other words, procedures must not present disproportionate hurdles

---

62 The problems that such an idea of quantitative intensity would cause for legal doctrine cannot be problematised here. What Brade has convincingly argued for German fundamental rights when delineating the phenomenon of "fundamental rights conflicts" ("Grundrechtskonkurrenzen") from the notion of additive fundamental rights interference will apply to IHRL, too: exceeding the limits of the scope of individual fundamental rights would pose "hardly solvable difficulties for the legal practitioner" as there is "simply no convincing category transcending the scope of fundamental rights to make the facts tangible", Alexander Brade, *Additive Grundrechtseingriffe: Ein Beitrag zur Grundrechtsdogmatik* (Nomos 2020), 200.

63 See Björnstern Baade, 'Due Diligence and the Duty to Potect Human Rights' in Heike Krieger, Anne Peters and Leonhard Kreuzer (eds), *Due Diligence in the International Legal Order* (Oxford University Press 2020), 97–99.

64 See *supra* 8.2.1.2.2.2.

for individuals to enjoy their human rights. Secondly, procedural protection *ex ante* can become necessary when the intensity of the expected interference with human rights is particularly high. The more the envisaged measure interferes with the human rights of an individual, the more careful must the state action be when making her decision. And the greater the relevance of *ex ante* legal protection.

9.1.4 The Individual Enforceability of Procedural Obligations

The next issue we shall turn to is the issue of whether the procedural guarantees are individually enforceable, i.e., whether subjective rights correspond to them. We will see that the committees consider obligations of administrative procedure to be generally enforceable (9.1.4.1). However, there is a caveat when it comes to the question of when procedural shortcomings constitute actual violations of human rights (9.1.4.2).

9.1.4.1 The General Enforceability of Obligations of Administrative Procedure

The HRC's relatively recent case of *S. F. v. Denmark* provides a starting point to understand whether the committees consider procedural obligations *ex ante* to be enforceable. In its views in this case, the HRC considered the expulsion of an Iranian national, who had applied for asylum in Denmark in 1998, to the Islamic Republic of Iran. The episode from the lengthy sequence of administrative steps leading up to the author's eventual deportation in 2014, which is of interest here, is the author's application with the Refugee Appeals Board—an administrative body—to reopen his proceedings in 2014. After the board had denied reopening the proceedings, the author alleged that the decision not to reopen the proceedings was in violation of his rights under Articles 6 and 7 ICCPR because they were not made by a competent tribunal and that he should have benefited from a new oral hearing before the decision was made.[65] The HRC rejected the admissibility of this claim by stating that "the author had failed to justify how *this in itself* affected his rights under the relevant provisions."[66]

Notably, with this statement, the HRC does not reject the possibility that a lack of *ex ante* legal protection can constitute a violation of human rights entirely. Instead, it seems to implicitly recognise the possibility and only rejects

[65] HRC, *S. F. v. Denmark* (Comm no 2494/2014, HRC, 17 May 2019), paras. 5.2–5.3.

[66] Ibid, para. 7.5. Emphasis added.

the author's claims because he did not substantiate how the procedural shortcomings constitute a violation. If a violation of the author's rights by a lack of procedural protection *ex ante* had not been possible to begin with, the HRC could have rejected the possibility that such a claim could be brought altogether and not made it dependent on the substantiation of the author. However, the committee makes clear that there must be something more than the mere violation of a procedural obligation for that violation to be enforceable. We will return to this point in the next section.

In its views in the case of *I.D.G v. Spain*, the CESCR considered "a communication that raises the possibility of a violation of the author's right to housing by reason of possibly inadequate notice of mortgage enforcement proceedings, which, it is claimed, prevented a proper defence in those proceedings" to be admissible without raising any objections.[67] And eventually, the HRC eventually states that "insufficient notice of an application for mortgage enforcement [...] represents a violation of the right to housing".[68]

Even more illuminating are the remarks found in the admissibility part of the CESCR's views in the case of *Trujillo v. Ecuador*[69]. The author had claimed that she was entitled to "access to information on eligibility for social benefits and to an administrative process that guarantees due process".[70] In response to this claim, Ecuador submitted that "the author's allegations relate[d] not to a violation of a Covenant right but to the right to due process and the right to information, and that the Committee [was] therefore not competent *ratione materiae* to consider the allegations".[71] The committee answered this challenge of its jurisdiction in a way that makes clear that it considers procedural rights to be enforceable by their right-holders:

> *The Committee recalls that the lack of adequate judicial protection may entail a violation of a right recognized in the Covenant, since it is the duty of States to guarantee effective judicial remedies for the protection of Covenant rights; there cannot be a right without a remedy to protect it. The Committee also considers that the failure to provide persons with appropriate information on how to access a right may entail a violation of that right. The Committee therefore considers that the author's allegations concerning due process and timely access to information are intimately linked to the complaint of a violation of the right to social security under article* 9 of the

[67] CESCR, *I.D.G. v. Spain*, para. 9.7.

[68] Ibid, para. 12.4.

[69] CESCR, *Trujillo v. Ecuador*.

[70] Ibid, para. 3.2.

[71] Ibid, para. 9.6.

> Covenant and are inseparable from it. The Committee concludes that it is competent ratione materiae to consider this part of the communication.[72]

Notably, the committee draws a parallel to the right to an effective remedy. That a lack of an effective remedy can constitute a violation of a human right is generally accepted for ICCPR rights as well.[73] Given that effective remedies *ex post* and legal protection *ex ante* work together in tandem to further the better implementation of human rights,[74] it seems sensible to draw conclusions from the enforceability of the right to an effective remedy for the enforceability of legal protection *ex ante*.

These examples show that the committees have no general objection to the enforceability of procedural rights derived from the rights of the covenants. In particular from the case law of the CESCR, we could see that it considers the "adequate procedural protection" which is an "essential element of all human rights" to give rise to subjective rights which are "inseparable" from the material contents of the rights and can thus generally be enforced in front of (quasi-)judicial bodies. This finding is in line with Alexy's point of a *prima facie* argument in favour of subjective rights which applies to IHRL as well.[75] Human rights—like the fundamental rights of the German constitution are individual rights. Hence, whenever someone would want to argue that certain elements or derivations therefrom are only objective in nature, she would bear the burden of proof for such an assertion.[76]

9.1.4.2 When Does an Interference with Procedural Rights Amount to an Enforceable Violation?

Does this general decision in favour of enforceability mean that every procedural shortcoming gives rise to an enforceable violation of the respective human right? The HRC's pronouncements do not yield a lot of information on the question of when a procedural shortcoming amounts to a violation of an ICCPR right. However, the case of *S. F. v. Denmark* which has already told us that the HRC has no general objection to the enforceability of derivative procedural rights, can

---

[72] Ibid, para. 9.7. Reference omitted.

[73] See Taylor, 78ff. While the HRC used to be of the view that, in order to find a violation of the right to an effective remedy, there needed to be a substantive violation of the right in question, it has in more recent jurisprudence developed what one might call an "arguability test", see Joseph and Castan, 869–870.

[74] See *supra* 8.2.1.2.

[75] Alexy, *A Theory of Constitutional Rights*, 333. See also *supra* 6.1.2.

[76] See *supra* 6.1.2.

be consulted for this question, too. As we have seen, the committee rejected the claim of the author of the communication that his rights were violated because he had not substantiated that the fact that an allegedly incompetent tribunal had made a decision and that he was not heard by this tribunal "in itself" affected his rights under Articles 6 and 7 ICCPR.[77] The committee seems to be of the opinion that there must be some additional detrimental effect on the enjoyment of human rights resulting from the procedural violation that goes beyond the mere procedural shortcoming. Otherwise, victim status as required by Article 1 of the first Optional Protocol to the ICCPR cannot be established.[78]

Once again, the pronouncements of the CESCR shed more light on the question. In its General Comment 17, we find a passage that would indicate that the CESCR has a more straightforward approach towards procedural shortcomings constituting a violation:

> *Examples [for violations of the obligation to fulfil] include [...] the failure to provide adequate opportunities for the active and informed participation of authors and groups of authors in any decision-making process that has an impact on their right to benefit from the protection of the moral and material interests resulting from their scientific, literary or artistic productions.*[79]

In this passage, the committee does not make the finding of a violation dependent on any conditions. However, its case law tells us that its approach is not that straightforward. As we have discussed in the previous section, in *I.D.G. v. Spain*, the CESCR found that Spain had not done enough to notify the author of a planned forced eviction from her home. Having found this breach of a procedural obligation derived from the right to housing, the CESCR raised the question of "whether the inadequate notice given to the author [...] *did or did not significantly affect her right to a defence*, such as to entail a violation of the right to housing".[80] Apparently, there are procedural shortcomings which are grave enough to entail a violation of human rights and such which are not. Only when other legal positions connected to human rights—in this case the right to defence—are "significantly affected" is the committee ready to find a violation.

In this case, Spain argued that the author's right to a defence was not significantly affected by the inadequate notice stating that the applicant would have

[77] HRC, *S. F. v. Denmark*, para. 7.5.

[78] See generally on the victim requirement Joseph and Castan, 71ff.

[79] CESCR, GC 17, para. 46.

[80] CESCR, *I.D.G. v. Spain*, paras. 13.4–13.5. Emphasis added.

had very few legal means to influence the mortgage enforcement procedure anyway and that she could have mounted "unlimited challenges to recovery of the mortgage loan" in an ordinary procedure.[81] The CESCR rejected this argument. It argued that legal challenges in an ordinary procedure would only be adequate to remedy an interference with the right to housing if they were able to stop the auction of the house. This was, however, not the case. Hence, the CESCR concluded that the inadequate notice of the enforcement proceedings amounted to a violation of the author's right to housing.[82]

Notably, the "right to a defence" which the CESCR refers to in the passage in *I.D.G. v. Spain* is itself a derivative procedural right. The committee does not directly refer to the material contents of the right to housing. Nevertheless, the committee establishes a connection with the material content of the right to housing, albeit indirectly. By holding that avenues of legal action are in compliance with the right to defence only if they are able to stop an eviction, the committee connects the procedural guarantees in question to the material contents of the right to housing.

Moreover, in the *Trujillo* case, when analysing the author's complaint, the CESCR stated that "[the author's] situation might not entail a violation of the right to social security if it had no significant impact on the author's life plan and her effective enjoyment of the right through a retirement pension".[83] Here too, the CESCR suggests that violations of a state's procedural obligations with regard to a certain right, do not necessarily entail a violation of that right. Only if the procedural shortcoming had a significant impact on the author's enjoyment of her rights does it amount to a violation of these rights. In the case, the CESCR answered the question of whether the procedural violation affected the author's right to social security severely enough in the affirmative. The committee referred to the "legitimate expectations" of the author in order to explain that the failure to share adequate information about her eligibility for a retirement pension had significantly impacted her right to social security.[84] The fact that the Ecuadorian Social Security Institute continued to receive voluntary contributions made by the author from 1990 to 1995 even though they were invalid, and that, in 2001, employees of the institute orally informed her that she was eligible for the special

---

[81] Ibid, para. 13.4.

[82] Ibid, para. 13.4–13.7.

[83] CESCR, *Trujillo v. Ecuador*, para. 16.3.

[84] For a general discussion of the concept see Soren Schønberg, *Legitimate Expectations in Administrative Law* (Oxford University Press 2000).

retirement pension scheme, created a "legitimate expectation" that led the author to make the arrangements she did. The CESCR held that the information she had not received on time "concerned a considerable proportion of the author's contributions" and was brought to her attention rather late "by which time she was an older person, faced with difficulties in gaining access to the labour market, in a critical economic situation and experiencing health problems."[85]

The approach of the committees is in line with their justification of procedural rights and obligations. As we have seen, except in the context of indigenous peoples' rights, the committees do not rely on dignitarian justifications.[86] Instead, they exclusively construe the participation of affected individuals in decision-making processes of the state to be a means to the end of better human rights realisation. According to the instrumental justification, the participation of an individual does not have a value in itself. This explains why the committees would seemingly not take issue with a procedural violation that does not have substantive effects on the enjoyment of an individual's human rights. If human rights are implemented adequately anyway, insisting upon the fulfilment of procedural obligations would seem formalistic.

This begs the question of whether the issue here must be approached differently if one were to follow the dignitarian justification.[87] On the one hand, the fact that according to the dignitarian justification, the participation of the individual has a standalone value, speaks in favour of any procedural shortcoming being a violation. On the other hand, the principle of human dignity in which the dignitarian justification rests is not a binding human right under international law. Given its relatively weak legal quality, it would be difficult to argue that any procedural shortcoming would amount to an enforceable violation of human rights because it does not do justice to the human being as a self-directed agent. Moreover, seeing an enforceable human rights violation in every procedural shortcoming would dramatically exacerbate the problems that come with the positive procedural obligations. We will address these issues in the next section.

[85] CESCR, *Trujillo v. Ecuador*, para. 16.3.

[86] See *supra* 8.1.

[87] See *supra* 8.2.2.

9.2 The Problem with the Positive Nature of Procedural Obligations

In the context of our analysis of the FCC's jurisprudence, we have concluded that due to their positive nature, obligations of administrative procedure may raise certain problems with regard to the principles of democracy and the separation of power. Similar problems arise under IHRL, albeit related to a different principle, i.e., the principle of state sovereignty. After explaining why and how these problems arise under IHRL (9.2.1), we will highlight the particular importance of the principle of subsidiarity (9.2.2) and assess whether the committees' approaches we have identified can adequately address the concerns (9.2.3).

9.2.1 The Problem with Positive Obligations Under IHRL and the Relationship Between International Human Rights Institutions and States

One main takeaway from our reflections about the FCC's jurisprudence was the realisation that positive rights and obligations create certain problems, especially when they are individually enforceable. Through their open-ended nature, they can pose challenges to the principles of democracy and the separation of powers. We have seen that, given these dangers, it is important for the judiciary of a state, when reviewing alleged violations of positive rights to be careful not to overstep their limits. They must make sure that they do not make demands which are too specific and take away too much leeway from the other branches of government, in particular from the (democratically elected) legislature.[88]

The open-ended nature that has proven problematic for positive obligations under German constitutional law,[89] has received critical scrutiny in IHRL scholarship, too. Under IHRL, too, positive duties are considered "quintessentially political".[90] It was, e.g., argued that endowing courts with the competence to demand positive action under socio-economic rights from the state would "turn

[88] See *supra* 6.1 and 6.2.

[89] See *supra* 6.1.

[90] Fredman, 92.

the judiciary into a political organ"[91]. Such statements are prompted by the same concerns as Böckenförde's fear of a "constitutional jurisdictional state".[92]

The decisive difference for IHRL in this regard is that the open-ended nature of positive rights and obligations does not clash with constitutional principles such as democracy or the separation of powers but with the principle of state sovereignty, i.e., states' "supreme authority" within their territories.[93] International law and its institutions may, according to classical theory, only interfere with this authority where the states have authorised such interventions. As the Permanent Court of International Justice put it in its famous Lotus Case of 1927:

> *International law governs relations between independent States. The rules of law binding upon States therefore emanate from their own free will as expressed in conventions or by usages generally accepted as expressing principles of law and established in order to regulate the relations between these co-existing independent communities or with a view to the achievement of common aims. Restrictions upon the independence of States cannot therefore be presumed.*[94]

Given their open-ended nature, one may ask how far the consent of states goes with regard to the positive obligations they have undertaken. However, the classical state-centred theory of international law resting on states' sovereignty predates the advent of codified IHRL which has drastically changed the international legal environment for states. Most importantly, it has pulled many, if not most aspects of the relationship between states and those subjected to their power out of the states' *domaine réservé*. Nevertheless, the argument that a certain action or a certain conduct is "within a state's sovereign authority" still has great normative force. Not so long ago, the Lotus case was still one of the most often cited cases in the context of international law.[95] And states still refer to their sovereignty when defending themselves against human rights-based criticism. Current examples are the treatment of the *Uyghur* minority in China and the quelling of protests

---

[91] E. W. Vierdag, 'The Legal Nature of the Rights Granted by the International Covenant on Economic, Social and Cultural Rights' (1978) 9 Netherlands Yearbook of International Law 69, 93.

[92] Böckenförde, 25–26. See *supra* 6.1.1.

[93] For a discussion of this "pivotal principle of modern international law", see Samantha Besson, 'Sovereingty' in Anne Peters (ed), *Max Planck Encyclopedia of Public International Law (MPEPIL)* (Oxford University Press 2011).

[94] PCIJ, *S.S. Lotus (French Republic v. Turkish Republic)*, PCIJ Rep Series A No 10, 18.

[95] Armin von Bogdandy and Markus Rau, 'The Lotus' in Anne Peters (ed), *Max Planck Encyclopedia of Public International Law (MPEPIL)* (Oxford University Press 2006), para. 15.

in Belarus in the aftermath of the obviously rigged Presidential election in 2020 or in Russia after the beginning of the full-scale invasion of Ukraine in early 2022. In a world in which populism, *inter alia* directed against IHRL, is on the rise,[96] such arguments must be taken seriously. This does, of course, not mean that sovereignty-based arguments which are obviously used as shields against a human rights embarrassment should stop the institutions of IHRL from fulfilling their function and defending human rights. A rising populist climate, however, should make them particularly aware of the dangers that judicial activism and judicial overreach in the field of human rights could pose. It could provide grist to the mill of populists and thus further delegitimise IHRL institutions. Hence, those who engage in IHRL, should be aware of their role and how they can achieve or maintain the necessary level of persuasion.[97] This must include being aware of the cultural and political environment in which human rights are implemented.[98] Against this backdrop, the dangers of positive rights have particular urgency.

9.2.2 A Particular Emphasis on Subsidiarity as the Necessary Consequence

Like all positive obligations under IHRL, the procedural obligations discussed here "stretch the competence"[99] of (quasi-)judicial bodies. The more open-ended a certain right is, the more leeway an international body has when adjudicating a claim under that right or making general pronouncements as to its implementation. This leeway can easily be abused in a way that would unduly restrict states' room for manoeuvre and might ultimately lead to the delegitimization of said international body.

The international legal order reflects an awareness of this issue that arises with all obligations under IHRL but are particularly pertinent when it comes to positive obligations. Like the relationship between the FCC and the other parts of government in Germany, the relationship between international (quasi-)

---

[96] For an analysis and categorisation of the challenges populism poses to international human rights institutions see Jan Petrov, 'The populist challenge to the European Court of Human Rights' (2020) 18 International Journal of Constitutional Law 476.

[97] See also Philip Alston, 'The Populist Challenge to Human Rights' (2017) 9 Journal of Human Rights Practice 1, 11–13.

[98] John Tobin, 'Seeking to Persuade: A Constructive Approach to Human Rights Treaty Interpretation' (2010) 23 Harvard Human Rights Journal 1, 40–48.

[99] Fredman, 92.

judicial bodies and states, is shaped by an awareness of the dangers of overstepping boundaries and competences. This has found a normative expression in the "structural principle"[100] of subsidiarity. It describes the idea that states are the primary guarantors of human rights. Their "vast corps of national officials", including their legislatures, their executives and their judiciaries are primarily responsible for implementing their human rights obligations. The international human rights system is merely in place to facilitate the enjoyment of human rights through assistance for states and by holding them to account.[101] The principle of subsidiarity "mediate[s] the polarity of pluralism and the common good in a globalized world".[102]

The subsidiarity principle has given rise to doctrines which essentially prescribe (judicial) deference and restraint of the international system of human rights *vis à vis* states. Interestingly, these (somewhat) correspond to the procedural safeguards in place for the constitutional complaint under Article 93 (1) (4a) Basic Law to ensure that the FCC does not overstep its mandate.[103]

Firstly, there is the exhaustion of the local remedies doctrine. Before an individual can lodge an application with an international human rights institution, she must exhaust all legal remedies available in the state allegedly violating her rights. We find this rule in Article 5 (2) (b) of the First Optional Protocol to the ICCPR, in Article 3 (1) of the Optional Protocol to the ICESCR, as well as in (almost) all other pertinent human rights treaties, e.g., in Article 35 (1) ECHR. This is parallel to the requirement that individuals exhaust all available remedies under section 90 (2) (1) AFCC and the "principle of subsidiarity" which the FCC has established.

Secondly, the doctrine of remedial subsidiarity stipulates that a human rights body finding a violation of a human right shall not specify which measure precisely is required to address the violation but that the duty to provide an effective remedy falls upon the state.[104] We found an equivalent of this doctrine

---

[100] Paolo G. Carozza, 'Subsidiarity as a Structural Principle of International Human Rights Law' (2003) 97 The American Journal of International Law 38.

[101] Gerald L. Neuman, 'Subsidiarity' in Dinah Shelton (ed), *The Oxford Handbook of International Human Rights Law* (Oxford University Press 2013), 364.

[102] Carozza, 'Subsidiarity as a Structural Principle of International Human Rights Law', 38.

[103] See *supra* 6.2.

[104] Neuman, 'Subsidiarity', 371–374. Neuman provides an interesting analysis of how different bodies perceive the scope of this principle differently and give more or less precise recommendations for the implementation of a remedy.

in section 95 AFCC according to which the FCC may void a law but not write a new one instead.

Thirdly, the "fourth instance doctrine" describes the fact that human rights courts and bodies do not exist to generally review the factual findings of national courts and their application of national law. Instead, those bodies must limit themselves to address human rights claims brought before them.[105] This doctrine starkly resembles the FCC's formula of "specific constitutional law"[106] and the idea that the FCC is not a *"Superrevisionsinstanz"*[107].

Finally, the margin of appreciation doctrine is a consequence of the principle of subsidiarity, too. The doctrine which was developed by the ECtHR describes the leeway states enjoy when implementing their human rights obligations.[108] The doctrine has rightfully been described as a doctrine of judicial deference rather than a doctrine of material margins of discretion, i.e., as being "more a matter of who takes the decisions, rather than what those decisions might be".[109] In that sense, it, too, is a "procedural doctrine".[110] We must mention here, however, that it was famously rejected by the HRC.[111]

These derivations of the principle of subsidiarity apply to all dimensions of IHRL, not just to positive obligations. However, as we have already stated in the context of German fundamental rights, reflections about the relationship between (quasi-)judicial institutions and those they oversee are particularly important in the context of positive obligations. Given the open-endedness of positive obligations, it is particularly important for international bodies to adhere to the principle of subsidiarity and to allow national courts to address the issues first, to allow the state itself to decide *how* to address a violation, to review the application of national law only in so far as a misapplication constitutes violations of specific

[105] Ibid, 370–371; Jo M. Pasqualucci, *The Practice and Procedure of the Inter-American Court of Human Rights* (2nd edn, Cambridge University Press 2012), 125–128.

[106] BVerfGE 1, 418 (420).

[107] BVerfGE 7, 198 (207); BVerfGE 18, 85 (92). For a discussion of the doctrine, see Schlaich and Korioth, paras. 283–285.

[108] For an explanation of the concept and its origins, see Michael R. Hutchinson, 'The Margin of Appreciation Doctrine in the European Court of Human Rights' (1999) 48 International & Comparative Law Quarterly 638, 639–640.

[109] Ibid, 640.

[110] Neuman, 'Subsidiarity', 369.

[111] Linus Mührel and Ivana Jelić, 'The Human Rights Committee—Challenges and Prospects for Enhanced Effectiveness and Integration' [2022] Journal of Human Rights Practice 17, 20–21.

human rights and, generally, to grant states a wide enough margin of appreciation for the implementation of their obligations.[112]

9.2.3 Assessment of the Committees' Pronouncements

While there is a relative paucity in the pronouncements of the HRC, the CESCR's pronouncements have revealed suitable approaches to address the risks that come with open-ended positive obligations under IHRL. In particular the awareness of context, the adaptability of procedural guarantees to different rights and situations as well as the cautious approach to finding violations are important here. These allow the committee to respond to different situations and contexts appropriately. The CESCR's approach is thus sufficiently flexible—at least theoretically—to always strike the right balance between states' sovereign interests and those interests of the individual in question protected by IHRL. The HRC would be well-advised to be guided by the explicit flexibility of its sister committee. The fact that we find fewer remarks in the pronouncements of the HRC may, however, already point to the fact that it leaves states great leeway in the implementation of procedural obligations, even if it does not do so as explicitly.

Two points that the committees have not explicitly mentioned in their pronouncements shall additionally be highlighted here. Firstly, obligations of administrative procedure are positive obligations. As such, their scope depends on the resources and capacities of a state.[113] Setting up and maintaining an administrative apparatus and its decision-making processes in line with human rights can be a costly endeavour. In this regard, the obligations discussed here are arguably comparable to those arising from Article 14 ICCPR, which are often referred to when arguing that the implementation of civil and political rights is not necessarily less costly than the implementation of socio-economic rights[114]. The HRC acknowledged the capacity-dependence of positive obligations explicitly for the obligation to protect the right to life, when it held that states were "under a due diligence obligation to take reasonable, positive measures that do not impose

[112] On question of positive obligations and the scope of review, see generally Heike Krieger, 'Positive Verpflichtungen unter der EMRK: Unentbehrliches Element einer gemeineuropäischen Grundrechtsdogmatik, leeres Versprechen oder Grenze der Justiziabilität?' (2014) 74 Zeitschrift für ausländisches öffentliches Recht und Völkerrecht (ZaöRV) 187, 187–188, 209–212.

[113] Kälin and Künzli, 105.

[114] See Koch, 84.

disproportionate burdens on them" to respond to threats from private individuals and entities the conduct of which is not attributable to the state.[115] Explicit recognition of this dependency is, however, just as crucial for (other) procedural obligations given that their open-ended nature as positive obligations can easily lend itself to requiring ever more implementation measures from states.

Secondly, with some notable exceptions such as the prohibition of torture, human rights are not absolute. Insofar as human rights are principles, they are relative not only to factual possibilities but also to the legal possibilities, i.e., the relative weight of counteracting legal interests.[116] This relativity must be kept in mind when assessing the implementation of procedural obligations. Other legal interests can prevail over *ex ante* procedural protection of an affected individual. Highlighting this relativity also of procedural obligations will add to the context-dependent approach found in the pronouncements of the CESCR. Relying on a rule and exception paradigm here could help to achieve even more nuance while following a context-dependent approach. In fact, it is one of the great advantages of this paradigm that governs the application of IHRL generally and the principle of proportionality that it allows one to make the case that a certain principle has to step back in a given situation while—at the same time—upholding its general and unchallenged validity and importance.

An illustrative example of a situation in which the procedural protection of individual rights was outweighed by public interests are the facts of the 2008 Kadi case before the Court of Justice of the European Union (CJEU)[117]. The case concerned a regulation that had implemented a UN Security Council resolution providing for "smart sanctions", *inter alia* the freezing of funds, against individuals suspected of being involved in terrorist activities. Before the implementation of these sanctions, the individuals had not been informed and had not been given an opportunity to lay out their view of the situation. The applicants argued that this omission had violated their right to be heard and their right to effective judicial review.

In its judgment, the CJEU first highlights that "[a]ccording to its settled case-law, the principle of effective judicial protection is a general principle of Community law" and—following an instrumental argument[118]—derives from it

[115] HRC, GC 36, para. 21.

[116] See Alexy, *A Theory of Constitutional Rights*, 47.

[117] *Kadi and Al Barakaat v Council and Commission* (Joined cases C-402/05 P and C-415/05 P, CJEU, 3 September 2008).

[118] The CJEU argues that this obligation to give reasons is meant to enable affected individuals to bring an action against the decision, thereby highlighting the facilitative function

an obligation of Community authorities to communicate the grounds for a decision to the affected individual.[119] However, the CJEU then moves on to reject the applicants' claims, convincingly arguing that "with regard to restrictive measures such as those imposed by the contested regulation, the Community authorities cannot be required to communicate those grounds before the name of a person or entity is entered in that list for the first time" and that "such prior communication would be liable to jeopardise the effectiveness of the freezing of funds and resources imposed by that regulation".[120] It continues that "[i]n order to attain the objective pursued by that regulation, such measures must, by their very nature, take advantage of a surprise effect and, as the Court has previously stated, apply with immediate effect".[121] It thereby makes use of the rule-exception-paradigm that allows it to limit procedural rights of affected individuals while—at the same time—highlighting their general validity.

The *Kadi* judgment exemplifies how the involvement of the affected individual can be rendered impossible by counteracting, oftentimes public, interests in a specific case. Effective counter-terrorism measures would not be possible if a terrorist suspect's rights to legal protection *ex ante* would be absolute. Especially in those areas of administration where a certain level of secrecy is required, involving the affected individual in the decision-making process can jeopardise the success of the measure. In such cases, the procedural rights of individuals must be carefully balanced against the public interests at stake. And in line with the principle of subsidiarity, international (quasi-)judicial bodies should give states considerable leeway in this regard.

9.3 The Potential of Process-Based Review for the Implementation of the Principle of Subsidiarity in IHRL

One last point shall be made here with regard to the review of procedural obligations under IHRL. In contrast to what we have just said regarding the problems that come with open-ended positive obligations, stricter, more robust procedural obligations can also have a conducive effect towards the implementation of

of *ex ante* procedural review for *ex post* legal action. See on this particular version of the instrumental justification, 5.1.1.3 as well as 8.2.1.2.2.3.

[119] CJEU, *Kadi and Al Barakaat*, paras. 335–336.

[120] Ibid, paras. 338–339.

[121] Ibid, para. 340.

the principle of subsidiarity. Perhaps somewhat paradoxically, obligations that are at odds with IHRL's traditionally posing obligations of result can—at the same time—become the subject of an international court's heightened scrutiny, when that court's aim is precisely to strengthen the principle of subsidiarity. In other words, stricter procedural obligations can facilitate "process-based review" of national decisions affecting human rights that leaves the states more leeway as to the substance of a decision.

The phenomenon of "process-based review" has been extensively discussed for some years in the context of the ECHR. In essence, process-based review is concerned with the way a decision was reached rather than the substantive legality of the decision itself.[122] Given that it leads to greater leeway regarding the substance of a decision, it has been understood as a strategy of the ECtHR to counter populist challenges to the system of human rights protection.[123]

How does "process-based review" work? Çalı calls the type of procedural review discussed here "letting good faith interpreters be".[124] This term aptly describes how this type of judicial deference works. As long as states can show that their competent state authorities have made their decision in good faith and that they have adhered to the applicable safeguards, the international organ tasked with reviewing that decision will defer the substance of that decision to them. International oversight bodies will "let them be". Hence, the object of the review shifts from the substance of a decision to the process by which this decision was made.

Most often, international courts and judicial bodies will employ this technique when it comes to decisions involving balancing. In that case, international human rights institutions will primarily reconstruct and evaluate the state authority's balancing *process*, i.e., they will look at *how* the balancing was done and not substitute their own balancing for the balancing of the competent state authority. In essence, this amounts to a "presumption of Convention compliance for

---

[122] Robert Spano, 'The Future of the European Court of Human Rights—Subsidiarity, Process-Based Review and the Rule of Law' (2018) 18 Human Rights Law Review 473, 480–481.

[123] Paul Lemmens, 'The European Court of Human Rights—Can there be too much Success?' [2022] Journal of Human Rights Practice 169, 182–184.

[124] Başak Çalı, 'Coping with Crisis: Whither the Variably Geometry in the Jurisprudence of the European Court of Human Rights' (2018) 35 Wisconsin International Law Journal 237, 256.

the outcome of the domestic proportionality assessment"[125]. Only if the judicial body finds flaws in the decision-making process will it have reason to look more closely at the substance of the decision. On the following pages, we will look at whether we can find process-based review in the pronouncements of the committees as well (9.3.1) and reflect on the potential of this judicial technique and how it relates to what we have stated in the previous part of this chapter, namely that too detailed and too strict rules for the implementation of procedural obligations can be problematic (9.3.2).

9.3.1 Process-Based Review in the Pronouncements of the Committees

While the phenomenon of process-based review is mostly discussed in the context of the ECHR, we find examples of process-based review in the pronouncements of the committees, too. In its views in the *Länsman* case, the HRC argued that Finland had fulfilled its obligations under Article 27 ICCPR as the authorities "did go through the process of weighing the authors' interests and the general economic interests [...] when deciding on the most appropriate measures of forestry management", and "considered specifically whether the proposed activities constituted a denial of article 27 rights".[126] The committee did not re-evaluate this decision itself but was content with finding that the authority had reached its decision in a certain way. This is a clear example of deference to the state party through process-based review.

The CESCR has taken a similar approach. A first example is the case of *I.D.G. v. Spain.*[127] Moreover, in its views in *López Albán*, the CESCR notes

> *that Madrid Criminal Court No. 28 did not conduct an analysis of the proportionality of the legitimate objective of the eviction to its consequences for the persons evicted. Specifically, the court did not weigh the benefits of the measure – in this case, protecting the right to property of the bank that owns the apartment – against its possible consequences for the rights of the evicted persons.*[128]

---

[125] Oddný Mjöll Arnardóttir, 'The Brighton Aftermath and the Changing Role of the European Court of Human Rights' (2018) 9 Journal of International Dispute Settlement 223, 230.

[126] HRC, *Länsman et al. v. Finland*, para. 10.5. Emphasis original.

[127] For a discussion of this case as an example for procedural review see Huijbers, 72–75.

[128] CESCR, *López Albán v. Spain*, para. 11.5.

In the views, the committee does not criticize that the measure was not proportionate in the end. Instead, the CESCR rebukes the Spanish court for not conducting the necessary analysis. It is not the outcome of the proportionality analysis that was decisive here but rather that no such analysis was conducted. In the subsequent paragraph, the CESCR then turns to the specifics of the case before it holds that the author's argument should have been taken up by the court and should have been included in their assessment of the eviction.[129]

The committee reiterated this reasoning even more clearly in its views on the *El Ayoubi* case which also concerned a forced eviction. In this case, the committee concluded that "there were legitimate reasons for [the] eviction and that it could therefore be justified".[130] However, the committee still found a violation because the Spanish court had not conducted a proportionality test:

> *Nevertheless, the Committee notes that [the court] did not conduct an analysis of the proportionality of the legitimate objective of the eviction to its consequences for the persons evicted. Specifically, the court did not weigh the benefits of the measure – in this case, protecting the right to property of the bank that owns the apartment – against its possible consequences for the rights of the evicted persons. [...]*
>
> *[A]lthough the authors claimed that the measure would affect their right to adequate housing, [the court] did not conduct any analysis of proportionality between the harm caused by the authors in occupying the apartment and the harm they were seeking to avoid by such occupation on finding themselves homeless. [...] Furthermore, the State party's legislation did not provide the authors with any other judicial mechanism through which to challenge the eviction orders that would have given another judicial authority the opportunity to analyse the proportionality of the eviction and the conditions in which it was going to be carried out. The Committee finds, therefore, that the absence of such an assessment constituted a violation by the State party of the author's right to housing under article 11 (1) of the Covenant, read in conjunction with article 2 (1).*[131]

Notably, in the *El Ayoubi* case, the CESCR has seen a violation in the way the Spanish court had conducted its proportionality analysis. It did not use a process-based review to defer to the states' authorities. Nevertheless, the passage is an example of how process-based review can also go if the procedural obligations of a state party are not fulfilled. And the case reminds us how administrative

[129] Ibid, para. 11.6.

[130] CESCR, *El Ayoubi and El Azouan v Spain* (Comm no 54/2018, CESCR, 19 February 2021), para. 14.5.

[131] Ibid, paras. 14.5–14.6.

procedure, and in particular the giving reasons requirement is a necessary precondition for process-based review. The giving reasons requirement makes the proportionality assessment which structures the balancing process interpersonally comprehensible.[132]

9.3.2 The Potential of Process-Based Review

While these examples concern the review of the process of balancing, it is entirely conceivable that a court may additionally review other aspects of a decision-making process, justifying that the decision itself is subject to limited review. The reasoning could be that, because the individual was sufficiently involved in the decision-making process, the decision-maker can be trusted as a good faith decision-maker and is therefore granted a wider margin of appreciation. So, is process-based review actually a "mechanism by which the Court implements the principle of subsidiarity in practice"[133]? Has it—as was held—ushered in an "age of subsidiarity".[134] Or do the risks that come with open-ended procedural obligations outweigh the potential process-based review has?

A universal answer to this question is arguably impossible to give. What states and their societies consider an intrusion with their sovereign rights depends on societal, cultural, and legal factors. Process-based review depends on a rather high level of scrutiny of the implementation of procedural obligations. Only with robust and enforceable procedural guarantees could such an approach work. The more robust the procedural protections granted would be, however, the higher the level of scrutiny they are subject to, the more they would be at odds with the tensions between positive obligations and state sovereignty we have discussed in the previous section. How comfortably states would accept such an "intrusion" with their internal decision-making processes will vary greatly between jurisdictions. While such an approach might be relatively easy to execute for a regional human rights mechanism such as the ECtHR given the similarities between the political, legal and constitutional traditions of the member states[135], it is infinitely

---

[132] See *supra* 8.2.1.1.2.3 and 8.2.1.2.2.3.

[133] Spano, 'The Future of the European Court of Human Rights—Subsidiarity, Process-Based Review and the Rule of Law', 481.

[134] Robert Spano, 'Universality or Diversity of Human Rights?: Strasbourg in the Age of Subsidiarity' (2014) 14 Human Rights Law Review 487.

[135] Christof Heyns and Magnus Killander, 'Universality and the Growth of Regional Systems' in Dinah Shelton (ed), *The Oxford Handbook of International Human Rights Law* (Oxford University Press 2013), 677. Heyns and Killander rightfully point out, however, that

more difficult in a much more diverse international system. The principles of *audi alteram partem* and the giving reasons requirement arguably come naturally to the European or American lawyer. Whether this is equally true for the participants of a legal system less focused on the individual and with less strongly developed rule of law traditions is at the very least questionable.

So, it comes down to a question of preference. If states were willing to pay the price of greater scrutiny over *how* they make their decisions, they might gain more leeway as to the substance of that decision. In a kind of overall combined assessment of material and procedural subsidiarity, they might find that greater leeway for the "what" is worth paying the price of more restriction as to the "how". In that sense, process-based review could indeed help "secure the increased effectiveness of human rights protection at the national level by moving towards a bottom-up strategy empowering national rights-holders and decision-makers to take the lead in securing human rights".[136] However, given the disruptive potential of the obligations discussed here—potentially for the whole state apparatus –, it might also be easier for (some) states to accept stronger restrictions on the outcomes of their decisions.

Moreover, there is a certain potential for abuse in procedural review. States might use their compliance with procedural obligations as a defence against accusations of material infringements upon human rights. Hence, procedural guarantees such as the ones discussed in this thesis cannot substitute material human rights guarantees. Especially in light of the instrumental as well as the dignitarian justification of procedural protection, procedures must not be used by a state to escape its material obligations. Procedural guarantees must not lead to a less effective implementation of the material contents of human rights. They must not be used to trick or even ridicule the individual subject to state power. This must be kept in mind when considering the potential of process-based review for the implementation of the principle of subsidiarity of IHRL.

---

after the fall of the Soviet Union, the group of member states has become somewhat less homogenous.

[136] Spano, 'The Future of the European Court of Human Rights—Subsidiarity, Process-Based Review and the Rule of Law', 486. Note that the quote acknowledges both, how process-based review can facilitate the realisation of subsidiarity, as well as how it can help taking the individual and the active role she plays in the realisation of her rights seriously.

9.4 Conclusion

In this chapter, we have seen that the implementation of procedural protection of international human rights is context-dependent. Nevertheless, some elements of administrative procedure are generally relevant to all human rights and in all situations. The implementation of procedural obligations must be guided by the rationale that the committees draw upon to justify the obligations. Moreover, we have seen that the principle of proportionality influences the implementation of procedural obligations in that it limits how the enjoyment of human rights may be made dependent upon the completion of procedures, and by requiring procedural compensation for particularly intensive interferences.

Given that the procedural obligations this thesis has reflected upon are positive in nature, the concerns of human rights overreach which are ascribed to positive IHRL obligations generally apply. Hence, when reviewing and commenting upon the implementation of procedural obligations, international (quasi-)judicial bodies should be aware of the risks and fulfil their tasks with due care. Beyond what we have seen in the committees' pronouncements, international bodies should take into account the capacities of a state as well as the relative nature of human rights when issuing statements on or assessing the implementation of procedural obligations. At the same time, we have seen that process-based review can also be conducive to the implementation of the subsidiarity principle. This would, however, require robust procedural rights and thorough scrutiny by treaty bodies which—when viewed in isolation—might be at odds with the idea of subsidiarity. Hence, it would come down to a trade-off between material and procedural subsidiarity. Whether such a trade-off would be considered worth it would probably depend *inter alia* on the legal, societal and cultural traditions of the specific state in question.

Conclusion 10

In the first part of the conclusion to this study, we will summarize its main findings (10.1) and point out potential avenues for further research (10.2). Afterwards, we will try to change our perspective. So far, we have looked at the administrative decision-making process and the involvement of the individual from the perspective of IHRL. At the end of this thesis, we shall add to this by taking the perspective of those who are bound by the obligations discussed here. Against the backdrop of the potential costliness of obligations of administrative procedure, we will ask what is in it for states (10.3). While this is by no means meant as a concession, implying that international law and its effectiveness are merely a matter of politics, the concluding reflections of this thesis will hopefully bolster the relevance of its findings. Finally, we will emphasise that—when done correctly, in accordance with IHRL—administrative procedure can be a real win-win undertaking (10.4).

10.1 Summary of Findings

This study has shown that, why and how—in the words of the CESCR—"adequate procedural protection and due process are essential aspects of all human rights".[1] States must—as aptly put by the HRC—"organize all State organs and governance structures through which public authority is exercised in a manner

[1] CESCR, GC 7, para. 15.

B. Behlert, *The Necessity of a Conversation between the Administration and the Individual*, Juridicum—Bochumer Schriften zur Friedenssicherung und zum Humanitären Völkerrecht | Bochum Studies on the International Law of Peace and Armed Conflict 72, https://doi.org/10.1007/978-3-658-50303-1_10

consistent with the need to respect and ensure [human rights]".[2] Most importantly, the procedures required by IHRL must involve the affected individual in an active capacity that enables her to vindicate her (human) rights *vis à vis* the administrative body.

Before turning to the analysis of the ICCPR and the ICESCR and the respective committees' pronouncements, this study has analysed the FCC's jurisprudence on procedural rights of individuals *vis à vis* the German state's administration. This way, we have developed an analytical foil through which we conducted our subsequent analysis of IHRL. We have seen that, after some developments of the idea of the protection of fundamental rights through procedure in the early jurisprudence of the FCC, the discourse arose most prominently in the 1970s, in the context of the rise of the welfare state. In his lecture at the *Staatsrechtslehrertagung* in 1971, Peter Häberle argued that the modern welfare state had created challenges to fundamental rights that could not effectively be addressed by *ex post* remedies. Because governance in the welfare state was more and more defined by open-ended blanket provisions, *ex post* legal protection had in some instances become ineffective to protect fundamental rights *vis à vis* the state. Instead, legal protection *ex ante* ("*vorverlagerter Rechtsschutz*") could facilitate more effective protection of fundamental rights.[3]

The discussion of the procedural safeguards necessary to protect the fundamental rights of German citizens *vis à vis* the administration of the German state gained more and more traction in the academic discourse and the jurisprudence of the FCC in the 1970s and 1980s. Eventually, the idea that the fundamental rights of the German Basic Law require the participation of potentially affected individuals in procedures that concern them and certain organisational features for the state became an important element of the general fundamental rights doctrine developed in the jurisprudence of the FCC.[4]

Fundamental rights under the German Basic Law are "first and foremost defensive rights against the state".[5] Hence, the FCC had to construct procedural obligations by deriving them from the so-called "objective value dimension" of German fundamental rights.[6] It justifies this creative exercise by relying on two justifications. On the one hand, it employs an instrumental justification according

[2] HRC, GC 36, para. 19.

[3] Häberle, 'Grundrechte im Leistungsstaat', 53.

[4] See *supra* Chap. 3 generally.

[5] BVerfGE 7, 198 (204).

[6] See *supra* Chap. 4 generally.

to which procedures are means to the end of better fundamental rights implementation.[7] The instrumental value of administrative procedure can be explained well in relation to judicial review. Legal protection *ex ante* adds to, facilitates, and can compensate for a lack of effective legal protection *ex post*. These functions all bolster the effective implementation of the fundamental rights of the Basic Law. On the other hand, the FCC employs a dignitarian justification according to which the participation of the individual in the decision-making process of the administration is required by her "subject status" under the German constitution, in particular under Article 1 (1) Basic Law.[8]

Regarding implementation, we have found that it is necessarily context-dependent, but must be guided by the justifications of administrative procedure, in particular by the ideal of effective fundamental rights implementation.[9] Importantly, we could make some reflections on the dangers that come with the enforceability of positive obligations.[10] Moreover, the principle of proportionality places two requirements on the implementation of procedural obligations[11]: firstly, procedures may not represent disproportionate hurdles for the enjoyment of fundamental rights. And secondly, particularly careful legal protection *ex ante* can be required when an envisaged measure is likely to constitute a particularly intensive or irreversible interference with a fundamental right. In other words, there is a proportionate connection between the intensity and the degree of irreversibility of the envisaged interference and the required procedural protection.

Looking at IHRL through the thus developed analytical foil, we have first considered the doctrinal bases of obligations of administrative procedure in the ICCPR and the ICESCR.[12] We have found that the committees derive obligations of administrative procedure as positive obligations from the general obligations provisions of the treaties. However, the committees' pronouncements leave considerable gaps regarding the details of the construction of the doctrinal basis for obligations of administrative procedure. We have tried to fill these gaps and argued that Article 2 (1), (2) ICCPR and Article 2 (1) ICESCR in connection with the specific rights in question are the precise legal anchors for obligations

[7] See *supra* 5.1.
[8] See *supra* 5.2.
[9] See *supra* 6.3.1.
[10] See *supra* 6.1.
[11] See *supra* 6.3.2.
[12] See *supra* Chap. 7 generally.

of administrative procedure. More precisely, it is the obligation to "fulfil" human rights which gives rise to procedural obligations.

We have then turned to the issue of justification.[13] In contrast to the FCC, the committees do not rely on dignitarian justifications at all. They justify the conversation between the administration and the individual and her involvement in decision-making processes entirely as a means to the end of better human rights implementation. However, the committees do not elaborate very concretely on how procedures can function to enhance human rights protection. We have, however, shown that the principle of effectiveness and, in particular the right to an effective remedy can function as a theoretical underpinning of the committees' instrumental justifications. Relying on these principles, we could make essentially the same pragmatic arguments which we found in the jurisprudence of the FCC. In relation to the right to an effective remedy—i.e., to legal protection *ex post*—legal protection *ex ante* can fulfil compensatory and facilitative functions as well as the function of providing additional protection. We have furthermore shown that a dignitarian justification based on the idea of the individual as a self-directed agent is conceivable under IHRL, too. According to such a justification, involving the affected individual in an administrative procedure can operationalise her human dignity under IHRL. Importantly, however, in contrast to the guarantee of human dignity under the Basic Law, the principle of human dignity under IHRL does not give direct rise to any binding obligations upon states. Its normative force is considerably weaker.

Finally, with regard to the implementation of obligations of administrative procedure, we have shown how context-specific these obligations are under IHRL, too.[14] Moreover, we have shown that, in the view of the committees, subjective rights correspond to the procedural obligations derived from the covenants, i.e., the rights are individually enforceable by their holders. At the same time, the committees do not consider every procedural shortcoming to be a violation of the respective human rights. With regard to the influence of the principle of proportionality on the implementation of the human rights in question, we have seen that they are twofold. On the one hand, procedures must not place undue burdens on affected individuals. On the other hand, the more intense the prospective interference with the human rights of the affected person is likely to be, the more comprehensive the procedural protection must be.

The findings of this study provide a fairly comprehensive overview of the relationship between IHRL and administrative procedure. They provide an insight

[13] See *supra* Chap. 8 generally.

[14] See *supra* Chap. 9 generally.

into what IHRL has to say about the relationship between a state's administration and individuals subjected to its power. While, in comparison with the German constitutional law discourse, the specifics have not been as comprehensively explored by the committees and—perhaps more strikingly—by the academic literature, this study has shown that IHRL does set standards for this relationship, and that those standards which IHRL sets can be justified by fundamental principles, most importantly the principle of effectiveness and human dignity.

10.2 Potential Avenues for Further Research

Despite the relatively comprehensive overview this study has given, it can only be a first tapping into the relationship between IHRL and administrative procedures. Hence, in this section, we will point to some potential avenues for further research.

Firstly, this thesis could address the issue of implementation only in a general manner and with rather broad brushstrokes. Future works might build on this and reflect on the requirements for the implementation of procedural obligations of states in specific circumstances, for specific rights and for specific procedures, and thereby develop the understanding of the context dependence of procedural protection *ex ante* further. Future case studies on the specific procedural needs for specific human rights will be helpful to gradually fill the rough lines of the picture that this study has sketched out. For example, what are the specific requirements regarding persons with disabilities? What are the specific requirements in relation to children? For vulnerable groups like these, specific human rights regimes exist which could give rise to specific requirements. Such in-depth analyses will yield results that can then be abstracted to the more general level again. So-inducted generalised abstractions can then be used (as starting-points) for the analysis of the procedural dimension of specific rights. Such a circular approach is a promising avenue towards a clearer and more complete understanding of the connection between IHRL and administrative procedure. Moreover, the same is true for case studies that analyse specific administrative procedures in greater detail.[15] Certain administrative procedures and their respective outcomes can affect human rights in very different ways. Tackling the connection between IHRL and administrative law from this perspective is a promising avenue for future research as well.

[15] Some time ago, the author of this study has attempted an analysis of the role of international human rights for the asylum procedure, see Behlert, 'The Obligation to Conduct Individual Refugee Status Determination Procedures under the ICCPR—Constructing a Convincing Legal Basis'.

Secondly, contributions from other jurisdictions would be interesting. In line with what we said about how a discussion in international law should be had,[16] it would be important to see how the connection between individual rights and administrative procedure is addressed by (constitutional) courts and academics in other states. Against the backdrop of their "legal upbringing", IHRL scholars from jurisdictions other than Germany will probably address the connection between IHRL and administrative procedure differently. Understanding how different an analysis of the connection between IHRL and administrative procedure from scholars from different jurisdictions would be would also contribute to a more complete picture and a more robust understanding of the procedural dimension of IHRL.

Thirdly, there is more theorizing to be done. This study set out to understand the legal, the doctrinal connection between IHRL and administrative procedure. There are highly interesting and lucrative connections between the findings of this study and legal theories. For example, our approach towards administrative procedure as the operationalisation of an actor-oriented understanding of human rights in line with human dignity gives rise to interesting potential connections to modern theories of IHRL which seek to construe the individual more as a self-directing agent[17]. Moreover, given the framing of the interaction between the administration of a state and the individual as a "conversation",[18] connections to communications theories might also be lucrative to explore. Most obviously, perhaps, connecting the research to governance, political science or sociological theories seems lucrative as well.

Fourthly, (some of) the findings of this study could be tested empirically. The necessity of empirical research is particularly pertinent for the effectiveness justification. The hypothesis is accepted widely and well enough to function as a justification for the HRC and the CESCR. And, as we have seen, it is certainly plausible enough to justify deriving procedural obligations from the provisions of IHRL. Nevertheless, an empirical test of the findings can shed more light on the factual connection between IHRL and administrative procedure. Does the participation of individuals in administrative procedures actually lead to better, i.e., more effective human rights implementation? In which way does it enhance the implementation? Some research into the effects of administrative procedure

[16] See *supra* 2.4.3.

[17] For an example, see Mann. For a brief summary of Mann's theory in this regard, see *supra* 8.2.2.3.

[18] See BVerfGE 45, 297 (335).

has already been done,[19] and there certainly are more promising avenues to be followed in this direction. It shall be said here, however, that any attempt to validate or falsify a thesis like the effectiveness justification would face considerable methodological challenges.[20]

Fifthly, current developments in technology pose difficult fundamental questions about the relationship between individuals and the (administration of a) state. What does the discomfortingly fast pace with which artificial intelligence develops mean for the state of the future and the relation to its citizens? Do human rights grant a right to a procedure led by a human being? Or could computers take over this task as well?[21] What would AI-based decision-making mean for the dignitarian justification? Can human dignity even be operationalised *vis à vis* a machine? Can the machine take a human being's agency seriously and reckon with her views?

On the less discomforting side, however, artificial intelligence also holds potential for a better, more effective enjoyment of human rights. The realisation that procedures can also present obstacles for the enjoyment of human rights and be a limitation of human rights in and of themselves has played a comparatively great role in the pronouncements of the treaty bodies. One important consequence derived from this is that administrative decision-making processes must generally be speedy. The use of artificial intelligence by state administration could help speed up certain processes and thus even have a positive effect on the enjoyment of human rights. Nevertheless, given the inherent dangers in that technology,[22] such a positive outlook should certainly be given more (critical) thought.

This study hopefully holds some lucrative starting or "attachment points" for these and other questions. In the best-case scenario, it will contribute to research

---

[19] Pascal Langenbach, *Der Anhörungseffekt: Verfahrensfairness und Rechtsbefolgung im allgemeinen Verwaltungsverfahren* (Mohr Siebeck 2017).

[20] For an exemplary methodological critique of research constituting an an attempt to show causality between the ratification of human rights treaties and a rise in human rights abuses, see Ryan Goodman and Derek Jinks, 'Measuring the Effects of Human Rights Treaties' (2003) 14 European Journal of International Law 171. There is, at least, a certain probability that attempts to verify the effectiveness justification would face similar headwind.

[21] For a recent example of a study devoted to this question from the perspective of German fundamental rights, see Dorothea Mund, *Das Recht auf menschliche Entscheidung—zu den verfassungsrechtlichen Vorgaben der technischen Erzeugung von Verwaltungsentscheidungen* (Mohr Siebeck 2021).

[22] Cf. Keving Roose, 'A.I. Poses 'Risk of Extinction', Industry Leaders Warn' *The New York Times* <https://www.nytimes.com/2023/05/30/technology/ai-threat-warning.html?searchResultPosition=5> accessed 26 August 2025.

on such interesting questions and, perhaps, spark even more interesting follow-up questions. Eventually, the picture of how the relationship between a state's administration and the individuals subjected to its power must be designed could then be filled more and more.

10.3 What Is in It for the States?

The obligations discussed in this thesis may turn out to be very costly for states, both financially and politically. After laying out these costs (10.3.1), we will explain how states can benefit from involving affected individual in the decision-making processes of their administration in the short and long term (10.3.2). This argument has the potential to make the findings of this thesis more relevant by raising the chances that states will accept the obligations discussed here. When the incentives are clear, states will arguably be more likely to implement their obligations.

10.3.1 The Financial and Political Costs of Administrative Procedure

States are obliged to "organize all State organs and governance structures through which public authority is exercised in a manner consistent with the need to respect and ensure [human rights]"[23]. It is obvious why an effective implementation of this obligation requires significant administrative capacities and is therefore rather costly—financially and otherwise. Just as this argument is often made with regard to the right to a fair trial and the organisation of the judicial system, the same can be said for states' administrations. An administration that realises the right to be heard and implements the obligation to give reasons, for example, binds more resources than an administration that does not. Decision-making processes that are designed to protect individuals' rights are not necessarily the most efficient ones in terms of time, personnel etc. The costliness of effective administrative procedures adds another factor that might make implementing the effective administrative procedures required by IHRL rather unattractive for states. Despite the fact that the obligations discussed here are relative to states' capacities, it is easily conceivable that states might be sceptical when it comes to accepting such

[23] HRC, GC 36, para. 19.

obligations. If resources are limited, states must be convinced, that allocating their resources to the obligations discussed in this thesis is "worth it".

Besides the financial costs, however, there are potential "political costs" that might incentivise states from refraining from implementing the obligations discussed in the present thesis. The findings of this study are potentially revolutionary for a lot of states as they might have to restructure the way their administration works rather significantly. While it is argued here that the image of the human being as a self-directed agent is part of human rights law and should be shared by states around the world, the reality in many states of the world is arguably rather different.

Administrative law is not only closely connected to the political system of a state, but also in some ways a reflection of it. Fritz Werner famously stated that administrative law was "concretised constitutional law".[24] It reflects the constitutional traditions of a state and—as we have seen from the German example—operationalises the human image of a constitution. Administrative law has from its very inception been intimately connected to the idea of *Rechtsstaat*, *etat de droit*, the rule of law and so on.[25] States without strong traditions in this regard might consider obligations of administrative procedure as an imperialist affront.

Of course, national law, including constitutional law, does not provide a justification for states to ignore the demands of IHRL for the administrative decision-making processes of states. This is expressed clearly by Article 27 VCLT which provides that states "may not invoke the provisions of its internal law as justification for its failure to perform a treaty".[26] This is obviously true for human rights law as well. So, states cannot reject their human rights obligations by referring to their different legal systems or traditions. Nevertheless, it is important to realise how heavily influenced administrative law by legal and constitutional traditions is. States might have difficulties accepting the obligations discussed in this thesis due to growing anti-Western sentiments. These have found more and more

[24] Fritz Werner, 'Verwaltungsrecht als konkretisiertes Verfassungsrecht' (1959) 74 Das Deutsche Verwaltungsblatt 527.

[25] Cf. Sordi.

[26] The provision is, of course, not directly applicable as the VCLT entered into force after the two covenants and is not retroactively applicable, Article 4 VCLT. Nevertheless, Article 27 VCLT reflects a fundamental principle of customary international law and can therefore be applied as such, cf. Oliver Dörr and Kirsten Schmalenbach, *Vienna Convention on the Law of Treaties: a commentary* (2nd edn, Springer 2018), 91–92 and 495.

resonance in large parts of the international community in recent times. It is therefore reasonable to assume that the close connection of administrative procedure to the "Western" rule of law concept could be a potential ground for scepticism, or even rejection of the kind of procedural involvement of individuals envisaged here in (large) parts of the world. Administrative procedure might be viewed as "yet another Western concept" to be forced upon non-Western members of the international community.

10.3.2 Legitimacy as the Potential Benefit for States

Against the backdrop of these financial and political costs for states, we will now change our perspective and ask: what is in it for them? This is certainly a somewhat cynical question. From a human rights perspective—which this thesis has decidedly taken –, the answer to the question of why states should implement their human rights obligations can only be: "because they have to!" Moreover, human rights scholarship (which does not count itself to the critical legal studies movement) is somewhat necessarily based on the assumption (or hope) that states want to comply with their human rights obligations. Otherwise, it would be a futile undertaking to begin with. Hence, it is important to emphasise again that the somewhat cynical question reflected upon in this part is not meant to question the normative force of the arguments put forward by this thesis.

However, human rights law research can sometimes be of questionable relevance when it is too idealistic and too ignorant of political realities. While a certain level of ignorance towards political realities is necessary to prevent legal scholarship from becoming apologetic, engagement with reality cannot be completely neglected. In this sense, asking the question of what is in it for states is not to question the validity claim of the procedural obligations derived in this study. Rather, engaging with this question is meant to offer states an *additional* incentive, beyond their will to comply with human rights law and thereby make the research this thesis has engaged in more realistic.

And indeed, there is another incentive for states to implement obligations of administrative procedure and involve affected individuals in decision-making processes, namely the well-established connection between procedure, participation, and legitimacy. Judges Simon and Heußner pointed to this important benefit of administrative procedure, in particular of involving the affected individuals in decision-making processes in their separate opinion to the *funk* order of the FCC:

> *Finally, it may be remarked that a fair application of procedural law in the sense set out above yields important additional advantages. It is a prerequisite for the indispensable acceptance of decisions […] by the population […].*[27]

Taking, for a brief moment, the cynical "what's in it for the states" angle, we would probably have to admit that this is arguably the more important incentive for states. Even if states were always acting in good faith regarding their human rights obligations, they would probably not deny that (long-term) legitimacy is at least an attractive extra incentive. The following pages will discuss the notion of legitimacy (10.3.2.1) and why it is attractive for states (10.3.2.2). Afterwards, the connection between procedure and legitimacy will be sketched out. We will argue that involving individuals in state decision-making processes can have both short-term (10.3.2.3) as well as long-term effects (10.3.2.4) on the legitimacy of state decisions and institutions.

10.3.2.1 The Notion of Legitimacy

Before we can discuss the connection between procedure, participation, and legitimacy, we must explain what this study means by legitimacy. The word is derived from the Latin word *"legitimare"*[28] which means "to make something conform to the law". In that sense, the Oxford English Dictionary names "[c]onformity to the law, to rules, or to some recognized principle; lawfulness. Also: conformity to sound reasoning; logicality; justifiability"[29] as the most important meaning for the word, today. These definitions are very close to "lawfulness" or "legality". Equating legitimacy with "lawfulness", however, falls short. "Legitimacy" is different from legality, it goes beyond it and requires more than mere conformity with the law.[30] The third meaning given by the Oxford English Dictionary comes closer to the actual meaning of the word in the context that it is used in in this thesis: "[t]he legal right to govern or to sovereignty".[31] However, this does not really hit the nail on the head, either, because it firstly ties on to legality again,

---

[27] BVerfGE 53, 30 (80–81): *"Abschließend mag noch bemerkt werden, daß eine faire Anwendung des Verfahrensrechts im vorstehend dargelegten Sinne noch gewichtige zusätzliche Vorteile erbringt. Sie ist Voraussetzung für die unerläßliche Akzeptanz atomrechtlicher Entscheidungen durch die Bevölkerung […]."*

[28] Oxford English Dictionary, *legitimacy, n* (Oxford University Press 2023).

[29] Ibid.

[30] Bianchi even goes so far to say that the notion of legitimacy is "[f]undamentally alien to the vocabulary of law", Andrea Bianchi, *International Law Theories: An Inquiry into Different Ways of Thinking* (Oxford University Press 2016), 53.

[31] Dictionary, *legitimacy, n.*

secondly, the entry specifies that it is about "descent" and, thirdly, the entry states that this meaning is "[n]ow chiefly merged in sense 1"[32].

The exact contours of the concept of "legitimacy" are contested and unclear; its meanings are manifold.[33] Some even question whether those who are discussing legitimacy are even talking about one and the same thing.[34] Most generally, however, one can say that legitimacy "concerns the question of when, or under what circumstances, the exercise of political power is rightful or justified"[35]; it refers to the justification and acceptance of political authority or the "rightfulness of power"[36]. This makes the attractiveness of legitimacy for governments immediately comprehensible. After all, which ruler would not want to justify her rulership? And which ruler in history has not somehow tried to do so?

Before we can explore the connection between administrative procedure and legitimacy some distinctions between different categories of legitimacy are in order. To begin with, normative and descriptive forms of legitimacy must be distinguished. Whether someone's rule is normatively legitimate is assessed against moral criteria. The question is whether an institution has a right to rule "as a matter of moral theory".[37] A ruler can have normative legitimacy, e.g., because she has a certain pedigree, a great human rights track record, a certain expertise, etc. Derivations of power from God would also fall under this category. Normative legitimacy focuses on the ruler and her characteristics and not on the ruled. Descriptive legitimacy, in contrast, focuses on the ruled. It asks whether the ruled accept someone's rule as legitimate and refers to the "belief by an actor that a rule or institution ought to be obeyed".[38] It is a "subjective quality, relational between actor and institution and defined by the actor's perception of the institution".[39]

---

32 Ibid.

33 Christopher A. Thomas, 'The Uses and Abuses of Legitimacy in International Law' (2014) 34 Oxford Journal of Legal Studies 729, 733ff.

34 Arthur Isak Applbaum, 'Legitimacy without the Duty to Obey' (2010) 38 Philosophy & Public Affairs 215, 216–217.

35 Fabian Wenner, *Liberal Legitimacy: The justifcation of political power in the work of John Rawls* (Nomos Verlagsgesellschaft 2020), 11.

36 David Beetham, *The Legitimation of Power* (Palgrave Macmillan 1991), 26.

37 Daniel Bodansky, 'Legitimacy in International Law and International Relations' in Jeffrey L. Dunoff and Mark A. Pollack (eds), *Interdisciplinary Perspectives on International Law and International Relations* (Cambridge University Press 2012), 327.

38 Ian Hurd, 'Legitimacy and Authority in International Politics' (1999) 53 International Organization 379, 381.

39 Ibid, 381.

A second distinction that can be made with regard to legitimacy is between input- and output-based legitimacy.[40] Output-based legitimacy is thought of as resulting from the substance of a decision. People accept a certain decision because they agree with its substance. Input-based legitimacy, in contrast, draws its normative force from the way authority is conferred upon an entity or how a certain decision is reached. People might not be happy with a decision but trust the process that leads to the decision well enough to accept it anyway. An obvious example of input-based legitimacy is democratic elections. A person is elected leader, and through this act authority is conferred upon him. Hence, she is considered legitimate. In a functioning democracy, her rule should therefore be accepted by the ruled, no matter whether they have voted for her or not. For its reliance on the process that leads to a decision, input-based legitimacy is sometimes also referred to as "process-based legitimacy".[41]

This study has been interested in the process that leads up to decisions affecting the human rights of individuals. While we have made the case that "adequate procedural protection" can at least enhance the quality of a decision from a human rights point of view, the substance of a decision is not of primary relevance to this study. Certainly, the outcome of a process is likely to improve when the process is made better. This is essentially, what instrumental justifications of procedural involvement are about. Nevertheless, when we will now discuss the legitimacy-enhancing function of procedural involvement, what we will be speaking of is input-based legitimacy. Moreover, this section is meant to make a practical argument as to what states can gain from the procedural involvement of affected individuals in their decision-making processes. Hence, the influence of the procedural involvement on the attitudes of the ruled are what interests us here. Thus, when this thesis speaks about legitimacy, it means descriptive, output-based legitimacy.

10.3.2.2 Why Legitimacy is so Attractive for Those in Power

So, why is this descriptive output-based legitimacy attractive for states and their governments? Surely, legitimacy refers to the "right to rule" of an institution or a person. Such a right is attractive as every leader seems to want to justify her rule

---

[40] Bianchi, *International Law Theories: An Inquiry into Different Ways of Thinking*C. Fritz Scharpf has expressed this distinction with regard to democratic self-determination poignantly when he argued that input-based-legitimacy designated "government *by* the people" and output-based-legitimacy designated "government *for* the people", see Fritz Scharpf, *Governing in Europe: Effective and Democratic?* (Oxford University Press 1999), 6ff.

[41] Daniel Bodansky, 'Legitimacy' in Daniel Bodansky, Jutta Brunée and Ellen Hey (eds), *The Oxford Handbook of International Environmental Law* (Oxford University Press 2008), 710.

somehow. At least, every leader in history has—in one way or another—sought to do so. Even brutal dictators without serious opponents still hold "elections". However, there is also a (practical) consequence that makes actually being regarded as having a right to rule attractive. It makes those over whom one rules more likely to follow one's commands.

According to popular theories, there are basically three ways to secure the compliance of the ruled with commands—beyond the obvious basis of "self-interest" of the ruled[42]. One way to champion public power is to use force against those who are subjected to the law. Two recent examples showing that brute force can work to make people follow the law are Belarus and the Russian Federation. After a rigged election in August 2020, the Republic of Belarus saw the greatest protests in its history.[43] Shortly after the protests had erupted, the Belarusian regime started clamping down on the protests harshly.[44] Finally, they managed to squash the protests more or less completely.[45] Similarly, in Russia, Wladimir Putin has been able to consolidate his power over the last 20 plus years with increasingly autocratic leadership. After the beginning of the full-scale Russian aggression against Ukraine on 24 February 2022, Putin's rule has become more and more repressive. Even the smallest protests were quelled brutally.[46] Unfortunately, the examples of autocratic regimes seeking to remain in power with brutal repression instead of by trying to secure legitimacy are numerous. And the Russian and Belarusian examples illustrate the potential effectiveness of brutal rule aptly. When Lukashenko's authority was challenged stronger than ever before,

---

[42] The idea that people follow the law because it is in their own self-interest, either because compliance brings them a reward, or because non-compliance has a sanction as a consequence, has been elaborated on by the so-called "deterrence literature". For an overview, see Tom R. Tyler, *Why People Obey the Law* (Princeton University Press 2006).

[43] See, e.g., Shaun Walker, "We will win': vast Belarus rally adamant Lukashenko must go' *The Guardian* (16 August 2020) <https://www.theguardian.com/world/2020/aug/16/we-will-win-vast-belarus-rally-adamant-lukashenko-must-go> accessed 26 August 2025.

[44] See, e.g., Shaun Walker and Andrew Roth, 'Belarusians seek justice for brutal beatings by riot police' *The Guardian* (18 August 2020) <https://www.theguardian.com/world/2020/aug/18/belarusians-seek-justice-for-brutal-beatings-by-riot-police> accessed 26 August 2025.

[45] For an example for a description of the current state of affairs, see Olga Loginova, 'A fake Ryanair hijack—and the fear that has stalked Belarus's people ever since' *The Guardian* (19 October 2023) <https://www.theguardian.com/global-development/2023/oct/19/a-fake-ryanair-hijack-and-the-fear-that-has-stalked-belaruss-people-ever-since> accessed 26 August 2025.

[46] Anton Troianovski, 'Police arrest more than 3,000 people as protests grow across Russia.' *The New York Times* (6 March 2022) <https://www.nytimes.com/2022/03/06/world/europe/police-russia-protests.html> accessed 26 August 2025.

his rule became more repressive than it has ever been, and so far, it has been working for him and many others.

While—at least for a limited amount of time—using force to make people comply works, such an approach is costly. It takes an enormous security apparatus, and often functions only when accompanied by measures that secure a certain standard of living to keep the people satisfied. Moreover, as we have seen in Belarus in 2020, from the perspective of a ruler, such an approach is risky, too. Once people become too angry with the system, they might fight back, and this will then require even greater police powers. Moreover, the approach is dependent on the repressive system's staying faithful to the leader. Finally—and most importantly –, securing one's power by using force, e.g., to quell protests, is entirely deplorable from a human rights perspective and therefore unacceptable to begin with.[47]

Another, less problematic potential basis for compliance is rational argumentation.[48] Those subjected to a decision may be willing to follow it because they are convinced by its content or by the arguments brought forward by the administrative body issuing it. From a human rights law perspective, there is nothing wrong with a state engaging in a rational discussion with its citizens and trying to persuade them. However, from the states' perspective, rational argumentation provides a rather risky basis for justifying the exercise of public power, too. Who guarantees that the argumentation that convinces one person will convince another? And who guarantees that an argument that convinces a person in 2023 will convince her again in 2025 when her situation has significantly changed? Moreover, having to constantly convince people of the rightfulness of a decision is very costly as well. A state cannot always negotiate with its nationals until they are convinced that they should accept a decision that's negative for them.

In light of the shortcomings of these two other potential bases for the exercise of public power, the attractiveness of legitimacy for states becomes apparent. In contrast to the other two potential bases, legitimacy possesses a "normative quality" which has important consequences for the ruler and the ruled.[49] When speaking about a particular act of the exercise of public power as "legitimate", we do not mean that the decision is substantively correct or good, rather, we mean that the entity handing down the decision had a right to exercise public

---

47 On the relationship between authoritarian rule and the suppression of civil and political rights, see Pierre Thielbörger, 'Flashbangs against Empowerment' (*völkerrechtsblog*, 14 August 2020) <https://voelkerrechtsblog.org/de/flashbangs-against-empowerment/> accessed 26 August 2025.

48 Bodansky, 'Legitimacy', 707.

49 Bodansky, 'Legitimacy in International Law and International Relations', 326.

power in the way they did because they are legitimate.[50] In that sense, (output-based) legitimacy has a "content-neutral quality", and "relates to the qualities of the decision-maker or the decision-making process [...] rather than the content of the decisions themselves".[51]

Metaphorically, legitimacy has very aptly been described as a "reservoir of favourable attitudes or goodwill".[52] When the reservoir is full, people are likely to accept a decision that is not favourable to them because of the benevolent attitude they have towards those rendering a certain decision. Legitimacy "involves the notion of deference".[53] In other words, legitimacy "allows people to maintain confidence in institutions' long-term decision-making [and] enables institutions to weather short-term shocks and crises without significant loss of public confidence".[54] Leaders will not need to exert outside influence or pressure on people to follow them or their decisions. They will not have to convince people by rational arguments. And they will not have to suppress them by forceful means in order to make them comply. It is this consequence which makes legitimacy so attractive for governments. It can lead to *"Herrschaft"* in a Weberian sense, i.e., to a "relationship of command and obedience, such that those subordinate to it can be expected to carry out an instruction regardless of its content"[55]. According to Max Weber, legitimacy is "the glue that keeps organisations functioning, ensuring the adherence of administrators to the organisation and its hierarchy, and the effectiveness of their actions with respect to their constituents".[56]

10.3.2.3 Procedural Involvement and Legitimacy

Now that we have established what legitimacy is and why it is so attractive for governments, we will look at the connection between involvement in a decision-making process and the legitimacy of the decision. Certain procedural features, such as transparency and participation have long been considered to enhance

[50] Ibid, 326.

[51] Bodansky, 'Legitimacy', 708.

[52] David Easton, *A Systems Analysis of Political Life* (Wiley 1965), 273, David Easton, 'A Re-Assessment of the Concept of Political Support' (1975) 5 British Journal of Political Science 435, 444.

[53] Bodansky, 'Legitimacy', 707.

[54] Sarah Kerkin, 'Designing for Legitimacy: A Systems Perspective' (2017) 15 New Zealand Journal of Public and International Law 67, 69.

[55] David Beetham, 'Max Weber and the Legitimacy of the Modern State' (1991) 13 Analyse & Kritik 34, 35. For Max Weber's definition of leadership, see Max Weber, *Economy and Society: A New Translation* (Keith Tribe tr, Harvard University Press 2019), 134–135.

[56] Weber, 335.

the legitimacy of a decision. We also find expressions of this in international law documents or documents issued by international organisations. For example, the two paragraphs from the preamble of the Århus Convention highlight the connection between participation and legitimacy:

> *Recognizing that, in the field of the environment, improved access to information and public participation in decision-making enhance the quality and the implementation of decisions, contribute to public awareness of environmental issues, give the public the opportunity to express its concerns and enable public authorities to take due account of such concerns,*
>
> *Aiming thereby to further the accountability of and transparency in decision-making* ***and to strengthen public support for decisions on the environment****[...].*[57]

Similarly, international bodies have made the connection too. For example, the Governance Evaluation of the International Monetary Fund (IMF) of 2008 held that a reform of the IMF's governance mechanisms was likely to increase the IMF's legitimacy.[58] The CESCR, moreover, has also acknowledged this connection when it connected the necessity of involving those affected in decision-making processes to the "acceptability" of a decision.[59]

In more recent literature, the connection between procedural involvement and legitimacy has been investigated more and more. Tom R. Tyler's research on procedural fairness and legitimacy has been described as the "dominant theoretical approach to legitimacy" in the fields of criminology and socio-legal studies.[60] In his seminal book "Why People Obey the Law" of 1990[61], Tyler investigates normative approaches to explain why people follow the law. In contrast to instrumental approaches, which assume that people follow the law because they expect a reward for following the law or fear sanctions in case of non-compliance, normative approaches view people as complying with the law because they view it

[57] Convention on Access to Information, Public Participation in Decision-Making and Access to Justice in Environmental Matters (adopted 25 June 1998, entered into force 30 October 2001) 2161 UNTS 447 (Århus Convention), Preamble.

[58] *Governance of the International Monetary Fund: an evaluation / [prepared by an IEO team headed by Ruben Lamdany]* (2008), 2.

[59] CESCR, GC 21, para. 16.

[60] Anthony Bottoms and Justice Tankebe, 'Beyond Procedural Justice: A Dialogical Approach to Legitimacy in Criminal Justice' (2012) 102 Journal of Criminal Law and Criminology 119, 120.

[61] Tyler.

as just or moral. According to this perspective, obeying the law is less about self-interest. People "will feel personally committed to obeying the law, irrespective of whether they risk punishment for breaking the law".[62]

The contrast between the two approaches becomes palpable with regard to balancing decisions made by public authorities. The exercise of public power often involves balancing human rights, be that when a state agent seeks to interfere with individual human rights, when they decide on whether to grant someone a positive right or when deciding a matter that involves contravening human rights of two or more private individuals. In the first two cases, human rights are regularly balanced against public goods, and in the latter example, two private rights are balanced against each other. In all cases, the possibility of the state agent's issuing a decision that will disappoint at least one individual is given—in the latter case, that possibility is even a certainty. And the individual whose interests could not be treated preferentially is likely to reject the outcome of the decision.[63] According to the instrumental theory of compliance with the law, the affected individual will likely view the negative outcome as illegitimate. According to the normative theory, in contrast, people would consider the legitimacy of the decision to be mostly affected by *how* the negative result was achieved. In other words, if the normative theory was right and procedural fairness played a central role in people's compliance with the law, it could ensure that individuals view the decision as legitimate, accept it and comply with it even though it is negative for them.

Tyler's book sought to answer *inter alia* the following questions:

> *Do people distinguish between procedures (how decisions are made) and outcomes (what the decisions are)? Do they distinguish between winning and being fairly treated? To the extent that they do, which of these judgments influences their reactions to their experience?*[64]

All three questions are highly important for our purposes. And, indeed, Tyler's book has shown that people follow the law when they consider it legitimate. Most importantly, his study has shown that "citizen's evaluations of the authorities are heavily influenced by their judgments about the fairness of the decision-making process used by the authorities"[65]. In fact, his study found that fair procedures provided a "cushion of support against the potentially damaging effects of

[62] Ibid, 3.

[63] Ibid, 20.

[64] Ibid, 5.

[65] Ibid, 97.

unfavourable outcomes".[66] Moreover, the study finds that "judgments about the fairness of the procedures used during respondents' personal experience influence[d] views about the legitimacy of legal authorities" and that "[t]hese views in turn influence[d] compliance".[67]

This two-step causal relationship that Tyler showed with a relatively large group of people empirically proves the assumption that has become such a commonplace in international legal literature and documents of international bodies: procedural fairness, involvement, transparency, etc matter. They have the potential to significantly bolster the legitimacy of the ruling institution in the eyes of the subjected individual. Hence, they are not only required by IHRL but are also a valuable instrument for the state to make compliance with its laws and (administrative) orders more robust. In other words, involving the individual in decision-making processes can enhance the legitimacy of decisions as the outcome of these processes.

10.3.2.4 Long-Term Effects on the Legitimacy of States' Organs

Beyond this short-term effect regarding the legitimacy of individual decisions, the involvement of individuals in decision-making processes can have indirect long-term effects for the legitimacy of the institutions that make a certain decision. Procedural fairness can enhance the legitimacy not only of an individual decision but also of the legitimacy of the decision-making institution and ultimately the state as a whole. This indirect and long-term consequence is arguably even more important for states. It is the kind of legitimacy that we have described as so attractive for states because it allows them to "weather short-term shocks and crises without significant loss of public confidence"[68]. Involving individuals in state decision-making processes can give states this ability by filling the reservoir of goodwill of their people. If the public believes in the legitimacy of individual decision-making processes, it "shores up the legitimacy of underpinning constitutional settings".[69] In the eyes of an individual subjected to the power of a state, each individual experience that enhances the legitimacy of the state is—to stay in the metaphor—a drop of goodwill in the legitimacy reservoir. And with each of these drops, the overall stability of the state's governing institutions is strengthened.

---

[66] Ibid, 101.

[67] Ibid, 102.

[68] Kerkin, 69.

[69] Ibid, 68.

10.4 Administrative Procedure: A Win-Win-Undertaking

Our short reflection on procedure, participation and legitimacy has shown that the obligations argued for in this thesis are not only required by and beneficial to the human rights of individuals. They can also be beneficial to states by enhancing their legitimacy. Hence, when a state implements its obligations of administrative procedure under IHRL, both sides can profit.

From the perspective of human rights law, it is important that administrative procedure is always construed as a device to implement international human rights in an effective way, and in a way that does justice to the autonomy of individual human beings. It must not be used as a device for states to whitewash their actions or deceive their citizens. It must not become a theatre in which states give the impression that they care, when actually, they do not. It must not become a charade or a farce. However, when administrative procedure is conceived of in a human rights-friendly way, it can become an actual conversation between the individual and the administration and be a win-win undertaking for both sides involved.

Bibliography

Ahmed F and Perry A, 'Expertise, Deference, and Giving Reasons' [2011] Oxford Student Legal Research Paper Series

Alexy R, 'Grundrechte als subjektive Rechte und als objektive Normen' 29 Der Staat 49

Alexy R, *A Theory of Constitutional Rights* (Rivers J tr, Oxford University Press 2002)

Alexy R, 'Constitutional Rights and Proportionality' (2014) 22 Revus [Online] 51

Alston P, 'Conjuring Up New Human Rights: A Proposal for Quality Control' (1984) 78 American Journal of International Law 607

Alston P, 'The Historical Origins of the Concept of 'General Comments' in Human Rights Law' in Boisson de Chazournes L and Gowlland-Debbas V (eds), *The International Legal System in Quest of Equity and Universality: Liber amicorum Georges Abi-Saab* (Brill | Nijhoff 2001)

Alston P, 'Book Review: Does the Past Matter? On the Origins of Human Rights, The Slave Trade and the Origins of International Human Rights Law' (2013) 126 Harvard Law Review 2043

Alston P, 'The Populist Challenge to Human Rights' (2017) 9 Journal of Human Rights Practice 1

Alston P and Quinn G, 'The Nature and Scope of States Parties' Obligations under the International Covenant on Economic, Social and Cultural Rights' (1987) 9 Human Rights Quarterly 156

Aman ACJ, 'Privatization, Prisons, Democracy, and Human Rights: The Need to Extend the Province of Administrative Law' (2005) 12 Indiana Journal of Global Legal Studies 511

Applbaum AI, 'Legitimacy without the Duty to Obey' (2010) 38 Philosophy & Public Affairs 215

Arai-Takahashi Y, 'Proportionality' in Shelton D (ed), *The Oxford Handbook of International Human Rights Law* (Oxford University Press 2013)

Arnardóttir OM, 'The Brighton Aftermath and the Changing Role of the European Court of Human Rights' (2018) 9 Journal of International Dispute Settlement 223

Baade B, 'Due Diligence and the Duty to Potect Human Rights' in Krieger H, Peters A and Kreuzer L (eds), *Due Diligence in the International Legal Order* (Oxford University Press 2020)

B. Behlert, *The Necessity of a Conversation between the Administration and the Individual*, Juridicum—Bochumer Schriften zur Friedenssicherung und zum Humanitären Völkerrecht | Bochum Studies on the International Law of Peace and Armed Conflict 72, https://doi.org/10.1007/978-3-658-50303-1

Baer S, 'Equality' in Rosenfeld M and Sajó A (eds), *The Oxford Handbook of Comparative Constitutional Law* (Oxford University Press 2012)

Bagaric M and Allan J, 'The Vacuous Concept of Dignity' (2006) 5 Journal of Human Rights 257

Barak A, *Proportionality: Constitutional Rights and their Limitations* (Cambridge University Press 2012)

Barak A, *Human Dignity: The Constitutional Value and the Constitutional Right* (Cambridge University Press 2015)

Barelli M, 'Free, Prior, and Informed Consent in the UNDRIP: Articles 10, 19, 29 (2), and 32 (2)' in Hohmann J and Weller M (eds), *The UN Declaration on the Rights of Indigenous Peoples: A Commentary* (Oxford University Press 2018)

Barnes J, 'Three generations of administrative procedures' in Rose-Ackerman S and Lindseth PL (eds), *Comparative Administrative Law* (2nd edn, Edward Elgar Publishing 2017)

Bates E, 'History' in Moeckli D, Shah S and Sivakumaran S (eds), *International Human Rights Law* (3rd edn, Oxford University Press 2018)

Bates J, 'Human Dignity—An Empty Phrase in Search of Meaning?' (2005) 10 Judicial Review 165

Beetham D, *The Legitimation of Power* (Palgrave Macmillan 1991)

Beetham D, 'Max Weber and the Legitimacy of the Modern State' (1991) 13 Analyse & Kritik 34

Behlert B, 'The Obligation to Conduct Individual Refugee Status Determination Procedures under the ICCPR—Constructing a Convincing Legal Basis' (2019) 2 Humanitäres Völkerrecht (Journal of International Law of Peace and Armed Conflict) 201

Behlert B, 'The Protection of Human Rights in Times of Public Health Emergencies' in Thielbörger P and Lüder SR (eds), *Die COVID-19-Pandemie als Herausforderung an das Völkerrecht, das Verfassungsrecht und das Verwaltungsrecht* (Berliner Wissenschafts-Verlag 2022)

Beitz CR, 'Human Dignity in the Theory of Human Rights: Nothing but a Phrase?' (2013) 41 Philosophy & Public Affairs 259

Besson S, 'Sovereingty' in Peters A (ed), *Max Planck Encyclopedia of Public International Law (MPEPIL)* (Oxford University Press 2011)

Bethge H, 'Grundrechtsverwirklichung und Grundrechtssicherung durch Organisation und Verfahren: Zu einigen Aspekten der aktuellen Grundrechtsdiskussion' [1982] Neue Juristische Wochenschrift (NJW) 1

Bianchi A, 'Textual interpretation and (international) law reading: the myth of (in)determinacy and the genealogy of meaning' in Waibel M, Bekker PHF and Dolzer R (eds), *Making Transnational Law Work in the Global Economy: Essays in Honour of Detlev Vagts* (Cambridge University Press 2010)

Bianchi A, *International Law Theories: An Inquiry into Different Ways of Thinking* (Oxford University Press 2016)

Binder C, 'Human Dignity in International Human Rights Law' in Donath PB and others (eds), *Der Schutz des Individuums durch das Recht: Festschrift für Rainer Hofmann zum 70 Geburtstag* (Springer 2023)

Bjorge E, *The Evolutionary Interpretation of Treaties* (Oxford University Press 2014)

Böckenförde E-W, 'Grundrechte als Grundsatznormen: Zur gegenwärtigen Lage der Grundrechtsdogmatik' (1990) 29 Der Staat 1

Bodansky D, 'Legitimacy' in Bodansky D, Brunée J and Hey E (eds), *The Oxford Handbook of International Environmental Law* (Oxford University Press 2008)

Bodansky D, 'Legitimacy in International Law and International Relations' in Dunoff JL and Pollack MA (eds), *Interdisciplinary Perspectives on International Law and International Relations* (Cambridge University Press 2012)

Bottoms A and Tankebe J, 'Beyond Procedural Justice: A Dialogical Approach to Legitimacy in Criminal Justice' (2012) 102 Journal of Criminal Law and Criminology 119

Boysen S, 'GG Art. 3 [Gleichheit vor dem Gesetz]' in von Münch I and others (eds), *Grundgesetz Kommentar* (8th edn, C. H. Beck 2025)

Brade A, *Additive Grundrechtseingriffe: Ein Beitrag zur Grundrechtsdogmatik* (Nomos 2020)

Bucher P, *Der Parlamentarische Rat 1948–1949, Band 2: Der Verfassungskonvent auf Herrenchiemsee* (Deutscher Bundestag and Bundesarchiv eds, Oldenbourg Wissenschaftsverlag 1981)

Buffard I and Zemanek K, 'The "Object and Purpose" of a Treaty: An Enigma?' (1998) 3 Austrian Review of International & European Law 311

Byrnes A and Renshaw C, 'Within the State' in Moeckli D, Shah S and Sivakumaran S (eds), *International Human Rights Law* (3rd edn, Oxford University Press 2018)

Çalı B, 'Specialized Rules of Treaty Interpretation: Human Rights' in Hollis DB (ed), *The Oxford Guide to Treaties* (Oxford University Press 2012)

Çalı B, 'Coping with Crisis: Whither the Variably Geometry in the Jurisprudence of the European Court of Human Rights' (2018) 35 Wisconsin International Law Journal 237

Cantor DJ, 'Reframing Relationships: Revisiting the Procedural Standards for Refugee Status Determination in Light of Recent Human Rights Treaty Body Jurisprudence' (2015) 34 Refugee Survey Quarterly 79

Carazo MP, 'Velásquez Rodríguez v Honduras Case' in Peters A (ed), *Max Planck Encyclopedia of Public International Law (MPEPIL)* (Oxford University Press 2008)

Carozza PG, 'Subsidiarity as a Structural Principle of International Human Rights Law' (2003) 97 The American Journal of International Law 38

Carozza PG, 'Human Dignity and Judicial Interpretation of Human Rights: A Reply' (2008) 19 European Journal of International Law 931

Carozza PG, 'Human Dignity' in Shelton D (ed), *The Oxford Handbook of International Human Rights Law* (Oxford University Press 2013)

Cassesse A, *Five Master of International Law: Conversations with R-J Dupuy, E Jiménez de Aréchaga, R Jennings, L Henkin and O Schachter* (Hart Publishing 2011)

Castellino J and Doyle C, 'Who Are 'Indigenous Peoples'?: An Examination of Concepts Concerning Group Membership in the UNDRIP' in Hohmann J and Weller M (eds), *The UN Declaration on the Rights of Indigenous Peoples: A Commentary* (Oxford University Press 2018)

Chinkin C, 'Sources' in Moeckli D, Shah S and Sivakumaran S (eds), *International Human Rights Law* (3rd edn, Oxford University Press 2018)

Clifford J, 'Equality' in Shelton D (ed), *The Oxford Handbook of International Human Rights Law* (Oxford University Press 2013)

Clooney A and Webb P, *The Right to a Fair Trial in International Law* (Oxford University Press 2021)

Cohen J, 'Minimalism About Human Rights: The Most We Can Hope For?' (2004) 12 The Journal of Political Philosophy 190

Connors J, 'United Nations' in Moeckli D, Shah S and Sivakumaran S (eds), *International Human Rights Law* (3rd edn, Oxford University Press 2018)

Corder H, 'A Right to Administrative Justice—'New' or Just Repackaging the Old?' in von Arnauld A, von der Decken K and Susi M (eds), *The Cambridge Handbook ofNew Human Rights—Recognition, Novelty, Rhetoric* (Cambridge University Press 2020)

Couronne V and Maurel R, 'Effective Domestic Remedy' in Ruiz Fabri H (ed), *Max Planck Encyclopedia for International Procedural Law* (Oxford University Press 2019)

Crawford J, *State Responsibility—The General Part* (Cambridge University Press 2013)

Cremer W, *Freiheitsgrundrechte* (Mohr Siebeck 2003)

Cremer W, 'Rechtsanwendungsgleichheit im Mehrebenensystem' in Sacksofsky U (ed), *Veröffentlichung der Vereinigung der Deutschen Staatsrechtslehrer, Band 78, Gleichheit, Vielfalt, Technischer Wandel* (De Gruyter 2019)

d'Aspremont J, 'The Rise and Fall of Democracy Governance in International Law: A Reply to Susan Marks' (2011) 22 European Journal of International Law 549

d'Aspremont J, 'Expansionism and the Sources of International Human Rights Law' (2016) 46 Israel Yearbook on Human Rights 223

Daly P, *Understanding Administrative Law in the Common Law World* (Oxford University Press 2021)

David V, 'The Expanding Right to an Effective Remedy: Common Developments at the Human Rights Committee and the Inter-American Court' (2014) 3 British Journal of American Legal Studies 259

Della Cananea G, *Due Process of Law beyond the State: Requirements of Administrative Procedure* (Oxford University Press 2016)

Denninger E, '§ 193—Staatliche Hilfe zur Grundrechtsausübung durch Verfahren, Organisation und Finanzierung' in Isensee J and Kirchhof P (eds), *Handbuch des Staatsrechts*, vol IX (3 edn, C. F. Müller 2011)

Denninger E, 'Government Assistance in the Exercise of Basic Rights (Procedure and Organization)' 12 German Law Journal 430

Detterbeck S, *Allgemeines Verwaltungsrecht* (21st edn, C. H. Beck 2023)

Dickerson H, 'Minimum Standards' in Peters A (ed), *Max Planck Encyclopedia of Public International Law (MPEPIL)* (Oxford University Press 2010)

Dictionary OE, *legitimacy, n* (Oxford University Press 2023)

Dictionary OE, *redress, n* (Oxford University Press 2023)

Dictionary OE, *remedy, n* (Oxford University Press 2023)

Djeffal C, *Static and Evolutive Treaty Interpretation: A Functional Reconstruction* (Cambridge University Press 2016)

Dolderer M, *Objektive Grundrechtsgehalte* (Duncker und Humblot 2000)

Dörr O and Schmalenbach K, *Vienna Convention on the Law of Treaties : a commentary* (2nd edn, Springer 2018)

Doswald-Beck L, 'Fair Trial, Right to, International Protection' in Peters A (ed), *Max Planck Encyclopedia of International Law (MPEPIL)* (Oxford University Press 2013)

Dupré C, 'Human Dignity in Europe: A Foundational Constitutional Principle' 19 European Public Law 319

Dupuy P-M, 'Evolutionary Interpretation of Treaties: Between Memory and Prophecy' in Cannizzaro E (ed), *The Law of Treaties Beyond the Vienna Convention* (Oxford University Press 2011)

Dürig G, 'Der Grundrechtssatz von der Menschenwürde: Entwurf eines praktikablen Wertsystems der Grundrechte aus Art. 1 Abs. 1 in Verbindung mit Art. 19 Abs. 2 des Grundgesetzes' (1956) 81 Archiv des öffentlichen Rechts 117

Dyzenhaus D, 'Dignity in Administrative Law: Judicial Deference in a Culture of Justification' in Grimm D, Kemmerer A and Möllers C (eds), *Human Dignity in Context: Explorations of a Contested Concept* (Nomos 2018)

Easton D, *A Systems Analysis of Political Life* (Wiley 1965)

Easton D, 'A Re-Assessment of the Concept of Political Support' (1975) 5 British Journal of Political Science 435

Elliott M, 'Has the Common Law Duty to Give Reasons Come of Age Yet?' [2011] Public Law 56

Feinberg J, 'The Nature and Value of Rights' (1970) 4 The Journal of Value Inquiry 243

Fenrich K, *The Evolving International Procedural Capacity of Individuals* (Springer 2019)

Fitzmaurice G, 'Vae Victis or Woe to the Negotiators—Your Treaty or Our Interpretation of It' (1971) 65 American Journal of International Law 358

Fitzmaurice M, 'Interpretation of Human Rights Treaties' in Shelton D (ed), *The Oxford Handbook of International Human Rights Law* (Oxford University Press 2013)

Fordham M, 'Reasons: The Third Dimension' (1998) 3 Judicial Review 158

Forst R, 'The Justification of Human Rights and the Basic Right to Justification: A Reflexive Approach' (2010) 120 Ethics 711

Forsthoff E, *Lehrbuch des Verwaltungsrechts*, vol 1 (10th edn, C. H. Beck 1973)

Franck TM, 'The Emerging Right to Democratic Governance' (1992) 86 American Journal of International Law 46

Fredman S, *Human Rights Transformed: Positive Rights and Positive Duties* (Oxford University Press 2008)

Gardbaum S, 'Human Rights as International Constitutional Rights' (2008) 19 European Journal of International Law 749

Gardiner R, 'The Vienna Convention Rules on Treaty Interpretation' in Hollis DB (ed), *The Oxford Guide to Treaties* (Oxford University Press 2012)

Gardiner R, *Treaty interpretation* (2nd edn, Oxford University Press 2015)

George T, 'Hermeneutics' in Zalta EN (ed), *The Stanford Encyclopedia of Philosophy* (Winter 2021 edn, Metaphysics Research Lab, Stanford University 2021) <https://plato.stanford.edu/archives/win2021/entries/hermeneutics/> accessed 17 December 2023

Gersdorf H, '§ 80 VwGO' in Posser H and Wolff HA (eds), *BeckOK VwGO* (67th edn, C. H. Beck 2023)

Gewirth A, 'Rights and Virtues' (1985) 38 The Review of Metaphysics 739

Goerlich H, *Grundrechte als Verfahrensgarantien* (Nomos Verlagsgesellschaft 1981)

Golder B, 'Theorizing Human Rights' in Orford A and Hoffmann F (eds), *The Oxford Handbook of the Theory of International Law* (Oxford University Press 2016)

Goodman R and Jinks D, 'Measuring the Effects of Human Rights Treaties' (2003) 14 European Journal of International Law 171

Grimm D, 'Freedom of Speech in a Globalized World' in Hare I and Weinstein J (eds), *Extreme Speech and Democracy* (Oxford University Press 2009)

Groves M and Weeks G, 'The Legitimacy of Expectations About Fairness: Can Process and Substance be Untangled?' in Bell J and others (eds), *Public Law Adjudication in Common Law Systems: Process and Substance* (Hart Publishing 2016)

Gurlit E, '§ 109 Dienende Funktion des Verfahrens und Prozeduralisierung' in Kahl W and Ludwigs M (eds), *Handbuch des Verwaltungsrechts*, vol IV (C. F. Müller 2022)

Häberle P, 'Grundrechte im Leistungsstaat' (1972) 30 Veröffentlichungen der Vereinigung deutscher Staatsrechtslehrer (VVDStRL) 43

Häberle P, 'Zeit und Verfassung: Prolegomena zu einen "zeit-gerechten" Verfassungsverständnis' (1974) 21 Zeitschrift für Politik 111

Häberle P, 'Grundrechtsgeltung und Grundrechtsinterpretation im Verfassungsstaat — Zugleich zur Rechtsvergleichung als „fünfter" Auslegungsmethode' (1989) 44 Juristen-Zeitung 913

Häberle P, '§ 22 Die Menschenwürde als Grundlage der staatlichen Gemeinschaft' in Isensee J and Kirchhof F (eds), *Handbuch des Staatsrechts* (3rd edn, C.F. Müller 2004)

Habermas J, 'The Concept of Human Dignity and the Realistic Utopia of Human Rights' (2010) 41 Metaphilosophy 464

Hailbronner K and Gogolin J, 'Aliens' in Peters A (ed), *Max Planck Encyclopedia of Public International Law (MPEPIL)* (Oxford University Press 2013)

Hare I, 'Extreme Speech under International and Regional Human Rights Standards' in Hare I and Weinstein J (eds), *Extreme Speech and Democracy* (Oxford University Press 2009)

Hartwig S, 'Grundrechtsschutz des Verfahrens: Der Mülheim-Kärlich-Beschluss' in Grimm D (ed), *Vorbereiter—Nachbereiter?* (Mohr Siebeck 2019)

Hassan P, 'The Word "Arbitrary" As Used In The Universal Declaration Of Human Rights: "Illegal" Or "Unjust"?' (1969) 10 Harvard International Law Journal 225

Hathaway JC, *The Rights of Refugees under International Law* (Cambridge University Press 2005)

Held J, *Der Grundrechtsbezug des Verwaltungsverfahrens* (Duncker & Humblot 1984)

Henkin L, 'Rights: American and Human' (1979) 79 Columbia Law Review 405

Henne T, '"Smend oder Hennis?": Bedeutung, Rezeption und Problematik der 'Lüth-Entscheidung' des Bundesverfassungsgerichts von 1958' in van Ooyen RC and Möllers MHW (eds), *Handbuch Bundesverfassungsgericht im politischen System* (2nd edn, Springer VS 2015)

Hepburn J, 'The Duty to Give Reasons for Administrative Decisions in International Law' (2012) 61 International and Comparative Law Quarterly 641

Herdegen M, 'Art. 1 Abs. 3' in Dürig G, Herzog R and Scholz R (eds), *Grundgesetz Kommentar* (107th EL edn, C. H. Beck 2025)

Heselhaus S and Hemsley R, 'Human Dignity and the European Convention on Human Rights' in Becchi P and Mathis K (eds), *Handbook of Human Dignity in Europe* (Springer Nature 2019)

Hesse K, 'Bestand und Bedeutung der Grundrechte in der Bundesrepublik Deutschland' [1978] Europäische Grundrechtezeitschrift (EuGRZ) 427

Heyns C and Killander M, 'Universality and the Growth of Regional Systems' in Shelton D (ed), *The Oxford Handbook of International Human Rights Law* (Oxford University Press 2013)

Hillgruber C, '§ 201: Inhalt und Schranken der Grundrechte' in Isensee J and Kirchhof P (eds), *Handbuch des Staatsrechts*, vol IX (C.F. Müller 2011)

Hollerbach A and al. e, 'Grundrechte im Leistungsstaat: Aussprache und Schlussworte' 30 Veröffentlichungen der Vereinigung deutscher Staatsrechtslehrer (VVDStRL) 142

Hong M, *Der Menschenwürdegehalt der Grundrechte: Grundfragen, Entstehung und Rechtsprechung* (Mohr Siebeck 2019)

Huijbers L, *Process-based Fundamental Rights Review* (Intersentia 2021)

Humphrey JP, 'The International Bill of Rights: Scope and Implementation Bicentennial Symposium: Constitutional Government—Strengths, Weaknesses, Future' (1975) 17 Wm & Mary L Rev 527

Humphrey JP, 'Political and Related Rights' in Meron T (ed), *Human Rights in International Law: Legal and Policy Issues* (Oxford University Press 1986)

Hurd I, 'Legitimacy and Authority in International Politics' (1999) 53 International Organization 379

Hutchinson MR, 'The Margin of Appreciation Doctrine in the European Court of Human Rights' (1999) 48 International & Comparative Law Quarterly 638

Ipsen K, 'Regelungsbereich, Geschichte und Funktion des Völkerrechts' in Epping V and Heintschell von Heinegg W (eds), *Völkerrecht* (7th edn, C. H. Beck 2018)

Isensee J, 'Verfassung ohne soziale Grundrechte: Ein Wesenszug des Grundgesetzes' (1980) 19 Der Staat 367

Isensee J, '§ 191—Das Grundrecht als Abwehrrecht und als Staatliche Schutzpflicht' in Isensee J and Kirchhof P (eds), *Handbuch des Staatsrechts*, vol IX (C. F. Müller 2011)

Jarass HD, 'Grundrechte als Wertentscheidungen bzw. objektivrechtliche Prinzipien in der Rechtsprechung des Bundesverfassungsgerichts' (1985) 110 Archiv des Öffentlichen Rechts 363

Jarass HD, 'Bausteine einer umfassenden Grundrechtsdogmatik' (1995) 120 Archiv des öffentlichen Rechts 345

Jarass HD, '§ 38 Funktionen und Dimensionen der Grundrechte' in Merten D and Papier H-J (eds), *Handbuch der Grundrechte in Deutschland und Europa* (C. F. Müller 2006)

Jarass HD, 'Art. 3 [Gleichheit]' in Jarass HD, Pieroth B and Kment M (eds), *Grundgesetz für die Bundesrepublik Deutschland Kommentar* (18th edn, C. H. Beck 2024)

Jellinek G, *System der subjektiven öffentlichen Rechte* (Reprint of 2nd edn, Scientia Verlag 1964)

Jestaedt M, 'Die deutsche Staatsrechtslehre im europäisierten Rechtswissenschaftsdiskurs: Kennzeichen, Kernkompetenzen und Rezeptionshindernisse' (2012) 67 Juristenzeitung 1

Jhering Rv, *Geist des römischen Rechts auf den verschiedenen Stufen seiner Entwicklung*, vol 3/4 (Breitkopf und Härtel 1858)

Joseph S, 'Extending the Right to Life Under the International Covenant on Civil and Political Rights: General Comment 36' (2019) 19 Human Rights Law Review 347

Joseph S and Castan M, *The International Covenant on Civil and Political Rights : Cases, Materials, and Commentary* (3rd edn, Oxford University Press 2013)

Kälin W and Künzli J, *The Law of International Human Rights Protection* (2nd edn, Oxford University Press 2019)

Kämmerer J-A, 'Art. 2 GG' in von Münch I and others (eds), Grundgesetz Kommentar (8th edn, C. H. Beck 2025)

Kavanagh A, 'Reasoning about proportionality under the Human Rights Act 1998: outcomes, substance and process' (2014) 130 Law Quarterly Review 235

Keller H and Moeckli D, 'Introduction' in Moeckli D, Keller H and Heri C (eds), *The Human Rights Covenants at 50: Their Past, Present, and Future* (Oxford Academic, Oxford University Press 2018)

Kelsen H, *Reine Rechtslehre: Einleitung in die rechtswissenschaftliche Problematik (Studienausgabe der 1. Auflage 1934)* (Jestaedt M ed, Mohr Siebeck 2008)

Kerkin S, 'Designing for Legitimacy: A Systems Perspective' (2017) 15 New Zealand Journal of Public and International Law 67

Kingsbury B, Krisch N and Stewart RB, 'The Emergence of Global Administrative Law' (2005) 68 Law and Contemporary Problems 15

Kirchhof G, 'Der besondere Schutz der Familie in Art. 6 Abs. 1 des Grundgesetzes: Abwehrrecht, Einrichtungsgarantie, Benachteiligungsverbot, staatliche Schutz- und Förderpflicht' (2004) 129 Archiv des öffentlichen Rechts

Kirchhof P, 'GG Art. 3 Abs. 1 [Gleichheit vor dem Gesetz]' in Dürig G, Herzog R and Scholz R (eds), *Grundgesetz Kommentar* (107th EL edn, C. H. Beck 2025)

Kischel U, 'GG Art. 3 [Gleichheit vor dem Gesetz]' in Epping V and Hillgruber C (eds), *BeckOK Grundgesetz* (62nd edn, C. H. Beck 2025)

Klein E and Kretzmer D, 'The UN Human Rights Committee: The General Comments—The Evolution of an Autonomous Monitoring Instrument' (2015) 58 German Yearbook of International Law 189

Koch IE, 'Dichotomies, Trichotomies or Waves of Duties' (2005) 5 Human Rights Law Review 81

Koskenniemi M, *From Apology to Utopia: The Structure of International Legal Argument* (Reissue with a new Epilogue edn, Cambridge University Press 2006)

Krieger H, 'Positive Verpflichtungen unter der EMRK: Unentbehrliches Element einer gemeineuropäischen Grundrechtsdogmatik, leeres Versprechen oder Grenze der Justiziabilität?' (2014) 74 Zeitschrift für ausländisches öffentliches Recht und Völkerrecht (ZaöRV) 187

Krieger H and Peters A, 'Due Diligence and Structural Change in the International Legal Order' in Krieger H, Peters A and Kreuzer L (eds), *Due Diligence in the International Legal Order* (Oxford University Press 2020)

Langenbach P, *Der Anhörungseffekt: Verfahrensfairness und Rechtsbefolgung im allgemeinen Verwaltungsverfahren* (Mohr Siebeck 2017)

Le Sueur AP, 'Legal Duties to Give Reasons' (1999) 52 Current Legal Problems 150

Lechner H and Zuck R, 'BVerfGG § 90 [Antragsberechtigung]' in Lechner H and Zuck R (eds), *Bundsverfassungsgerichtsgesetz—Kommentar* (8th edn, C. H. Beck 2019)

Lehnhardt C, 'Private Military Companies' in Peters A (ed), *Max Planck Encyclopedia of International Law (MPEPIL)* (Oxford University Press 2011)

Lemmens P, 'The European Court of Human Rights—Can there be too much Success?' [2022] Journal of Human Rights Practice 169

Letsas G, 'Rescuing Proportionality' in Cruft R, Liao SM and Renzo M (eds), *Philosophical Foundations of Human Rights* (Oxford University Press 2015)

Loginova O, 'A fake Ryanair hijack—and the fear that has stalked Belarus's people ever since' *The Guardian* (19 October 2023). https://www.theguardian.com/global-development/2023/oct/19/a-fake-ryanair-hijack-and-the-fear-that-has-stalked-belaruss-people-ever-since. Accessed 26 August 2025

Macklin R, 'Dignity is a Useless Concept: It Means no More than Respect for Persons or Their Autonomy' (2003) 327 British Medical Journal 1419

Mann I, *Humanity at Sea: Maritime Migration and the Foundations of International Law* (Cambridge University Press 2016)

Maurer H and Waldhoff C, *Allgemeines Verwaltungsrecht* (21st edn, C.H. Beck 2024)

Mayer O, *Deutsches Verwaltungsrecht*, vol I, II (Unedited reprint of the 3rd edition published in 1924 edn, Duncker & Humblot 2004)

McCrudden C, 'Human Dignity and Judicial Interpretation of Human Rights' (2008) 19 European Journal of International Law 655

McCrudden C, 'Human Rights Histories' (2015) 35 Oxford Journal of Legal Studies 179

McDougal MS and Lasswell HD, 'The Identification and Appraisal of Diverse Systems of Public Order' (1953) 53 American Journal of International Law 1

Mechlem K, 'Treaty Bodies and the Interpretation of Human Rights' (2009) 42 Vanderbilt Journal of Transnational Law 905

Mégret F, 'Nature of Obligations' in Moeckli D, Shah S and Sivakumaran S (eds), *International Human Rights Law* (3rd edn, Oxford University Press 2018)

Merten D, '§ 68 Verhältnismäßigkeitsgrundsatz' in Merten D and Papier H-J (eds), *Handbuch der Grundrechte in Deutschland und Europa* (2009)

Möllers C, *Gewaltengliederung* (Mohr Siebeck 2005)

Möllers C, *Die drei Gewalten* (Velbrück Wissenschaft 2008)

Möllers C, *The Three Branches: A Comparative Model of Separation of Powers* (Oxford University Press 2013)

Mowbray A, 'The Creativity of the European Court of Human Rights' (2005) 5 Human Rights Law Review 57

Mührel L and Jelić I, 'The Human Rights Committee—Challenges and Prospects for Enhanced Effectiveness and Integration' [2022] Journal of Human Rights Practice 17

Mund D, *Das Recht auf menschliche Entscheidung—zu den verfassungsrechtlichen Vorgaben der technischen Erzeugung von Verwaltungsentscheidungen* (Mohr Siebeck 2021)

Neuman GL, 'The Uses of International Law in Constitutional Interpretation' (2004) 98 The American Journal of International Law 82

Neuman GL, 'Subsidiarity' in Shelton D (ed), *The Oxford Handbook of International Human Rights Law* (Oxford University Press 2013)

Niesler A, 'BVerfGG § 90 Abs. 2' in Walter C and Grünewald B (eds), *BeckOK BVerfGG* (19th edn, C. H. Beck 2025)

Nowak M, *UN Covenant on Civil and Political Rights: CCPR Commentary* (2nd revised edn, N.P. Engel, Publisher 2005)

Nowak M and Schabas W, *U.N. International Covenant on Civil and Political Rights: Nowak's CCPR commentary* (3rd revised edn, N.P. Engel, Publisher 2019)

Nußberger A and Hey J, 'Art. 3 [Gleichheit vor dem Gesetz]' in Sachs M (ed), *Grundgesetz Kommentar* (10th edn, C. H. Beck 2024)

Online I, 'In Small Places, Close to Home: The Beginnings of Universal Human Rights'. https://ironline.american.edu/blog/our-basic-human-rights/. Accessed 26 August 2025

Opsahl T, 'The General Comments of the Human Rights Committee' in Jekewitz J and others (eds), *Des Menschen Recht zwischen Freiheit und Verantwortung: Festschrift für Karl Josef Partsch zum 75 Geburtstag* (Duncker & Humblot 1989)

Ossenbühl F, 'Kernenergie im Spiegel des Verfassungsrechts' [1981] Die Öffentliche Verwaltung 1

Panaccio C-M, 'In Defence of Two-Step Balancing and Proportionality in Rights Adjudication' (2011) XXIV Canadian Journal of Law and Jurisprudence 109

Pasqualucci JM, *The Practice and Procedure of the Inter-American Court of Human Rights* (2nd edn, Cambridge University Press 2012)

Peat D and Windsor M, 'Playing the Game of Interpretation: On Meaning and Metaphor in International Law' in Bianchi A, Peat D and Windsor M (eds), *Interpretation in International Law* (Oxford University Press 2015)

Perelman C, 'Pragmatic Arguments' (1959) 34 Philosophy 18

Peters A, 'Realizing Utopia as a Scholarly Endeavour' (2013) 24 European Journal of International Law 533

Peters A, *Beyond Human Rights: The Legal Status of the Individual in International Law* (Cambridge University Press 2016)

Petersen N, 'Human Dignity, International Protection' in Peters A (ed), *Max Planck Encyclopedia of Public International Law (MPEPIL)* (Oxford University Press 2020)

Petrov J, 'The populist challenge to the European Court of Human Rights' (2020) 18 International Journal of Constitutional Law 476

Pietzker J, '§ 125 Der allgemeine Gleichheitssatz' in Merten D and Papier H-J (eds), *Handbuch der Grundrechte in Deutschland und Europa* (C. F. Müller 2013)

Pollicino O, 'Judicial Protection of Fundamental Rights in the Transition from the World of Atoms to the Word of Bits: The Case of Freedom of Speech' (2019) 25 European Law Journal

Randall MH, 'The History of the Covenants: Looking Back Half a Century and Beyond' in Moeckli D, Keller H and Heri C (eds), *The Human Rights Covenants at 50: Their Past, Present, and Future* (Oxford University Press 2018)

Reiertsen M, *Effective Domestic Remedies and the European Court of Human Rights* (Cambridge University Press 2022)

Riedel E, 'Einführung—Allgemeine Bemerkungen zu Bestimmungen des Internationalen Paktes über Wirtschaftliche, Soziale und Kulturelle Rechte der Vereinten Nationen' in Deutsches Institut für M (ed), *Die »General Comments« zu den VN-Menschenrechtsverträgen: Deutsche Übersetzung und Kurzeinführungen* (Nomos 2005)

Riedel E, 'Reflections on the UN Human Rights Covenants at Fifty' (2016) 54 Archiv des Völkerrechts 132

Riedel E, Giacca G and Golay C, 'The Development of Economic, Social, and Cultural Rights in International Law' in Riedel E, Giacca G and Golay C (eds), *Economic, Social, and Cultural Rights in International Law* (Oxford University Press 2014)

Rietiker D, 'The Principle of "Effectiveness" in the Recent Jurisprudence of the European Court of Human Rights: Its Different Dimensions and Its Consistency with Public International Law—No Need for the Concept of Treaty *Sui Generis*' (2010) 79 Nordic Journal of International Law 245

Rodenhäuser T, 'Another Brick in the Wall: Carrier Sanctions and the Privatization of Immigration Control' (2014) 26 International Journal of Refugee Law 223

Rodley NS, 'The Role and Impact of Treaty Bodies' in Shelton D (ed), *The Oxford Handbook of International Human Rights Law* (Oxford University Press 2013)

Roose K, 'A.I. Poses 'Risk of Extinction', Industry Leaders Warn' *The New York Times*. https://www.nytimes.com/2023/05/30/technology/ai-threat-warning.html?searchResultPosition=5. Accessed 26 August 2025

Roßbach M and Wischmeyer T, 'Grundrechtsschutz durch Organisation: Das erste Fernsehurteil und das Hochschulurteil' in Grimm D (ed), *Vorbereiter—Nachbereiter?* (Mohr Siebeck 2019)

Sachs M, 'Art. 20 [Verfassungsgrundsätze; Widerstandsrecht]' in Sachs M (ed), *Grundgesetz Kommentar* (10th edn, C. H. Beck 2024)

Saul B, Kinley D and Mowbray J, *The International Covenant on Economic, Social and Cultural Rights: Commentary, Cases and Materials* (Oxford University Press 2014)

Schachter O, 'The Invisible College of International Lawyers' (1977) 72 Northwestern University Law Review 217

Schachter O, 'Editorial Comment: Human Dignity as a Normative Concept' (1983) 77 American Journal of International Law 848

Scharpf F, *Governing in Europe: Effective and Democratic?* (Oxford University Press 1999)

Scheinin M and Åhrén M, 'Relationship to Human Rights, and Related International Instruments' in Hohmann J and Weller M (eds), *The UN Declaration on the Rights of Indigenous Peoples: A Commentary* (Oxford University Press 2018)

Scheuner U, 'Pressefreiheit' (1965) 22 Veröffentlichungen der Vereinigung deutscher Staatsrechtslehrer (VVDStRL) 1

Schlaich K and Korioth S, *Das Bundesverfassungsgericht: Stellung, Verfahren, Entscheidungen* (12th edn, C. H. Beck 2021)

Schmidt-Aßmann E, 'Die Wissenschaftsfreiheit nach Art. 5 Abs. 3 GG als Organisationsgrundrecht' in Becker B (ed), *Festschrift für Werner Thieme zum 70 Geburtstag* (Heymann 1993)

Schmidt-Aßmann E, '§ 26 Der Rechtsstaat' in Kirchhof P and Isensee J (eds), *Handbuch des Staatsrechts*, vol II (3rd edn, C. F. Müller 2004)

Schmidt-Aßmann E, 'Art. 19 Abs. 4' in Dürig G, Herzog R and Scholz R (eds), *Grundgesetz Kommentar* (107th EL edn, C. H. Beck 2025)

Schønberg S, *Legitimate Expectations in Administrative Law* (Oxford University Press 2000)

Schulze-Fielitz H, 'Art. 19 Abs. 4' in Dreier H (ed), *Grundgesetz Kommentar* (3rd edn, Mohr Siebeck 2013)

Schwarze J, *Der funktionale Zusammenhang von Verwaltungsverfahrensrecht und verwaltungsgerichtlichem Rechtsschutz* (Duncker & Humblot 1974)

Seibert-Fohr A, 'Domestic Implementation of the International Covenant on Civil and Political Rights pursuant to its article 2 para. 2' (2001) 5 Max Planck Yearbook of United Nations Law 399

Shane S and Nixon R, 'In Washington, Contractors Take On Biggest Role Ever' *The New York Times*. https://www.nytimes.com/2007/02/04/washington/04contract.html. Accessed 26 August 2025

Shelton D, 'Human Rights, Remedies' in Peters A (ed), *Max Planck Encyclopedia of Public International Law (MPEPIL)* (Oxford University Press 2006)

Shelton D, *Remedies in International Human Rights Law* (Oxford University Press 2006)

Shue H, *Basic Rights—Subsistence, Affluence and U.S. Foreign Policy: 40th Anniversary Edition* (40th anniversary edn, Princeton University Press 2020)

Smits JM, 'Comparative Law and Its Influence on National Legal Systems' in Reimann M and Zimmermann R (eds), *The Oxford Handbook of Comparative Law* (Oxford University Press 2006)

Sommermann K-P, 'Artikel 20' in Huber P and Voßkuhle A (eds), *Grundgesetz Kommentar* (8th edn, C. H. Beck 2024)

Sordi B, 'Révolution, Rechtsstaat and the Rule of Law: historical reflections on the emergence and development of administrative law' in Rose-Ackerman S, Lindseth PL and Emerson B (eds), *Comparative Administrative Law* (2nd edn, Edward Elgar 2017)

Spano R, 'Universality or Diversity of Human Rights?: Strasbourg in the Age of Subsidiarity' (2014) 14 Human Rights Law Review 487

Spano R, 'The Future of the European Court of Human Rights—Subsidiarity, Process-Based Review and the Rule of Law' (2018) 18 Human Rights Law Review 473

Ssenyonjo M, *Economic, Social and Cultural Rights in International Law* (2nd edn, Hart Publishing 2016)

Staubach P, 'Das Verhältnismäßigkeitsprinzip' in Grimm D (ed), *Vorbereiter—Nachbereiter?, Studien zum Verhältnis von Verfassungsrechtsprechung und Verfassungsrechtswissenschaft* (Mohr Siebeck 2019)

Stone Sweet A, 'Sur la constitutionnalisation de la Convention européenne des droit de l'hommes: Cinquante ans après son installation, la Cour européenne des droit de l'homme conçue comme une Cour constituionnelle' (2009) 80 Revue trimestrielle des droits de l'homme 923

Taylor PM, *A Commentary on the International Covenant on Civil and Political Rights: The UN Human Rights Committee's Monitoring of ICCPR Rights* (Cambridge University Press 2020)

Thielbörger P, 'Flashbangs against Empowerment' (*Völkerrechtsblog*, 14 August 2020) https://voelkerrechtsblog.org/de/flashbangs-against-empowerment/. Accessed 26 August 2025

Thielbörger P, *The Right(s) to Water: The Multi-Level Governance of a Unique Human Right* (Springer 2014)

Thielbörger P, 'Re-Conceptualizing the Human Right to Water: A Pledge for a Hybrid Approach' (2015) 15 Human Rights Law Review 225

Thiele A, 'GG Art. 3 Abs. 1 [Gleichheit]' in Brosius-Gersdorf F (ed), *Dreier Grundgesetz-Kommentar* (4th edn, Mohr Siebeck 2023)

Thomas CA, 'The Uses and Abuses of Legitimacy in International Law' (2014) 34 Oxford Journal of Legal Studies 729

Tobin J, 'Seeking to Persuade: A Constructive Approach to Human Rights Treaty Interpretation' (2010) 23 Harvard Human Rights Journal 1

Tomuschat C, 'Human Rights in a World-Wide Framework—Some Current Issues' (1985) 45 Zeitschrift für ausländisches öffentliches Recht und Völkerrecht 547

Tomuschat C, *Human Rights: Between Idealism and Realism* (3rd edn, Oxford University Press 2014)

Troianovski A, 'Police arrest more than 3,000 people as protests grow across Russia.' *The New York Times* (6 March 2022) .https://www.nytimes.com/2022/03/06/world/europe/police-russia-protests.html. Accessed 26 August 2025

Tyler TR, *Why People Obey the Law* (Princeton University Press 2006)

Vierdag EW, 'The Legal Nature of the Rights Granted by the International Covenant on Economic, Social and Cultural Rights' (1978) 9 Netherlands Yearbook of International Law 69

Villiger ME, 'The Rules on Interpretation: Misgivings, Misunderstandings, Miscarriage? The 'Crucible' Intended by the International Law Commission' in Cannizzaro E (ed), *The Law of Treaties Beyond the Vienna Convention* (Oxford University Press 2011)

von Arnauld A and Theilen JT, 'Rhetoric of Rights: A Topical Perspective on the Functions of Claiming a 'Human Right to …'' in von Arnauld A, von der Decken K and Susi M (eds), *The Cambridge Handbook of New Human Rights* (Cambridge University Press 2020)

von Arnauld A, von der Decken K and Susi M (eds), *The Cambridge Handbook of New Human Rights—Recognition, Novelty, Rhetoric* (Cambridge University Press 2020)

von Bernstorff J, 'The Dispute About Human Dignity and Ethical Absolutism in the Field of Fundamental and Human Rights Protection: Defending a Deontic Understanding of Rights' in Grimm D, Kemmerer A and Möllers C (eds), *Human Dignity in Context: Explorations of a Contested Concept* (Nomos 2018)

von Bogdandy A and Rau M, 'The Lotus' in Peters A (ed), *Max Planck Encyclopedia of Public International Law (MPEPIL)* (Oxford University Press 2006)

Voßkuhle A, 'Multilevel Cooperation of the European Constitutional Courts: Der Europäische Verfassungsgerichtsverbund' (2010) 6 European Constitutional Law Review 175

Wahl R, *Herausforderungen und Antworten: Das Öffentliche Recht der letzten fünf Jahrzehnte* (De Gruyter Recht 2006)

Waldhoff C, '§ 11 Verwaltung und Verwaltungsrecht' in Kahl W and Ludwigs M (eds), *Handbuch des Verwaltungsrechts*, vol I (C. F. Müller 2021)

Waldron J, 'Dignity and Rank' in Waldron J and Dan-Cohen M (eds), *Dignity, Rank, & Rights* (Oxford University Press 2012)

Waldron J, 'How Law Protects Dignity' (2012) 71 Cambridge Law Journal 200

Waldron J, 'Law, Dignity and Self-Control' in *Dignity, Rank, & Rights* (Oxford University Press 2012)

Walker S, ''We will win': vast Belarus rally adamant Lukashenko must go' *The Guardian* (16 August 2020). https://www.theguardian.com/world/2020/aug/16/we-will-win-vast-belarus-rally-adamant-lukashenko-must-go. Accessed 26 August 2025

Walker S and Roth A, 'Belarusians seek justice for brutal beatings by riot police' *The Guardian* (18 August 2020). https://www.theguardian.com/world/2020/aug/18/belarusians-seek-justice-for-brutal-beatings-by-riot-police. Accessed 26 August 2025

Walter C, 'Subjects of International Law' in Peters A (ed), *Max Planck Encyclopedia of Public International Law (MPEPIL)* (Oxford University Press 2007)

Walter C, 'GG Art. 93 [Bundesverfassungsgericht, Zuständigkeit]' in Dürig G, Herzog R and Scholz R (eds), *Grundgesetz Kommentar* (107th EL edn, C. H. Beck 2025)

Wapler F, 'GG Art. 1 Abs. 1 [Menschenwürde; Menschenrechte; Grundrechtsbindung]' in Brosius-Gersdorf F (ed), *Dreier Grundgesetz-Kommentar Band I* (4th edn, Mohr Siebeck 2023)

Ward T, 'The Right to Free, Prior, and Informed Consent: Indigenous Peoples' Participation Rights within International Law' (2011) 10 Northwestern University Journal of International Human Rights 54

Weber M, *Economy and Society: A New Translation* (Tribe K tr, Harvard University Press 2019)
Weller M, 'Self-Determination of Indigenous Peoples: Article 3, 4, 5, 18, 23 and 46(1)' in Hohmann J and Weller M (eds), *The UN Declaration on the Rights of Indigenous Peoples: A Commentary* (Oxford University Press 2018)
Wenner F, *Liberal Legitimacy: The justifcation of political power in the work of John Rawls* (Nomos Verlagsgesellschaft 2020)
Werner F, 'Verwaltungsrecht als konkretisiertes Verfassungsrecht' (1959) 74 Das Deutsche Verwaltungsblatt 527
Wheatle S-S, 'Access to Justice: From Judicial Empowerment to Public Empowerment' in Elliott M and Hughes K (eds), *Common Law Constitutional Rights* (Hart Publishing 2020)
Wolf B, 'Free Speech versus Human Dignity: Comparative Perspectives on Internet Privacy' (2014) 23 Tulane Journal of International and Comparative Law 251
Wollenschläger F, 'GG Art. 3' in Huber P and V0ßkuhle A (eds), *Grundgesetz Kommentar* (8th edn, C. H. Beck 2024)
Yaffe N, 'Indigenous Consent: A Self-Determination Perspective' (2018) 19 Melbourne Journal of International Law 703
Young KG, 'Rights and Obligations' in Moeckli D and others (eds), *International Human Rights Law* (4th edn, Oxford University Press 2022)
Ziekow J, '§ 14 Verwaltungsrecht und Verwaltungsprozessrecht' in Kahl W and Ludwigs M (eds), *Handbuch des Verwaltungsrechts*, vol I (C. F. Müller 2021)

MIX
Papier aus verantwortungsvollen Quellen
Paper from responsible sources
FSC® C105338

If you have any concerns about our products,
you can contact us on
ProductSafety@springernature.com

In case Publisher is established outside the EU,
the EU authorized representative is:
Springer Nature Customer Service Center GmbH
Europaplatz 3, 69115 Heidelberg, Germany

Printed by Libri Plureos GmbH
in Hamburg, Germany